THE LIBRARY
ST. MARY'S COLLEGE OF MARYLAND
ST. MARY'S CITY, MARYLAND 20686

THE STRATEGIC DEFENSE INITIATIVE

D0160999

THE JOHNS HOPKINS
FOREIGN POLICY INSTITUTE

FPI

Harold Brown
Chairman

Simon Serfaty
Executive Director

Philip Geyelin
Editor-in-Residence

Wilfrid Kohl
Director
International Energy Program

Michael Vlahos
Codirector
Security Studies Program

Nancy McCoy
Editorial Coordinator

George R. Packard
Dean, School of Advanced International Studies, The Johns Hopkins University

The Johns Hopkins Foreign Policy Institute (FPI) was founded in 1980 and serves as the research center for the School of Advanced International Studies (SAIS) in Washington, D.C. The FPI is a meeting place for SAIS faculty members and students as well as for government analysts, policymakers, diplomats, journalists, business leaders, and other specialists in international affairs. In addition to conducting research on policy-related international issues, the FPI sponsors conferences, seminars, and roundtables.

FPI publications include the *SAIS Review*, a biannual journal of foreign affairs, which is edited by SAIS students; the SAIS Papers in International Affairs, a monograph series copublished with Westview Press in Boulder, Colorado; the FPI Policy Briefs, a series of analyses of immediate or emerging foreign-policy issues; and the FPI Case Studies, a series designed to teach analytical negotiating skills.

For additional information regarding FPI publications, write to: FPI Publications Program, School of Advanced International Studies, The Johns Hopkins University, 1740 Massachusetts Avenue, N.W., Washington, D.C. 20036.

ABOUT THE BOOK AND EDITOR

Strategic defense is now an integral part of political-military planning and diplomacy and has emerged as the most serious challenge in decades to the U.S. nuclear strategy of the past thirty-five years. But is strategic defense constructive, or is it dangerous? Already, SDI has emerged as a new source of tension in the arms-control community and within the Western Alliance, largely because of uncertainties about its feasibility, specifically its technical-economic, political, and military-strategic aspects.

This book presents the major issues on both sides of the debate. Contributors address the program's range of possible objectives, which include providing an alternative to deterrence by the threat of nuclear response, enhancing deterrence achieved by increasing the survivability of retaliatory forces, and gaining nuclear advantage through technological superiority. They also examine the interaction between offensive and defensive forces in force structure and arms control as well as the problems SDI raises for the balance of conventional forces and the stability of allied relations. Soviet perceptions of ballistic missile defense and the potential of a Soviet breakout from the ABM Treaty are also considered. Regarding the issue of feasibility, the contributors describe the availability and limits of technology, the survivability of a defense against attack, the cost-exchange ratio for the defense, and the direct and opportunity costs of SDI to the nation.

Harold Brown is chairman of the Foreign Policy Institute at the School of Advanced International Studies, The Johns Hopkins University, and he is the author of *Thinking About National Security* (Westview, 1984). He was secretary of defense in the Carter administration.

Published in cooperation with
The Johns Hopkins Foreign Policy Institute,
School of Advanced International Studies

THE STRATEGIC DEFENSE INITIATIVE
INITIATIVE
Shield or Snare?

edited by
Harold Brown

Westview Press / Boulder and London

The opinions expressed in this book are solely those of the individual authors.

This Westview softcover edition is printed on acid-free paper and bound in softcovers that carry the highest rating of the National Association of State Textbook Administrators, in consultation with the Association of American Publishers and the Book Manufacturers' Institute.

All rights reserved. No part of this publication may be reproduced or transmitted in any form or by any means, electronic or mechanical, including photocopy, recording, or any information storage and retrieval system, without permission in writing from the publisher.

Copyright © 1987 by The Johns Hopkins Foreign Policy Institute, School of Advanced International Studies (SAIS)

Published in 1987 in the United States of America by Westview Press, Inc.; Frederick A. Praeger, Publisher; 5500 Central Avenue, Boulder, Colorado 80301

Library of Congress Cataloging-in-Publication Data
The strategic defense initiative: shield or snare?/edited by Harold Brown.
    p.   cm.
  Contents: The nature of SDI/Stephen J. Hadley—The American ethos and national-security traditions/Michael Vlahos—SDI and U.S. foreign policy/Robert W. Tucker—The challenge of SDI/George Liska—Is SDI technically feasible?/Harold Brown—The macroeconomics of strategic defenses/Barry M. Blechman and Victor A. Utgoff—Is SDI politically durable?/Dave McCurdy—Soviet policy toward BMD and SDI/Bruce Parrott—Heavenly gains or earthly losses?/Richard K. Betts—The implications of SDI for U.S.-European relations/Robert E. Osgood.
  ISBN 0-8133-0469-5
  1. Strategic Defense Initiative. I. Brown, Harold, 1927–
UG743.S775 1987
358′.1754–dc19   87-21314
                                                            CIP

Composition for this book originated with conversion of the editor's word-processor disks. This book was produced without formal editing by the publisher.

Printed and bound in the United States of America

The paper used in this publication meets the requirements of the American National Standard for Permanence of Paper for Printed Library Materials Z39.48-1984.

6   5   4   3   2

To the memory of our friend and colleague,
Robert Endicott Osgood

CONTENTS

TABLES AND FIGURES

INTRODUCTION

Harold Brown

On March 23, 1983, President Reagan set forth his vision of a strategic defense to protect the United States from the nuclear threat of ballistic missiles. Nuclear strategists, political leaders in the United States, Western Europe, and the Soviet Union, technologists, and editorial writers responded in the weeks that followed with arguments for and against such a change in strategic objective and the program that it foreshadowed. The issues ranged from the scientific and technological through the economic, military, and strategic to the ethical and political.

Considerable analysis has since been done, and additional technological information has emerged from the research and development program, both about how a defense against ballistic missiles (and implicitly a corresponding defense against air-breathing delivery systems) might work and about how the offense might be structured so as to deceive, overwhelm, or directly attack it. But the issues and arguments have not changed much since the spring of 1983. The papers in this book confront these issues and examine the arguments from diverse perspectives. They were developed in the course of research by a study group at The Johns Hopkins Foreign Policy Institute. The program was sponsored by the Carnegie Corporation to study the issue of the military uses of space and quickly identified the Strategic Defense Initiative (SDI) as the new driving force likely to dominate military efforts in space over the coming decade.

A variety of motives and purposes are comprised in the advocacy of a strategic defense program. As reviewed in Stephen J. Hadley's paper, skeptics and opponents also have varying attitudes toward the possible objectives. The purpose of SDI in its purest form has been rather consistently expressed by President Reagan and Secretary of Defense Weinberger. It is to replace the strategic doctrine (some would call it a fact of life) of deterrence of nuclear attack (or, in the form of extended deterrence, of conventional warfare as well) by the threat of a nuclear response, holding at risk the military, economic, urban-industrial, and political control capabilities of the Soviet Union.

The ethical and political problems of relying on such a deterrent have troubled American publics and political leaders since the nuclear age first emerged. Maintaining the doctrine of deterrence has become only more difficult as antinuclear movements have gained strength and as the Soviet Union has achieved parity with the United States in strategic nuclear forces. But before Reagan, all American presidents in the nuclear age concluded that there was no alternative to relying to some degree on such deterrence. Michael Vlahos points out that by seeking to overcome the situation by technological advance, President Reagan has touched a chord that resonates to certain American national characteristics and historical experiences. But even if feasible, replacing deterrence through rendering ballistic missiles (and, by extension, all nuclear weapons) "obsolete" also poses well-known problems in terms of the balance of conventional forces between NATO and the Warsaw Pact, which Robert W. Tucker and Robert E. Osgood discuss in their contributions.

A more modest goal for SDI would balance the strategic offensive and defensive forces of both superpowers so that if deterrence failed, the damage to U.S. society would be greatly decreased, perhaps even enough to ensure what could be called national survival. A mix of this sort might be consistent with an imperfect defense that allowed the explosion of as many as a few tens of nuclear weapons even on urban-industrial areas. One question that immediately arises is whether and how much the chances of nuclear war would be increased by the expectation of the superpowers that they could survive it, albeit in a badly damaged state. A second is whether such a balance is technically and politically feasible.

A still less ambitious goal would reinforce deterrence by means of strategic defense, through protecting strategic offensive forces and strategic command, control, and communications (C^3), making them less vulnerable to preemptive attack. This would leave nothing of President Reagan's stated objective and little of his proposed program (which is intended to defend the whole country, not simply a few hard points). But hard-point defenses would be much easier to achieve technologically and militarily because the targets are less fragile and more mobile than urban-industrial targets. Such defenses could, however, be augmented to have some capability to defend the entire country. In any event they could intercept many warheads. But the effect of improving deterrence through increased survivability of U.S. forces could well be more than counterbalanced by the increased capability that a corresponding Soviet strategic defense would provide to intercept those forces before they hit Soviet targets. Moreover, different basing modes for strategic offensive forces and strategic C^3, and arms reductions as well, could also reduce the vulnerability of U.S. forces, and they may prove more effective at doing so—in a two-sided game—than active defense.

Another way of looking at the objective of SDI is that the program might allow the United States to gain an advantage by virtue of its superior technology. The global political implications of such an objective are discussed by George Liska. It is, however, rather hard to reconcile this objective with President Reagan's repeated indications that, at the proper time, the United States would be prepared to share that technology with, or make its benefits available to, the Soviet Union. Another, possibly related, objective would be to replace the need for strategic arms control; the paradox is that many analyses suggest that for SDI to succeed and, in particular, for a stable transition to a defense-dominated strategic balance to be possible, elaborate and effective control and reduction of strategic offensive forces would be necessary.

The feasibility of each of these possible objectives for strategic defense depends on the answers to various technical and military-strategic questions. Those answers cannot be definitively known now or for many years. Indeed, the study issued by the American Physical Society (APS) in April 1987 suggests that not only engineering questions but some scientific questions may take a decade or longer to answer. But some judgments are possible about what the answers are likely to be. In 1984 Paul Nitze, perhaps the most knowledgeable senior figure on these matters in the Reagan administration, set forth criteria for an effective strategic defense: a favorable cost-exchange ratio for the defense at the margin—that is, the defense would be able to offset at lower cost increments of offensive capability; survivability of the defense against a direct attack; and stability. Some cost factors are covered in the paper by Barry M. Blechman and Victor A. Utgoff, and judgments about whether the criteria can be met appear in various of these essays. Yet, unfortunately, many proponents and opponents of SDI make their cases unfairly by comparing rungs that do not truly correspond to each other on the ladders of measures, countermeasures, and counter-countermeasures. If one takes present offenses and future defenses, the latter look better; if one takes present defenses and future offenses, the offense will win. The nicety of judgment consists in comparing what is actually likely to be available on each side at various times in the future. My own judgments on this matter are contained in my own chapter, a version of which first appeared early in 1986; nothing has happened since to change them.

Most informed judgments (and I share them), including that of the recent APS study, are at best skeptical about the prospects of SDI. The question may be asked, then why are the Soviets so evidently concerned about the U.S. program? First, the Soviets dislike having to change their own force plans. Until 1983 those plans did not have to consider the possibility of a U.S. antiballistic missile (ABM) program. The possibility of having to revise their military programs in response to U.S. initiatives is an uncomfortable one. Second, the Soviets fear and tend to overrate U.S. technological prowess. Though their technical and military advisers probably have assured Soviet political leaders that a Soviet strategic offensive force can be reconfigured and enhanced to destroy, deceive, overwhelm, or penetrate U.S. strategic defenses, these leaders must nevertheless ask themselves what the consequences would be for Soviet power if that advice proved wrong: the severity of those consequences, however unlikely, must concern them.

SDI challenges the Soviets to competition on a ground that seems relatively unfavorable to them—that of high technology. Their resources, while great and almost certainly adequate to respond, are nevertheless in short supply. Moreover, the challenge comes at a time when the political leadership hopes to overcome economic stagnation by the application of technology, which it can ill afford to divert elsewhere. The Soviets must also be concerned that devotion of U.S. resources to a challenging technological goal, even if the goal is not reached, will stretch U.S. capabilities and produce useful spin-offs in the civil area and especially in military areas. Though an equal effort applied directly to developing such technologies would be more likely to achieve them, the Soviets are as aware as we that those direct efforts might not be made in the absence of SDI. Soviet concerns about spin-offs have been expressed especially about the use of space-based weapons to attack targets on the earth.

And, finally, it should be noted that SDI and its putative dangers have provided the USSR with a useful stick with which to beat the United States in international forums. For all these reasons the Soviets have tried to restrict the U.S. SDI program as much as possible, even while conducting an extensive program of their own on directed-energy weapons, some space-based components, and especially a massive development program for ground-based antiballistic missile systems that provides them with a capability to break out of the Anti-Ballistic Missile Treaty much more easily than the United States. Soviet attitudes are discussed in Bruce Parrott's paper.

That Soviet program, the unanswered technical and strategic questions, the relationship to arms control and SDI's possible use as a lever or bargaining chip in such negotiations, all argue the need for a substantial

U.S. research and development program on SDI. One purpose would be to find out which of the possible goals of SDI are technically and militarily feasible; expert judgments and predictions can be wrong and need to be informed by such a program. Most of the past examples that proponents of SDI give about the possibility of achieving various technological capabilities are inapplicable. The cases cited are engineering accomplishments not forbidden by the laws of physics and did not have to survive attempts by military opponents to mount a response that negates the accomplishment. The SDI program needs to consider such responses. A second purpose would be to deter or if necessary respond to a Soviet breakout from the ABM treaty. A third would be to preserve the option for a hard-point defense of strategic offensive forces and strategic C^3. Finally—though very inefficiently—a demanding technological goal would indeed help technological advance in general by providing funds that might not otherwise be made available.

The real questions are the appropriate level and nature of an R and D program. A level of 9 percent of the defense R and D budget (that is, $3.5 billion or slightly more in 1988) may seem high, but it should be noted that during the 1950s and 1960s a combination of air defense and ballistic missile defense research and development was allocated a similar percentage of the then much smaller defense R and D budget. As to the nature of the program, one devoted to research and technology development consistent with the narrow (and, for fourteen years, generally accepted) interpretation of the ABM treaty, with particular emphasis on the longer-range possibilities of boost-phase intercept by directed-energy weapons and of midcourse discrimination by whatever means, would seem to offer the most promise.

The Strategic Defense Initiative Office, which directs the program, appears to take a different approach, pressing for early decision on full-scale engineering development, and even deployment beginning in the mid-1990s, of a primitive capability (using kinetic-energy weapons based in space as well as ground-based systems) and trying to get ahead, and by improvements stay ahead, of the Soviet response to that capability. The reasoning may be that if the program does not grow rapidly in size and gives little or no promise of early deployment, it will lose the support of its strongest congressional and public supporters and die. This concern is intensified by the knowledge that President Reagan, who is much more supportive than almost any of his likely successors, will leave office in January 1989. There is some validity to that political judgment. But the program has been kept alive only by the rather reluctant support of congressional skeptics who are willing to accept an R and D program specifically intended to answer the technological questions about whether SDI makes any sense. They are likely to be turned against the program by any commitment to early deployment in advance of answers to those questions, and their numbers greatly exceed those of the true believers.

There is a paradox also in the relationship of arms control to SDI (a relationship analyzed in Richard K. Betts's paper). Strategic offensive force limits, and indeed reductions, are vital if SDI in any of its more ambitious forms is to have any prospect for success. At the same time, both Soviet attitudes and the logic of the situation ensure that such limitations can be achieved only if limits on SDI development and testing are also accepted. It would be irresponsible for a nation that relies on deterrence, as the United States does and the Soviets say they do, to reduce its strategic offensive forces in the face of an expected adversary deployment of a defense against those forces. Defenses on the other side must be penetrable if deterrence is to be preserved; and that penetration will rely, among other things, on large numbers of offensive forces. Agreements limiting and reducing strategic offensive forces at the same time as they limit the nature of SDI development are feasible in principle, although the prospects appear poor over the next couple of years. Perhaps the gravest danger is that the erosion of the ABM treaty will become an abandonment or denunciation of the treaty. This would make the future even more uncertain and would create potential instability. That instability, however, probably would not be as serious as some of the more anxious opponents of SDI maintain, because strategic defense of urban-industrial targets against offensive forces designed by a determined opponent so as to survive and penetrate that defense appears infeasible at least for decades and probably for the foreseeable future.

In practice, the U.S. SDI program is unlikely to grow in budgetary terms even as fast as 10 percent a year, as noted in the paper by Congressman McCurdy. In that light, the greatest risk to U.S. security from SDI could be that the Soviets will prove less constrained in their ABM activities, when budgetary and political constraints are considered, than the United States. One other possibility is that the Soviets could propose limiting antiballistic missile capabilities to ground-based development and deployment alone. That would not be in the U.S. interest because the Soviet Union has a production base for ground-based systems while the United States has not.

To conclude, what are the long-term effects of the Reagan administration's adoption of strategic defense as a preferred alternative to earlier nuclear strategies? SDI has clearly changed the emphasis in the U.S.-Soviet military competition and arms-control negotiations. Under certain circumstances, that could be useful. It has been a useful lever in gaining Soviet concessions, conditioned on limitation of SDI, on strategic offensive forces. The Reykjavík summit in October 1986, however, displayed the administration's determination to trash the idea of deterrence—that is, holding important Soviet values hostage to ballistic missile attack—and to seek the elimination of ballistic missiles and perhaps of all nuclear forces in an attempt to make strategic defense more feasible. Secretary Shultz's Moscow meetings of April 13–15, 1987, produced a tentative agreement on intermediate-range nuclear forces that has intensified European concerns about denuclearization. In that light, it seems very likely that a major effect of SDI will be to accelerate the decline in support by U.S. and European publics for existing nuclear policies. Since no reliable substitute for those policies is apparent, this will create strains for U.S. political-military planning and between the United States and its allies.

The balance between these two sets of factors will determine whether the Strategic Defense Initiative will prove constructive or erosive. At the moment, the latter seems more likely.

Part One

THINKING ABOUT SDI

1

THE NATURE OF SDI

Stephen J. Hadley

In the almost four years since President Reagan launched the Strategic Defense Initiative (SDI), his commitment to it has grown rather than diminished. It now appears that he views SDI—not an agreement with the Soviets reducing offensive nuclear arms—as his principal legacy to future generations dealing with the problem of nuclear weapons.

Yet while the president's own commitment to SDI has grown, the public remains uncertain. Although Congress has generally supported the program, it has done so reluctantly, with substantial reductions in the funding levels requested by the president. The Gramm-Rudman legislation will severely challenge even this level of support. At present there is substantial public uncertainty as to whether SDI is worth having—particularly if it comes at the price of a U.S.-Soviet agreement reducing offensive nuclear weapons. The debate during the next year could well be critical.

This chapter explores the rationale for the SDI program. It begins by providing some background on the current SDI effort—where SDI fits into the current U.S.-Soviet nuclear standoff, how U.S. planners hope to use SDI technology, and what can be known already about the defensive systems that are likely to result from SDI research.

The chapter then examines the arguments for and against SDI. As to the critics, most of their arguments focus on the actual deployment of defensive systems. They offer little guidance into the underlying rationale for the current SDI effort or help in assessing its value. The claims of SDI supporters provide somewhat greater assistance. They focus quite properly on SDI's potential contribution to correcting deficiencies in current U.S. nuclear strategy and in the forces designed to

---

This chapter is expanded in the FPI Policy Brief, *Thinking About SDI* (Washington, D.C.: The Johns Hopkins Foreign Policy Institute, 1986).

implement that strategy. This potential contribution, although considerably more modest than many SDI supporters claim, nonetheless justifies a significant research effort. The nature of this potential contribution also suggests a number of guidelines for structuring that effort.

SDI: THE CONCEPT AND THE SYSTEM

How It All Began

It was President Reagan's speech of March 23, 1983, that made SDI a central feature of the administration's nuclear policy. At the end of a speech primarily devoted to arguing against cuts in his proposed defense budget, President Reagan offered an alternative to the traditional approach to dealing with the threat posed by Soviet power—and, particularly, the threat posed by Soviet nuclear weapons. He described this traditional approach as "deterrence of aggression through the promise of retaliation."

This approach is based on the expectation that a large portion of the strategic offensive nuclear systems deployed by both superpowers—including land-based intercontinental ballistic missiles (ICBMs), submarine-launched ballistic missiles (SLBMs), and a much smaller number of long-range bombers—will survive a nuclear attack. Further, although the Soviets have extensive air defenses designed to shoot down U.S. bombers, neither side currently has any credible defense against the ballistic missiles of the other. Thus, both sides are confident that a large portion of their strategic nuclear forces can survive a nuclear first strike and then be launched in an effective retaliatory second strike—inflicting an "unacceptable" level of damage on the territory, military forces, economy, and population of the other side. It is the very prospect of such assured retaliatory capability that, even in crisis, is supposed to deter each side from launching a strategic nuclear attack.

In his March speech President Reagan sought to make a clean break from the past and to offer an alternative to this approach. The human spirit, he said, must be capable of "rising above dealing with other nations and human beings by threatening their existence." He proposed "a program to counter the awesome Soviet missile threat with measures that are defensive," so that U.S. security would rest not on "the threat of instant U.S. retaliation to deter a Soviet attack" but on the United States' ability to "intercept and destroy strategic ballistic missiles before they reached our own soil or that of our allies."

As a first step, President Reagan directed that a long-term research and development program be defined for achieving this capability. His goal was nothing if not ambitious: to use "the very strengths in technology that spawned our great industrial base" to render nuclear weapons "impotent and obsolete." The SDI effort was configured in response to this directive. As originally conceived, it was a five-year, $26 billion research program designed to investigate alternative technologies that might provide a defense against ballistic missiles. Congress subsequently reduced funding for the program, however, raising the prospect that the program will have to be either cut back or funded beyond five years. The rationale advanced for the program was that at its conclusion the United States would have the necessary technical information to determine whether a defense against ballistic missiles is feasible and whether it is worth pursuing.

SDI was soon to be acclaimed a brilliant political and diplomatic success. Politically, it largely stole the thunder of the political Left, and particularly the nuclear freeze movement, on the nuclear issue. It put President Reagan firmly on record as favoring the total elimination of nuclear weapons and wanting to rid the world of the nuclear nightmare. This objective would be achieved, not by giving in to the temptation of unilateral disarmament or by negotiating unenforceable arms-control agreements with the nation's principal adversary, but by turning to the genie of Western technology. Perhaps owing to the remarkable special effects of the *Star Wars* trilogy or the artists' conceptions of SDI on the network evening news, the plan appeared to many Americans as a plausible alternative to reliance on the threat of nuclear retaliation.

Diplomatically, SDI was a major factor in the Soviet decision in January 1985 to return to the negotiating table after having walked out of the Strategic Arms Reduction Talks (START) late in 1983. The Soviet return was in part a tacit recognition of the failure of their bare-knuckle effort to halt the deployment of U.S. intermediate-range nuclear missiles in Europe. Yet it seems clear that the return was also motivated by a desire to launch a propaganda attack on SDI. This required the posture of a reasonable, peace-loving Soviet Union. A return to the bargaining table was a necessary precondition to such a posture—the admission ticket to the subsequent "propaganda wars."

Further, it seems clear that SDI has created substantial negotiating capital for the United States. Since the Soviets have an overall numerical advantage over the United States in strategic nuclear delivery systems (2,502 to 1,910 in 1986[1]), reductions to parity at lower force levels would require greater reductions by the Soviets than by the United States. The Soviet Union has generally been reluctant to consider such reductions. But the prospect of a major U.S. effort in ballistic missile defense, even if years away, has given the Soviets something to be concerned about— and something for which they may be willing to pay, in terms of asymmetrical reductions in the level of offensive forces.

The Current Concept

The SDI concept currently being considered by U.S. defense planners involves a complex system of layers of defensive weapons that would engage Soviet ballistic missiles and the nuclear warheads they carry at various points in their progress from launch to target. The complete flight of a ballistic missile lasts only twenty-five to thirty minutes. The first three to four minutes after launch are known as the boost phase, during which time all the warheads are atop the missile as it moves up through and then beyond the earth's atmosphere to over 100 miles above the earth. At this point the warheads, along with decoys and other "penetration aids," separate from the missile. Once separated, the warheads actually coast to their targets in what is called a ballistic trajectory, continuing upward to a point well over 500 miles above the earth and then moving back downward until they begin to reenter the earth's atmosphere. This is the midcourse phase of the warheads' flight and lasts around twenty minutes. During the third phase, the reentry phase, the warheads move down through the earth's atmosphere toward their targets in just a couple of minutes.

The problems presented in each of the three phases vary substantially. Critical to the effectiveness of the system of strategic defense is the boost-phase intercept, or the ability to attack and destroy a ballistic missile after it breaks through the earth's atmosphere but before the warheads have separated. Destruction of the missile at this point would render ineffective all the warheads it carried—which currently could be anywhere from 1 to 10. The task would be technically demanding, however, involving a roughly contemporaneous attack on well over 2,000 ballistic missiles, given an all-out Soviet attack at current force levels. Within the first three to four minutes after launch, the launch would have to be detected, the missiles tracked, and a successful attack made on each missile. For the attack on the ballistic missiles U.S. defense planners have considered large satellites carrying directed-energy weapons (laser and particle-beam weapons) coupled with many more smaller satellites carrying kinetic-energy weapons, each firing high-speed, nonnuclear homing projectiles that would destroy the ballistic missiles on impact.

During the midcourse phase, time would be less of a constraint, since the warheads would coast for perhaps twenty minutes. However, the warheads would be scattered among decoys and other devices designed to disguise them. A midcourse attack would demand a system that could track all these objects, discriminate between the true warheads and the decoys, and then attack the warheads. Without a successful boost-phase attack the numbers involved would be impressive—perhaps

10,000 warheads and a much larger number of decoys. To detect, track, and discriminate among these objects would pose a substantial challenge in terms of both sensors and computer data-processing/battle management capability. For attack on the warheads during the midcourse phase, planners have considered space-based directed-energy and kinetic-energy weapons combined with clouds of small pellets or aerosols dispensed in space to help discriminate between the warheads and the decoys. One scenario uses directed-energy weapons to help distinguish between warheads and decoys, with kinetic-energy weapons attacking the warheads.

Potential problems during the reentry phase are in many ways more familiar, having been addressed in detail during the antiballistic missile (ABM) debate of the 1960s. The earth's atmosphere acts as a sieve to strain out the decoys, which either burn up or lag behind the true warheads. The technical problems in this phase would involve tracking and intercepting the fast-moving warheads at a safe distance from their targets. Planners have examined a system of ground-based radars and two types of ground-launched rocket interceptors. One interceptor would attack incoming warheads above the earth's atmosphere (an exo-atmospheric attack, in which the problem of discrimination from decoys would still remain). The other interceptor would attack the warheads after they had entered the atmosphere (an endo-atmospheric attack).

Such defensive systems themselves present a problem in that they too would be subject to attack or "suppression." There is particular concern about the vulnerability of the space-based satellite systems, which could be attacked by antisatellite (ASAT) systems. This danger might introduce new instabilities into the U.S.-Soviet strategic nuclear relationship and tempt either side during a crisis to launch a preemptive attack against the other's satellite systems. It is for this reason (as well as possibly lower cost) that U.S. defense planners have considered systems that would be deployed in space only shortly before their actual use (the so-called pop-up systems) or, alternatively, that would rely more heavily on ground-based components. This latter type of system might include fairly exotic ground-based lasers coupled with orbiting mirrors that would retarget their beams.

A second problem of these defensive systems is their vulnerability to countermeasures designed to reduce their effectiveness. These include steps to harden or otherwise modify the outer shell of the ballistic missiles against attack; deployment of fast-burn boosters, which would shorten the time between launch and dispersal of the warheads; greater use of penetration aids to help the warheads reach their targets; and simple proliferation of missiles and warheads to overwhelm any defensive system by sheer numbers. To the extent that it is easier and less costly for one side to field effective countermeasures than it is for the other to increase the capacity or effectiveness of the defensive system itself, the defense would be at a distinct disadvantage.

It is certainly too soon to draw much in the way of conclusions about the effectiveness of any of these technologies or the feasibility of the overall concept. Yet, because of the nature of the task that the system is to perform and what the performance of this task would necessarily require, there are some things that can be said about any ballistic missile defense system that is likely to emerge from the SDI effort.

Characteristics of the System

SDI Is Truly a System. SDI is not a typical military program. Its research is directed not toward a single weapon, such as a new bomber or ballistic missile, but rather toward a series of different weapons linked by computer to form an integrated, multilayered defense capability. It is a "weapons system" in the true sense of the term. In this respect it is less like the MX missile and more like an antisubmarine warfare or air defense system—linking sensors that would detect the targets with computers that would distinguish and track them; requiring different kinds of weapons to attack the targets in different ways; and necessitating a command, control, and communications (C^3) system to coordinate the attack.

Full Deployment Is a Long Way Off. It generally takes from ten to fifteen years to develop and deploy an individual weapons system. Because basic research on the applicable technologies is still required and a complex, interrelated system of different weapons is involved, a full ballistic missile defense will require substantially more time. Indeed, it is a fair assumption that it will be twenty to thirty years before either the United States or the Soviet Union could complete deployment of a full ballistic missile defense system based on the concept currently envisioned by U.S. defense planners.

Each Side Will Have Ample Time to Plan and Respond. Consequently, each side will have ample time in which to modify its force structure and defense plans in response to the prospect of a full ballistic missile defense system developed and deployed by the other side. This response could involve deployment of additional offensive weapons to overwhelm the defense by sheer numbers, or the use of countermeasures or changes in tactics to reduce its effectiveness. The more technologically sophisticated the response, of course, the less ample would be the available time. The development and deployment of new offensive systems designed with a particular defensive system in mind would require substantial lead time. But less ambitious alternatives are likely to be available.

Generally, therefore, there is much time for both sides to plan and respond.

All Components Will Not Be Fully Developed at the Same Time. The technologies being examined in the SDI program are at different levels of maturity. Presumably, this means that some parts of a ballistic missile defense system could be ready for development and deployment before others. For instance, interception of incoming warheads during the reentry phase was extensively studied in the 1960s, and one might expect that either side could deploy a substantial system for this purpose at the near end of the twenty- to thirty-year period described above—and probably sooner. Indeed, the Soviets still maintain, and are in the process of modernizing, their ABM system around Moscow. By contrast, the directed-energy technologies mentioned in connection with boost-phase and midcourse intercept are less well developed and could be deployed in substantial numbers only at the latter end of that twenty- to thirty-year period. The computer software and data-processing/battle management capability necessary for a fully effective system may indeed appear only after the weapons for actually knocking out the missiles or warheads have been developed.

Both Sides Will Have the Option to Deploy Imperfect Systems. For the foregoing reason, both sides will have to consider whether they want to develop and deploy pieces of an overall defense system as particular technologies or capabilities mature. A land-based defense against incoming warheads during the reentry phase is an obvious example. A boost-phase intercept system using kinetic-energy weapons giving substantial (but less than total) effectiveness against ballistic missiles is another. Even with the combined capability of both systems, however, the decision to develop and deploy such imperfect systems would not be an easy one. The current concept of U.S. defense planners assumes that each layer of defense would "leak" missiles or warheads into the next, but with ever decreasing numbers getting through each layer. Assuming a 10,000-warhead attack and a four-layer defense system, for example, a 75 percent effectiveness at each level would be required in order to reduce the attacking force to less than 50 warheads (which would still be enough to cause massive damage). At a 75 percent level of effectiveness, however, a two-layer defense (a boost phase and reentry phase) would leave an attacking force of about 600 warheads. Thus, both sides will have to decide whether development and deployment of such imperfect systems is desirable.

SDI Involves Two Distinct Concepts. In a sense the SDI effort suggests two different concepts. One entails the use of primarily ground-based systems in the reentry phase to protect specific targets of great importance (so-called site defense). The other puts greater emphasis on space-based systems that would attack the warheads (or missiles) earlier in the flight path and provide protection to large areas of the country (population or area defense). These concepts involve very different technologies and would have substantially different consequences for the relationship between the nuclear forces of the two sides.

Even If SDI Works, the Air-Breathing Threat Would Remain. Even at its best, a ballistic missile defense system offers only a partial solution to the threat posed by Soviet nuclear weapons. The SDI effort announced by President Reagan, and the concept now being pursued by U.S. defense planners, does not purport to deal with the threat posed by strategic bombers or cruise missiles. These weapons are generically called the "air-breathing threat" because, unlike ballistic missiles, they never leave the earth's atmosphere. Even with an effective ballistic missile defense, the United States would still face a threat from Soviet air-breathing systems. The development and deployment of defenses against these systems is generally not limited by any U.S.-Soviet arms-control agreement. The Soviets, for their part, have put a substantial effort into developing and deploying such defenses. The United States, however, has not made any comparable effort.

Policy Consequences May Outstrip SDI's Actual Capability. It is hard to recall a research program that has generated political and policy fallout comparable to that associated with SDI. The SDI effort has in some measure undercut support for the United States' existing nuclear strategy at the same time that the country is decades away from an effective alternative to it. It has touched off a passionate political debate and threatens to provoke significant Soviet strategy and force posture changes before U.S. defense planners have concluded that a defensive system is even feasible, much less desirable. The result has been destabilizing in and of itself. This may suggest the need to lower the decibel level of the SDI debate. It may also suggest that both sides should forbear from overemphasizing the results of whatever demonstration experiments are conducted as part of the SDI effort. The gap between such experiments and an operational system is too enormous.

THE SEARCH FOR A RATIONALE

For the U.S. public and its elected officials to make up their minds as to the value of the current SDI, they need to be clear as to its rationale. One may look to the arguments of SDI critics for guidance. To a large extent, however, these arguments are directed toward the ultimate question of whether deployment of a ballistic missile defense system is in the U.S. interest. They are of little use in clarifying the underlying rationale for the current program and assessing its value.

The Arguments of the Critics

The System Will Not Work. One particularly unhelpful consideration in assessing the value of the SDI effort is whether or not ballistic missile defense will "work." The SDI effort is, after all, a research program, justified precisely on the ground that substantial technical uncertainties must be resolved before any judgment can be made as to the feasibility of effective defense against ballistic missiles. To require proof of feasibility as a precondition for a research program is to put the cart before the horse.

This consideration might be a more forceful argument if it could be shown that ballistic missile defense would require a capability that the laws of physics simply will not permit or that is plainly beyond the nation's current engineering capability. Yet, so far at least, this does not appear to be the case. The problems are basically engineering problems, not problems of physics, and there is a substantial body of opinion that says they can be solved.

A variant of the "it won't work" argument is the claim that further work on SDI is a waste of money because it is simply far easier and cheaper to develop measures to defeat a ballistic missile defense system than it is to build one. If true, this would be a serious objection to actual deployment of such a system. However, it seems wholly appropriate at this point to pursue a research program that would have as one of its tasks the exploration of this issue.

Finally, it is somewhat misleading to talk in terms of whether ballistic missile defense will work. As already noted, the concept of ballistic missile defense currently under consideration involves not a single weapon but a series of weapons using potentially different technologies. Some of these technologies (such as that required to intercept warheads during the reentry phase) involve much less uncertainty than others (such as the more exotic laser and directed-energy technologies). There is a tendency, on the part of those who argue that ballistic missile defense will not work, to point to the uncertainties associated with these latter technologies or to the monumental data-processing/battle management capability required for a perfect defense against an all-out Soviet attack. This ignores, of course, the less uncertain prospects of some of the more conventional technologies and the option of deploying less-than-perfect systems.

The System Will Cost Too Much. As in the case of questions about the feasibility of a defense against ballistic missiles, it is also too soon to abandon the SDI effort on the ground that actual deployment would simply cost too much. The concept of "too much" suggests a judgment made by weighing capability against cost. In order to make this judgment, one must know what the system could do, and that requires completion of the research effort. Further, estimates of cost much beyond order-of-magnitude calculations may be just too speculative at this time. All that should be asked for the present is that, given other budgetary priorities, there be some reasonable proportionality between the amount of money spent on SDI and what that effort could potentially contribute to U.S. national security.

The Soviets Will Be Furious. It is also not helpful in deciding whether to pursue SDI to focus on the official Soviet reaction to the SDI effort. This is largely because that reaction is so predictable. The United States should expect its principal adversary to protest any initiative that offers the prospect of improving the United States' relative military or political posture, especially in the all-important arena of strategic nuclear weapons. This is in fact what the Soviets have always done, whether the initiative was the MX, the development of cruise missiles, or the deployment of U.S. intermediate-range missiles in Europe. Why should anything different be expected regarding SDI?

Some may argue that the United States should not pursue a research program on SDI for fear of provoking a comparable or even more ambitious Soviet effort. There is, however, substantial evidence that the Soviet Union is already making a major effort in this field. While SDI may cause the Soviets to expand their research program somewhat, there is no guarantee that a discontinuation or scaling back on the U.S. side would cause the Soviets to discontinue or scale back their program. To the contrary, the Soviet Union traditionally has been more defense oriented in its military planning than has the United States, having made, for example, a much greater commitment to air defense and civil defense. Continued research on ballistic missile defense, regardless of the U.S. effort, would be more consistent with this history.

SDI Will Destroy Arms Control. Critics also contend that the SDI effort will destroy the arms-control process between the United States and the Soviet Union. More specifically, they argue that the negotiation of substantial reductions in the level of strategic offensive forces cannot be achieved so long as the United States does not forgo its SDI effort. One need only look at the discussion between the two sides at Reykjavík to see that this need not be so. Since deployment of a full ballistic missile defense is so far in the future, an interim agreement for deep offensive reductions in return for a time-limited ban on SDI deployment should be attractive to both sides. More important, however, arms control is not an end in itself. It is only one means of dealing with the problem posed by Soviet possession of nuclear weapons. If greater reliance on defensive systems is a better way of dealing with this problem, then it might sensibly be chosen, even at the expense of negotiated restraints on strategic nuclear weapons.

The Arguments of the Supporters

On the question of the rationale for the SDI effort—whether the potential benefits of greater reliance on defensive systems justify more than a token SDI effort, and what priority any such effort should be given—the arguments of SDI supporters provide some relevant guidance. They focus on what a ballistic missile defense system would contribute to U.S. nuclear strategy and capability. By analyzing these arguments, some judgments can be made about the kind of contribution that plausibly can be expected from ballistic missile defense.

SDI Will Free the United States from the Threat of Nuclear War. President Reagan initially described the objective of what became the SDI effort as the ability to render nuclear weapons "impotent and obsolete." In the State of the Union address on February 4, 1986, he asserted that "[a] security shield can one day render nuclear weapons obsolete and free mankind from the prison of nuclear terror." Supporters of SDI have used the same image, sponsoring advertisements in cartoon form that show an American family smiling under a rainbow-like "peace shield" protecting it from nuclear attack.

These are images of great political power and appeal. They respond to a real concern, which has increased as the nuclear arsenals of the two sides have grown, about the potential consequences of a failure in the current system of "deterrence through promise of retaliation." What if the prospect of an assured retaliatory strike by the United States were not sufficient to deter a Soviet first strike? The promise of the peace shield is that it would free the United States from the consequences of nuclear attack; that the United States would regain control over its own national survival; that the United States would no longer be dependent on the "deterrence calculation" and on Soviet forbearance.

The problem is that the current SDI effort does not promise all these things. It does not seek a defense against the Soviet air-breathing threat. Further, to the extent the peace shield provided only an imperfect defense against ballistic missiles, the nuclear threat would remain substantial. If the justification for SDI rested solely on the prospect of rendering nuclear weapons "impotent and obsolete," the implausibility of that prospect might lead one to question the size of, and the priority already accorded to, the SDI program. A substantial SDI effort, particularly in light of Gramm-Rudman, requires a much more immediate rationale.

SDI Will Restore U.S. Strategic Superiority. Some SDI supporters suggest that the deployment of a ballistic missile defense might restore

U.S. strategic nuclear superiority. They hearken back to a time in the late 1940s and early 1950s, when the United States had either a nuclear monopoly or, once the Soviets acquired nuclear weapons, a clear numerical advantage in long-range bombers that were then the only means of delivery. Although President Reagan has disavowed any intention of seeking U.S. strategic nuclear superiority, it is still fair to ask whether SDI offers the prospect of a return to anything like the former U.S. advantage—and of what this new superiority would consist.

• A Unilateral U.S. Deployment: A unilateral U.S. deployment of an effective ballistic missile defense system could, at least theoretically, provide some kind of superiority. For example, it might give the United States the capability of launching a limited strategic nuclear attack with some confidence that the remainder of its nuclear arsenal would deter the Soviets from all-out retaliation—and that any more limited Soviet response could be handled by the U.S. ballistic missile defense system (coupled with some enhanced air defense capability). Regardless of whether the United States would ever take such an action, the capability of doing so could result in at least a perceived margin of superiority for the United States in the strategic arena.

However, even assuming that the United States could achieve anything like the kind of system effectiveness that this scenario would require, it is unlikely that the Soviets would permit such a unilateral U.S. deployment. The Soviets have already stated that they would view any U.S. deployment as an effort to convert strategic offensive forces into first-strike weapons—and that they would not permit such a result. The better assumption, therefore, is that any deployment of even a marginally effective ballistic missile defense system is likely to be two-sided, with systems deployed by both the United States and the Soviet Union. Would a two-sided deployment permit a return to U.S. strategic nuclear superiority? Although it might be contended that the Soviets would be unable to deploy a ballistic missile defense system (or one of any significant effectiveness), history suggests that, while it may take an enormous effort, the Soviets would ultimately develop and deploy a passable system—even a system of considerable technical sophistication. The United States might enjoy a substantial head start, which could translate into a temporary U.S. advantage, but it is likely that the Soviets would eventually catch up.

• A More Effective U.S. System: A possible source of a more permanent, if less substantial, U.S. advantage would be a U.S. system more effective than that deployed by the Soviets, whether by virtue of superior U.S. technology or differences in the geography and environment of the two countries. If this greater effectiveness could be maintained, it could offer the prospect of a permanent margin of U.S. superiority.

Some SDI supporters argue that one of the deficiencies in the current U.S. strategic posture is that the Soviets have greater war-fighting capability. The concern is that a greater Soviet investment in air defense, civil defense, and offensive weapons able to attack U.S. strategic nuclear forces successfully has put the USSR in a position to survive a U.S.-Soviet nuclear exchange with substantially less damage and fewer casualties. This permits the Soviets, the argument continues, credibly to threaten the use of their nuclear weapons in time of crisis. It can be argued that a more effective U.S. system of ballistic missile defense would not only correct this imbalance but also shift the advantage in the direction of the United States. Presumably, this would permit the United States to threaten more credibly the use of its own nuclear weapons in time of crisis. Yet substantial uncertainties remain.

U.S. ability to contemplate realistically a more effective ballistic missile defense system will depend on the progress of U.S. and Soviet technology over the next five to fifteen years, the timing of deployment decisions, and the specifics of the systems deployed. The numbers of warheads deployed by the two sides on their ballistic missiles are so large (almost 9,000 by the United States and almost 10,000 by the Soviet Union) that the U.S. system would have to be quite effective before any marginal advantage would have any real significance. If the U.S. system would still permit 1,000 Soviet warheads to leak through, could the United States credibly threaten to use its strategic nuclear weapons? Even if the U.S. system were twice as effective as the Soviet system, would the United States be in any better position simply because 1,000 warheads would leak through its system while 2,000 would leak through the Soviets'?

• More Emphasis on Air-Breathing Systems: A margin of U.S. strategic superiority might alternatively result from the renewed emphasis on bombers and cruise missiles that would result from deployment of ballistic missile defenses. This focus would seem to favor the United States. This country currently has a modest lead in the number of heavy bombers (260 U.S. B-1B, B-52G, and B-52H aircraft to 160 Soviet Bears and Bisons) and plans to add 81 more B-1B bombers by about 1990. The United States is also conceded to have a lead in long-range nuclear-armed cruise missiles for deployment on bomber aircraft, submarines, and surface ships.

There are a number of reasons, however, to think that the prospect of any permanent U.S. advantage—much less, superiority—based on this rationale is illusory. The Soviets are producing a new variant of one bomber (the Bear H) and are building another (the Blackjack). Further, if medium-range bombers are included in the comparison, any U.S. advantage shifts decisively toward the Soviets, with 510 Soviet Badgers, Blinders, and Backfires outnumbering the 55 U.S. FB-111As. Thus, to the extent medium-range bombers—particularly Backfires—are considered to be strategic systems, any U.S. bomber advantage disappears. So far as cruise missiles are concerned, the Soviets appear to have comparable programs under way. The Soviets also have a greater number of platforms on which to deploy them. Thus, the U.S. lead in cruise missiles may be only a head start, not a permanent advantage.

• More Emphasis on SLBMs: A different argument for U.S. strategic superiority might be based on the superiority of the U.S. SLBM force. If it could be shown that the trajectories or other flight characteristics of SLBMs (and their warheads) make these missiles less susceptible than ICBMs to ballistic missile defense, the U.S. quantitative lead in the number of warheads in its SLBM force (6,656 to 3,216 in 1986) could provide some measure of advantage. This lead is, however, in large part due to the earlier U.S. effort to equip its SLBMs with multiple independently target reentry vehicles (MIRVs). A Soviet SLBM MIRVing program is proceeding apace. Thus, the U.S. numerical advantage may be only a temporary lead.

U.S. submarines, however, are much harder to detect than their Soviet counterparts, are generally deployed more flexibly, and operate at greater distances from their homeland. Thus, they may be deployed nearer the Soviet Union, decreasing their time to target when compared to Soviet ICBMs or even SLBMs. To the extent that this reduced flight time (and perhaps lower trajectory) makes them harder to detect, track, and kill (at least by area or population defense systems), the United States might have some claim to a qualitative strategic superiority. This advantage would be enhanced by the deployment of the D-5 missile, which will have substantial capability against Soviet land-based missiles and other hard targets. Counterbalancing any such advantage, however, is the relatively higher proportion of major U.S. cities located on its ocean coasts (and thus vulnerable to short flight-time SLBM attack).

• Summary: Under a deployment of ballistic missile defenses by both the United States and the Soviet Union, the prospect of any margin of U.S. strategic nuclear superiority appears to be highly speculative. One would be hard pressed to justify a substantial SDI effort on this basis alone—assuming, President Reagan notwithstanding, that the United States did want to pursue such superiority. Further research and analysis may provide greater insight, however.

SDI Will Enhance Extended Deterrence. A margin of strategic nuclear superiority would enhance the security of both the United States and its allies. Historically, the United States has used its strategic nuclear weapons not only to deter Soviet nuclear attack but also to deter a conventional attack by Soviet army and air force units on U.S. allies in Europe and Asia. The United States has declared that if the Soviets launched such a conventional attack (one that many analysts believe would meet with quick success), the United States would consider responding with nuclear weapons—including strategic nuclear weapons launched against the territory of the Soviet Union. For this "extended deterrence" strategy to be effective, the U.S. threat must have some credibility. The question is whether deployment of ballistic missile defenses would enhance or reduce the credibility of this threat and, with it, extended deterrence.

A unilateral U.S. deployment of an effective ballistic missile defense system (coupled with enhanced air defense capability) might help the United States to threaten credibly a limited use of strategic nuclear weapons in response to Soviet conventional attack. The balance of the U.S. strategic arsenal would deter all-out Soviet retaliation, and U.S. defense systems would handle any more limited response. As already pointed out, however, a unilateral U.S. deployment is not likely.

It is also hard to see how any margin of superiority that the United States might acquire under a two-sided deployment could contribute much to enhancing extended deterrence. A substantially more effective U.S. system offering comparatively greater protection of U.S. population and territory might arguably enhance the credibility of the U.S. nuclear threat. However, the number of Soviet nuclear warheads deployed is now so high that, unless that system was very effective indeed, the number of warheads likely to penetrate in a Soviet attack would still be large enough to undermine the credibility of the U.S. threat.

Even if the U.S. and Soviet systems achieved roughly comparable and fairly high levels of effectiveness, it is possible that the systems would differ in their effectiveness against certain kinds of attacks (for example, against close-in SLBMs) that would favor the United States. This might permit the United States to threaten credibly to respond with these kinds of attacks in the event of a Soviet conventional attack. At this point, however, such possibilities are quite speculative.

Ballistic missile defenses might, indeed, erode the credibility of the U.S. threat. If the U.S. and Soviet systems were fairly effective against low-level strategic nuclear attacks but became relatively ineffective against attacks above a certain threshold, this might make *less* credible a U.S. threat to use strategic nuclear weapons for extended deterrence. For the U.S. attack to be effective (in the face of Soviet defenses), it would have to be of such a size that it would in all likelihood provoke all-out Soviet retaliation—retaliation that the U.S. defenses could not handle.

In sum, ballistic missile defense does not appear to offer the prospect of the kind of major breakthrough that would significantly enhance the U.S. ability to use nuclear weapons to deter conventional attacks and thereby contribute to extended deterrence. It may marginally increase the credibility of the U.S. threat, but the precise manner and extent of this contribution is quite speculative. While the issue warrants further research and analysis, as yet it appears to be an uncertain basis of support for the SDI effort.

SDI Will Improve Crisis Stability. The concept of crisis stability provides a separate rationale for the SDI effort. Although not part of the justification offered by the president in his March 1983 speech, it was part of his speech to the European Parliament in early May 1985. In that speech President Reagan characterized the Soviet nuclear forces as "clearly designed to strike first, and thus disarm their adversary," thereby "undermining stability and the basis for mutual deterrence." He reviewed three alternative responses. The first was to press the Soviets to reduce these forces through equitable, verifiable arms-control measures—an effort already being made at the negotiations in Geneva. The second was to step up the United States' own modernization efforts to keep pace with Soviet deployments. As to this alternative, President Reagan said: "Even if this course could be sustained by the West, it would produce a less stable strategic balance than the one we have today." Instead, the president proposed "to offset the continued Soviet offensive build-up in destabilizing weapons by developing defenses against these weapons."

This is a rationale for the SDI effort that is consistent with the scope of that effort—defense against Soviet ballistic missiles—and that is a part of the overall U.S. goal of improving crisis stability. In a simplified form, crisis stability means eliminating any military advantage to being the side that initiates a nuclear attack. Conversely, it means having confidence in the ability of one's own nuclear forces to survive such a first strike and to execute a devastating retaliatory second strike in response.

Ballistic missile defense potentially could enhance crisis stability in several ways. First, it could ease the problem of the potential vulnerability of the U.S. ICBM force and other high-priority targets. In the 1970s the Soviets deployed ICBMs (the SS-17, SS-18, and SS-19) much greater in size than their U.S. counterparts. Once MIRVed (or fitted with multiple nuclear warheads capable of hitting separate and distinct targets), these Soviet missiles carried 4, 10, and 6 warheads, respectively. Concern developed in the United States that with improvements in the accuracy of these MIRVed ICBMs, the Soviets would, in time of crisis, be tempted to launch a preemptive attack against high-priority U.S. civil and military targets, including the U.S. ICBM force.

During the last decade a debate has raged over the plausibility of this preemptive attack scenario and how serious a problem ICBM vulnerability is for the overall U.S. strategic nuclear force. The Scowcroft Commission report in 1983 suggested that concern about ICBM vulnerability was overblown. That being said, it still persists as a problem, though of arguable dimensions.

The Carter administration sought to solve this problem by deploying the MX missile in a survivable basing mode, called the racetrack. However, the Reagan administration rejected this approach. It attempted to find its own survivable basing mode, including dense pack. Technical, environmental, or political problems intervened, however, until the search was finally abandoned. SDI, by contrast, offered a solution to ICBM vulnerability that seemed environmentally sound (President Reagan has continually emphasized that the system would be nonnuclear), politically acceptable (passing as it artfully does as a way to render nuclear weapons "impotent and obsolete"), and technically feasible. Of all the capabilities that are part of the current SDI effort, a site defense system attacking incoming warheads in the reentry phase seems to be the most appropriate for defense of U.S. ICBM fields. It also involves the least technical risk and could be available for earliest deployment.

This being said, it must be pointed out that to be effective, site defense would require some rebasing of the U.S. Minuteman force. Further, if the United States opted for deployment of the Midgetman missile, some would argue that site defense no longer would be required to ensure survivability of the U.S. ICBM force. Thus, much analysis would be required before any deployment decision on site defense would be in order.

The Soviets may also be interested in a site defense system to defend their own ICBMs. The deployment of the MX missile into old Minuteman silos, and of the D-5 missile into U.S. ballistic missile submarines, will vastly improve U.S. capability to destroy Soviet ICBMs. Since the Soviet Union has a much more significant investment in its fixed land-based systems than does the United States (6,420 warheads to 2,110 in 1986, and vastly greater throw weight), the deployment of a defense for fixed ICBMs may be more important to the Soviets.

Indeed, it might be asked why the United States should encourage a system that will serve to defend Soviet investment in the very weapons that give the United States greatest concern. The answer is crisis stability. Because they are accurate, reliable, and vulnerable, ICBMs are both the best Soviet first-strike weapon and the one—because of their vulnerability—the Soviets would be most likely to use. Thus, the United States may have some interest in letting the Soviets reduce the vulnerability of these systems, at the same time that the United States reduces the vulnerability of its own, so as to reduce the incentives for the Soviets to use these weapons in a first strike.

Other aspects of the SDI effort involving not just site defense but area or population defense (such as systems for boost-phase or midcourse intercept) could also contribute to crisis stability. They could complicate a Soviet first strike by denying the Soviets confidence that they could succeed in destroying the targets of their choosing. Further, to the extent that these defenses are effective against ballistic missiles, they create some incentive for both sides to move toward aircraft and cruise missiles. Because these weapons take so much longer to reach their targets, they are less suitable as first-strike weapons. Finally, imperfect area defenses of modest effectiveness also may deter small nuclear attacks. Neither side would run the risk of such attacks if they could not be effective. Yet a larger attack would run the risk of provoking greater (and unacceptable) retaliation. Thus, area defenses might "raise the nuclear threshold" and decrease the likelihood of resort to strategic nuclear weapons (although, as has been discussed, this will erode the credibility of extended deterrence).

Three caveats should be observed. First, it may be argued that the instability caused by Soviet land-based ballistic missiles will gradually disappear. With their new SS-24 and SS-25, the Soviets appear to be moving away from silo-based missiles toward mobile missiles, which are less vulnerable. It may be further argued that mobile Soviet ICBMs will of necessity be smaller, of lower throw weight, and therefore less threatening to the United States. While these trends are to be encouraged, however, they will not eliminate the threat to U.S. ICBMs. Further, it is likely to be politically more difficult for the United States to deploy mobile ICBMs than for the Soviets. Even should it deploy mobile ICBMs, the United States might still need to deploy the defense systems for them. Second, it seems unlikely that ballistic missile defenses will achieve such effectiveness as to render ballistic missiles obsolete. Thus, while greater emphasis may be placed on air-breathing systems, ballistic missiles are likely to continue for some time to be the backbone of the weapons inventory of the two sides. Third, if area defenses achieve too much effectiveness, they may begin to threaten crisis stability. Either side may lose confidence that it would retain enough capability after a first strike to conduct effective retaliation. This, in turn, might generate renewed pressure for a first strike.

SDI Will Limit Damage If Deterrence Fails. A very straightforward argument on behalf of ballistic missile defense is that it would save

U.S. lives in the event that "deterrence through promise of retaliation" fails and nuclear war starts. This would appear of itself to be an almost unassailable argument for pursuing SDI, and particularly the population defense elements, so long as it did not increase the likelihood of a failure of deterrence or enhance the incentives of either side to launch a first strike. That consideration aside, the ultimate decision to deploy such a system would turn on a simple judgment that the number of lives potentially saved justified the cost of the system.

SDI Will Protect the United States Against Nuclear Accident. It can be argued that even a very imperfect ballistic missile defense system could provide some protection in the event of an accidental Soviet launch of a small number of ballistic missiles. This rationale alone probably would not justify much of an SDI research effort. However, there is certainly no reason why the effort that is made should not have, as part of its charter, investigation of thin defenses for handling accidental attacks.

The United States Needs to Hedge Against a Soviet Breakthrough. Even without any other justification the United States needs some sort of SDI research effort simply because of the existing Soviet program. A Soviet breakthrough in ballistic missile defense technology, which enabled it to deploy unilaterally even an imperfect system significantly in advance of the United States, would risk affording the Soviets a margin of superiority in the strategic nuclear arena.

CONCLUSIONS

It seems fair to say that SDI promises much less than some of the claims made on its behalf. As presently conceived, it does not offer in the foreseeable future a realistic prospect of rendering nuclear weapons "impotent and obsolete." Such an ambitious goal would require that the program be expanded to include research into improving the technology for, and prospects of, defense against bombers and particularly cruise missiles.

Nevertheless, four separate arguments in support of SDI, when taken together, seem to justify a significant ballistic missile defense research effort. These arguments focus on SDI's potential contribution to: (1) crisis stability, (2) limitation of damage to the U.S. territory and population in the event of nuclear war (even if a peace shield is a somewhat unrealistic objective), (3) protection against an accidental launch of Soviet ballistic missiles, and (4) hedging against a breakthrough in Soviet research efforts.

This conclusion and the foregoing discussion provide some guidance as to the nature of the SDI program that should be pursued. Given the crisis stability rationale (the argument for reduced vulnerability of U.S. ICBMs, in particular), the technologies supporting site defense probably should have priority. Area defense technologies should be pursued that would limit damage, protect against accidental launches, and hedge against Soviet technological breakthroughs. The payoff in the medium term from these technologies, however, may be small. The SDI effort should examine potential differences in effectiveness between possible U.S. and Soviet ballistic missile defense systems. It should in particular consider any inherent factors, geographical or other, that may suggest permanent differences in performance in the systems of the two sides. Research is also needed into the way U.S. and Soviet systems and technologies would respond to different kinds of offensive forces and attack scenarios (such as close-in SLBM attack). It may be that a basis for a margin of U.S. superiority can be found here.

U.S. defense planners must understand clearly the potential vulnerabilities of, and countermeasures against, various ballistic missile defense systems. The SDI effort should include a vigorous "red team" approach to studying the vulnerability of such systems to attack as well as possible Soviet responses, including likely countermeasures and the cost of such countermeasures. Finally, the United States must monitor Soviet efforts in this field so as to be able to plan and respond effectively.

NOTES

1. Data on U.S. and Soviet forces in this chapter are drawn from *The Military Balance 1986–87* (London: International Institute for Strategic Studies, 1986).

2

THE AMERICAN ETHOS AND NATIONAL-SECURITY TRADITIONS

Michael Vlahos

America is talking again about how to defend itself from attack. For decades, since Hiroshima, this nation has wrestled with the possible consequences of a war in which nuclear weapons were launched against the United States. With the advent of the hydrogen bomb, we faced the prospect of potential national extinction if such weapons hit America. Still, we tried to develop defenses, aircraft and missiles that would shoot down the bombers that could attack the United States with nuclear bombs. Then came the ICBM—*Sputnik*—the intercontinental ballistic missile. Against this weapon, arcing into space and back at hypersonic speed, there was no defense.

There was an alternative doctrine, a simple concept really, that could substitute for real defenses. This was a doctrine called deterrence. It meant, quite simply, that the United States would deter nuclear attack with the threat of disproportionate counterattack. If the Soviet Union launched nuclear missiles at the United States, we would retaliate by launching nuclear missiles back at them. We would threaten their ultimate destruction. Although we might not initially respond by destroying the Soviet Union, we would do so if the Soviets attempted to incinerate America. Nuclear war could not be "won" if both sides were destroyed. Checkmate. Deterrence works.

The problem, however, was not so simple as the concept. It was complicated by how America redefined the geography of national security

This chapter is expanded in *Strategic Defense and the American Ethos: Can the Nuclear World Be Changed?* (Boulder, Colo.: Westview Press with The Johns Hopkins Foreign Policy Institute, SAIS, 1987).

after global war. After 1945 it was no longer possible for Americans to equate national security with merely a North American continent or even Western Hemisphere free from attack. The United States got into the business of defending something called a Free World. We had become our brother's keeper, at least for the community of democratic peoples.

We defended this world with nuclear weapons. Throughout the 1950s we declared that the United States could use atomic bombs if freedom was abridged anywhere in the world. Since that time we have softened publicly the conditions under which America might use nuclear weapons to defend its allies. In addition, by the 1970s the number of our allies had dwindled, and our commitment to defend to the death had shrunk to NATO Europe, Japan and the Republic of Korea, and Australasia.

But defending others with nuclear weapons implied the distinct possibility that using them would lead to the ultimate nuclear use: what came to be known as mutual assured destruction (MAD), the very heart of deterrence itself. This possibility made any crisis between the United States and the Soviet Union in the public mind the potential "first step" to "nuclear holocaust."

Add to this apprehension the growth in Soviet nuclear strength. There had been a time, enshrouded in myth for many today, when only the United States possessed "the bomb." Then there was a generation or so when the Soviets had bombs, but of a kind and number and delivery distinctly inferior to the U.S. nuclear arsenal. This meant that the same generation of Americans could have confidence in the frightening concept of deterrence because it was a concept that we controlled.

The theory of deterrence has been rooted in two assumptions: U.S. nuclear superiority and the extension of deterrence—the will to escalate from conventional war—that only U.S. nuclear superiority can guarantee with confidence. Now there is no such confidence. The Soviet nuclear buildup has exposed the fragility of deterrence without strategic advantage. The United States has been unable to keep pace with recent Soviet nuclear programs. It has been unable to restrain them through arms control. It has been unable to counter them with sufficient new nuclear programs.

The issue of strategic defense is really an issue of change. More important, it is also change in the readiness of the American people to endure a strategy that can no longer promise security.

Debate over "Star Wars" is a struggle over unspoken values. It is a part of a tension stretching back to America's beginnings. One part is a tension over the proper American role in the wider world. Can we forever defend other peoples on the basis of inevitable American destruction? Another part is a tension over the very nature of our national security. Can we continue to trust our way of life to a strategic concept of retaliation that is believed both immoral and unworkable?

The president's Strategic Defense Initiative (SDI) was presented as a visionary fork in the road. It may never bring us back to a former time when we felt safe from attack, when our security seemed to rest on our free will. It is nonetheless a potential turning point for Americans.

SDI is not just another future weapons system. It is both an instrument and a signal of historical change. Strategic defense did not reemerge as a result of technology alone. Defense against nuclear attack has arisen from an eroding American strategic position, a stance that many believe is losing the respect of allies and adversary and, at last, of Americans themselves.

The surface debate may look like just another arcane tug-of-war in the Washington strategic community. It is not. The Strategic Defense Initiative is a response to something much bigger.

The issue of strategic defense emerged from change in the nuclear world, a shaking of tradition, and its origins must be probed. This exploration looks at the American past. This is a place that few in the strategic community visit. But our ultimate architecture of national security will be shaped by the needs of American culture, however unpalatable this may seem to strategic thinkers.

Many questions must be asked. How did persistent national attitudes lead to the Strategic Defense Initiative? Are there traditions in the American style of national security that have found voice in strategic defenses? Is SDI an authentic expression of the American ethos?

Technology has recently encouraged a rethinking of defense against nuclear missiles. If new defensive technology had been incorporated into traditional deterrence doctrine, defenses could have been pursued to strengthen deterrence and in part avoid the loss of confidence in the doctrine itself. Why not? Why was it left to a visionary presidential speech to set a course ahead? How and why did a national consensus committed to nuclear deterrence splinter? Why did change in the nuclear world lead to the Reagan vision and not to an attempt to shore up tradition?

It is my thesis that an impending American cultural rejection of a strategy of deterrence through the promise of mutual annihilation led to renewed interest in strategic defenses.

Deterrence through threat of nuclear retaliation has kept the peace for forty years. It has not failed. The deaths of hundreds of millions have not been entered on its ledger. But it is in the process of cultural rejection by Americans. Change cannot be forever delayed. It is my hope to examine its origins and, by implication, its future.

AMERICAN ETHOS AND NATIONAL SECURITY

National-security policies reflect the culture of the society creating them. The culture of a society—its ethos—defines distinctive patterns of individual and group behavior. Culture shapes the way we look at the world: our worldview. Whatever our immediate group membership, our final sense of identity is shaped by larger cultural patterns. Each human culture is unique, and each society's forms of war and politics express this uniqueness.[1]

The United States has taken this truth as its own. From the beginning this nation imposed upon itself a self-conscious identity in contrast to the European world. It was a "New World" torn from the "Old." Americans need to strengthen their self-described uniqueness, and our national-security policy has always been asked to reinforce our identity.

National security in American life exists as an icon and instrumentality lying between the Old World and the New. Society has shaped its armed forces not simply to defend, but to represent America and serve as the physical mechanism of its separation from or involvement in the larger world.[2]

The issue of separation or involvement is central to the American experience. It has created continuing tension over the use of military force. It is a force pulling against itself, a tension at the root of the American mission. America is marked by its sense of mission, for it was a concept before it was a place, and a place before it was a nation. America began as a sanctuary, a religious and political refuge from European tyranny; Americans have defined themselves according to the charge of a national "mission." America was both removed from Europe and created by Europeans. It existed as a refuge from all that was evil there, but also as a symbol of Europe's eventual reformation. The United States has a national mission that is both protective and proselytizing. But which interpretation of national mission will prevail?

This fundamental stress can be called a struggle between "progress" and "purification." It is a conflict over the direction of national identity. What we are is dependent on what we will be. America is a concept forever in the process of "becoming." Where we are going is the key to becoming. The right path must be taken. And there have always been two righteous paths for America. Calling them "progressive" and "purifier" is not meant to imply formal, or even conscious, political affiliation in the galaxy of American interest groups. But it is a way of describing how all Americans, at the unspoken core of their meaning, speak in ways that form significant variations within the common sense of what it is to be an American.

This dualistic identity shares common religious roots. The impact of Protestant thought is felt in the ways we talk about mission, service, sacrifice, restraint. It underlies the sense that Americans share as serving a higher calling. If America's core values can be defined, they would begin with this sense of calling. It is linked to the broader and secular notion of national mission.

Both progressive and purifier visions of national identity also began with the belief that America was to be the temporal enactment of God's will and purpose. The progressive focused on national becoming through physical experience: manifest destiny. The purifier saw an American realization through spiritual example, as in American Christian missionary movements.[3]

The progressive part of our ethos calls for a literal realization of national mission. From the beginning, mission involved a place. This place was called many things, from an American "empire" to a "New Jerusalem." At first it was an alternative world to the tyranny of Europe. Eventually the progressive New World sought to reform the Old.

The key is that American values and goals are to be realized through the physical growth of the United States. Nineteenth-century expansion was territorial. Twentieth-century expansion was contractual. The United States became committed to the world.

For the progressive, there is a role for war. War can be both just and necessary. In the American Revolution, war created liberty. In the Civil War, war preserved it. American intervention in the two world wars rescued humanity. War is fought both to defend America and to realize its mission. The horrifying weapons of the nuclear age were wedged reluctantly within this tradition.

War is seen as corrupting. Progressives, however, believe that the American calling is righteous enough to defy war's corruption. This will be true as long as the American way of war is true to the American ethos.[4]

Theodore Roosevelt embodied the progressive approach to war and military force. For Roosevelt, this approach actually mirrored a self-styled, "progressive" domestic political agenda. Roosevelt put strategy into practice. U.S. military power was used to promote world stability, and U.S. naval forces became an active instrument of an American mission. This set a twentieth-century precedent.[5]

The other cause is no less "righteous." It can demand more of American society. The purifier demands that the United States attain earthly perfection before it preaches to others. Reform thyself, and be a model to the world. The power of American virtue will spread the word. The United States will uplift through example.

For the purifiers, American expansion means war. War is always morally corrosive. There is no defense against its poison. The growth of the United States in the 1840s was seen as an extension of slavery. Expansion in the 1890s perpetuated an unjust economic system. Today, America's "global reach" is called an economic enslavement of the Third World.

Daniel Webster said it all: "You have a Sparta, embellish it!" He meant that America lives in the uprightness of its citizens, that spiritual purity is in inverse proportion to physical size, that an American empire would equal imperialism, and that physical expansion would destroy American democracy and the American soul.[6]

The impulse to national expansion is seen as an expression of domestic disease. It is a symptom that our society is in need of healing.

Purifiers are not always pacifists. Their suspicion of military estab- lishments is an American tradition. In eighteenth-century Europe, armies were the agents of monarchy and the tools of tyranny. The original American army was the militia. It was the first "peoples" army. In contrast, a large standing military was seen as a separate political force in society. It would "militarize" America and promote war. In this sense purifiers hearken to the America of the 1790s.[7]

There is no formal allegiance by groups as progressives or purifiers. Interest groups in society tend to have special concerns. They consider an embracing American mission only when parts of it connect with their own objectives. The very words "purifier" and "progressive" describe two basic approaches to an American sense of mission. The core values are shared—constitution, democracy, economic opportunity, a conviction of the universal rightness of the values themselves—but the path to promoting or safeguarding them differs profoundly. Groups in U.S. society tend to lean toward either the purifier or the progressive, without using those terms. Most individuals and groups think in terms of political allegiances: whether Whig or Republican or Democrat. Yet political parties have shifted over time from progressive to purifier worldviews, and back again. Superficial political labels can often disguise the deeper currents of worldview.

For example, there have been salient occasions in our history when those who followed a purifier current in American worldview suddenly shifted course. The political context of American society can always change, and groups are forced to discard one means—progressive or purifier—to attain their goals. Groups that have been solid purifiers can turn to progressive means. William Lloyd Garrison and the American Peace Society championed pacifism as radical "nonresistance" in the 1850s. They deserted the cause, however, and flocked to the colors in April 1861 when Lincoln called for volunteers. At the annual meeting of the American Peace Society in May, one society member recalled how purifiers at once became progressives:

> The course of the Society, on that occasion, was a surprise to all: a stranger, unapprised of the purpose of the meeting, would have supposed it for the vindication of war, rather than that of peace.[8]

In the 1930s purifiers on the socialist Left vocally denounced isolationism and demanded U.S. involvement against "Fascist aggression" in Abyssinia and Spain. Their "internationalism" ironically encouraged what would become the ultimate expansion of the American progressive mission after 1945. And there were progressives that became purifiers. Those who followed Woodrow Wilson's call and fought with the American Expeditionary Force in France in 1918 later renounced U.S. intervention in European affairs. Many A.E.F. veterans helped to shape the neutrality legislation that marked the high tide of "isolationism."

Purifiers and progressives do not wear neat and correspondent political colors. The Right was a bastion of American antiwar chastity during the era of the Ludlow Amendment, as was the populist Left. Today, extreme right- and left-wing constituencies share an unusual intimacy. Both seek American withdrawal and purification. Libertarians and Unitarians, for example, reflect a curious convergence as they call for strategic withdrawal, disarmament, and social reform.[9]

The apparent irony of this convergence is superficial. Progress and purification are ultimately linked for Americans. They are different means to a common end. The ability of the rigid disciples of radical nonviolence to "lock-and-load" with the Grand Army of the Republic, the readiness of A.E.F. veterans to champion isolation in Congress, evokes the strong if hidden bridge between progress and purification.

The images of "progressive" and "purifier" are intended to evoke two basic and still unresolved paths for an American mission. The tension between them is reflected in a historically confused American approach to national security. Since the end of World War II the United States has maintained a progressive construction of national security. It has been upheld longer than any former expansive interpretation of the American mission. Yet many believe it is eroding. Purifier groups in U.S. society have grown strong in recent years. Although the debate over national security is really a contest between progressive and purifier, between two directions for the American future, the visible issues emerge through slogans like "No More Vietnams" and "No Nukes" and, now, with "Star Wars."

THE SDI DEBATE AS A LEGACY
OF AMERICAN TRADITIONS

The debate over strategic defense—"Star Wars"—is being waged over these fundamental issues: Who are we? Where do we come from? Where are we going?

The voices defending and attacking the Strategic Defense Initiative (SDI) are full of passion. The language may sound like a debate over national security. But the emotions expressed emerge from out of our visions and fears about the American future. We define ourselves in our future. The stress we feel discussing strategic defense is related then to our sense of national identity.

The voices raised for and against strategic defense are descended from earlier progressive and purifier visions of American mission. They seek roots in the world before 1945. They look to an America that linked national-security policy to traditional values. This must be recognized.

The debate over SDI is a reemergence of the passionate over the pragmatic in American national security. Strategic defense implies much more than change in strategic nuclear posture. It is a potential departure by society from a goal of "nuclear stability" to a kind of nuclear disestablishment.

Star Wars supporters are certainly within the progressive tradition. The vision of SDI evokes an earlier age of American manifest destiny. SDI describes a new place for the physical expansion of the United States: "space, the final frontier." SDI renews an American precept lost after 1945: control of our own destiny. The progressive argument reads like this: Nuclear weapons are not the only immorality. It is immoral as well for American citizens to live exposed to destruction. It is wrong to yield their safety to the restraint of a potential enemy.[10]

The Star Wars iconoclasts—those who see SDI as unmitigated immorality—are purifiers. They, too, believe that prevention of nuclear war ultimately hinges on nuclear disestablishment. But they see SDI as an attempt to substitute other kinds of military force for nuclear deterrence. If successful, this would perpetuate the legitimacy and reality of war. If unsuccessful, they insist, SDI would promote, not prevent, a nuclear war. Finally, SDI threatens the primacy of arms control as the only accepted process to an eventual nuclear disestablishment. Arms control is the only way to control the threat of war. An armed world cannot secure "real peace," with or without nuclear weapons.[11]

However defensive, weapons are still weapons. This has been a tenacious tenet of American purifiers since the beginning. They opposed first the big sailing frigates of 1797 and then the battleships of 1890 or

1935 as contributing to a general world climate of antagonism and confrontation. They insist that limited weapons actually tend to make nuclear war more "thinkable," their way of saying more acceptable, and so, more possible. Nuclear weapons paradoxically are cherished by purifiers. Their natural persistence lends inarguable moral force to the call for disarmament. It is the ultimate "horror of war." SDI is to be especially condemned for both eroding the future moral force of the nuclear threat and for doing this with another weapon.

Ironically, then, although purifier and progressive visions of national direction remain juxtaposed, both groups share the goal of nuclear disestablishment. The progressives have embraced change that will strip nuclear weapons of political and military value. The purifiers seek to imprison nuclear weapons through arms control, which they believe is the first step to a disarmed world. Both worldviews promote old ideas of American mission. Both reject the more classically European policies—in particular, the national-security policies of the past forty years—of the postwar pragmatists.[12]

The pragmatists emerged from the wreckage of traditional American mythology. The received truths of World War II indicted U.S. policies of the 1930s. American isolation from the world had encouraged evil states to start aggressive wars. Eventually, it led them to attack the United States itself. Pearl Harbor showed brutally that the United States lived in a harsh world. The lesson to both isolationists and internationalists (who in the 1930s sought American involvement in the world without corollary rearmament) was that their prewar policies were foolish and dangerous.[13]

Even in 1945 this lesson was still not fully accepted. Global war seemed to finish the issue of Nazi evil, and the United Nations and great power détente seemed sufficient solution to keep the peace. The hammer blows of Berlin and China and Korea finally drove the lesson home: the world was forever changed, and America's approach to the world must be recast.

The old American traditions of "manifest destiny and mission," in which Yankee forays into the world hewed to an episodic and crusading character, were buried in 1950 by Korea and the cold war. U.S. global responsibilities demanded pragmatic policymaking. The United States, it was said, was a mature great power. It should be guided in the British manner, according to cool and classical calculations of national interest and intervention. The pragmatists sought to "manage" America and the world. They bent their knees to traditional national ideals. But they seemed assured that former notions of national identity would intrude only at the margins of political debate.

Since 1980 all that has changed. Both Left and Right margins unexpectedly unseated the centers of their political parties: they came in from the margins. Pragmatists are now accused of "realism," in tones not dissimilar to epithets of "Old World realpolitik," like Woodrow Wilson's charge against "secret treaties."

The pragmatic center can claim today to have guided the United States through forty years of nuclear peace. The center was shocked then to be judged by purifiers as morally guilty of wishing to perpetuate the nuclear world. It was no longer sufficient to say that peace was possible only through preparation for nuclear war.

The postwar pragmatists have sought to defend their postwar strategic architecture. By their measurement, it has sheltered the liberty of the West and upheld a nuclear peace. Yet change is the core of both progressive and purifier challenges to the pragmatic center. The center in contrast has pushed stability, the opposite of change.

Always, technology is the touchstone of change. Technology is a symbol of the American mission for both progressives and purifiers. For SDI supporters, technology is assurance of achievement. Technology is the sign of America's calling. It is America's special gift. The impact of this nation on world history can be seen through the impact of technology.

For the iconoclasts, technology is in itself suspect. It may even be an agency of evil. A few SDI opponents in the popular press sound like Luddites. They are as full of anger and fear as were their ancestors during the industrial revolution.[14]

Anti-Star Wars diatribes describe SDI as technology "gone mad." SDI becomes a symbol of a larger problem. Technology worship in American society is destroying the environment and dehumanizing Man. SDI symbolizes an unnatural course for Man. Weapons in space, to the extreme purifier are, like the clarion of "Man in space," an image of celestial violation. Although couched in the sober language of pragmatism, the distaste for the physical-heroic in space is ultimately a rejection of the progressive half of the American ethos.

> The real Niñas and Pintas today are unmanned probes . . . the most lofty justification for manned space travel is that it satisfies, as all 'Star Trek' fans know, the urge 'to boldly go where no man has gone before.' But a mission to Mars would be timidly revisiting a place we went years ago. As an expression of the human spirit, manned space exploration is rather complacent. . . . Sally Ride on Mars would be nothing more than a $100 billion flag-planter.[15]

Both progressives and purifiers understand that SDI means change. Progressives would embrace change as relief, even sanctuary, from a frightening and uncertain present. Purifiers also fear and loathe the nuclear present. Unrelenting change brought us the dilemmas of the present, and increasing the pace of change can bring only more danger. They want a different kind of change.

To the progressive, technology is the instrument of American destiny: it is what made us and preserved us. It created the hope of a free world. To the purifier, technology has been the instrument corrupting America and endangering the world. To the postwar pragmatists, technology represented a mechanism of balance, the eccentric of a stable-state political universe.

"Technology" for each group is simply a part of the litany of our hope or despair for the future.

By offering a unified national goal, SDI has already linked progressives and purifiers (and transcended the pragmatists). By encapsulating motifs that both visions share, by aspiring to a righteous construction of national security free of the cynicism of nuclear deterrence through threat of annihilation, it might even seem to be a potential means of binding two strands in the American ethos. SDI does not promote an agenda of arms control, however, so it is rejected by the purifiers. SDI is embraced by the progressives, but often for the wrong reasons. It is seen as a national deus ex machina, the intervention of an ancestral, almost godlike instrumentality that will return us to the romantic landscape of security we once enjoyed. SDI is scourged and worshipped, ultimately, for its sense of promise. It is almost instinctively understood by Americans. It resonates to our national hymn.

Because it strikes so deep a chord, SDI represents a potential point of departure from the pragmatists' sense of an American mission. It can overturn the world as it was remade after 1950. But maybe that world is already changed. Maybe SDI only brings the recognition of change. Even its most impassioned critics, stirred up by the Nuclear Freeze, push for a departure, at least from the nuclear world. While purifier and progressive directions for an American character diverge, their goals for Americans somehow merge on the horizon.

The desire for escape from the present nuclear world is in itself important. It implies perhaps a desire for Americans to escape the entire sum of commitments and entanglements snared since the last great war. The promise of SDI, and the ways in which it might change the context of American national security, raise these questions:

- How, after forty years, did the idea of fundamental change become politically legitimate?
- Why the groundswell for nuclear disestablishment, and how did a yearning for nuclear abolition lead to SDI?

- How did the center, the guiding postwar pragmatists, lose the American consensus?
- How did a president come to inspire a vision for progressives and renounce the status quo of seven predecessors?

Is the vision of SDI a rejection of a "pragmatic" postwar American mission, or is it ultimately a more basic rejection of a national-security doctrine of deterrence rooted in nuclear determinism?

THE CHALLENGE TO NUCLEAR DETERRENCE

Genesis: Change in a Nuclear World

The "nuclear world" as it came to be known after 1945 seemed a new place. All former notions of the uses of military force in international relations were swept away. Everything had changed. The atomic bomb magnified the dynamism of modern strategy, which had been scarred already by city bombing, poison gas, and "total war." The twentieth century was a century of change, change wrought by technology. Nuclear fission was now its most visible symbol. Atomic weapons and their deadly delivery systems multiplied. The "arms race" was reality, bomber and missile "gaps" the perceptual norm. It was frightening. And it was inescapable.

The face of the nuclear world appeared to change in the 1960s. The fear of the threat of nuclear war was assuaged by a national confidence in U.S. nuclear capability. President Kennedy had rekindled faith in American strength; the military buildup of his administration erased the public uncertainties created by bomber and missile gaps.

Moreover, Americans assumed that the technology of nuclear systems had reached an evolutionary plateau and that the U.S. nuclear advantage could, conceivably, be extended forever. It was even said that the Soviets also accepted this notion of a nuclear plateau. They understood that a condition of stability naturally encouraged a "stable nuclear balance." Kremlin leaders, so it was argued, could no longer hope to achieve a nuclear advantage over the United States. Conviction replaced uncertainty as American policymakers came to believe that the United States could control the strategic nuclear balance to its advantage.[16]

World War II had added a leitmotiv to the American mythic symphony. The United States had experienced no national failure after its victory in 1945. Its energies seemed equal to the threat of nuclear war. Kennedy's inaugural charge radiated national confidence. A nuclear world could be harnessed by the United States, just as a turbulent world could be uplifted and an implacable adversary ultimately reformed.

An authentic American school of strategy, nurtured after the war at places like Yale and MIT and Rand, seemed to have grown to maturity. It added to these other strengths. Among its tenets, as announced by secretary of defense Robert McNamara in 1967, was the conviction that Soviet behavior could be conditioned by U.S. actions, just as the United States could control the dynamics of the arms race. These assumptions formed a kind of cultural projection. American policymaking perspectives were pasted onto the adversary to become our understanding of Soviet strategic worldview. It was all too easy to conclude, after assuming they possessed a rational approach to strategy, that the Soviets accepted our tenets of nuclear stability as well.[17]

This new reality was capped by an arms-control policy that tied American military posture to a reform agenda. No longer was Western nuclear capability focused simply on deterrence of war: it existed now to encourage arms limitations. Nuclear forces resembled the Roman god Janus, with one face looking to war, and one to peace. Before, SAC (Strategic Air Command) could say with a straight face that "Peace Is Our Profession." Weapons' existence preserved the peace. Now, the government was implying that only a decline in weapons could be described as promoting peace.[18] Confidence in U.S. nuclear strength, an assumption that the Soviets would not bid for nuclear advantage, and a desire among pragmatists to pursue goals of stability and arms limitation integral to the American tradition led to a promise of change in the nuclear world.

By the 1970s it appeared that the path of stability was fully cleared, if not yet paved. At its policy terminus it offered a seductive vision with strong Early American roots: détente. The "peaceable kingdom" seemed possible. The assumptions of the policymakers of the 1960s had been proved. The nuclear balance remained stabilized. Arms-control agreements were edging toward real arms limitation.

Darker undercurrents, however, were at work, which would erode American confidence in the strategic theories of the 1960s, while at the same time, perversely, strengthen their goals. The pragmatists who shaped these theories framed goals of nuclear stability and arms limitation through a posture of American nuclear strength. The goals were consonant with national core values, but the means to achieve them were borrowed from classical, European strategic tradition.

National failure in Vietnam undermined the policy hold of the pragmatic center and ended in destroying its fragile postwar legitimacy. Ultimately, Vietnam was a failure that penetrated to the core of the pragmatists' strategic premises. Theories implying almost scientific principles were applied in Vietnam. They were devoid of the traditional emotional content of American wars, which focused on a kind of crusading reformation of the enemy. The callous theories of "graduated response" and "escalation control" failed to reinforce the core values of national ethos. Vietnam was not seen as a failure of theories misapplied. The theories themselves, it was said, and those who made them, were wrong.[19] Yet these theories had also been applied wholesale to the doctrine of nuclear deterrence.

National failure in Vietnam led not only to a partial American retreat in the Third World. It also inspired a reemergence of progressive and purifier worldviews. Among Democrats, these had been in uneasy coalition since 1950. Largely as a function of internecine political combat over Vietnam policy, the challenge to pragmatist strategy emerged first in the Democratic party. In the 1972 convention, purifier constituencies seized control of the party. Although ameliorated since, purifier views have remained ascendant among Democrats. Their planks have exalted arms control and détente as a new American strategy, along with a kind of "soft internationalism" as a substitute for containment. This geopolitical vision of containment, created by the Truman progressives of the late 1940s, was in eclipse, labeled as "neo-imperialism."

The Republican pragmatists under Nixon survived a while longer. They sought to limit the damage of American defeat by accommodating the Soviet Union. This was presented for public consumption, however, as a kind of "peace in our time." Intended to buy time for Western recovery, the Nixon course only promoted eventual rebellion among radical and populist Republicans, who saw in accommodation with evil a corruption of American righteousness and, ultimately, of the American mission. To Republican purifiers reminiscent of the old isolationists and Republican progressives driven by a globalist anticommunism, Watergate was the rallying cry for a rejection of the Nixonian pragmatists. This led to Reagan's eventual coup de main.

Nixon's "atmospherics" of arms control and détente, however, publicly altered the image of the adversary in the early 1970s. The Soviets were now mirror-image instead of mirror-opposite. Arms control became a problem of communication, not of ideology. This implied that the weapons themselves were the problem. Real security could be based on mutual understanding. Impending superpower rapprochement made nuclear deterrence based on American strategic advantage look passé. The question that underlay Nixonian détente: "What in the name of God is 'strategic superiority'?"

In this climate of political upheaval, national defeat, and hopeful accommodation with the enemy, an intellectual pressure may have been the most insidious. An academic school of historical "revisionism" poisoned all that was positive in our public myths of the postwar era. The American mission was a sham, revisionists wrote. A strategy of global leadership and containment was retold as a crude kind of nineteenth-century manifest destiny. The revisionists, dominated by purifiers and penitent progressives, called for a return to the spiritual sources of American conduct. In their writings, an American mission informed by the historical "lessons" of global war and prewar appeasement was renounced. Traditional American morality meant abstention from corrupting policies.

The United States had transgressed. It had lost its original sense of purpose. It was now no more than a sordid empire. Since 1945 it had initiated two evil wars against the Third World. It had threatened all Humankind with nuclear holocaust. Historical dispensation required penance. This meant nuclear disarmament, social reform, and good works in the form of alms to the Third World. In this vein, a standard claim was:

> People talk about nuclear weapons as an aberration or something horrible that's just sort of happened. And I think the reality is that nuclear weapons are the dominant force in U.S. foreign policy since 1945, and they've been a major part of the United States dominating the world—economically, socially, and politically.[20]

By the mid-1970s the pragmatic center was under terrific pressure from two traditional directions in the American ethos. A reemergence of purifiers, generally but not wholly identifying themselves on the political Left, pressured the dominant Democratic center during and after the Vietnam War. With the nomination of George McGovern in 1972, the purifier vision, long buried during decades of world wars and cold wars, reassumed the mantle of 1932. Pragmatists in the party accommodated the change, attempting after 1976 to pull the Democrats' agenda back to the center. Progressives in the party, the cold warriors of NSC-68 and Korea, fought back, but their last bastion crumbled after the death of Senator Henry Jackson in 1982. Many, like Jeanne Kirkpatrick and Richard Perle, became renegades and joined the newly progressive Republican camp.

Nixon's stigmata of Watergate ultimately impugned the pragmatists in the Grand Old Party. Republican populists under Reagan attacked in 1976 and were narrowly defeated by the Ford coterie. It was a pyrrhic victory for them, however, and by 1980 Reagan's time had come. Although not burdened by direct culpability for Vietnam, as were the Democrat pragmatists, their association with Kissinger and classical grand strategy tainted the pragmatists fatally. It also infected the credibility of their strategic policies. The assumed failure of these policies permitted the

Reagan progressives eventually to conjure an alternative in the form of SDI.

But in the later 1970s it was purifier political pressures that burdened both the Ford and Carter administrations. Responding first to the political and military failures of the 1970s, the purifiers eventually came to fasten on the evil of nuclear weapons. This process of political fixation was intensified by the twin failures of arms control and strategic modernization after 1975.

Failure of the Nuclear Elite

The struggle for power within the arms-control community after 1975 can be traced to domestic stresses and to Soviet behavior, which chafed away at pragmatist policies of nuclear deterrence. First, the pragmatists' moderate arms-control strategy had not made the world a safer place. In fact, the world had very quickly become a more dangerous place. The Soviet response to arms control had been to use it to their own advantage: to build up their nuclear forces while holding back U.S. strategic programs. The achievements of early arms-control agreements, especially SALT I, were seen by many as clearly damaging to the U.S. strategic nuclear position. SALT II was merely a protracted attempt to limit its damage. Consequently, internal strife flared up about the utility— even the safety—of arms control as the centerpiece of U.S. strategic policy.[21]

Second, pragmatist efforts at strategic modernization crumbled from public pressures unintentionally created by détente and purifier political lobbies, which slowed attempts to modernize America's aging nuclear arsenal. Even in 1983 enormous political effort was needed to put intermediate-range nuclear forces (INF) into Western Europe. Finally, strategic modernization failed with its critical capstone: the MX ICBM.

The self-evisceration of the strategic community came at the end of the 1970s with the final collapse of détente. The pragmatic center showed itself incapable of passing SALT II and, then, of getting reelected. It could not achieve its moderate arms-control agenda. With the coming of Reagan, it would not get another chance.

Many pragmatists yielded to the purifiers, abandoning the course of long-term goals through moderate change for the road of rapid and radical solutions. Many from the postwar center converted. The "Gang of Four" was one sharp highlight of pragmatists-turned-purifiers. Within the Republican camp, the pragmatic center had been banished momentarily for abetting the decline of American power. But for this group, the answer was not to be found in a purifier agenda for arms control. Quite the reverse. Strategic pragmatists, like Harry Rowen and Albert

Wohlstetter, embraced the progressive worldview and called for a reassertion of U.S. nuclear advantage.

The postwar strength of the pragmatic center, built on the received "truths" of the 1930s and 1940s, was diminished. Its nonpartisan political unity—the unity of deterrence—was gone. The margins had conquered the center.

The situation was unusual. Policymaking elites were now visibly dominated by traditional notions of national security. Extreme progressives and purifiers holding media center-stage spoke in lurid language for public consumption. Together, they generated a kind of national-security symbiosis. They needed each other for the consummation of their passion. These voices were comfortable with radical agenda and spectral futures inevitable if prophesy and Cassandra-warning were not heeded.

The result of fear-mongering after 1980 was fear itself. The collapse of détente and civil feuding within the arms-control community inspired real public apprehension. When the Soviet Union rushed to take advantage by stoking the fires of the "Euromissile" crisis, they inflamed only a latent hysteria.

At first startled by the intensity of the nuclear debate, the public began to question the notion of nuclear deterrence. For more than a generation they had accepted the pragmatists' "nuclear reality" and grown accustomed to a certain balance and moderation of tone in elite language describing such policies as "deterrence," "retaliation," and "assured destruction." But the elites had fractured, and public trust drifted. After the failures of the 1970s public confidence in national policy waned. No longer could Americans be consoled or comforted by nuclear deterrence. And in the face of a remorseless Soviet nuclear buildup, postwar strategic theories seemed especially fragile. This time of fear was to have serious cultural consequences; ultimately, it changed the terms of reference for national-security policy.

The Rebellion Against Nuclear Deterrence

American worldview shifted between 1979 and 1983. Not only were popular attitudes transformed but the group agenda of influential social "guilds" changed as well. What had been lost was more than superficial political support for deterrence. It was the confident belief that underlay it: that the best—the only—way to secure the United States from nuclear attack was through the credible threat of nuclear retaliation. Could confidence and security continue if this threat was no longer believed? And if it was believed, but simply wrong, could it be continued?

The change in public perceptions was sensationalized in a spate of television and cinema portrayals of nuclear war. Films of the early 1980s exceeded those popular in the early 1960s; *The Day After, Testament,* and *Threads* attempted an emotional devastation in sharp contrast to *Fail Safe* and *Doctor Strangelove.* Those earlier movies merely looked at how war might start and warned of our inability to control a nuclear "accident."

Today's films, however, focus on war and a postwar world. Unlike *Fail Safe,* they are not sanctimonious. Unlike *Doctor Strangelove,* they dare not risk humor. They are proselytizing films: not political propaganda, but American secular missionary tracts. Their appeal is much like a fire-and-brimstone sermon, and through fear they seek to convert and reform.[22] Instead of insisting that we vigilantly keep the cork tight on the "nuclear genie," they preach that these weapons will destroy us unless we repent our evil ways and rid ourselves of them soon. These films form the catechism of the purifiers. Their verses read like this:

- Nuclear evil is in the weapons themselves, like a monstrous incubus. We and the Soviets are in their thrall.
- Peace is not the absence of war, but the absence of nuclear weapons. As long as there are nuclear weapons, there will one day be nuclear war. (Of course, one might say that this is implicit in President Reagan's vision as well.)
- Imagined Soviet crimes are less important than nuclear disestablishment. The Soviets are people and can be reformed. The weapons are irreconcilable evil.
- The longer the United States keeps nuclear weapons, the more their evil will enter into us. Absolute weapons corrupt absolutely.
- We created nuclear weapons; we are therefore guilty of a cardinal sin. We must take the first step, and the major risk, to their abolition.

As Jonathan Schell wrote, in *The Abolition,* "Nuclear weapons are truly an evil obsession: they can somehow drag us down even as we try to fight them. They soil us."[23]

Three legitimate groups enshrined these theses: a political coalition for a Nuclear Freeze; the Union of Concerned Scientists and those who have pushed the Nuclear Winter nostrum; and the U.S. Catholic Conference (USCC), which promoted the pastoral letter of American bishops. Seeking to create electoral pressure to achieve radical arms control, these groups have employed many tactics reminiscent of the nineteenth-century abolitionist movement: they have made it politically dangerous, intellectually dangerous, and morally dangerous to defend the status quo.

The Nuclear Freeze tried to create a bandwagon that would be politically dangerous for any officeholder to oppose. The key declaration was that the potential for nuclear war was a function of the size of nuclear stockpiles. The freeze movement tried to force a consensus that equated nuclear armaments to nuclear war. Once this connection was made, it was imagined that anyone so foolish as to support nuclear armaments would by definition be in favor of nuclear war.[24]

Nuclear Winter was to be unopposable because those who asserted it were unimpeachable. The Sagan set sought to manipulate the abject respect most Americans have for their scientists. The "concerned scientists" also tried to make it seem as though all scientists with any principles were with them. "Scientists" would redefine strategic reality. Scientific fiat would deny all forms of nuclear utility. The most limited nuclear war would be impossible if even a small atomic dose could trigger nuclear winter and lead to human extinction. Nuclear weapons might be in the hands of the military, but their value would be negated by a higher consciousness.[25]

The Bishop's Pastoral was embraced by the entire purifier community—even the very secular professional Left. The Pastoral had the virtue of declaring in its highly publicized first draft that national defense through threat of nuclear retaliation was immoral. Anyone defending the theory of deterrence was either a very bad man or a fool. Nuclear disarmament was offered as the only and ultimate solution to the nuclear dilemma. Until nuclear weapons could be abolished, their possession would be acceptable only if assurance was given that they would never be used. Some bishops and USCC leaders even declared that capitulation was preferable to the *threat* of nuclear destruction.[26]

These condemnations indicted postwar strategy and undermined the pragmatic center. The importance of the freeze movement was its ability to ingest what had been the center and to shift the boundary markers of national debate. Nuclear abolition was made the center, and nearly every centrist political group now jumped the bandwagon. In order to seize the center, the freeze and its resolutions were watered down to inoffensiveness, but the terms of reference for nuclear debate nonetheless had been changed. The old center, the strategic worldview of the postwar pragmatists, had been replaced by a purifier vision, however hazy, of nuclear abolition.

Progressives supporting the Reagan administration fulminated against purifier groups. They retained a large, if uneasy, following. The "moral high ground," however, was in the hands of the "abolitionists." By 1983 the purifiers had succeeded in damaging public faith in peace through threat of nuclear retaliation. Deterrence had been informally labeled as MAD: Mutual Assured Destruction. Now there seemed no security in the notion of assured destruction. Four administrations had tried to increase U.S. capacity to respond to the threat of Soviet attack with options other than assured destruction, but options short of MAD sought only to limit damage in the event that basic deterrence failed.

The Reagan administration attempted to extend this set of options in what some called a "prevailing" strategy. This promised limited damage, at least, from the application of the threat of nuclear retaliation. The attempt failed. In fact, it added volatile fuel to the purifier movement. The Reagan nuclear strategy, adamantly resisting the freeze formula, was a ready-made mask for purifier portrayal of progressives as warmongers.

WHAT WAS TO BE DONE?

The pragmatists were innocent of the political need to manipulate a skittish public. They lacked the tools to orchestrate a campaign for public confidence. They were equally incapable of defending their nuclear strategy from an unexpected angle of attack: from former members of their own corps and from legitimate political groups—not just from the margins of the American Left or from Soviet propaganda. Revitalizing the morale of Western strategy was a task beyond pragmatic strategists, whose careers had been spent in the pursuit of the unquestioned premises of their strategic world.

The pragmatists faced seemingly insurmountable obstacles. How could they renew American strength and confidence? Strategic modernization was failing. Arms control had failed. The Western publics were losing faith in basic nuclear deterrence.

In response the pragmatic center tried to reassert a strategic nuclear posture that Americans, allies, and adversary had long believed to be "credible." It was hoped that restoration of U.S. strategic posture might reclaim Western public confidence and encourage a Soviet return to the "arms control table." This notion of credibility reposed in a concept called "extended deterrence." Extended deterrence has been called the existential concept from which all U.S. postwar strategy has been derived. The Soviet ICBM buildup of the last fifteen years, however, has rent the confidence in American nuclear advantage necessary to sustain it.

Today, the Soviet capability to strike U.S. ICBM fields and nonalert bomber strips is intended to dissuade U.S. strategic nuclear "first use" in the context of preventing a Soviet theater victory. The Soviet ICBM is, like the U.S. strategic force of old, a *political* tool to show confident escalation control. In the words of two Soviet generals,

Soviet military strategy primarily reflects the political strategy of the Communist Party of the Soviet Union. . . . Only political leadership can determine the scale and consistency of bringing to bear the most powerful means of destruction. . . . Of all factors which affect military strategy, the most important are political factors.[27]

Political goals explain the recent Soviet attempt to abort U.S. theater nuclear reinforcement in NATO. U.S. Pershing and cruise missiles were a very modest addition to local NATO forces. The missiles are vulnerable to Soviet conventional attack in a theater war and are insufficient by themselves to extend deterrence. If they had been blocked, however, the Soviet Union could have announced an American withdrawal of will. The Euromissiles were America's stopgap response to a world of parity. They were to show that the United States was still committed to extended deterrence. They were a symbol of American resolve. Cancellation of the Euromissiles would have made them a symbol of the end of extended deterrence, and it would have strengthened Soviet political leverage over Western Europe.

Strategic modernization, as described by former secretary of defense Harold Brown, was an attempt to reassert extended deterrence. Knowing that only substance, not symbol, would work, he programmed nuclear forces that would create uncertainties in Soviet target planning against U.S. ICBMs. Under Brown's concept, MX deployment was not intended to make U.S. ICBMs invulnerable or to threaten the entire Soviet ICBM force. However, because enough U.S. missiles would survive an attack to derail Soviet war aims, the Soviets would not be able to strike the MX with confidence. Soviet planners would be unable to deter U.S. strategic nuclear response in a theater war. They would find themselves deterred, therefore, at lower levels, thus conceding to the United States the escalation control it assumed in 1945.[28]

The MX deployment envisaged by Brown, however, never saw concrete. The token MX voted by Congress during the Reagan tenure cannot do the job. The so-called Midgetman, or mobile ICBM, highly touted for the role of stand-in, is in equally deep trouble politically. Vulnerable to barrage attacks, Midgetman's lasting utility, let alone its ability to correct Soviet nuclear advantage, is uncertain. More important, it is still an ICBM. A new missile on American soil is unwanted. This is part of the change in the nuclear world.

The Trident D-5 submarine-launched ballistic missile has been hailed by some as a working substitute for the ICBM. It can hit Soviet military targets accurately, including ICBMs. The Trident D-5 is to be deployed, however, in a limited number of submarines (perhaps two dozen at most), and only about half of these will be on patrol. Furthermore, command and control of prompt, countermilitary attacks launched from submarines is more uncertain than is the direction of land-based missiles. Sea-based missiles have served as a strategic reserve, not as a weapon of initial use. Will enough D-5s be at sea, available, and under control to be seen as a confident ICBM understudy? Without new ICBMs, and a survivable place to put them, the Soviet path to advantage is clear.

A limited ballistic missile defense (colloquially, BMD) could serve in theory as a substitute for strategic modernization. Its primary function would be to deny the Soviets confidence in a war-winning option. BMD could potentially reestablish confidence in U.S. escalation control, which would at one stroke reestablish extended deterrence. An exposed alliance would be less vulnerable to Soviet action or U.S. inaction.

There are a number of reasons why limited ballistic missile defense would seem attractive from the vantage of 1980: BMD could work to subtract from Soviet strike capability, just as strategic modernization would add to our own. A deployment of ICBM defenses could help achieve the original goals of strategic modernization. Defenses, unlike ICBMs, might seem less frightening to nuclear-sensitive publics.

Traditional ground-based BMD, however, is inherently limited. It might be able to cope with single-warhead ICBMs; however, multiple-warhead missiles could overwhelm land-based interceptors. Land-based ICBM interceptors could attack the swarm of Soviet warheads only in their terminal flight stage. In this phase it would be effective against incoming nuclear warheads, where the atmosphere would slow and pick out lighter decoys from heavier warheads. But against thousands of RVs, there would not be enough time to save the targeted U.S. silos.

Successful terminal defenses would need the help of thousands of ICBM aim points to overload a Soviet strike force with more targets to destroy than they have warheads. Traditional terminal defenses require U.S. ICBMs to be shuttled between fields of empty silos in order to waste the cross-targeting of thousands of Soviet warheads. It was this very notion of an expansion of ballistic missile infrastructure—even if it meant only a proliferation of multiple empty silos—that the American people rejected in 1981.

U.S. defense planners were faced with only one alternative: multiplying the opportunities for shooting down ICBMs. This meant essentially that U.S. defenses would have to intercept Soviet ICBMs at earlier stages of their flight. Ground-based ballistic missile defenses are useful, even as a limited defense. The problem is not that such a defense would be limited, but that its limits are inherently predictable. Even with a mix of high-atmosphere and terminal defense missiles, however, there is only the short final phase for interception.[29] The issue, however, is not the imperfection of defenses against ICBMs. It remains the promise of damage limitation, if only to our own nuclear forces. Defenses can unseat the fragile calculations and perfect scoring needed for a disarming ICBM strike.

Strategic defenses have been built before, even during the nuclear age. There is plenty of precedent. The Soviets have long believed, and invested, in strategic defenses. However inefficient their effort has appeared to some Western analysts, it is consonant with Soviet strategic doctrine, which seeks to limit damage from attack, even if only at the margins.

The Soviets have continually expanded and upgraded their own defensive ring around Moscow. They believe in its limited utility. The Soviets have exploited the chance to test and experiment with the BMD field allowed under the ABM treaty. Arguably, the treaty has aided the overall Soviet effort in strategic defenses, for it would be possible to plan a "breakout" from the treaty. Stockpiling for this eventuality is a resource issue. A long-term lead preparation would make just such a move possible: the erecting of a crude but quick nationwide ballistic missile defense.

Should the United States seek to justify limited BMD deployment, it could do so on several grounds. First, the ABM treaty was designed with revision in mind, at least in the Soviet mind. The treaty terms have built-in room for modification and could be altered to include mutual ground-based BMD deployments (the only kind known when the treaty was signed) if weapons emerged "based on new physical principles." If mutually agreeable, a limited U.S. BMD deployment could be possible within an arms-control regime.

Second, limited BMD would reinforce, rather than unseat, traditional nuclear strategy. It would not compromise deterrence through threat of mutual annihilation. It would not destroy the political usefulness of extended deterrence. And U.S. nuclear policymakers, a distinct part of the ruling class of postwar pragmatists, are comfortable with defensive systems that conform to their worldview.

But the United States essentially rejected limited, ground-based ballistic missile defenses at the end of the 1960s. We even dismantled the single BMD installation allowed under the ABM treaty after 1975. Why and how could strategic defenses return?

THE RETURN OF BMD

There are two reasons why ballistic missile defenses reemerged in the late 1970s to offer a limited defense option: technological progress and a reversal of political judgment. Combined, these two facts changed the attitudes that, in the 1960s, led to a rejection of BMD.

Ballistic missile defenses originally emerged as a U.S. response to Soviet ICBM buildup. The antiballistic missile was intended to counter the ICBM threat, just as U.S. surface-to-air missiles had made Soviet air-breathing bombers of the 1950s vulnerable. By 1969 the United States could define—if not prove—a defense against the Soviet ICBMs, which also, like jet bombers, had at first seemed invulnerable.

But strategic defenses did not clinch a political leap of faith from Congress as nuclear delivery shifted from bomber to ballistic missile. By signing the ABM treaty, U.S. policymakers reaffirmed their belief in MAD, which demanded invulnerability of strategic systems as well as absolute exposure of U.S. and Soviet societies. Although BMD research was allowed to continue, the treaty killed development of the Safeguard ABM system and essentially buried any hopes of a U.S. ballistic missile defense.

The decision to forgo ABM development was not unduly lamented. Although the United States had managed to fashion a rudimentary defense against Soviet ICBMs, it was still difficult in 1969 to shoot them down. Moreover, the Soviets had already taken countermeasures against potential unrestricted ABM deployment by the United States. By creating their own multiple independently targeted reentry vehicle (MIRV), they had greatly complicated the task of U.S. defense and doomed the development potential of Safeguard. Consequently, prevailing political opinion judged strategic defenses impossible. Not until the late 1970s would technology begin to change these attitudes.[30]

There were three grounds for the political judgment that scuttled the ABM: An ABM program was expensive. It was also considered unnecessary, as it could be expected to yield only marginal benefits to the U.S. nuclear advantage of the 1960s. Finally, the ABM offered only modest increased security for the U.S. nuclear deterrent. Such small gains were offset by contemporary fears of the ABM's potential for changing the strategic balance. The Soviet Union might gain more than the United States in a full-scale defense program, and they might begin to whittle away U.S. advantage in offensive nuclear forces.

However, by 1980 the strategic equation was uncertain and altered in ways unimagined in 1969. The United States now had the short end of stability. In addition, Soviet strategic defensive programs were beginning to suggest an eventual instability not unlike that which the strategic community, a decade earlier, had feared would result if both sides embarked on strategic defense programs. The Soviets seemed to be gaining an advantage and were beginning to violate the same treaty that was to preserve U.S. advantage. And now only the Soviets were competing. It remained for quiet research programs in the U.S. Department of Defense to explore new technologies, mostly as a hedge against technological breakout by the Soviets at the expiration of the ABM treaty. However, by the end of the 1970s a potential synergy in these technologies appeared to offer a renewed potential for strategic defenses: from space.[31]

Yet, no national-security market existed for the BMD technologies of 1980. There was no political champion, no man on a white horse. Reagan's announcement in 1983 of his intention to pursue SDI demarcated a political and cultural watershed in terms of strategic defenses. In a single televised breath, he took strategic defenses from "black programs" to the glare of public policy. He could risk this in part because BMD technologies in the 1980s have greatly improved on those that the Safeguard system offered in the late 1960s.

Limited space defenses are an option now. Performance of systems put in place by the year 2000 can be predicted. Several authorities, never enthusiasts of BMD, have suggested system performance for a "near-term" deployment. Harold Brown has written,

> Against an unresponsive threat, the over-all system could possibly have a 50 percent effectiveness—that is, destroy 50 percent of the offensive force before it reached the terminal defenses. Even claims of 90 percent effectiveness might plausibly be advanced.[32]

Brown does not foresee completion of actual systems until at least the late 1990s. Moreover, he does not believe that during the interim the Soviet threat would remain unresponsive, and he is right. Any conclusions we draw about the effectiveness of our own BMD efforts must take into account the development of Soviet countertechnologies.

However, as a response to Reagan's vision of a "defended world," Brown's comments suggest important changes in the old status quo. Before the Reagan speech, that was a world of increasing Soviet strategic strength, uncertain U.S. response, and domestic disenchantment over deterrence. Projections of even 50 percent effectiveness of nonnuclear systems against Soviet nuclear offensive forces can begin to redefine the nuclear world.

By 1980 the eternal stability of a nuclear balance based solely on offensive systems was in question. As pragmatists agonized over possible destabilizing effects of BMD, the existing nuclear balance was itself threatening to become unstable. The pragmatists might have accepted strategic defenses as a way out of a cultural cul-de-sac. With proper political presentation, strategic defenses might have been deployed as a means to reassert the credibility of U.S. extended deterrence, without necessitating a return to multiple protective shelters for the silos of a new ICBM. But they could not bring themselves to return to an option—

strategic defense—that they had rejected with such finality in 1972. The pragmatists, even under domestic political attack, still clung to a national-security doctrine that continued to erode and yet could no longer be shored up with crumbling nuclear mortar.

They refused to see that the prospects for the future might be worse without strategic defenses than with them in a controlled, limited form. Part of the appeal of SDI is a promise that the pragmatic center cannot easily deny. Without popular support for strategic modernization, without the means to halt Soviet nuclear expansion, BMD offers strategic refuge. Limited strategic defenses under an arms-control regime might also rein in rogue Soviet strategic programs, now pushing the threshold of an unratified SALT II spirit.

A PRESIDENT'S VISION

If Reagan had never spoken, perhaps the pragmatic center finally might have cemented its own SDI. But speak he did. The images are worth remembering.

> Up to now we have increasingly based our strategy of deterrence upon the threat of retaliation. But what if free people could live secure in the knowledge that their security did not rest on the threat of instant U.S. retaliation to deter a Soviet attack; that we could intercept and destroy strategic ballistic missiles before they reached our soil or that of our allies. I know this is a formidable task . . . but is it not worth every investment necessary to free the world from the threat of nuclear war?[33]

It was an authentic presidential dream: "This is not a speech that came up; it was a top down speech . . . a speech that came from the President's heart."[34]

The language of Reagan's vision of a strategic defense initiative recalled the sonorous cadences of Franklin Delano Roosevelt:

> If those days are not to come to pass—if we are to have a world in which we can breathe freely and live in amity without fear—peace-loving nations must make a concerted effort. . . .[35]

Reagan's speech, like FDR's address in Chicago in 1937, unconsciously shared basic unifying sentiments in the American worldview. Its call was not merely authentic, it was autochthonous, as from the ancient Greek sense of the word: a vision springing from ancestral land.

Reagan is not the first U.S. leader to lament the nuclear predicament and to explore some escape clause. Yet, unlike his predecessors, Reagan lacks the political luxury of simple presidential "dissatisfaction" with the all-or-nothing final option represented in a strategy of deterrence. It has been said that he received a dramatic shock of recognition. When he was taken, before the 1980 election, to the heart of Cheyenne Mountain and briefed on the awful, target-by-target, missile-by-missile truth of the SIOP—the Single Integrated Operational Plan, the final script for full nuclear war—he was stunned. The shock he so visibly revealed, the recognition of the terrible responsibility that would soon be his burden, might be called a prefiguration of tragedy. He just said, "There must be another way."

For former presidents the dilemma must have been easier to digest. The ethical problems associated with a potential failure of deterrence were offset by two powerful, reassuring truths: U.S. nuclear strength (if not advantage) and a generation of popular national-security consensus. Reagan faced not only the possibility of Soviet strategic advantage, a fear to which he was by inclination attuned, but a gathering shift in the worldview of American society.[36]

Reagan faced a far more intractable national-security problem than faced by other postwar presidents, for the need to find a military remedy to strategic fragility was not the whole problem. The Soviet buildup and the postponement of U.S. response were difficulties hardly unique to the Reagan administration and had been held at bay before. The significant change in the problem was the corrosion of confidence in deterrence within American society.

The national consensus sustaining deterrence had been riven: or, more precisely, the higher strategic consensus was split. This was not insignificant. The very underpinning of American grand strategy, the nuclear posture of extended deterrence, had always relied on the unstated but wholesale support of the American people. It was less important that a majority of Americans still supported the U.S. strategic posture than that the vocal lobbying of elites stalled needed nuclear programs. They tore at the cohesion of national will central to deterrence.

This splintering of the basic belief system upholding national-security policy has extended to congressional policymaking. Past presidents have had the comfortable option of throwing up their hands and saying: It's a dirty job to keep the peace with nuclear weapons, but somebody's got to do it. Congressional support would generally be assured. That is no longer true.

Given a strategic balance slowly tilting toward the Soviet Union, the Reagan administration had very little time and very little running room to reestablish a shattered consensus. During his first term, Reagan made statements intended to underscore extended deterrence. These were given as strong signals to the Soviets. They had an unintended but destructive domestic impact. Much public support for strategic modernization trickled away in the ensuing storm of purifier protest.

Domestic alienation aside, the pace of Soviet strategic programs demanded prompt response. A very rough deterrent posture could be maintained for some time. Long-term stability in the nuclear balance, however, could not be assured simply by the Trident D-5 missile, the B-1B bomber, and improvements in the command and control of nuclear forces. New ballistic missile defense technologies seemed to promise an escape clause that had eluded former postwar presidents.

But Reagan did not call for a limited BMD deployment. Cultural pressures made limited objectives seem insufficient. The denial of Soviet advantage or a more confident extension of deterrence were hard now to sell. The puzzle facing Reagan was bigger than the familiar charge of deterrent credibility. The very strategic worldview of the American public and policymaking elite seemed to be changing, and the change had an air of permanence. Furthermore, the final extent of potential change could not be gauged.

In 1983 protest over deployment of Pershing and cruise missiles in Europe was still high and freeze sentiment still visible and strong. It was natural to assume rising domestic opposition to the U.S. nuclear posture. The fate of MX seemed murky. The best that could be hoped for was a minimal buy of missiles to be housed in exposed Minuteman silos—a far cry from Brown's original concept. Fifty MX missiles would be a pathetic counter to an approaching Soviet strategic advantage.

SDI, then, emerged from a milieu of cultural pressure, technological possibility, and political opportunity. These were blended in Reagan's own imagery. The president's presentation increased the force of change by giving it two strengths: prominence in national debate and a potential for remaking a national consensus. The defended world envisaged by Reagan is intended to embrace both progressive and purifier manifestos in the nuclear debate.

- It is officially nonnuclear, so it does not perpetuate evil. Indeed, it will eventually "make nuclear weapons obsolete."
- It is defensive and thus builds on American traditions of emphasizing a defensive national security.
- It embraces the postwar construction of the American mission. It seeks to strengthen U.S. alliance commitments by detaching an extension of deterrence to protect friends from inevitable escalation to assured destruction.

Finally, SDI attempts to play upon some received postwar truths, approaches to national defense that Americans understood and fully supported. One of these truths was the defense of American cities and citizens from attack. Only in the 1960s was defense against nuclear attack abandoned, and it was not until the ABM treaty of 1972 that this abdication was made official doctrine. The defense of the American people has always been a major presidential responsibility. In the 1950s, it was declaratory policy. There were many reasons why strategic defense was later dropped. It is important to remember, however, that the Safeguard ABM system was first a city defense. This is, after all, a natural goal.

The reaction to Reagan's vision has been mixed. Purifier groups do not believe that SDI, or Star Wars, as they call it, is a useful way to rebuild an American national-security consensus. Old-line pragmatists also oppose SDI, although they might support a very limited ballistic missile defense. Unfortunately, the pragmatists have been unable to contribute to the debate over strategic defenses. Their position was cemented in the Anti-Ballistic Missile Treaty and the scrapping of both strategic defense and the idea behind it.

Strategic defenses, with or without an orbiting component, represent a bridge between the goals of progressives and purifiers. Purifiers cannot openly support defensive weapons, because they are weapons. Only arms control, not more arms, can bring lasting peace. But arms control cannot repress the unconscious appeal of SDI, which is why purifiers continue to attack SDI on the grounds that it cannot "work," and not on the grounds that if it did work, it would be "bad." For the progressives, SDI has become a sounding bell for an almost atavistic retelling of traditional American approaches to security.

There is a convergence of domestic dissatisfaction with deterrence and Soviet nuclear programs that corrode its fragile legitimacy. Together, these saline currents make strategic defense a double deus ex machina for the United States. Defenses are a way of meeting both the cultural and the military imperatives of national security.

NOTES

1. For a further discussion, see Michael Vlahos, "Cultural Variation, Strategic Planning, and War Performance," American Political Science Association conference paper, August 1985.

2. See Michael Vlahos, *America: Images of Empire* (Washington, D.C.: The Johns Hopkins Foreign Policy Institute, 1982).

3. My use of the term "progressive" is unrelated to the brief, formal era of the Progressive party, and it should be detached from the more persistent, informal usage of the descriptive "progressive" in Left or neo-Left circles before and after World War II.

The religious roots of both purifier and progressive worldviews have been addressed by a number of American scholars. For example, see Perry Miller, *The New England Mind: From Colony to Province* (Cambridge, Mass.: Harvard University Press, 1953); also, Perry Miller, *The Puritans* (New York: Harper & Row, 1963); Sidney Ahlstrom, "The Puritan Ethic and the Spirit of Democracy," in George L. Hunt, ed., *Calvinism and the Political Order* (Philadelphia, Pa.: Westminster Press, 1965).

William Wolf underscored this slow process of religious to secular metamorphosis when he wrote of Abraham Lincoln, "The Puritan background of Lincoln's confidence in American destiny under God had become rationalized in the nineteenth century into the dream of world democracy with the original religious perspective rapidly disappearing into the distance . . . [but] Lincoln sustained that vision in its original religious rootage and reference to God's will." ("Abraham Lincoln and Calvinism," in Hunt, *Calvinism and the Political Order*)

This rooting is especially direct in American pacifism. "The major pacifist sects that were transplanted to America had begun as outgrowths of the great religious movements that transformed the intellectual climate of . . . northern and central Europe in the sixteenth and seventeenth centuries. Mennonitism and its offshoots formed the radical wing of the Protestant Reformation, which at the beginning was collectively known as Anabaptism, and the Quaker Society of Friends, for all the differences that set it apart from the parent movement, was a genuine child of mid-seventeenth century English Puritanism." (Peter Brock, *Pacifism in the United States* [Princeton, N.J.: Princeton University Press, 1968], 3)

4. Woodrow Wilson reacted strongly to media criticism during his intervention in Vera Cruz, and his reply resonated to this inner virtue in Americans. "I never went into battle . . . but I fancy . . . that it is just as hard to do your duty when men are sneering at you as when they are shooting at you. . . . The cheers of the moment are not what a man ought to think about, but the verdict of his conscience and of the consciences of mankind."

In his very declaration of war in April 1917 he showed that means will remain proportionate to ends as long as unique American moral values rule the uses of force. "Our object . . . is to vindicate the principles of peace and justice in the life of the world against selfish and autocratic power. . . . We are now about to accept the gage of battle with this natural foe of liberty. . . . We are glad . . . to fight thus for the ultimate peace of the world and for the liberation of its peoples. . . . The world must be made safe for democracy." (Quoted in Robert Dallek, *The American Style of Diplomacy* [New York: Alfred A. Knopf, 1983], 70, 84–85)

5. Roosevelt's powerful vision of America and world order emerge in two recent, sympathetic interpretations by Burton and Collin. (See David H. Burton, *Theodore Roosevelt: Confident Imperialist* [Philadelphia, Pa.: University of Pennsylvania Press, 1982], and Richard H. Collin, *Theodore Roosevelt, Culture, Diplomacy, and Expansion* [Baton Rouge, La.: Louisiana State University Press, 1985].) Beale's classic is more critical but of course views Roosevelt from the

vantage of the mid-1950s. (See Howard K. Beale, *Theodore Roosevelt and the Rise of America to World Power* [Baltimore, Md.: The Johns Hopkins University Press, 1957].) At that point the United States seemed to have learned all the right lessons on the issue from two world wars, and Roosevelt could be presented as a representative of a failed paradigm of "imperialism." The newer interpretations see more continuity between Roosevelt and succeeding American approaches to the world. He becomes at once an authentic spokesman of American values and a visionary of the American future.

6. *Writings and Speeches of Daniel Webster*, vol. 16 (Boston, Mass.: Little, Brown & Co., 1903), 423. Also, Frederick Merk, *Manifest Destiny and Mission* (New York: Vintage Books, 1966); Richard W. Van Alstyne, *The Rising American Empire* (Chicago, Ill.: Quadrangle Books, 1965); Robert L. Beisner, *Twelve Against Empire: The Anti-Imperialists, 1898–1900* (New York: McGraw-Hill, 1968); Ernest May, *Imperial Democracy* (New York: Harcourt Brace Jovanovich, 1961).

7. Some of these issues are reawakened in Eliot Cohen's *Citizens and Soldiers: The Dilemmas of Military Service* (Ithaca, N.Y.: Cornell University Press, 1985). The true Jeffersonian cast of the purifiers is captured by the words of Thomas Jefferson, who clearly linked republican virtue with "the necessity of obliging every citizen to be a soldier; this was the case with the Greeks and Romans and must be that of every free state." (148) The leveling process of citizen soldiering is underscored in the same book by Ralph Barton Perry. "That which most entertained and impressed the country was the spectacle of the rich man or the favored of fortune digging trenches with a pick or otherwise deliberately submitting to unaccustomed toil and strange hardships. People read about it because it was funny, but they saw what it meant. They saw that the spirit of service could redeem physical labor from ignominy, and sweep away the external differences and inequalities that divide a man from his fellows." This was written by one of the founders of the Plattsburg military camps. A professional military, in contrast, would smack of European militarism and monarchism. Instead of leveling, it would discriminate. Instead of promoting republican virtues, it would foster sinister elitism.

8. The observer on this occasion was Joshua P. Blanchard. (Brock, *Pacifism in the United States*, 690.) This can also be said of pacifist-universalist leftists in Germany in August 1914. Such conversions are temporary and fade when the crisis blows itself out. So the conversion of purifiers attained after 1941—as in 1861—has dissipated over cold-war time and Vietnam disenchantment. Today, purifier attitudes are resurgent.

9. Manfred Jonas, *Isolationism in America, 1935–1941* (Ithaca, N.Y.: Cornell University Press, 1966). The Ludlow Amendment, introduced by Senator Thomas P. Gore of Oklahoma on August 31, 1917, was the first attempt to introduce a constitutional amendment requiring a national referendum before a declaration of war. Similar proposals were made in every subsequent Congress, except the sixty-sixth.

The Ludlow Amendment and its clones, although sponsored by stolid conservative legislators, were also supported by the Women's International League for Peace and Freedom, the National Council for the Prevention of War, and the Brotherhood of Locomotive Firemen and Engineers, among others.

The spate of House and Senate resolutions in the 1930s attempting to limit U.S. involvement in a war is retro-reminiscent of the "nuclear freeze" era burst of parliamentary high rhetoric. It is worth noting that both periods of rhetorical self-exaltation came at times of increasing tension abroad and increasing domestic unwillingness to counter these threats with defense dollars. (Jonas, *Isolationism in America*, 158–64.)

"Ludlowism" has revived recently in the form of this gem of a concept, highlighted by *The New York Times*. Jeremy Stone, director of the Federation of American Scientists, in the Fall 1985 issue of *Foreign Policy*, recommended that presidents be required to obtain the consent of a congressional committee before ordering the first use of nuclear weapons. *The New York Times*, "Nuclear First Use Is Revived as Issue," September 9, 1985.

10. A recent brochure of the High Frontier fixates on the vulnerability of the United States to attack.

Picture this . . .

It is 4:45 a.m. Sunday morning in the
nation's capital . . .

The streets are nearly deserted.
Washington seems asleep and quiet . . .

. . . Except in the Security Room of the
White House and the War Room in the
Pentagon, which are in near chaos.

After twenty minutes of confusion and
conflicting information, they have just
received 100% confirmation by satellite and by radar that six Soviet ICBM's
have been launched from Yedrovo, a
Soviet missile base at the edge of
the Arctic Circle.

They are headed for America.

Etc., etc. But the intriguing aspect of this fearful vision, actually indistinguishable from the antinuclear motifs of the Left, is its reaching for core myths in the American experience. How else to explain an early Sunday morning attack, à la December 7, 1941? Or the arrangement of words, as though they are a kind of verse in another American tragedy?

11. Richard Falk, "one of the philosophers of the freeze movement," carefully scolded the moderate purists. "Most current action within the peace movement is dedicated . . . to *stabilizing* rather than *eliminating* nuclearism. The goal is to shift from certain *adventurist* forms of nuclearism . . . toward some variant of a *defensive* nuclear posture. . . . [But] . . . reliance on nuclear weapons inevitably concentrates anti-democratic authority in governmental institutions and builds a strong permanent disposition to engage in ultimate war as to negate the atmosphere and structure of genuine peace. We can never taste real

peace again until we find the means to eliminate nuclear weapons altogether." (Quoted in Adam Garfinkle, *The Politics of the Nuclear Freeze* [Philadelphia, Pa.: Foreign Policy Research Institute, 1984], 5)

12. The term, "postwar pragmatists," should not be confused with more narrow political designations, like Garfinkle's "pragmatic center" in *The Politics of the Nuclear Freeze*. The postwar pragmatists embraced most of the foreign-policy community after 1950, after Taft and Wallace vestiges of another age were banished. They maintained superficial domestic party attachments, but they shared a common strategic worldview.

13. Robert E. Osgood, *Ideas and Self-Interest in America's Foreign Relations* (Chicago, Ill.: The University of Chicago Press, 1953). Osgood describes the emergence of an American strategic worldview by placing postwar conditions in a broad context of American historical behavior. He articulates the need for a pragmatic vision to avoid a return to prewar immobility in U.S. foreign policy.

14. William Broad uses the old metaphor of evil science to show how science enslaves the young engineers engaged in America's dark Star Wars sorcery, entrancing them, as Mephistopheles, to sell their souls for alchemic secrets. "High-tech Gulags such as O-Group (a subdivision of Lawrence Livermore Laboratory) are seductive. They push science and technology to the limit and impose none of the terrible physical privations of their Soviet counterparts. But in some respects they may be more insidious. The prisoners are there of their own accord, serving both science and war, creating in order to destroy, part of any elite, yet pawns in a terrifying game." (William Broad, *Star Warriors: A Penetrating Look into the Lives of the Young Scientists Behind Our Space Age Weaponry* [New York: Simon and Schuster, 1985])

15. Tina Rosenberg, "Mission Out of Control," *The New Republic*, May 14, 1984, 18–21. These sentiments, in slightly milder form, are also echoed in James A. Van Allen, "Space Science, Space Technology, and the Space Station," *Scientific American*, vol. 254, January 1986, 32–39, and Alex Roland, "Triumph or Turkey?" *Discovery*, November 1985.

16. See, especially, "Remarks by Secretary of Defense Robert S. McNamara Before United Press International Editors and Publishers," San Francisco, California, September 18, 1967, printed in *Scope, Magnitude, and Implications of the United States Antiballistic Missile Program*, hearings before the subcommittee on military applications of the Joint Committee on Atomic Energy, 90th Cong., 1st sess. (Washington, D.C.: GPO, 1967), 107. "The more frequent question that arises in this connection is whether or not the United States possesses nuclear superiority over the Soviet Union. The answer is that we do. . . . Furthermore, we will maintain a superiority over the Soviet Union for as far ahead in the future as we can realistically plan."

17. These ideas were presented in a September 1967 speech by Robert S. McNamara. "What is essential to understand here is that the Soviet Union and the United States mutually influence one another's strategic plans. Whatever their intentions, actions—or even realistically potential actions—on either side relating to the build-up of nuclear forces necessarily triggers reactions on the other side. It is precisely this action-reaction phenomena that fuels the arms

race. . . . The result has been that we have both built up our force to a point that far exceeds a credible second-strike capability against the forces we each started with. In doing so neither of us has reached a first-strike capability." (Robert S. McNamara, "The Dynamics of Nuclear Strategy," speech of October 9, 1967, Department of State Bulletin, #57)

18. Colin Gray insists that "contemporary arms control theory was an invention of the strategic studies community in the period 1958–60." *Strategic Studies and Public Policy* (Lexington, Ky.: The University of Kentucky Press, 1982), 72. By the end of McNamara's tenure at the Department of Defense, the theoretical "doctrines" of the public policy community had permeated fully the official strategic worldview. From McNamara's 1967 San Francisco speech: "We do not want a nuclear arms race with the Soviet Union . . . what we would much prefer to do is to come to a realistic and reasonably riskless agreement with the Soviet Union, which would effectively prevent such an arms race . . . since we now possess a deterrent in excess of our individual needs, both of our nations would benefit from a properly safe-guarded agreement first to limit, and later to reduce, our strategic nuclear forces." (Printed in *Scope, Magnitude, and Implications of the United States Antiballistic Missile Program,* 109)

19. Stephen Rosen suggests some of the ways in which the existential postulates of strategic theory permeated the conduct of war in Southeast Asia. See Stephen Peter Rosen, "Vietnam and the Theory of Limited War," *International Security,* Fall 1982 (VII/2), 83–114.

20. The words are those of Steve Leeds, of the War Resisters' League, quoted in Garfinkle, *The Politics of the Nuclear Freeze,* 7. These sentiments became legitimate within more "centrist" intellectual circles. Robert Karl Manoff, a sometime editor of *Harper's* magazine, laid this national corruption at the feet of "nuclearism." "Thirty-eight years after Hiroshima, it is time to come to grips with the central political fact of modern American life: the epistemological structure of the nuclear regime is incompatible with the epistemological structure of democracy itself. Nuclearism and democracy embody antagonistic ideals of knowledge. . . . This suggests a disturbing but unmistakable conclusion: The United States cannot long endure as both nuclear and democratic." (Quoted in Garfinkle, *The Politics of the Nuclear Freeze,* 26)

The accession of these attitudes to the highest levels of the old establishment can be measured in the words of George F. Kennan, as he accepted the Albert Einstein Peace Prize in 1981. "But we must remember that it has been we Americans who, at almost every step of the road, have taken the lead in the development of this sort of weaponry. It was we who first produced and tested such a device; we who were the first to raise its destructiveness to a new level with the hydrogen bomb; we who introduced the multiple warhead; we who have declined every proposal for the renunciation of the principle of "first use"; and we alone, so help us God, who have used the weapon in anger against others, and against tens of thousands of helpless non-combatants at that." (Quoted in Robert F. Drinan, *Beyond the Nuclear Freeze* [New York: The Seabury Press, 1983], 159) The revisionists themselves are assessed in Robert James Maddox's *The New Left and the Origins of the Cold War* (Princeton, N.J.: Princeton University Press, 1973).

21. This unraveling within the pragmatic center is well covered in Gray, *Strategic Studies and Public Policy*, 129–33, 160–67, and by Lawrence Freedman, *The Evolution of Nuclear Strategy* (New York: St. Martin's Press, 1983), 344–51, 354–58.

22. The fundamentalist tone of contemporary antinuclear films is underscored by the number of video experiences targeted on children and nuclear war: *Bombs Will Make the Rainbow Break, In the Nuclear Shadow, There's a Nuclear War Going on Inside of Me, What Soviet Children Are Saying About Nuclear War*. (From a list in the "Nuclear War Prevention Kit" [Washington, D.C.: Center for Defense Information, 1985])

It should be remembered also that the nuclear films of the very early nuclear age did not scold or preach. They simply presented the terror of nuclear war as a kind of fact of life. Neville Shute's *On the Beach*, for example, a nuclear movie of the 1950s, was extremely "civilized." Sure, the world was coming to an end as a result of nuclear war. But there was a kind of majesty to the ending of humankind: the very process of attenuation was a dramatic opportunity to unearth the core issues of human existence in the face of extinction. The viewer was left to his own conclusions, and agenda. This sense of fatalism permeated the visions of the 1950s. Rod Serling's "Twilight Zone" episode, "Incident on Maple Street," employed the motif of nuclear war again as a vehicle, a means for exploring the human condition.

23. Jonathan Schell, *The Abolition* (New York: Alfred A. Knopf, 1984), 163.

24. Frank Donner wrote that "opponents of the freeze [are] all paladins of unlimited weaponry . . . committed to the modern secular religion of a long, twilight struggle with the Soviet Union." This characterization infected some in Congress. Fortney Stark (D.-California) thundered, "[Our people] do not want to be incinerated so some Dr. Strangelove theorist can test his belief that nuclear war is winnable." Tom Harken (D.-Iowa) weighed in with, "No longer will the people of the United States allow their lives to be held in constant peril by the decisions of an elite group of generals, politicians, and scientists." See Garfinkle, *The Politics of the Nuclear Freeze*, 15, 25.

25. "Study Says 4 Billion Could Starve in 'Nuclear Winter' After Attack," *The New York Times*, September 13, 1985. Dr. Mark Harwell, coauthor of the report by the International Council of Scientific Unions, wrote: "We are left with images of Ethiopia and the Sudan as being more representative of what the world would look like after a nuclear war for most of the people than the sorts of images we have of Hiroshima and Nagasaki." The chairman, Sir Frederick Warner, added: "The potential environmental damage of a nuclear war demands that we develop a new perspective when considering such a conflict. . . . This effort represents the consensus of a prestigious body of scientists. It would be a grave error to ignore their findings."

The more celebrated Nuclear Winter personality, Carl Sagan, makes sure to remind us of the rogue variables that might unleash a nuclear war, variables over which the enlightened have no control. "And in the present time, there is certainly the possibility that some concatenation of communications failure, computer malfunction, misapprehension, madness in high office, could conspire to produce this global climatic catastrophe." ("World Chronicle," taped June 5, 1984, UN Radio and Visual Services, Department of Public Information, transcript, 3–4, 7)

26. National Council of Catholic Bishops, *The Challenge of Peace: God's Promise and Our Response: A Pastoral Letter on War and Peace* (Washington, D.C.: The United States Catholic Conference, 1983). See also Episcopal Diocese of Washington, *The Nuclear Dilemma: A Draft Report of the Committee of Inquiry on the Nuclear Issue* (Washington, D.C., August 1985).

Edward Doherty, one of the principal advisers to the bishops, was angered by an article in *Policy Review*. In a letter, published in the Winter 1986 issue, he wrote: "In refusing to legitimate nuclear deterrence, I argued that I did not will all the horrible consequences that might flow from nuclear disarmament, but did argue that they were nowhere near as horrible nor as permanent as those that would ensue in a major nuclear exchange. . . . Mr. D'Souza's reporting of this whole conversation exposes his lack of interest in moral discourse and the basic chauvinism of his approach to security questions: The United States is justified in employing any measures, including the use of nuclear weapons, to frustrate Soviet aggression. This may seem to him and to many other Americans as the only practical, realistic policy, but that does not make it square with traditional Christian ethics." (6–7)

Russell Shaw, secretary of public affairs, USCC, added this illuminating perspective for those who wrote for the bishops. "Someone might object that it is morally obligatory to retain the nuclear deterrent, considering what might happen (loss of political and moral liberties). This, however, is not an ethically coherent argument. We are morally responsible for the evil we will do (or, as with deterrence, that we will to be done on our behalf). But we are not morally responsible for—guilty of—the evil that is done to us, even though we may foresee it as a consequence of our own ceasing to do evil. I am obliged to cease being willing to do evil to an adversary even though I may anticipate that the adversary will then do evil to me." (Ibid., 7)

27. Lieutenant General G. Sememov and Major General V. Prokhorov, "Scientific-Technical Progress and Some Questions on Strategy," *Military Thought*, no. 2, February 1969, found in Lee, "Soviet Nuclear Targeting Strategy," 8–9.

28. As Harold Brown described the "countervailing strategy": "We have concluded that if deterrence is to be fully effective, the United States must be able to respond at a level appropriate to the type and scale of a Soviet attack. Our goal is to make a Soviet victory as improbable (seen through Soviet eyes) as we can make it." (Department of Defense, *Report of Secretary of Defense Harold Brown*, 68)

29. As William J. Perry characterized the limitations of the latest terrestrial BMD system, the LoAD, to defend a "thin" MX deployment in fixed silos: "The last time I made a careful evaluation of it, I believe that it was or could be designed to be capable of extracting a 2-to-1 or perhaps a 3-to-1 cost from the Soviets wanting to attack our silos . . . I have never seen the evidence which would suggest that we could with confidence extract any higher cost . . . therefore, the question about a LoAD system, in my judgment, is not whether

it works or does not work. The question is . . . will it do you any good defending 36 silos or 50 silos or 100 silos? In my judgment, the answer to that is no." (*Strategic Force Modernization Programs*, hearings before the subcommittee on strategic and theater nuclear forces, Senate Committee on Armed Services, 97th Cong., 1st sess. [Washington, D.C.: GPO, 1981], 483)

30. *Diplomatic and Strategic Impact of Multiple Warhead Missiles*, hearings before the subcommittee on national security and scientific developments, House Committee on Foreign Affairs, 91st Cong., 1st sess. (Washington, D.C.: GPO, 1969); *Strategic and Foreign Policy Implications of ABM Systems*, hearings before the subcommittee on international organization and disarmament affairs, Senate Committee on Foreign Relations, 91st Cong., 1st sess. (Washington, D.C.: GPO, 1969), especially statements by Drs. George B. Kistiakowsky, Hans A. Bethe, Herbert York, and James R. Killian.

31. On implied potential of BMD in 1981, see *Strategic Force Modernization Program*, hearings before the Senate Committee on Armed Services (Washington, D.C.: GPO, 1981).

32. Harold Brown, "SDI Technology and SDI Policy," 19, speech before IISS conference at Windsor Park, October 15, 1985.

33. Ronald Reagan, television address, March 23, 1983.

34. Paul Stares, *The Militarization of Space: U.S. Policy, 1945–1984* (Ithaca, N.Y.: Cornell University Press, 1985), 225.

35. From FDR's "Quarantine" speech made on October 5, 1937, in Chicago, an isolationist bastion: "If those things come to pass in other parts of the world, let no one imagine that America will escape, that it may expect mercy, that this Western hemisphere will not be attacked and that it will continue tranquilly and peacefully to carry on the ethics and the arts of civilization. . . . If those days are not to come to pass—if we are to have a *world in which we can breathe freely and live in amity without fear*—peace-loving nations must make a concerted effort to uphold laws and principles on which alone peace can rest secure." (Emphasis added)

36. Some of the interplay between postwar presidents and domestic pressures over issues of war and peace is discussed by Charles DeBenedetti, *The Peace Reform in American History* (Bloomington, Ind.: Indiana University Press, 1980).

3

SDI AND
U.S. FOREIGN POLICY

Robert W. Tucker

THE IMPLICATIONS OF MUTUAL DETERRENCE

For a generation we have pursued a nuclear strategy of mutual deterrence through the threat of retaliation. At the time of its acceptance mutual deterrence was generally seen to reflect far more a necessity than a choice. Once accepted, efforts were directed to making mutual deterrence as safe and reliable as possible. How this might best be done gave rise to differences that remain unresolved today. The idea of mutual assured destruction provided one answer. Readily caricatured, if only by virtue of its acronym MAD, and clearly startling in its implications, it nevertheless expressed the prevailing view of the nuclear predicament, which was nothing other than the inordinate destructiveness of nuclear weapons and the apparent impossibility of mounting an effective defense against them. In these circumstances, the reasoning went, wisdom consisted in making a virtue of the nuclear vice by pursuing arrangements that would ensure that the use of nuclear weapons resulted in the common ruin of the attacked and the attacker. Given the prevailing inaccuracy of missiles, this meant a level of industrial and civilian destruction (cities) that would be unacceptable to either side. And given the state of defensive technology, it meant that efforts at defense would not only prove ineffective but destabilizing because of the fears and illusions they might encourage.

It is now largely forgotten that mutual deterrence through the threat (and presumably the certainty) of retaliation provided the answer for

This chapter is taken from "General Considerations on SDI and U.S. Foreign Policy," in Robert W. Tucker et al., *SDI and U.S. Foreign Policy* (Boulder, Colo.: Westview Press with The Johns Hopkins Foreign Policy Institute, SAIS, 1987).

many who had taken a strong antinuclear position—indeed, who often had taken a position indistinguishable from nuclear pacifism. Yet the change from a position akin to nuclear pacifism to one strongly supporting deterrence was not so difficult to make. It followed, quite simply, from the conviction that mutual and assured destruction was the next best thing to the ideal—though impossible—solution. If we could not simply rid the world of nuclear weapons, then we could at least ensure that these weapons would never be used in view of the consequences to which their use must lead. To tamper in any way with this form of insurance must, it was thereafter argued, run the risk of leading us back to a world in which nuclear weapons might be used. It was not until the 1980s that a significant breach occurred in the ranks of the deterrence faithful, with many reverting in full or in part to a position they had earlier taken.

Mutual assured destruction was the latest version of the very old idea that war would disappear once its destructiveness promised to become sufficiently great. It was not the officials of the Kennedy and Johnson administrations who gave us this allegedly novel concept—as Reagan administration officials appear to believe—but a succession of eighteenth- to twentieth-century thinkers who were persuaded that advances in the technology of war must ultimately do away with war by making it too destructive. The same persuasion was voiced from the outset of the nuclear age. Indeed, the once most widely quoted expression of this theme came not from a visionary—or from a technocratic U.S. defense secretary—but from one of the century's greatest practitioners of statecraft, Winston Churchill, who remarked on the effect of nuclear weapons: "It may well be that we shall, by a process of sublime irony, have reached a stage in this story where safety will be the sturdy child of terror, and survival the twin brother of annihilation."

U.S. nuclear strategy continues to rest on the pervasive uncertainty attending any nuclear conflict between the superpowers. The various innovations in strategic doctrine since the early 1970s—from limited "nuclear options" through "countervailing" to "prevailing"—have not affected this uncertainty over whether meaningful limits can be placed on the use of nuclear weapons. Nor has this uncertainty been affected significantly by the many refinements in nuclear weapons and, above all, by changes in their accuracy. The difference between the mutual assured destruction of a generation ago and the mutual deterrence of today is a difference of degree rather than kind. The vision of apocalypse has been slightly blurred, but it is still very much apparent.

The advent of mutual deterrence was a development of the first order of magnitude. It meant, quite simply, that the nation's historic security experience had come to a sudden and dramatic end. For the first time in our history, our physical existence had been put directly and completely to risk. The significance of this abrupt and wrenching change can scarcely be exaggerated. From the period of its infancy the United States had enjoyed an almost uniquely benign security experience, which was one of the great determinants in shaping the American character. It helped account for the optimism and sense of confidence with which, as a people, we have faced the future.

The two world wars had not brought this experience to an end, for the nation's physical security had not been directly threatened in either conflict. Although the United States had finally intervened in these wars, and particularly in World War II, out of balance-of-power considerations, an adverse outcome of either was not generally seen to threaten directly the country's core security. Instead, a fascist victory was seen to threaten the nation's greater-than-physical security, since it carried the prospect of a world in which the political and economic frontiers of the United States would have to become coterminous with its territorial frontiers, a world in which the American example and influence would become irrelevant.

But the Soviet acquisition of nuclear weapons and the means of their delivery did directly threaten, and with a vengeance, our physical security. Mutual deterrence was the U.S. government's response to this novel condition. Given formal sanction in the 1972 strategic arms agreements with the Soviet Union, mutual deterrence meant that this nation was now in the most literal sense a hostage to the power and intentions of the Soviet Union, just as the Soviet Union was a hostage to the power and intentions of the United States.

Nothing that has happened since World War II is comparable in significance to this change in U.S. security. Nothing has offset, or balanced, this change. Many intervening developments, of course, have profoundly altered the global power structure and, in consequence, U.S. security. The economic and political restoration of Western Europe and Japan and the breakup of what was once seen as a monolithic communist camp directed from Moscow are the most salient and notorious. These and other developments have, with few exceptions, worked to the advantage of the United States in its contest with the Soviet Union. But even if we take adequate account of the growing external and internal constraints on Soviet power, there remains the sea change in the U.S. position. Nothing, to repeat, quite compensates for this change.

The new strategic order of mutual deterrence through mutual vulnerability not only implied a radical change in the nation's security condition, it also implied a considerable change in our diplomatic tradition of unilateralism. This tradition, with its insistence upon complete independence of action, had always formed an essential part of the country's historic isolationism. Long seen as the virtual touchstone of an isolationist policy and outlook, unilateralism was not, in fact, abandoned during and immediately following World War II. The conventional view that it was abandoned, surviving only within the minority of right-wing isolationists, rests on a confusion of form with substance. Given the United States' vast power, the weakness of its major allies, and its continuing immunity from direct attack, an apparent devotion to multilateral forms in the postwar years masked the substance of what was largely unilateral action.

Mutual deterrence constituted a novel and significant constraint on what had previously been the scope of the nation's freedom of action. It did so if only by tying our fate to the fate of our great adversary, and in a way that was unprecedented. Even had the Soviet Union been a different type of state, this sudden involvement in a common fate represented a major change. Given the nature of the Soviet regime, given the fact that it represented the antithesis of what the United States stood for, and given our postwar aspirations to preside over an international order increasingly receptive to and reflective of American values and institutions, this mutual relationship should have been particularly difficult to accept.

Nor was the advent of mutual deterrence significant only for America's historic security position and its diplomatic tradition of unilateralism. The new nuclear strategy also carried important implications for the security of our major allies by measurably worsening the U.S. strategic predicament. The root of that predicament is found in the asymmetrical structure of interest that imposes more difficult and exacting deterrence requirements on the United States than on the Soviet Union. While the requirements for the Soviet Union extend no farther than Eastern Europe, for the United States they extend to Western Europe, Japan, and (possibly) the Persian Gulf. To a degree far greater than for the Soviet Union, deterrence for the United States has always been, and is today, an extension that includes others. By its very nature, extended deterrence must have much less credibility than self-deterrence. The liability of extended deterrence, moreover, cannot be fully compensated for by greater conventional forces. Greater conventional forces will raise the threshold of nuclear conflict, but they cannot preclude nuclear conflict. Ultimately, compensation must be found either at the strategic nuclear level or nowhere. It cannot be found at the strategic level by forces that are roughly equivalent to the Soviet Union and, especially, that are equally, if indeed not more, vulnerable. In these circumstances, the credibility of deterrence is bound to erode, the only question being how much.

STRATEGIC PARITY AND THE CHALLENGE
TO EXTENDED DETERRENCE

In retrospect, it is remarkable how readily the nation adjusted to a strategy that carried these, and still other, adverse implications. In part, of course, the explanation lies in the widespread conviction that there was no real alternative to a nuclear strategy based on the mutual vulnerability of the United States and the Soviet Union. Mutual deterrence through the threat of retaliation was not seen as the result of theory or doctrine but of the nature of nuclear weapons and of technological prospects. Offensive weapons of ever-increasing accuracy and defensive systems based on exotic new technologies began to alter these prospects by the mid-to-late 1970s. But in the preceding decade, despite the interest in antiballistic missiles, the outlook appeared quite different. In the technological conditions of that period, mutual deterrence seemed far more a matter of necessity than of choice. The task of statesmanship, it was believed, was to recognize and to bow to this necessity, while directing one's efforts to making it as safe and reliable as possible. Moreover, it was assumed that in time the Soviet Union would also recognize and accept the condition of mutual vulnerability. The 1972 SALT I agreements were generally seen to validate this assumption.

These same years, roughly the decade following the Cuban missile crisis, were also marked by a significant change in outlook toward the political usefulness of nuclear weapons, a change that today is all too apparent. It finds frequent expression, particularly among those who were once high officials. One of them, a former secretary of defense, has recently declared: "Nuclear weapons serve no military purpose whatsoever. They are totally useless—except only to deter one's opponent from using them."[1] This revised attitude greatly eased the transition from a position of strategic superiority to one of rough equivalence characterizing mutual deterrence. For if it is accepted, very little—if, indeed, anything at all—is sacrificed in moving from a position of nuclear superiority to a position of nuclear parity. If strategic superiority is useless, in that it cannot be translated into diplomatic power or strategic advantage, then abandoning it must appear only reasonable.

What may be termed nuclear revisionism first appears as an influential view in the years following the Cuban missile crisis. Marking the end of the cold war, the Cuban missile crisis thereafter provided the prime illustration for those intent on demonstrating the political disutility of nuclear weapons. The marked disparity in nuclear forces, it has been argued, had no effect on the outcome of the crisis. Indeed, several of the members of the executive committee constituted to advise the president on the crisis have since testified that the possibility of using nuclear weapons was never considered. They have also noted that the disparity between the strategic forces of the two sides still could not have prevented the Soviet Union from imposing unprecedented destruction on this country, a prospect that by all accounts appalled president Kennedy. These considerations, however, do not disprove that the strategic superiority we enjoyed at the time had no effect on Soviet leadership and on the outcome of the crisis. They only show that it did not affect U.S. leadership in the sense that it did not prompt the Kennedy administration to attempt directly to exploit this superiority. To the contrary, president Kennedy and his associates explicitly refused to do so. There was no disposition, however, to refuse the indirect exploitation of strategic superiority. Such exploitation followed simply from the existence of a crisis in which the distinct possibility arose of the superpowers becoming directly engaged in a conventional military conflict.

The merit of nuclear revisionism apart, there is no question that the attitude it reflected aided the U.S. adjustment to the loss of strategic superiority. The Soviet achievement of strategic parity was an event of first-order importance, requiring a rethinking of the entire U.S. security position. Even if strategic superiority did not make extended deterrence *entirely* credible, it still made extended deterrence *more* credible, and it was on this credibility that the structure of American interests and commitments rested at the time and, in more difficult circumstances, continues to rest today. Strategic superiority made it much easier for the public to sustain a faith in U.S. ability to prevent nuclear war while protecting American vital interests. Yet, at the time, the effects of accepting a nuclear strategy of mutual vulnerability attracted only moderate attention and caused even less anxiety. In marked contrast to the early 1960s, the early 1970s gave rise to almost no agitation in the body politic over the nuclear issue, despite the momentous changes that had occurred.

It is in the prevailing political circumstances of the time that one finds the principal reason for the absence of much concern over the long-term consequences of mutual deterrence. There was, of course, the war in Vietnam and the almost obsessive preoccupation of government, elites, and public with the war. Vietnam aside, the reason for the relative lack of concern over the extraordinary change that was taking place was because we were in the floodtide of détente. Having developed slowly and unevenly in the course of the 1960s, by the early 1970s, détente had become the centerpiece of the Nixon policy reformulation. In the context of détente, the loss of strategic superiority was seen by some as an event without great significance and by others as an event that, although regrettable, could be taken in stride. Instead, greater attention was directed to SALT I, although the tangible results of the talks were almost inconsequential compared with the Soviet Union's achievement of strategic parity. But the arms-control negotiations were considered almost from the outset a litmus test of the overall relationship of the superpowers. If this relationship was relatively good, it was assumed, the possible consequences of the new strategic dispensation afforded little ground for concern.

The relative equanimity that marked the transition of the world of strategic parity provides eloquent testimony to the primacy of politics in nuclear matters. It demonstrates vividly that what is ultimately at issue in the persisting debate over nuclear weapons and strategy are not technical considerations but varying judgments about the character and aspirations of the Soviet regime. In this debate, how the opposing sides interpret the necessary and sufficient conditions of deterrence depends in large measure on what they believe about the nature of the U.S.-Soviet conflict. For most of the decade leading up to the 1972 SALT I agreements, the predominant view of this conflict was one of rising optimism. This accounts for the relative ease with which the nation adjusted to a nuclear strategy based on the mutual vulnerability of the United States and the Soviet Union. And more than any other factor, this accounts for the continuing credibility of extended deterrence.

The hopes and expectations placed in détente were not realized. By the middle of the 1970s, détente was giving way; by the end of the decade, it had collapsed. During these same years the belief grew that the Soviet government had not accepted the U.S. view of mutual deterrence but was engaged instead in a serious and sustained effort to overcome its own vulnerability. In these circumstances anxiety over the credibility of extended deterrence steadily increased. Evidence of this is found in the evolution of American strategic doctrine. Since the early 1970s strategic doctrines have increasingly assumed the function of bridging the apparently growing gap between the forces needed for a credible extended deterrence and the forces in being. If the gap could no longer be satisfactorily bridged in fact, it could still be bridged in word. Without ever claiming strategic superiority—indeed, even while expressly disavowing an interest in seeking superiority—the United States has attempted to salvage at least some residual benefits of superiority. Thus the claim of the Carter administration that we could still ensure that the Soviets would always lose more than they would gain from resorting to any kind of armed aggression ("countervailing"). Or the more pretentious claim of the Reagan administration that in a nuclear conflict our forces would have the capability of imposing an early termination of the conflict on terms favorable to this country ("prevailing").

THE RISE OF THE ANTINUCLEAR MOVEMENT

With the coming to office of Ronald Reagan, the nation had for the first time a president and an administration whose hostility to the nuclear strategy of the 1960s and 1970s was deep-seated and well advertised. Yet it was not the Reagan administration that mounted the first great assault on mutual deterrence but the antinuclear movement that suddenly arose during Reagan's first year in office. The antinuclear movement, which dominated the scene from 1981 to 1984, was unprecedented both for the abruptness with which it arose and for the breadth of support it appeared to enjoy. As late as the winter of 1979–80, there was little to indicate that nuclear weapons would become the critical issue of public discourse they did become by the fall of 1981. And whereas the antinuclear movements of the past (particularly the early 1960s) represented little more than the stirring of a few, the movement of the 1980s assumed mass proportions. Not only was the later movement far stronger than its predecessors, its effect on the Reagan administration was far greater.

At the outset the Reagan administration set its face against the peace movement and rejected its principal demand of a freeze on the deployment, testing, and manufacture of nuclear weapons. But despite an initial insensitivity and resistance to public anxiety on the nuclear issue, after scarcely a year in office the administration began, slowly but surely, to respond to public concern. The occasional lapses in discussing the use of weapons, lapses that many found so alarming, stopped. More significantly, the virtually dismissive attitude toward arms control changed, and if the change was scarcely in the nature of a conversion, it was nonetheless a change both in rhetoric and even in policy. Finally, and perhaps most significantly, the administration came forth in March 1983 with its real response to the anxiety and dissatisfaction reflected by the antinuclear movement—the Strategic Defense Initiative.

At the time, and even now, the prevailing view of the antinuclear movement found its origins in the statements and, even more, the outlook of the Reagan administration. But the lapse of faith in deterrence, which was the most important characteristic of the movement, is largely trivialized by this explanation. The initial behavior of the Reagan administration may be regarded as triggering the antinuclear movement; it cannot be plausibly seen as the deeper cause of this movement and the lapse of faith it represented. For this, we must look primarily to the decline and fall of détente. While it lasted, faith in deterrence went largely unquestioned. It did so despite the fact that many of the developments that so alarmed the peace movement in the 1980s were apparent enough in the mid-to-late 1970s. But so long as a semblance of détente remained, anxiety over the "arms race" and the dangers it presumably holds, as well as alarm over the political and moral hazards of the present structure of deterrence, were apparently held to modest levels. It is in the fall of détente and the rise of a new cold war that we must find the simple but critical explanation for the antinuclear arms movement.

At the same time the deeper implications of this movement may, and very likely do, have an enduring significance. Thus, the faith once generally held in mutual deterrence seems unlikely to be restored. This is plausible, even without taking into account the impact of the Reagan administration's Strategic Defense Initiative and the justification given on its behalf, although the effect of both is to deal a further blow to what was once a quite robust faith.

A decline of faith in the effectiveness of the deterrent structure of the past generation has been accompanied by an erosion in our moral judgment of that structure. The extent of this change is indicated by comparing the position taken in 1965 by Vatican Council II with the position taken in 1983 by American Catholic bishops.[2] A generation ago the Vatican Council pointedly refrained from condemning a structure of deterrence that rested, in the last resort, upon the threat of indiscriminate warfare. While warning that deterrence was "not a safe way to preserve a steady peace," the council nevertheless approved of deterrence. Nor did it condemn nuclear war. What it condemned, and all that it condemned, was "total war" and any acts of war "aimed indiscriminately at the destruction of entire cities or extensive areas along with their population."

By contrast, the American bishops condemn virtually any and every possible form of nuclear war. The use of nuclear weapons is rejected, whether they are used against military targets or against civilian centers of population, whether in a first strike or a retaliatory second strike, whether in a central or in a theater nuclear war. The bishops take this position because they are convinced nuclear weapons cannot be controlled or their effects limited. On the other hand, Vatican Council II limited itself to a careful statement of the circumstances in which the use of nuclear weapons must be condemned.

The moral condemnation of nuclear war—any and every nuclear war—is a position that is generally shared by the deterrence faithful. But for those who believe strongly enough in the effectiveness of mutual deterrence, the immorality of nuclear war need not present a considerable problem. Even if the price for holding an evil intent is the moral deformation of the holder, it makes a great difference whether one believes that while the prospects of doing evil are nearly nonexistent, the consequences of not threatening to do evil are very real. The matter is otherwise, however, for those who do not entertain a strong belief in the effectiveness of mutual deterrence or have experienced a lapse of faith. Once mutual deterrence is deprived of its saving grace—the promise that it will never have to be put to use—it must give rise to a growing sense of despair, moral and otherwise.

The American bishops' letter points in this direction as do similar recent pronouncements on the illegitimacy of ever using nuclear weapons. Although the "strictly conditioned moral acceptance" it gives to deterrence contrasts with its almost flat rejection of the use of nuclear weapons, the meaning of the apparent contrast depends on the optimism with which deterrent structures are viewed. Once the confidence formerly invested in them declines, as it has today, the illegitimacy with which the use—any use—of nuclear weapons is increasingly viewed will characterize the moral judgment made of mutual deterrence.

SDI AND THE NATURE OF DETERRENCE

The peace movement of the early 1980s helped to create an environment receptive to the Reagan administration's Strategic Defense Initiative. It did so by its attack on mutual deterrence. To be sure, the motives of those who led the antinuclear movement differed markedly from the motives of those supporting the president's program. Even so, this consideration may be less important than the fact that both the peace movement and the administration's supporters have contributed to the same general result. Moreover, in one decisive respect there is clearly an essential similarity in motivation. Whatever the other differences separating a Jonathan Schell from Ronald Reagan, both have been motivated by a deep unhappiness with and grave apprehension over the structure of deterrence we have lived with for the past generation. For both, the escape from a world in which it is "necessary to rely on the specter of retaliation," to use the president's words, is not deemed only desirable but necessary. Time alone, Schell has urged, must transform the possibility of nuclear war into a probability. The crisis in deterrence stems, at bottom, from nothing more than the "continuing reliance on nuclear arms."[3] Schell's view is only a step removed from the president's conviction that it is "inconceivable . . . that we can go on thinking down the future, not only for ourselves and for our lifetimes, but for other generations, that the great nations of the world will sit here, like people facing themselves across a table, each with a cocked gun, and no one knowing whether someone might tighten their finger on the trigger."[4]

The president's aversion to the present system of deterrence should have come as no surprise. He had expressed hostility to mutual deterrence on many occasions during the preceding decade. Reagan's views were, by and large, similar to those generally entertained on the political Right. For many years the Right had expressed skepticism over mutual deterrence, attacking it not only on strategic grounds but on political and moral grounds as well. Time and intervening developments served to sharpen this criticism. Although the essential critique of mutual deterrence remained substantially unchanged from the early 1970s to the mid-1980s, its persuasiveness did change. Intervening developments— technological, strategic, and political—did appear to lend greater persuasiveness to the critique, while placing supporters of mutual deterrence increasingly on the defensive. Technological developments alone had this effect. The advent of offensive missile systems of greater accuracy and the prospect of missile defenses combined to call into greater question than ever before the condition of mutual vulnerability.

It also became increasingly apparent that the Soviet leadership never really shared American acceptance of this condition. Instead, from the outset it pursued a strategy designed to limit the Soviet Union's vulnerability by developing a strategic force with the capability of attacking the U.S. land-based missile system. The Soviet pursuit of a first-strike capability (or, if one prefers, of a damage limitation capability) has prompted the conclusion by critics of mutual deterrence that a "stable relationship of mutual deterrence" has never existed.[5] The conclusion goes much too far. It equates the fact, or condition, of stability based on mutual deterrence with the effort to upset this condition. Even so, save for those who believe that deterrence is not only an inherent property of nuclear missile weapons but very nearly a self-sufficient property, the Soviet strategic effort since the early 1970s has served to strengthen the Right's case against the present system of deterrence.

This case, it needs to be emphasized, goes well beyond the vagaries of technological development and the vicissitudes of Soviet strategic programs. In its broader dimensions it rests on the contention that the strategic order of deterrence based on mutual vulnerability is flawed at its very core. For that order presumably incorporates two incompatible elements that, like oil and water, will always separate. Fred Iklé puts the matter thus:

> [T]he accord on a stable equilibrium of mutual restraint is psychologically incompatible with the constant threat of reciprocal annihilation. The first ingredient of this mixture represents the best in international relations: a continued willingness to cooperate in restraining one's own military power, coupled with a serene reliance on the opponent's prudence and his common sense. The second ingredient of the mixture represents the worst in international relations: an endless effort to maintain forces that are constantly

ready to annihilate the opponent, coupled with an unremitting determination
to deny him escape from this grip of terror.[6]

The believers in a viable, that is, a stable system of mutual deterrence
based on mutual vulnerability, Iklé argues, fail to appreciate the dynamic
of this incompatibility. They do not see the essential instability of this
order with its ceaseless tilting and its never-ending adjustments of a
quivering balance. But if this order is essentially unstable—a judgment
the record does not yet vindicate—it is so primarily for other reasons.
Iklé's incompatible ingredients are essentially the same ingredients that
have made up most international orders we have known. His criticism
of the order based on mutual deterrence is more properly a criticism
of the paradox that characterizes international order as such, and that
does so of necessity. Every international order rests on a "willingness
to cooperate in restraining one's own military power" as well as a
reliance, though not necessarily a "serene reliance," on the opponent's
prudence. At the same time, every international order rests on the threat
of punishment if the tacit "social contract" is broken. If the order of
mutual deterrence holds the threat of annihilation, as Iklé notes, this
results more from the nature of the weapons on which this order rests
than from the particular strategic disposition of these weapons. It is
true that the order of mutual deterrence pushes this conventional wisdom
respecting the basis of international order to its *reductio ad absurdum*.
But this, again, is less the result of the doctrine of consensual vulnerability
than of the character of the weapons themselves.
    If the present order of mutual deterrence is inherently flawed, as
Iklé and others believe, this results less from the principles on which
the order of deterrence is based than from the parties that compose it.
The oil and water, it turns out, are the United States and the Soviet
Union. If the mutuality required of deterrence can lead only to disaster,
this is because it must be entered into with a state like the Soviet
Union. This has always been the essential point in the Right's critique
of mutual deterrence. What is seen as the failure of mutual deterrence
and of concomitant efforts at arms control is not primarily the result
either of conceptual error or of technical misjudgment—though these
played a role—but of political misjudgment. Mutual deterrence, along
with the arms-control measures undertaken to strengthen it, depended
centrally on a certain assessment of the party with whom we would
undertake this relationship. This assessment was badly in error, in this
view, because of the nature of the Soviet regime and, to a lesser although
still important degree, because of the nature of democratic societies.
    Ultimately, this is the crucial reason why, according to the conservative
critique, the present system of mutual deterrence holds for us a peril

that can only grow. The Western democracies, Iklé has written, "will have to defend themselves for the foreseeable future against the military might and political ambition of the Soviet ruling class, still dominated by men imbued with Lenin's totalitarian philosophy." Iklé eschews speculation on the ways by which the threat of nuclear destruction may be turned into the "ideal instrument for totalitarian expansion." But he is confident that the "'balance of terror' cannot favor the defense of a democratic alliance. Sooner or later it will favor those most at ease with, those most experienced in, the systematic use of terror." Moreover, a continued reliance on the present system of mutual deterrence foreordains the West's demoralization, a condition that will result simply from the vision of a future in which we are resigned to "the possibility of an atrocity unsurpassed in human history."[7]

The promise of the Strategic Defense Initiative is to redress this pervasive pessimism by holding out the prospect of escaping its consequences. Technology, and technological optimism, will presumably provide the answer to politics, and political pessimism. In the short term, supporters of the initiative promise, technology can deliver us from the immediate perils of vulnerability by strengthening a now defective system of deterrence and through a point defense of missile sites. In the longer run, the promise is held out of fashioning an effective defense against ballistic missiles. Such a world will still fall far short of the president's vision of a world in which nuclear weapons are rendered impotent and thus no longer play a role, for this world would require denying the strategic use of not only space, and therefore of ballistic missiles, but of air space as well, and therefore of air-breathing conveyances. A defense against ballistic missiles would still leave us in a world of nuclear weapons. Moreover, it would leave us in a world of mutual deterrence through the threat of retaliation. It may well be, as Iklé has argued, that this would represent a great gain for the following reasons:

> Bombers and cruise missiles, compared with ballistic missiles, are less suited for surprise attack because of their longer time of travel. And bombers are safer as deterrent forces since, by taking to the air, they can be made nearly invulnerable to an alert, yet could safely return to their bases should the warning be false. Also, using in part the same technologies and systems, air defense could later complement our ballistic missile defenses.[8]

Even if these reasons are at once accepted, a world in which ballistic missiles played a diminishing role would still be a world of mutual deterrence. The U.S.-Soviet strategic relationship would still be characterized by mutual vulnerability and might be more stable than it is today for the reasons Iklé advances. People's anxieties might be lessened and their hopes strengthened. But these considerations do not affect the point that essentially the present system of mutual vulnerability will have been improved. It will still be mutual and, one is forced to add, it will still be just as much—or as little—"consensual" as it is today.

Altogether different, of course, is a world in which Reagan's grand vision is realized and nuclear weapons are rendered impotent altogether. The promise of transcending the age of deterrence makes up the political appeal of SDI. The world this vision encompasses is not one in which faith in deterrence is somehow restored by altering the technical arrangements on which this system rests, but one in which there is no longer a need to restore faith. In this world the deterrence of today, and possibly of tomorrow, will be replaced by a new relationship. This relationship, if we are to credit the president and supporters of his vision, will differ profoundly from the present one. Whereas the current relationship is constituted by a sword—a devastating sword—without a shield, the new one presumably will be constituted by a shield without a sword. The mutual deterrence of yesterday and today threaten an opponent with terrible retaliation should he resort to aggression. The deterrence of tomorrow and the day after tomorrow must rest on the same threat, for the movement from ballistic missiles to bombers and cruise missiles would signal no change in this respect. But in the world of President Reagan's sweeping vision, the greater aggressor might well be visited with no punishment at all. "Our goal," Secretary Weinberger has stated, "is to destroy weapons that kill people."[9] The other and better means of deterring war, Reagan has said of his defense initiative, is "by means other than threatening devastation to any aggressor—and by a means which threatens no one."[10]

The contention that this "new" deterrence will destroy weapons rather than people forms the basis of its claim to a higher morality. If ever realized, the claim would certainly prove justified. Although the deterrent arrangement under which we presently live differs in critical respects from the deterrence known in ages past, it does at least preserve this continuity with the past: it rests on a social principle, reciprocity, which has nearly always been the most reliable in setting restraints on man's collective behavior. It differs from the past by not carrying but threatening to carry this principle to an extreme limit. But the deterrence under which we will presumably live one day has no apparent continuity with the past. While holding out the "threat" of disarming an aggressor, it does so for no ostensible purpose other than defense. The destruction of an aggressor's weapons is not a step preparatory to the imposition of one's will, let alone the wreaking of vengeance. Instead, it is presented as an end in itself, and this despite the fact that it will have been taken to ward off an annihilating act of aggression. In the history of state relations, this idea of saving all lives rather than avenging some lives would surely represent, if ever acted upon, something new under the sun.

THE APPEAL OF SDI

The issue of motivation may be briefly considered against this general background. In regard to the prime movers of the defense initiative, there is little to add to accounts already available.[11] The story of how President Reagan came to embrace the idea of strategic defense and to make it one of the great projects of his administration has been told many times. His antipathy to the present system of deterrence goes back many years and was expressed in the presidential campaigns of 1976 and 1980. Mutual deterrence based on the threat of destruction has been likened by Mr. Reagan to two men holding cocked pistols to each other's heads. Aside from eliciting his strong moral disapproval, mutual deterrence is condemned because it holds out a future devoid of hope. Iklé's description of this expected future—"a prospect of anxiety without relief, an intellectual legacy crippling the outlook of each new generation, a theme of desolate sadness"[12]—is a more elegant statement of the president's view and explains his conviction that "there must be another way."

Moreover, the appeal of SDI is not only that it is another way but that it has particular appeal to the president and to those who share his outlook. If the true believers in SDI, beginning with the president, are technological optimists, it is partly because they are political pessimists. At bottom, they entertain little expectation that we will ever achieve a political relationship with the Soviet Union that finds expression in a more satisfactory strategic military relationship. Given this outlook, the only prospect for changing an unsatisfactory and even dangerous strategic relationship, while not surrendering vital political interests, is of necessity technological. It has special appeal, not only because it relies on exploiting our vaunted technological superiority, but because it can be pursued independently of the will or desire of the Soviet Union or, for that matter, of allies. SDI suggests to many the recapture of an independence of action, which was lost with the onset of the period of mutual deterrence.

If these were the general considerations that marshaled the president's advocacy of SDI, there were other more specific, and pressing, considerations that affected decisionmakers. SDI was undertaken at a time when the antinuclear movement enjoyed considerable momentum. At the very least, the movement indicated an erosion in the support that deterrent arrangements had formerly enjoyed. More than this, the movement suggested to many within the Reagan administration the beginning of a trend that might end by challenging in toto the legitimacy of mutual deterrence. Certainly, a number of signs—the Catholic bishops' letter being the most notorious—pointed in that direction.

While the antinuclear (freeze) movement had not deterred the Reagan administration from undertaking a strategic force modernization program, it did make it more difficult to line up congressional and public support for the program. This was apparent in the case of the MX missile. Clearly, the administration had only itself to blame for a large part of the difficulty it had with Congress over the MX when it betrayed an inadvertence that was impressive by almost any standard. Even so, a part of the administration's difficulties with Congress over the MX would very likely have arisen regardless of its behavior. The not unreasonable conviction grew that the apparent fate of the MX might well be the fate of any land-based missile system proposed in the future. And if this should prove to be the case, it was increasingly asked, what might happen to the U.S. land-based deterrent, if the Soviets continued unchecked their efforts in offensive land missiles?

In some measure, then, the defense initiative responded to apprehensions over what was seen as a growing domestic challenge to the order of mutual deterrence. SDI was to be the instrument for creating a new political consensus in place of the former one, which was now plainly eroding. An emphasis on defense, on destroying weapons rather than killing people, would appeal across the political spectrum. So too, it was and is believed, the prospect of a world ultimately free of the threat of nuclear weapons would appeal to those in the peace movement who had increasingly lost faith in mutual deterrence.

To these attractions of SDI must be added the quite different appeal the program holds for many whose interests are of a different order. Those within the administration who were initially surprised by, and even opposed to, the president's initiative, soon showed a remarkable degree of support. One explanation, of course, is that faith in SDI—or at least the appearance of faith—at once became the litmus test of loyalty to the president. Yet another explanation is simply that SDI began to appeal considerably to those persuaded that the nation's strategic position was constantly eroding. From this perspective SDI could be supported if only as a measure of insurance against the danger of being surprised by Soviet developments in missile defense (and, more generally, as a program to deepen our own understanding of the prospects for missile defense).

This purely precautionary rationale for SDI, however, scarcely accounts for the impressive early momentum of the program and the bureaucratic support it has elicited even among many who were initially skeptical of it. In part, the enthusiasm among the once-reserved lies in the promise SDI is seen to hold out as a solution to the predicament of extended deterrence. Strategic defense is expected to restore the cohesiveness of our major alliance by restoring the credibility of extended deterrence. It will presumably do so, however, without attempting to recapture strategic superiority. Indeed, from the outset administration officials have emphatically disavowed strategic superiority as a goal of the U.S. defense effort.

Is this denial to be taken at face value? It is not easy to do so. The contention that SDI will largely restore the credibility of extended deterrence follows from the claim that it will, at the very least, enhance mutual deterrence by markedly improving the prospect that a substantial portion of the U.S. land-based intercontinental ballistic missile (ICBM) force will survive a first strike. This prospect, moreover, is expected to materialize in the early stages of the defense transition, since it will result largely from the effective defense of missile sites. Thus, the technologically easiest and economically cheapest part of the defense initiative will soon relieve us of much of the anxiety we presently experience.

The strengthening of mutual deterrence, however, is not the same thing as the restoration of a credible extended deterrence. Clearly, stable mutual deterrence forms the essential precondition of all else. Even so, it will not be sufficient to restore the credibility extended deterrence once enjoyed, or was believed to have enjoyed. Indeed, critics of the present system have long contended that what is required for the credible deterrence of an attack on this country must be sharply distinguished from what is required for the credible deterrence of others. The requirements of extended deterrence, they have argued, are much more onerous and exacting, and this is particularly so for a strategy of extended deterrence that continues to rest on the threat to use nuclear weapons first in response to a Soviet conventional attack on our European allies. The unwillingness to confront squarely this growing predicament of extended deterrence and to take the needed measures, critics have contended, has become a major cause of today's strategic instability. "The absence of war probably reflects," one critic has recently written, "the fact that nuclear deterrence has not undergone the severe test of an acute military crisis in over two decades. There is now little basis for confidently assuming that deterrence stability will survive the next acute military crisis—whenever it may occur."[13]

From the perspective of those who have always emphasized the exacting requirements of extended deterrence and have persistently stressed the inadequacy of meeting these requirements by a strategy of mutual assured destruction, SDI is attractive because it holds the promise of restoring at least some semblance of strategic superiority. And from this perspective the disclaimers that "the United States patently has no plans to restore its former advantage in global nuclear arms"[14] are difficult to credit. Particularly when considered together with present programs for developing offensive counterforce weapons, SDI must appear as part of an overall effort to recapture what the United States lost a generation ago. Certainly, to the Soviet Union, the pursuit of counter-silo weapons and of strategic defenses must be, and is, seen as an attempt by the United States to regain a credible first-strike capability, thereby altering substantially, if not eliminating, the vulnerability to Soviet nuclear attack we have experienced since the early 1960s.

SDI AND THE PROSPECTS FOR PEACE

Any speculation on the general implications of SDI for the future of U.S. foreign policy must begin by making certain assumptions, particularly about technological prospects, which remain very much at issue today. Of almost equal importance to technological considerations are the pace at which and the determination with which the two sides proceed with their respective efforts. Then, too, the impact of SDI on the U.S.-Soviet relationship cannot be considered in isolation from the general geopolitical setting. Much will depend on the state of the overall political relationship between the two states in the years during which the defense initiative proceeds.

At one extreme, we may assume that successive administrations proceed apace with SDI, that the effort enjoys strong public support, that it is marked by striking technological successes, that the several stages of the defensive transition are accordingly telescoped, that the Soviet Union fails to match U.S. efforts (whether in devising counter-measures or in developing comparable defensive systems of its own) and falls steadily behind in the competition, and that the general geopolitical environment is no better than it is today and, what is more likely, is somewhat worse. In these circumstances, it seems reasonable to assume, the arms-control process must either break down altogether or, even if continued, become devoid of any meaning.

On the basis of these assumptions, an alarming scenario may be drawn. The Soviets find their strategic position steadily eroding. A mounting anxiety over this development is in no way assuaged by the geopolitical environment. Whether they look to the West, the East, or the South, political trends point to increasing difficulties in maintaining their present position, let alone in improving it. Rather than remaining passive in the face of these developments, it has been argued that

Moscow may feel driven to launch an attack on some central component of our as yet unprotected strategic defenses, which—though falling short of a first strike against the U.S. retaliatory capability—would still represent an act of war, with all its attendant dangers. It would do so for the same reasons that great powers in the past have struck out once they have concluded that they are being increasingly pressed on all sides and that time is working to their disadvantage.

From this perspective, SDI raises the prospect of precipitating a war—and perhaps a nuclear war—between the superpowers. Nor is it necessary, in this view, to add unfavorable political developments to what the Soviet leadership is already likely to see as sufficient reason for taking extreme measures, that is, the unilateral deployment by the United States of an increasingly effective defense against ballistic missiles. The Reagan administration understandably has soft-pedaled this contingency either by ignoring the prospect altogether or by assuming the "parallel deployment" of defensive systems. What if this assumption is not borne out and the other side begins to lag considerably behind? The prospect that it will do so was, after all, the expectation and hope of many who initially pushed for the defense initiative. U.S. technological superiority, it was urged, would enable us to make an end run around the Soviets. But in that event, Moscow would be confronted with the prospect of unilateral deployment that has so frightened the Reagan administration. If the Soviet Union deployed such systems unilaterally, administration officials have contended, deterrence would collapse and, according to a White House pamphlet, "We would have no choices between surrender and suicide."[15] It would not be surprising if Soviet officials took a similar view of their prospects in contemplating U.S. unilateral deployment of an effective defense.

The view outlined above ought not to be confused with the position that SDI is dangerous because it will intensify or heighten the risks of the dynamic of the arms race. The position that SDI will increase the pressure on both sides to use their nuclear weapons in a crisis, if only because defensive systems will dramatically reduce already short reaction times, finds the danger primarily in the technology itself, or rather in man's inability to control the technology. The fear is not the result of technology as such. Instead, it is the age-old fear of falling behind and losing one's place. The great danger of SDI does not result from technological determinism but from the Soviet fear that they will lose, or are losing, their hard-earned position of strategic parity with all that this loss entails.

The evident strength of this view is its appeal to history. Our experience with great-power conflicts does appear to support the position that in circumstances roughly comparable to those sketched out above, great powers have often gone to war. Is it plausible, though, to assume these circumstances in the present case? Does the history of the arms competition between the United States and the Soviet Union support the assumption of a critical U.S. technological triumph that goes unmatched—or uncompensated—by the Soviet Union? Certainly, this particular arms competition, now stretching over almost four decades, does not appear to bear it out. What it does point to is the ability of the more technologically backward of the two states either to match the strides of its adversary or to devise compensatory measures. It is true that we are told that this time will be different because the technological race is more difficult than ever and the Soviets are less prepared than ever to run it. But we have been told the same before, and we have been startled more than once to find that the adversary has not only run the race but finished in good time.

The critical assumption of a great disparity between the results of the respective efforts of the two sides is one that the history of the past forty years does not appear to support. Yet, it does support the assumption that a modest disparity may arise and has arisen without resulting in dangerous instability. Of course, it may be argued that the past is largely irrelevant to the present and future because the position of the Soviet Union has now fundamentally changed. In the past the Soviet Union was bent on establishing strategic equality with the United States. As the contender, it had to accept, and could afford to accept, disparities that it will find incompatible with its status as a strategic coequal.

This argument—as well as the larger view of which it is a part—does not share the belief that nuclear weapons have fundamentally altered the outlook and calculations of great powers and, particularly, the interests over which great powers have been willing in the past to go to war with other great powers. If this is indeed the case, then the implications of the defense initiative may well be as somber as they are often depicted by critics. For even if it is accepted that the circumstances corresponding to those assumptions earlier summarized are not likely to arise, they may do so. And if they do, the one remaining barrier to a catastrophic conflict is precisely the barrier posed by nuclear weapons themselves, a barrier that is largely brushed aside, however, by assimilating the conflicts between great nuclear powers to the conflicts between great powers in the past.

What must be questioned, though, is precisely this assumption of a continuity with the past. Admittedly, the appeal to experience is limited. Still, the view that nuclear weapons have effected a basic change in the nature of great-power conflicts rests on something more solid than intuition. During the past generation a common persuasion has grown that, short of surrender, no outcome of a crisis, however grave, could be worse than initiating a nuclear war. This persuasion is novel. Its effect is to confine the prospects of war between the great nuclear powers within limits that are far narrower than they have ever been. The significance of this persuasion is that it makes the risk of nuclear war virtually synonymous with the danger of miscalculation. It is the risk of miscalculation in severe crises that now defines the residual risk of nuclear war.

Nor is this all. While it may be said that many wars resulted from miscalculation, this consideration is almost irrelevant today because a war between nuclear superpowers would be one of miscalculation in a sense heretofore unknown. Given its expected speed and destructiveness, a nuclear war enables us to see the future as we have never before been able to see it. The calculations, and miscalculations, that once extended over months and years now extend over hours and days. The uncertainties that formerly attended the decision for war, and did so as late as World War II, have been replaced by the near certainties attending nuclear war between the superpowers. What does remain uncertain is not the minimum extent of destruction each side would suffer, but whether this destruction would permit the continuity and cohesiveness of national life in its wake. This is not the question national leaders literally asked themselves in 1914 or, for that matter, in 1939. And even if they had, they were not confronted with the direct and brutal answer nuclear weapons present.

Seeing the future as they have never before been permitted to see it, governments—the Soviet government included—may be expected to resist accepting it more determinedly than ever before. Even so, a risk of miscalculation will remain so long as the possibility exists that in a severe crisis the moment may come when circumstances conspire to make nuclear war appear inevitable. Logically, that time should never come. If no outcome of a crisis, short of outright surrender, could be worse for either side than the outcome represented by nuclear war, neither side should ever be tempted to miscalculate. The danger, we know, is that this logic will break down in a severe crisis and that one side or both sides will become increasingly persuaded of the inevitability of nuclear war.

Once that persuasion takes hold, a very different logic becomes operative. If nuclear war is once considered inevitable, striking first may be a considerable advantage, even in the absence of defensive systems. At any rate, the temptation to believe in such advantage may prove irresistible, and particularly so once even a limited defense system is in place. Even a terminal defense system must encourage the expectation (and, on the other side, the fear) that by striking first, the adversary's

remaining forces may be sufficiently depleted to be employed effectively
in a counterforce strategy. In these circumstances the side that has been
struck first may well face the painful choice between escalating the
exchange or accepting defeat. This is, of course, the same choice that
those alarmed over the Soviet land-based missile buildup have long
emphasized. The "window of vulnerability" to which this buildup has
supposedly led is to be overcome, however, by creating another window
of vulnerability, one that is likely to represent an even greater danger.

Still, these considerations do not essentially affect the point that the
conclusion of inevitability is the decisive factor. At most, they suggest
that the definition or scope of inevitability must be slightly broadened.
But the view that assimilates the conflicts between the great nuclear
powers to past great-power conflicts does not, need not, make the
contingency of nuclear war dependent on the conclusion of inevitability
that could emerge in a severe crisis. Nor does it consider that this
conclusion is of necessity a miscalculation in the sense that if each party
has sufficient information about the other party's intentions, there would
be no nuclear war. Instead, it finds the calculations leading to nuclear
war to differ little from the calculations that led to war in the past.
The conclusion of inevitability that is decisive in its calculations is one
that emerges outside the context of a severe crisis because it no longer
has the quality of immediacy.

If this view is accepted, we live in a more dangerous world than
even most pessimists have imagined. If nuclear weapons have not
essentially altered the motivations and calculations that led great powers
to war in the past, the avoidance of nuclear conflict in the future will
require more than simply the abandonment of SDI. Instead, such
avoidance may well depend upon holding out to the Soviet Union the
assurance that the present strategic relationship will not be altered in
any significant manner by this country.

SDI AND THE PROSPECTS FOR AN ARMS AGREEMENT

A quite different view of the future from the foregoing follows from
the assumptions that beyond terminal defense, the U.S. effort will prove
no more than moderately successful, that this effort will extend over a
generation, that the Soviets will compensate for U.S. efforts in part by
their own more modest progress and in part through taking effective
countermeasures, and that the political climate marginally improves in
comparison to the past five years. While these assumptions may turn
out to have been mistaken, from the present perspective they seem
reasonable. A defense effort that is moderately successful may be
considered as one comprising both endo- and exo-atmospheric elements

and capable of destroying one-half to three-quarters of warheads in a Soviet first strike. This may fall well below the expectations of SDI enthusiasts, but it would nevertheless represent a considerable technological achievement and one that many experts continue to doubt. Whether it would give this country a "damage limiting" capability remains doubtful if only given the prospect of Soviet proliferation in order to keep the same target coverage.

If these assumptions about the future are granted, what are their implications for U.S. foreign policy? What changes might follow from them? I would argue that very little may be expected to change—at least, very little that would not have changed for other reasons. This conclusion is at variance with the view that an increasing U.S. commitment to defensive systems will, if persisted in, largely destroy any remaining prospects for further arms-control agreements. One response to this is that the prospects for arms control do not appear very bright in any event, despite the apparent centrality the issue now has in the U.S.-Soviet relationship. Any future major arms-control agreement must be negotiated against the background of an experience that will make further agreements very difficult to reach. This experience is regarded as one tantamount to betrayal by a critically important political constituency. Having found our security interests weakened by the arms-control agreements of the 1970s and having been persuaded that Moscow will enter into a pact with this country only when it can gain political advantage from doing so, the Right's disposition (or inclination) to resist further agreements will be quite strong. It is not at all clear that this resistance could be overcome.

In any case, the prospects—such as they are—for a major agreement on strategic weapons are likely to decline with the passage of time, especially if we equate the prospects for limiting strategic weapons with those for reaching some kind of overall trade-off between our effort in defensive systems and a substantial Soviet reduction in land missiles. In making such an agreement we would be trading a still largely unknown asset against a known liability (the large Soviet land missile force). The Soviets would be trading a known asset against an unknown liability, but a liability that makes their present economic planning more difficult and one they fear they might not be able to overcome even if they concentrated on overcoming it at the possible cost of domestic economic reform.

The prospect of an agreement, therefore, rests largely on an approximate balance of one side's hopes and the other side's fears. But five years or so from now, this balance is likely to show signs of erosion. It may turn out that we are strikingly successful in our research and development effort, and that the Soviet Union can neither match this effort nor devise effective countermeasures. In that event, we might prove much more unwilling than today to compromise our effort. More likely is the prospect we have already argued for, namely, one in which our efforts are moderately successful but are nevertheless roughly matched or otherwise compensated for on the Soviet side. In that case, Soviet fears will partly recede from where they appear to be today. Soviet leadership will probably have already made the painful decision to commit substantial resources to the defensive effort. Having made the decision and braved the initial consequences, the incentive for making other substantial concessions to the West will have been markedly reduced.

If this reasoning has merit, the impact of a substantial U.S. commitment to defensive systems on Soviet incentives to reduce its offensive forces is greater today than it is likely to be in the years ahead. Unless the U.S. effort is attended by early and striking success, our leverage may be expected to decline by the late 1980s or shortly thereafter. Does it follow that we should therefore push toward concluding an agreement along now familiar lines? Advocates have urged that by doing so we would not only be capitalizing on an asset whose value is undetermined but would not really be compromising, let alone sacrificing, this asset. For we might conclude an agreement that broadly confines our effort to the research phase in return for a substantial Soviet reduction of offensive land missiles. Whereas we would have agreed only to slow down an effort that might always be intensified if the agreement was terminated for some reason, Moscow would have sacrificed a very real asset here and now. If this is indeed the case, however, the question arises: why should the Soviets conclude an agreement in which they give up a large, fixed-capital investment for what is only a moderation of our research effort, an effort that by comparison has cost us to date very little? On the other hand, those who view this effort as promising may find that the "bargain" in getting Moscow to surrender a substantial portion of its land missiles is no bargain at all. As they point out, once such an agreement is concluded, it is likely to be difficult to sustain the kind of effort that makes it worthwhile for the Soviets to remain strictly within the limits of the agreement. From this perspective, such an agreement is likely to impose somewhat greater risks for us than it does for Moscow because we will have to wind down an effort that could be quite difficult to pick up again. By contrast, this argument runs, the Soviets will surrender an asset that could be readily replaced should circumstance or interest so decree. Opponents of this kind of agreement insist that there is no way by which this presumed asymmetry might be compensated for, let alone removed. Even in the absence of our experience with the arms-control agreements of the 1970s, it poses a considerable obstacle to a future agreement.

THE IMPLICATIONS OF SDI FOR U.S. FOREIGN POLICY

The prospects for arms control apart, there remains the broader issue of how a move to defensive systems will affect the overall conduct and objectives of U.S. foreign policy. To the supporters of SDI, the general effect of the program will be to give new strength and vitality to our role and commitments in the world. Having once changed the present structure of deterrence, we will be in a position to act with greater confidence and assurance. The short-term effects of SDI will presumably lead to an increase in strategic stability and a strengthening of extended deterrence. The long-term effects, which are expected to result in something close to the restoration of our historic security, will give us a freedom of action we have not enjoyed since the 1950s.

To critics, the principal effect of the defense effort will be to encourage the illusion that, in the words of one, "Our national safety can be secured by acting alone."[16] From this perspective, SDI betokens the attempt to return to a past that cannot be restored, to a past when we were secure from physical attack and could pursue a unilateralist foreign policy. SDI thus reflects the refusal to recognize that we must learn to live with our adversary and that we have no safe alternative to a political resolution of our differences. And in the pursuit of political, rather than technological, solutions of the great conflict, our major alliances remain as important as ever.

The debate over the likely effects of SDI on foreign policy reveals more than anything else the basic political outlook and disposition of the parties to it rather than their varying assessments of the possibilities of technology. Whereas supporters of SDI are apt to be political pessimists and technological optimists, critics are apt to be technological pessimists and political optimists, at least relatively. The debate reflects, above all, varying assessments of the nature of the great conflict between the United States and the Soviet Union and the possible means of our safe deliverance from it. The debate has persisted throughout the postwar period. The differences today over the broad implications of SDI on the nation's foreign policy are simply the latest version of it.

Is it useful to go beyond these well-defined and entrenched positions and speculate about the general policy implications of SDI? Only if one also speculates on the kind of success SDI could ultimately enjoy. Here again, a choice must be made among possible future worlds, the choice that has already been elaborated in preceding pages. Thus, I forgo extended speculation on the implications for foreign policy of a world in which nuclear weapons are rendered impotent because we have acquired an effective defense against ballistic missiles and air-breathing conveyances as well. In this world, we would indeed have largely restored our historic security position, for we would no longer be subject to the threat either of nuclear or even conventional weapons carried by missiles or aircraft. Unable to use the air as a medium of warfare, except tactically, we would move back to an age dominated by land and naval forces. Of even greater importance, we would very likely return to a world dominated by conventional balance-of-power calculations. The prospects of entering such a world, however, are so meager and removed in time as to make any discussion of its policy consequences verge on the fanciful.

More realistic, if only by comparison, is the consideration of the general policy consequences of an effective defense against ballistic missiles, an effective defense possessed by both the United States and the Soviet Union. This, too, is a world far removed from the present one. In the judgment of many scientists it will remain an unobtainable world. But suppose it is obtainable. Would it entail significant effects for U.S. foreign policy? The view that it would rests on the argument earlier noted: that bombers, cruise missiles, and any other air-breathing conveyances that may be employed are much slower than ballistic missiles and therefore less suited for surprise attack. They are also considered safer as deterrent forces, given their relatively greater invulnerability and, for bombers at least, their ability to be recalled.

This world, let it be emphasized, would still remain one governed by mutual deterrence through the threat of retaliation. Thus the essential calculus that many, including the president, have found politically hazardous and morally repellent would remain in force. Would it nevertheless be a much safer deterrent system, since its dependence on bombers, cruise missiles, and the like would make it markedly more stable? This, after all, is the critical claim made on behalf of SDI, a claim that is not insubstantial. But even if it is conceded, the other general effects are not easy to discern.

Thus, it is not easy to assess the consequences of the new strategic dispensation for extended deterrence. The claim has been made that extended deterrence would be strengthened by becoming more credible, but the reasons are not apparent. The one change that clearly would strengthen extended deterrence—at least if cold logic prevailed—would be the restoration of something approaching our former invulnerability. But the new dispensation would not restore this; it would instead alter the character of our vulnerability to nuclear weapons. However important for strategic stability generally such alteration may be, its effects in improving extended deterrence do not appear substantial.

These considerations, moreover, simply assume that the effectiveness of a defense against ballistic missiles will in time come to enjoy such credibility as to go virtually unquestioned. Although ballistic missile systems will remain in place for an indefinite period, they will cease to play a role in the calculations of either side because of the common persuasion that in a severe crisis the defense against them would not be put to the test. And it would not be put to the test, presumably, because of the common perception that the defense on either side is reliable in its effectiveness. The likelihood of this perception arising, however, is not a solid one. Thus, it seems we are destined to repeat the now familiar experience of uncertainty over whether meaningful limits can be placed on the use of nuclear weapons. Yet, we will not and cannot know whether a defense system will work—particularly one that is extraordinarily complex and dependent on several new technologies—short of putting it to a test that may prove fatal. This being the case, even a defense system that is viewed as close to perfect in its effectiveness will, in fact, add yet another uncertainty about nuclear war to those we already have experienced. The great gain in strategic stability that such a system is supposed to confer will rest on this uncertainty, an uncertainty that in a severe crisis will depend for its resolution on an even shorter time span than that characterizing the present system of deterrence.

If these are the likely consequences attending what is deemed to be a near-perfect system of defense against ballistic missiles, then we can conclude that the consequences attending a much more modest system will be less significant. And it is, to repeat, a much more modest system that represents the one prospect over which it is useful to speculate. As such, it seems strained to argue that the defense transition will result in a new global unilateralism, let alone in a new isolationism. It may be that in the years ahead, the conduct of U.S. foreign policy and the character of commitments in the world will undergo substantial change. But in this event, it is unlikely to occur because the results of SDI provided what would otherwise have been a missed opportunity. A much more plausible argument is that the same motivations that at least partially account for SDI may also be expected to give rise to significant change in foreign policy. Major change toward a more unilateralist policy, one intent on contracting present commitments, might occur quite independently of the results of SDI. Indeed, if there is a relationship between the two, it would seem to be of the opposite nature. Rather than result from a successful SDI, a more unilateralist and even isolationist policy might follow more expectedly from the failure of SDI because the existing lapse of faith in deterrence would deepen.

It is not likely, though, that the essential role and commitments of the nation will change significantly in the decade ahead. The view that we are at the beginning of a lengthy defense transition does not alter this conclusion, for the results of this transition will in all likelihood leave U.S. foreign policy substantially where it would be without SDI. The stability of the present structure of deterrence may well be enhanced, a not inconsiderable achievement, although scarcely a revolutionary one. In a world marked by a greater commitment to defensive systems, the basic patterns of conflict will nevertheless remain unaltered. The super-power rivalry may undergo some alteration. If it does, SDI will not figure prominently as a cause. Perhaps the greatest potential effect of a defensive transition will be to reassert the primacy of the United States and the Soviet Union in the international system. The transition is bound to illuminate once again, as it is doing now, the great gap that separates the two from the rest of the world, including the rest of the present nuclear powers.

NOTES

1. Robert McNamara, "The Military Role of Nuclear Weapons," *Foreign Affairs* (Fall 1983), 79.

2. Second Vatican Council, *Pastoral Constitution on the Church in the Modern World,* December 7, 1965, National Catholic Welfare Conference, 1966. The Pastoral Letter of the U.S. Bishops on War and Peace, "The Challenge of Peace: God's Promise and Our Response," *Origins* 13, no. 1 (May 19, 1983). The quotations in the text are taken from these documents.

3. See Jonathan Schell, *The Abolition* (New York: Alfred A. Knopf, 1984). Similar views have been expressed by others. See, for example, George F. Kennan, *The Nuclear Delusion* (New York: Pantheon, 1983).

4. Presidential Press Conference, March 25, 1983, *The New York Times,* March 26, 1983.

5. Fred Charles Iklé, "Nuclear Strategy: Can There Be a Happy Ending?" *Foreign Affairs* (Spring 1985), 813.

6. Ibid., 817. It will be apparent that the force of Iklé's argument depends, in part, upon a selection of descriptive terms that gives to his two "ingredients" a connotation that does some violence to the actual state of affairs at present while idealizing, if only by implication, past international orders.

7. Ibid., 822–24.

8. Ibid., 816.

9. Quoted from *The Wall Street Journal,* January 2, 1985, excerpt of a speech by Defense Secretary Caspar Weinberger to the Foreign Press Center, Washington, D.C., December 19, 1984.

10. From a January 12, 1985, speech by President Reagan on defensive technology, "Weekly Compilation of Presidential Documents," March 28, 1985, vol. 19, no. 12.

11. Among the more discerning are: "The Origins of 'Star Wars,' " *The New York Times*, March 4, 1985; Don Oberdorfer, "A New Age of Uncertainty . . . ," *The Washington Post*, January 4, 1985; David Hoffman, "Reagan Seized Idea Shelved in '80 Race," *The Washington Post*, March 3, 1985; Frank Greve, "Out of the Blue: How 'Star Wars' Was Proposed," *Philadelphia Inquirer*, November 17, 1985.

12. Iklé, "Nuclear Strategy," 823–24.

13. Keith B. Payne, *Why SDI?* (National Institute for Public Policy, 1985), 4.

14. Iklé, "Nuclear Strategy," 820.

15. "The President's Strategic Defense Initiative," The White House (January 1985).

16. Townsend Hoopes, " 'Star Wars'—A Way of Going It Alone," *The New York Times*, January 2, 1986.

4

THE CHALLENGE OF SDI: PREEMPTIVE DIPLOMACY OR PREVENTIVE WAR?

George Liska

With the emergence of space-based defenses as the chief subject of military-strategic debate, the United States stands at the threshold of a new technology whose political implications will extend well into the next century. If these long-term effects are to govern choice among present options, the debate must transcend purely technical questions and seek to anticipate a hypothetical future. Unavoidably tentative at this stage, an inquiry into the implications of the Strategic Defense Initiative for political policies will achieve little if it does not aim for the "big picture." It must not, therefore, be intimidated by the greater rigor of the exact sciences and specificity of technological data but must scrutinize the laws of politics which, while less reliable and compelling than the laws of physics, nonetheless indicate the range of the probable on the strength of historical evidence.

Correcting for biases that stress operational efficacy and technical feasibility is nowhere more important than in the American culture, including the political subculture. It is a culture that typically favors a strictly defined perspective but now faces a question with far-reaching implications for societies with a radically different orientation and hierarchy of values. Embracing a technology such as the one underlying defenses in space in the alleged interest of humanity at large requires taking into account the human factor in its many facets without, for all that, getting mired in pacifist or any other sentimentality.

This chapter is reprinted from Robert W. Tucker et al., *SDI and U.S. Foreign Policy* (Boulder, Colo.: Westview Press with The Johns Hopkins Foreign Policy Institute, SAIS, 1987).

STABILITY IN NUCLEAR AND PRENUCLEAR SETTINGS

The effectiveness of mutual deterrence in creating strategic stability can be ascribed to the great uncertainty of the outcome of a nuclear exchange. The uncertainty, and its relation to stability, reflects the fact that there is and can be no reliable identification of the requisites of stability in terms of numbers of weapons and kinds of technology alone. Between major adversaries, one man's or side's stability is another's instability just as, as between the United States and its principal allies, the same deployment can be viewed as coupling or decoupling the two theaters of the Euro-American ecumene. Even in the prenuclear military context, the existence of equilibrium (another word for stability or its foundation) could be established in most instances only by inference from the restrained behavior of the main actors, not by counting muskets in one era and mortars or machine guns in the next. In fact, the impossibility of quantifying "power" was the precondition that allowed the balancing mechanism to work as well as it did. If the outcome of a military conflict could be predetermined by precise measurements, the marked initial advantage in ready capabilities that will prompt a state to challenge the existing order would make resistance decidedly unpromising and, therefore, in many instances less likely.

For strategic stability to be more than contingent—to rest on more than uncertainty revealed in cautious conduct—it must reliably inhibit states from employing military means to do the opposite from exploiting a real or imagined advantage: to wit, counteract a radically worsening political situation. Within a halfway rational universe of action, such total or absolute stability obtains when unleashing a military conflict means signing the death warrant of the attacker himself. A "balance of terror" of this kind has been fading, and with it unconditional stability, as the technology of counterforce has progressed to the detriment of strategies targeting populations as the first or last resort. By once again making war thinkable (because it is escalation-resistant even if not escalation-proof), the increasing efficacy of both nuclear and conventional weaponry has reinforced the shift from total stability to one highly susceptible to pressures from the political arena. The importance of that arena increases also insofar as a major power is most likely to initiate war for objectives more psychological or diplomatic than military. To the extent that they intensify political stress while reducing destruction, partial defenses against ballistic missiles are apt further to weaken stability on the nuclear level. A failproof protection of not only retaliatory capability but also population would go one better and, in effect, restore the traditionally unstable conventional military balance.

Without the threat of assured self-destruction, the issue of war as a practical resort returns to its habitual context as a "continuation of policy by other means," to be analyzed by reference to general principles of statecraft. When the future is at stake, the inquiry must reach beyond actually transpired behavior and consider underlying motives and determinants of action. If certain inferences can be drawn from the observed absence of conflict (for example, existence of equilibrium reflecting widespread satisfaction with the status quo relative to the costs of changing it forcibly), what are the commonly operative incentives to conflict? What will make a major power resort to substantial military action against another great power? Immediately at issue is rationality in statecraft, as distinct from the reasonable person's common sense. Moreover, where narrowly pragmatic or strictly military-strategic criteria would stamp certain conduct as irrational, a particular value system growing out of a specific political heritage might not. In particular to be considered is the hierarchy of values generated by a system (such as the classic European) stressing the absolute primacy of corporate autonomy and by a culture (such as the continental European) that is state- rather than homocentric. A social ethic emphasizing sacrificial heroism, as distinguished from essentially hedonistic needs, will further reinforce the primacy of the state; and this primacy will be portentous in its implications when coupled with a political culture (such as the East European ones, including Russian) whose tendency is to project menacing trends pessimistically into a future jeopardy to be forestalled in the present from still available strength.

Even before the nuclear age set in, great-power regimes had gone to war increasingly for essentially defensive (or preclusive) rather than unqualifiedly offensive (or predatory) reasons. They acted militarily not so much to aggrandize themselves further as to survive as great powers according to the standards of the age. The last purely acquisitive war, Prussia's mid-eighteenth century conquest of Silesia, was initiated as a means of becoming a great power, whereas Austria's diplomatically aggressive counteraction was designed to recover the lost province in order to restore the empire's standing in the Euro-Germanic theater. Similarly motivated was France's self-assertion on the continent and globally, then and increasingly after 1815 and 1871. All parties to World War I acted for reasons they thought to be, and that largely were, defensive. In a state system that was itself aging, the fear, well-grounded or not, of irreversible decline could not but produce a deep insecurity in an increasing number of regimes, a condition that made an offensive enactment of an essentially defensive posture more or less compelling. For the British, the threat came from Germany; for the Germans, from Russia; whereas for Austria-Hungary and Russia, and increasingly also for France, fear was largely generated from within, from the prospect of instability in the short run or also organic decline in the long.

When pre-World War II conditions and perceptions are given due weight, even the aggressions of Hitler's Germany to a large extent fit the preemptive model, which finds a classic expression in the strategy of Tojo's Japan. Finally, actions calculated to keep open the path to world power by shutting out unacknowledged competitors, decried as unprovoked aggressors, can be considered defensive. In this category belongs U.S. participation in the two world wars. It differs from earlier American wars waged for territorial aggrandizement within an essentially secure milieu under the banner of manifest destiny.

Notably on the part of the non-American polities, the political conditions of individual well-being and the material conditions of individual livelihood related only secondarily to the dominant statist value of corporate autonomy. They were of moment just enough to sustain the sociopolitical order against debilitating stress. Contemporary regimes may be said to remain all the more sensitive to status issues, the less they enjoy assured stability and security of tenure, while the state-centered ideal continues to predominate among the governed so long as the polity has not achieved the condition of material satiety. If true, even an ostensibly "materialistic" ideology, such as the Marxist-Leninist, and a scientific-technological bias, such as that of the Soviet regime and political culture, do not significantly alter matters. Neither feature abolishes the greater-Russian-than-American propensity to respond forcefully to major threats defined by nonutilitarian criteria. Such threats include hostile denial of a still unrealized claim to national self-fulfillment conditioned by the geography and history of "holy Russia." The nuclear context has not altered the crucial equations any more than can or will any foreseeable implementation of strategic defense in space. In fact, the latter may restore them to fuller applicability.

STRATEGIC (AND POLITICAL) STABILITY AND STRATEGIC DEFENSE

Exploring the policy implications of strategic defense requires distinguishing two stages of the scientific-technological progression: the condition of having arrived at a certain plateau and the process of getting there. In both stages, one must consider how far, if at all, one superpower is ahead of the other.

An actual defensive system is likely to extend in the foreseeable future only to the protection of strike forces, constituting terminal or point defense. Such a system, if in place on both sides about equally, could be said to maintain or even increase relative stability contingent on the uncertainty of the immediate consequences of a military engagement. However, such an assessment of deterrence will largely depend on ignoring impulsions from geopolitically focused competitive dynamics and its political-cultural context. When there is a sufficiently strong inducement, a first strike against the offensive or defensive capability of the adversary becomes more attractive than before: while the first strike partially cripples the retaliatory response (makes it "ragged"), even a but limited defense of the initiating side can be expected further to blunt the counterstrike. Stability is preserved only to the extent that the side that has been struck retains "objectively" the capability and "credibly" the will to intensify the exchange, on pain of setting off further rounds of retaliatory escalation. Such a retributory reaction becomes less likely the more one assumes that it would be the party initiating the first strike that was under greater pressure to defend itself offensively and was, therefore, more prepared to incur major damage and run ultimate risks. Under the same hypothesis the side receiving the first strike has less to gain from escalation because it faces the loss of no more than its prior geopolitical advantage. It can look forward to remaining or soon again becoming competitive in both the organic and the diplomatic dimensions of "national power."

More effective defenses aimed at the boost and midcourse phase of enemy missiles are significant in the near future mainly as remotely possible developments. They are all the more threatening to stability if one side is lagging technologically and the technology can be used offensively against command-control-communications facilities. Given the high probability that in an uneven race for improved strategic defense the lagging side would be the Soviet Union, the situation risks enhancing any existing incentives for the Russians to act preemptively before the race was over. Should it by contrast be the Soviets who win a head start in the higher-level defense capability, the incentive to use their advantage before it disappeared would be stronger than any comparable stimulus on the part of a similarly positioned United States. Since Soviet head start is apt to be both precarious and provisional, the likelihood highlights the risks implicit in any arms race when one party expends great effort to match or outstrip a resource-richer adversary only to see the nonrepeatable advantage fade and turn into its opposite unless it is used for a less reversible effect.

Thus, unless one is prepared to hypothesize a situation wherein the balance of both resource-related and geopolitical factors moves clearly from the U.S. to the Soviet side, the Soviets will continue to be the party more strongly motivated to initiate a nuclear exchange. The seemingly optimal state—both sides having a foolproof bubble-like strategic defense over their populations—would only place the United

States at a psychopolitical (next to military) disadvantage for a different reason, on the assumption that such a defense would restore the primacy of conventional military force.

Any deterioration in the Soviets' already adverse geopolitical situation would only fuel their urge to act. Since the United States is a saturated conservative power, it cannot be indifferent to the probability that the existence of limited, and the prospect of more advanced, U.S. defenses would make a Soviet first strike more likely. Would the same military-strategic condition enhance U.S. options for offensive (or counteroffensive) self-assertion in the world arena?

In principle, a U.S. effort to exploit strategic defenses politically for a "rollback" would merely increase the pressures on the Soviets to be more aggressive or subversive abroad and to repress or mobilize more intensely at home and regionally. In practice, an offensive U.S. self-assertion on a significant scale would be "rational" only if keyed to major strategic goals worthy of the attendant risks. Among such goals would be the elimination of Soviet dominance in Eastern Europe, using local disaffection from behind the shield of strategic defense. It is most unlikely that the mere possession of a capability would or could be used to push back the Soviets in peacetime. In a more likely contingency, deterrence would have broken down at least partially into a protracted conventional-military conflict. A serious threat to Soviet regional hegemony extending to the Soviet homeland would then tend to elicit a matching assault on the territorial United States, a substantial escalation apt either to overcome less-than-perfect defenses of military installations or to bypass them via countervalue strikes. Comparable, if less drastic, scenarios can be envisaged with respect to other focal areas, such as those abutting on the Persian Gulf.

The hypothetical scenarios point to the real danger latent in partial defenses, even if these are on balance favorable to the United States. They could tempt the leader of the West into theater strategies that promised spectacular results, while being inherently unpredictable as to their military and political effects locally as well as globally on foe and friend alike.

At issue is fundamentally the relation of strategic defenses to offensive political or politico-military behavior at the peripheries of either of the superpowers or the global system itself. It can be (and has been) argued that both of the superpowers seek an advantage in defense sufficient to neutralize the adversary's nuclear capability. The difference begins when the aggressive-expansionist Soviets are said to equate stability with possessing the advantage as a shield not so much against a hypothesized U.S. first strike (as they would claim) but for releasing superior instruments and techniques of lower-level violence for safe employment on behalf of an offensive self-assertion at their and the system's periphery. In the same interpretation the United States as a status quo power needs the advantage for retaining the ability to stage defensive political or nonnuclear military action abroad. Leaving aside the ambiguity of the distinction between offense and defense, the argument points to a glaring asymmetry between routinely limited geopolitical goals to be achieved incrementally and an imminent possession of qualitatively upgraded military-strategic means. The question remains: Would achievable defenses in themselves impart a sufficient advantage to either side to alter substantially the cost-benefit calculations in regard to moderate, at best, gains in mostly inessential areas or on marginal issues? Would they raise sufficiently the nuclear threshold? Or would the peripheral issues continue to be approached and decided on the basis of locally available conventional capabilities and, if in terms of a balance, then one weighing the relative importance of competing national interests and the relative strengths of supporting communal will rather than high-technology military instruments?

GEOHISTORICAL CONSTRAINTS
AND EXTENDED DETERRENCE

Hypothetical scenarios will unavoidably proliferate so long as the U.S. (or Soviet) security community is primarily interested in short-term perspectives on tactical or technical military settings of policy and continues to defy the theoretically conceded disutility of nuclear weapons for achieving results offensively. The presumption against usability is unlikely to be significantly altered by presently conceivable technological innovations. Moreover, to repeat, conclusions or inferences drawn from purely military scenarios about the utility of this or that kind of defense will be flawed so long as they rest on assumptions about Soviet geopolitical objectives and behavior that, bemused by the imputation of a world-conquering goal, ignore the more real fundamental issue of survival in great-power role and status.

As terror oozes out of the deterrent balance via counterforce and defense capabilities, the weight of geopolitical (including geographically conditioned historical, or geohistorical) factors necessarily increases. And as the latest American defense initiative injects high drama into the U.S.-Soviet discourse, the time span within which controversial issues and the relationship itself can be constructively addressed grows shorter.

An enhanced capacity to defend retaliatory facilities may well give the United States a diplomatic advantage over Soviet Russia. However, it risks inverting the larger psycho- and geopolitical equations to the United States' detriment. So long as Russia is exposed to confinement between the United States (and Western Europe) and China (and Japan), and especially if the encirclement shows signs of tightening and the comparative development ratios worsen (for example, by virtue of U.S.-aided industrial buildup of China), the incentives will grow for the Soviets to arrest the adverse drift before it is too late. Moreover, just as the Soviets might acquire the stronger incentive to act preemptively by virtue of negative trends, they are likely to retain the greater positive capacity to absorb damage to population and other material assets owing to their communal culture and political system. A political culture that absorbed the loss of twenty million in World War II and was, if anything, morally invigorated by the bloodletting, is on the face of it psychologically fit to face up to a nuclear exchange. It may be better equipped for the ordeal than a society that has been spared any comparable testing throughout its existence, that recently lost its nerve under the stress of casualties in the tens of thousands, and that tends to be traumatized by terror- and accident-induced casualties in the hundreds or less.

By the same token, the temptation for the Soviets to act "while there is still time" becomes an imperative once their options begin to narrow in relation to a neighbor (China), which, more hostile than is the United States and gaining in the capacity to inflict matching damage, exhibits a political and communal culture even more capable of absorbing human and material devastation than Soviet Russia. Tolerance for the loss of life increases along the west-to-east culture spectrum, while impediments to civil-defense preparations decrease. In such a setting anything that might set off a controlled nuclear exchange, only to risk degenerating into an uncontrolled one, constitutes an unevenly weighted deterrent working against the United States in the short run and against Russia in the long. It adds to the hypothetical cost of space-based defenses.

Less hypothetical are the political costs of enhancing U.S. defenses insofar as the attendant dangers would need to be forestalled by appeasing the Soviets politically. To achieve the necessary calming effect in time to avert an impending crisis, the geopolitical setting would have to be reshaped both abruptly and drastically. In the likely absence of compensating Soviet adjustments, the entailed diplomatic revolution would affect adversely U.S. alliances at the center as much as U.S. containment policies at the periphery of the global system. Conversely, absent the "appeasement," instead of staging a technological "breakout" via an unmatched SDI equivalent of their own, the Soviets might more plausibly try to break out of the ring of geopolitical encirclement. They could do so in either direction: through China, possibly by way of a surgical or wider strike using Moscow's nuclear advantage while it lasts; or through Western Europe, most probably by means of a limited conventional thrust dramatizing the Soviet perception of the developing configuration as lastingly intolerable.

Short of such an extremity, the development of strategic defenses by the United States will still have a profound effect on its alliances and, equally important, on Soviet conduct with respect to those alliances. As the United States develops a more independent capacity to protect its own territory, its stake in extending deterrence to allies will decline even if its ability remains intact or grows—and it will be perceived as declining by ally and enemy alike. So long as Western Europe is less effectively defended than the territorial United States—a situation unlikely ever to change despite parallel defenses against shorter-range Euromissiles—the Soviets will aim pressure or action in the direction of their nearer neighbors. Should such action take a military form, an effectively defended United States would be perceived as being able to defer a climactic confrontation with the Soviets indefinitely while buttressing further its extra-European alliances.

The temptation to sidestep irreversible decisions grows with the ability to defer them. This cliché cannot but impress, and its implications discourage, America's Western allies if U.S. defenses grow faster than those of both the Soviets and themselves. Intra-alliance stress would only intensify if a raised nuclear threshold (due to inter-superpower defenses and/or nuclear force reductions) increased emphasis on conventional-military buildup and related expenditures. Unlike the United States, the politically weak West European governments and their strongly economics-minded publics would rather live dangerously under the shelter of mutual assured destruction (MAD) than slowly atrophy from the strains and costs of adequate conventional or any other defense. Increasing the role of air-breathing delivery systems, such as bomber-carried cruise missiles, in conditions of antiballistic missile defense would not fundamentally alter the intra-alliance equation. The long travel time of such weapons, which makes them susceptible to recall, multiplies occasions for exerting psychological pressure on U.S. allies, who will be responsive to popular anxieties because they have representative governments and who will be free to respond because they are members of a noncoercive multimember alliance. This dual susceptibility augments the Western handicap in relations with an adversary not only comparatively immune to similar pressures but capable of manipulating the scope of military initiatives and the presentation of political intentions in ways calculated to sharpen dissent from radical deterrence or defense on the part of the more vulnerable side.

If extended deterrence is subject to weakening in relation to Western Europe, it is apt to fade in relation to China even before taking on a clear shape. To compensate, a partially and preferentially defended

United States might soon see itself compelled to reassure a volatile eastern protégé as much or more than the more solid Western partners. The compensations might be no less military-strategically irrational for being seemingly reasonable (because necessary) politically. The most ironic consequence of upgrading China's military resources and militarily relevant industrial-technological potential might then surface only gradually. Whereas strategic defenses have been initiated against Russia, their development might be eventually vindicated against the furthermost eastern power, positioned as the next challenger in the process.

ARMS CONTROL AND CONTROLLED COMPETITION

It is conceivable that the danger of an uncontrolled competition over strategic defense could lead the superpowers to coordinate its development within the framework of a fresh approach to arms control. However, concerted progress in a militarily critical technology seems impossible without prior or at least concurrent movement toward political accommodation. The military-strategic competition, despite its superficially autonomous dynamics, remains a mere reflection and symptom of relations in the geopolitical base. This does not mean that pressures emanating from a dramatically new phase in the military-strategic sphere cannot extend into the geopolitical theater and create there new incentives and possibilities as well as accentuate existing perils. Any Soviet gains that would result from continuing to extend a previously conceded military-strategic parity incrementally into the geopolitical sphere would be marginal when compared with the adjustments that might be necessary to neutralize the explosive effects of disparate developments in strategic defenses. Moreover, barring a growing disparity of that kind, Soviet self-restraint would be apt to grow as the Soviets developed a stake in the consensually revised order, resting on a henceforth legitimized access to areas and transactions critical for the dispersion of material and military capabilities among lesser regional powers within an evolving international system.

Mutual confidence-building behavior in the sphere that counts most in the final analysis, that of geopolitical competition, would inevitably extend to arms control. The latter's principles and provisions could begin to deemphasize quantitative levels of current weapons allocations and deployments. Instead, they would address primarily the middle- to long-term intentions of the superpowers in regard to research and development initiatives planned in support of their specific security strategies. Such long-term planning is inseparable from the aims pursued in the geopolitical arena. Consequently, a halfway serious attempt to coordinate weapons developments would not only reflect the degree of current consensus but also generate supplemental inducements to concert political policies. It might accelerate the convergence of more fundamental foreign-policy postures to culminate in the sharing of potentially disruptive scientific and technological innovations as they took shape and before they irreparably unbalanced political relationships.

Just as isolating the evolving military instruments from the larger context in the stage of preliminary planning may create new dangers, so conjugating arms development with corrective policy dynamics can open up new opportunities. Optimum defense technologies can mature only in the remote future. But they might still be focused upon now because intermediate improvements would not be sufficient to warrant diverting resources and attention from the eventual optimum. By the same reasoning, political strategies might usefully be keyed to the long-term best in U.S.-Soviet relations, in preference to problematically enhancing questionably vital American interests at the cost of making the relations more antagonistic than they are, or need be, when judged by the standard of uncontestably valid stakes.

However far in the future the positive or negative outcomes might mature, the basic decisions are apt to be taken in the remainder of the present century and some at least in the present decade. The contingency to avoid most—by creating the impression of it being the unchanging U.S. objective—is demotion of the Soviet adversary that compounds the risks from tactical rollback and strategic encirclement. Although the costs to the United States might be greatly deferred, they could still be more than materially devastating. The moral burden is greatest on a polity that has had the less immediate or compelling reason to set the stage for the military resolution of a conflict, should it come to pass for reasons not wholly free of its prior responsibility. In such a perspective, it would be reckless to proceed with the planning and development of defense technologies that (1) do not guarantee a substantial net increase of defense over defense-suppressant or offensive capabilities and (2) are conceived and deployed in isolation from the largest possible psycho-political context, one made up of divergencies in geopolitical situations and both communal and political cultures.

U.S. preference is for technological and organizational shortcuts to the solution of political problems rooted in ambiguities spanning space and time, geography and history. The impatience has been saved so far from spawning a major catastrophe, let alone a terminal one. In fostering this immunity, the U.S. margin for errors has exceeded the measure of foresight and the quality of design mobilized on America's behalf. It may be that if the latest of Pandora's boxes is opened recklessly too wide, it will disclose a hidden mechanism for evil stronger than the good fortune of history's most favored people. It would then not suffice that it was one of the luckiest political leaders ever who first set the challenge to Fortuna in motion.

RESTATEMENTS AND ELABORATIONS

Basic to the U.S.-Soviet relationship is the projection of each party's fears and ambitions onto the other, resulting in the mutual attribution of aggressive intent. In the Marxist view, "internal contradictions" in capitalism make the West "objectively" the aggressor. They will eventually induce—if not force—the leading Western power to strike out first to improve its ability to survive among the competing and less militarily burdened capitalist economies. The propensity of the American ethos to emphasize (material) damage limitation in choosing between alternative strategies would not, in such a doctrinaire view, withstand compulsions from the military-technological advantage vanishing amidst accelerating fiscal or widening economic stress. However, ideological self-exculpation to the contrary notwithstanding, the Soviets, too, face conditions that make them susceptible to a first strike should threats from East or West undermine the chief basis for the regime's claim to internal legitimacy: Russia's position as a world power. If the Western powers increasingly define survival primarily in quantitatively assessed human and material terms, the Soviet embodiment of Russia as a nation built around the state looks first and foremost to the qualitative factor of role and status. Yet again, despite differences in basic mind-sets, either superpower could be impelled toward the abyss of war by a valid kind of strategic rationality, one that meets the test of minimizing loss rather than maximizing gains. The resulting calculations may well prevail under sufficient stress over the contrary counsels of a prudence construed as nothing more profound than risk-avoiding caution.

In terms of historical analogies, a Soviet preemptive strike—and the political culture motivating it—would replicate Japan's offensively defensive response at Pearl Harbor to the prospect of an unmatchable U.S. naval buildup (combined with geopolitical and economic denial). Future U.S. behavior could be tentatively inferred on the same principle from the importance of economic incentives behind America's entry into World War I and II (interest in recovering Allied debts in the first conflict and in frustrating the German bid for succession to Britain's imperial assets and advantages in both). More pertinent is the analogy with the pre-World War I Anglo-German naval competition. Like the British dreadnoughts, defense in space raises military technology to a quali-tatively higher new level, restarting the arms race, as it were, from zero and reducing the value of the previous generation of weapons. One perceived result is to elevate the two main competitors categorically over other parties, just as the Anglo-German naval race overshadowed the resources as well as the stakes involved in the receding Anglo-French and Anglo-Russian naval competitions. Another consequence, more galling for the Soviet Union than it was for Germany, lies in reopening the issue of military-strategic parity.

For the Russians, as for the Germans earlier, the purpose of achieving (or closely approximating) such parity was to advance, by one stroke, a twin goal: to deter the established rival for the sake of military self-protection and to exert pressure on it as part of an expansive design aimed also at geopolitical parity. The similarities may be potent enough to outweigh a difference. Rapid technological change endangers the effort to attain and maintain parity most for an eastern power. Such a power tends to favor size and scale over versatility in weapons, more germane to the Western polity: to wit, specifically, Soviet missiles with superior throw-weight capacity, as against the U.S. triad stressing sea-borne and air-breathing deterrents. Thus, also, before losing out to Rome, the eastern Mediterranean Hellenistic powers futilely enlarged the Greek military instruments (four- to five-deck ships in lieu of smaller and more mobile three-deck ships, just as war elephants were used in lieu of only human phalanxes), while overly large and immobile Ottoman siege guns proved no match for the western powers' mobile field artillery. Soviet gigantism in weaponry, too, would in the end prove much less effectual within an environment dominated by antimissile strategic defenses.

Meanwhile, the U.S.-Soviet conflict parallels the Anglo-German pattern most alarmingly by stimulating fears and encouraging mutual suspicions of surprise attack. The real surprise might eventually come, for better or worse, from the high-technology nuclear weapons that generate so much concern on both sides playing as small a role in actual combat as the dreadnoughts did in World War I. The impracticality of actually using the "ultimate" weapon would then result in a shift to lower-grade weapons, such as directed conventional munitions, performing the substitute role of torpedo boats and light cruisers.

Should strategic defense play a key role in decreasing the importance of nuclear weapons in favor of conventional forces, U.S.-West European relations might face even greater political strains as more of the burden of matching Soviet conventional strength fell on the European allies. The cohesion of the Atlantic coalition, like that of any hegemonic alliance, requires that the protection provided by the leading ally exceed the ally's provocation of the enemy. The level of U.S. protection of Western Europe might well decline if strategic defenses shielded mainly U.S. territory while they reduced Washington's incentives to run the ultimate risk for Europe's defense. As for provocation, it might, in unbalanced conditions of defense, emanate not only from the U.S. side directly but from related developments on the German side of Russia's two-front situation that makes Russia (and its clients) vulnerable to territorial revision. Should the Soviets respond with nothing more serious than their own version of strategic defenses, it would substantially undermine the French and British nuclear deterrent forces, further aggravating the no-win situation for NATO's European members. Just as European military security and diplomatic status risked being substantially degraded in a peace that has been made more precarious, so the potential for physical survival would not be enhanced in a war that has become more likely. In these conditions the strategic defense initiative might well point less to a pot of gold at the end of the envisioned rainbow than to the end of the alliance itself.

On the extended East-West spectrum, China has begun to be for Russia in this century, and will be increasingly in the next century, what the Russian empire was in the nineteenth for the Germans and what Persia had been for the Ottoman empire still earlier. When the more centrally located polity confronts the day's principal western power, it typically interacts strategically with the western power or powers as an occasion and impetus for imitating innovative technologies. These are equally or more useful or necessary for dealing with the comparatively backward, but more directly threatening and instinctively feared, power still farther to the east. In the present setting, just as deploying intermediate-range missiles has been more important for the Soviets' undermanned Asian theater than the European theater, so current and future Soviet antiballistic missile defenses are likely to have a similar bias.

How explosive the eastward bias will be, and how intense the preemptively defensive Soviet urge in the western direction, will depend on the prospect for a cooperative transition to a defense-reliant world between the superpowers, attended by political accommodation. Just as any trade-off between U.S. and Soviet assets and liabilities in various regions of the globe is impossible on a one-to-one basis outside an overarching global bargain, so arms-control transactions can be neither individually satisfying nor cumulatively productive so long as they merely trade individual weapons or weapons systems against one another. The "trade" must be the most comprehensive one possible if it is to link present capabilities to compatible concepts of the future.

Near-utopian correctives to competitive power politics become possible only when they are no longer necessary to forestall serious conflict. This truism was progressively revealed as a truth in connection with the League of Nations type of collective security system. It applies equally to apolitical approaches to conflict and security, characteristic of single-minded arms-control efforts. They threaten to elevate a mere procedure that is not even an ongoing process to the status of panacea, while in fact harboring a dangerous illusion insofar as it fails to relate military capabilities consciously to political intentions.

The issue becomes acute whenever efforts at arms control escalate to schemes for substantial reduction, nearing elimination, of strategic nuclear weapons centered on intercontinental ballistic missiles. In contrast to an incrementally evolving politico-military concert attended by weapons coordination, such a leap of faith into the unknown sidesteps the resulting imponderables for strategic stability—unless, of course, the military-strategic and -technological turning point is recognized as entailing repercussions in the geopolitical arena sufficiently far-reaching to actualize its symbolic significance. In the absence of wide-ranging political accommodation, the issue of possible bad faith and deception on one side or the other cannot but inhibit the implementation of a reduction-to-elimination design that equals totally effective strategic defense in transferring prime dependence from nuclear weapons to conventional military weaponry. Related concerns will almost certainly frustrate the benign expectations from curtailing strategic offense, as will the threatening asymmetry with regard to third parties that are likely to resist a self-denial matching the one bilaterally and (in third-party eyes) collusively agreed upon by the dominant superpowers. Even a partial failure to conform on all sides would require extending the degree of superpower accommodation sufficient to defuse their competition to a virtual comanagement of the worldwide military-strategic chessboard. In brief, a thoroughgoing U.S.-Soviet "deal" on strategic defense and offense, to be militarily safe and politically stable, entails a multifaceted global bargain with selectively condominium-like overtones of truly revolutionary proportions.

In making a judgment whether the bargain is feasible and desirable, the first step is to grasp the nature of the U.S.-Soviet conflict. Just as the United States does not behave as it does because it is, in Soviet parlance, imperialist, but rather because it is insular, so the Soviet Union is better understood as continental than as communist. It follows that the United States is not inherently aggressive but acts expansively when it seeks to preserve the advantages of its position first across geopolitical space and now in outer space. The Soviet response aims to approximate and ultimately match the defensive advantage of the insular counterpart by all possible means. But whereas the insular power by nature employs the more discreet political-economic instruments of persuasion, the less-favored continental power has to rely on more direct and dramatic politico-military means. Its appearing all the more aggressive and expansionist as a result accounts in large part for the temptation to rationalize the need for hypothetically feasible defense by the fact of unchanging Soviet aggression. The imputation feeds readily into the Soviet suspicion that the initiative is but the latest medium for realizing an unalterable plan for undermining the peaceable Soviet state.

Similarly, in an earlier era, the Soviets branded NATO as an instrument for Western aggression impelled by resurgent German revanchism, when, in fact, the more plausible threat lay in NATO's politically offensive purposes aimed at the structural weaknesses of the Soviet bloc. By the same token, U.S. proponents of SDI may rationalize the need for something like it (as, before, for NATO) by the need to prevent the Soviets from using an actual or asserted advantage in intercontinental ballistic missiles (as, before, in armored divisions and massed infantry) to possess themselves militarily or only politically of Western Europe and, now, also of much of the Third World. In reality, NATO was in all probability no more necessary to prevent a Soviet invasion of Western Europe than space-based defenses are likely to be required for precluding cumulative Soviet gains either at the Third World margins or the West European center of the international system. What NATO did accomplish—and it was not negligible at the time—was to impede a precipitate all-out Finlandization of a war-shocked Western Europe, and to do this at a bearable cost in terms of intensifying the emergent conflict. SDI's object of forestalling a Soviet grab at geopolitical parity or more is likely to be fraught with greater risks for a lesser reason.

PRODUCTIVE ACCOMMODATION OR PREVENTIVE WAR?

Why, it might be asked, and to what end pursue geopolitical parity? The simplest answer to that question is another query: Why else attain and for what other end seek military-strategic parity, a condition the United States previously conceded to the Soviets? Beyond that, geopolitical parity (combining increased Soviet presence in Europe with no more drastically decreased U.S. preeminence worldwide) is both an alternative and a possible intermediate stage: an alternative to a contentiously prosecuted balance of quantitatively defined power, continuously raising the issue of one party's predominance so marked as to constitute hegemony; and a stage on the road to inter-superpower partnership, one that helps resolve the dialectic of defense and offense in the technological and strategic-military dimension and disposes of the offense-defense ambiguity in politically critical perceptions, while the parties embark on an evolutionary process pointing toward cooperation and convergence.

For evolutionary convergence to speed up and deepen has meant continuing to replace monocentric Stalinist totalitarianism with a political system that embraces functionally plural technocratic features in response to external opportunities and challenges that neither can nor need be managed militarily. The United States for its part would have to evolve toward modes of formulating and implementing foreign policy that impose longer-term and wider-ranging perspectives on the anarchy of individual and group biases. In that they make a society more flagrantly freewheeling in style than free in substance, the biases inevitably distort the manner of implementing the notion of the national interest. By playing upon the indeterminate content of the "national" and maximizing the particularistic connotation of "interest," they deform the thrust of the superficially similar but intrinsically contrasting norm of the "reason" of "state."

As the key by-product if not principal goal of convergence, a mutually acceptable evolution of the international system cannot have as its goal a world order based only on American-type values. A more plausible goal is an environment that is congenial to the continued validity of the more inclusive—and essentially Europeanist—diplomatic culture shared by the two superpowers and supportive of their prolonged viability as major actors among emerging ones.

Within an evolving system, the offense-defense dialectic compounds the interplay between primarily land- and sea-based powers, each offensively defensive in its own fashion. Any provisional resolution of the offense-defense dialectic in the military-strategic sphere will take the form of an institutionalized mix of defensive and offensive technologies and strategic applications, conducive to the moderation of militarily achievable goals. The analogous opposition of insular and continental powers will be periodically dissolved into a multiplicity of more symmetric land- *and* sea-oriented—that is, amphibious—powers, a process already initiated in the transition from the sharp Anglo-German to the more qualified U.S.-Soviet dichotomy as respectively insular and continental.

Thus the Greek and the Italian city-state systems, organized around the land-sea power cleavage, yielded in time to the Hellenistic and the early European pan-Mediterranean systems, composed of unevenly amphibious larger powers. Currently, the transition to a new offense-defense mix in military technology and strategy is already entangled with the initial stirrings of the other transition: from U.S.-Soviet maritime-continental asymmetry, one that has carried the European antecedents forward into the era of continent-wide powers, to a more polycentric world of major amphibious powers.

The development entails some demotion of the Big Two to the profit of not only China but also other aspirants to expanded regional roles. For the superpowers to monitor and channel the diffusion of functionally diversified power into a pattern viable for both is, meanwhile, the alternative to the center of gravity in an updated as well as inverted land-sea power spectrum moving away from both. If Japan replacing the United States as the key insular power and China supplanting Russia as the key continental power is the scenario that comes first and easiest to mind in that connection, it is not the only possible one over time.

Replacing the land-sea power schism with a polycentric configuration of amphibious powers does not bring a guarantee of eternal peace. Nor would cosmic bliss result from transcending the continental-maritime disparity through outer space, a more fundamental modifier of the traditional cleavage than was air power beginning with World War I and transcontinental missiles have been since World War II. Least promise resides in outer space becoming the locus of permanent defensive or offensive military installations, conceived and emplaced competitively. For the two superpowers cooperatively to manage the dispersion of power on earth and jointly develop new resources in outer space has the more positive potential. More realistic, it is also a more inspiring goal than is one of merely denuclearizing an unresolved conflict. Space-based defense, notably when advocated in the millenarian version bound to arouse apocalyptic visions on the Soviet side, injects an unnecessary irritant into an unavoidably precarious and protracted process of evolution. If the politics of such evolution are to contain the side effects of a multistage military-technological revolution, they must be nursed with the patience genuine conservatism owes to all organic change— not least when it involves bodies politic with constitutions that, markedly disparate in outward forms, are equally a historically validated outgrowth of distinctive conditions and situations.

The constituents and the promise of a strategy that promotes processes of change that heal old wounds, rather than opening new ones, must first assume a discernible shape on earth. Only then can any incidental benefits and the consummating reinforcements become manifest in outer space. There is nothing wrong with gradually developing a new defensive-offensive mix in both inner and outer space. On the contrary, such a development can be desirable if it promotes stability by enhancing the uncertainty of military outcomes, not least in regard to a first strike and a whole range of third parties that are harder to deter and penalize than either of the contemporary superpowers because they are hardier in either cultural or material makeups. The wrong sets in when military deterrence is outmatched by psychopolitical "impellence": when one side is swayed toward running a more than hypothetical risk of annihilation in order to preclude a not necessarily greater possibility that the other side is alone about to achieve the capacity for strategic compellence, by virtue of developing complete invulnerability against the key weapon on which deterrence rests. The asymmetry deepens when the challenge offered dramatically in the skies combines with a policy designed to perpetuate also the geopolitical inferiority of an ambitious rival: when, that is, the objective is to make a fiat from the heavens consolidate the rewards of meritorious works performed on earth.

The problem of sin assumes a secular face in world politics when the quest for an abnormal measure of protection by one party spells unbearable provocation for another, inviting desperate reaction. In the guise of a preventive war, such a reaction is inspired less by the expectation of success over the rival party than by the urge to avoid surrender to an irreversible process. The question of expediency rests, then, more fundamentally than on the probabilities of the immediate outcome, on the predictability of larger developments over a longer period of time: Can prediction be based on the projection of current trends? Is a present generation either obligated or entitled to run the risks of violent death to ensure bearable living for the next? As political expediency becomes indistinguishable from moral validity, the arrogance of the party that strikes out consists of acting to prevent a future it cannot know. The yet greater conceit is of the side that, failing to ask itself similarly pertinent questions before creating the situation calling for the fatal choice, has presumed to take upon itself the very shape of fate.

Part Two

IS SDI FEASIBLE?

5

IS SDI TECHNICALLY FEASIBLE?

Harold Brown

The program known as the Strategic Defense Initiative (SDI) includes research on a variety of technologies—many aimed at distinct phases of the ballistic missile flight path. For each phase—boost, post-boost, mid-course and terminal[1]—a defense would require successful surveillance, target acquisition, tracking, guidance of the weapons, and kill mechanisms. Are the objectives of SDI technically feasible?

The answer will depend primarily on what specific objectives strategic defenses ultimately seek to achieve—protection of population, of missile silos, of other military targets. Within that context, the answer will further depend on the capabilities of the technologies and on the potential countermeasures and counter-countermeasures of each side.

This article will assess the prospects for the various defensive technologies for both the near term (10 to 15 years) and the longer term. It will include recommendations on how to proceed with a realistic research and development program. It will also make tentative judgments on the technical feasibility of various SDI objectives, though definitive answers are not yet possible. The political desirability of SDI is a separate question, not addressed here.

Finally, in considering the prospects for the various SDI technologies, it is important to remember how long it takes to move from technological development through full-scale engineering to deployment. That time is governed by the budgetary and legislative process, as well as by the state of technology.

Reprinted by permission of FOREIGN AFFAIRS, America & the World 1985. Copyright 1986 by the Council on Foreign Relations, Inc.

- After the technology is proven out, full-scale engineering development of a moderately complex system will typically take five to eight years (a new ICBM is a good example).
- The course of deployment (unless there is concurrency of development with deployment, which has almost always proven counterproductive) takes five to seven years after completion of engineering development.
- Thus, if proven technology exists now, it will take 10 to 15 years before a new system employing the technology could be substantially deployed.
- If the technology needs to be further developed, even though the phenomena exist and are well understood, the time for that technology development will have to be added to such a period.

II

What kinds of technologies could be embodied in defenses against ballistic missiles that could begin deployment before or about the year 2000?

Terminal hard point defenses (e.g., defending ICBMs), using hardened ground-based radars and interceptor rockets, would require about ten years between a decision to deploy and having a significant force; the time to completion of deployment would approach 15 years from decision. The necessary technology exists now, and some subsystems have already been partially developed. What would be required would be the design of a new system involving—in sequence—some additional prototype development, full-scale engineering development, production and deployment. Such a system would include an interceptor like the Spartan missile aimed at reentry vehicles (RVs) outside the atmosphere, and another, rather like the Sprint missile, for intercepting RVs that have already entered the atmosphere.

Present designs of both missiles would require the use of nuclear warheads. Alternatively, non-nuclear versions could be developed using terminal homing devices in the interceptor. There is some question about how heavy a conventional warhead (and therefore the interceptor missile) would need to be in order to provide high probability of destroying the incoming RV and missile warhead; it depends on how close to the reentry vehicle the terminal guidance could bring the interceptor. If a non-nuclear interceptor is chosen, this would lengthen by at least a few years the time to a substantial deployed capability.

An additional optical sensor, the Airborne Optical Adjunct (AOA), which would track reentry vehicles by detecting their infrared emissions or viewing them with visible light, could also be included at about the same time as a non-nuclear warhead.[2] Such a capability is feasible technologically and likely to be helpful in discrimination during or shortly before the offensive missile's reentry, but the technology would need some additional development.

Over the next 10 to 15 years it also appears technologically feasible to develop the components of a system using *space-based kinetic-energy weapons*. These chemically propelled rockets would intercept the offensive missile during its boost phase and destroy the target by impact or by detonation of an exploding warhead. The chemical rockets would be similar in nature to air-to-air missiles, but steered with reaction jets rather than aerodynamic surfaces. The targets could be designated to the interceptors by laser or radar tracks, provided by a set of tracking and fire-control satellites orbiting at a higher altitude than the satellites from which the interceptors would be fired. Short-range laser designation of ground or airborne targets exists, but the accuracies required for ICBM tracking would require significant additional technological development, as would imaging and processing the infrared data, and looking close to the horizon.

The interceptors would home onto the target, guided by their own passive observation of the infrared emissions from the target missile or by receiving reflections from the target of radar signals emitted from satellites (semiactive radar homing). Such a system, however, must find a way to direct the killer rocket to the actual ICBM booster rather than to its plume (exhaust), which emits the infrared signal. While presumably this can be done, it will add complexity and offer an opportunity for offense countermeasures. Though the technology for components of kinetic-energy kill and boost-phase intercept systems exists, solution of problems of this sort would require a considerable developmental process.

Several years of additional technical development could significantly decrease the weight of the intercept rocket for a given kill probability. That approach is indicated because the weight determines a significant part of the total system cost. The cost of putting payloads in orbit with either the present shuttle or expendable boosters is thousands of dollars per pound. To reduce those costs to an acceptable level, a new "super" shuttle would probably have to be developed. This would involve up to a ten-year development and production process and a delay in deployment of a space-based kinetic-energy system.

Missile boosters in the upper atmosphere and in space can be detected, tracked and attacked through the infrared emissions of the missiles' exhaust plumes while their propulsion stages are burning; however, the actual effectiveness of such an approach will depend not only on the technical features of the defense, but on the actions of the offense in employing decoys, adopting countermeasures and suppressing the defensive system itself. For example, modest deliberate fluctuations in booster propulsion ("jinking") could require the kinetic-energy interceptor to make significant changes in its cross-trajectory velocity, and this would involve a large weight penalty for the defense. Fast-burning boosters would effectively negate such a defense system.

Nevertheless, the technology for a space-based boost-phase intercept system of some capability, using kinetic-energy weapons, could be ready for a decision as early as 1990–92 to initiate full-scale engineering development, with a significant deployment able to begin some time between 1995 and 2000. Soon after the year 2000 there could thus be deployed a space-based kinetic-energy kill system along with a high-altitude and low-altitude terminal defense. These would constitute three layers of a possible multilayered defense, the purpose of which would be to compound modest kill probabilities in each defensive layer so as to produce a high overall kill probability.

III

For the period five to ten years beyond 1995–2000, more elaborate space- and ground-based technologies *may* be feasible, with a corresponding period of deployment beginning some time between 2000 and 2010. Increased uncertainty, however, naturally attaches the further out we look.

Among the less uncertain of these later technologies are *space-based directed-energy weapons* such as neutral particle beams and chemical lasers.

- A *neutral particle beam* (NPB) would be made up of atomic particles, accelerated to a high speed in charged form by electric fields in an accelerator, then steered and pointed by a magnet, and then neutralized so that it will not be deflected by the earth's magnetic field.
- A *chemical laser* uses the energy created by chemical reactions[3] to create a highly focused, intense, highly ordered ("coherent") beam of infrared light, directed by a mirror.

As a measure of their status, both of these technologies could well be used toward the early end of the period 2000–10 for antisatellite purposes, which are less demanding than the antiballistic missile task. Demonstrations of the capability to kill an individual satellite by such means—most likely on cooperative targets—could be made still earlier, but these would not represent an operational military system.

Neutral particle beams are, in their present state of development, much brighter than any existing laser in terms of energy into a given solid (cone) angle. Today they produce particles of energy corresponding to acceleration by a few million volts of electric field (and could in the future be improved to 100 million "electron-volt" energies). Protecting ballistic missiles from such high-energy NPBs would require much heavier shielding than would protection from lasers. During the next 10 or 15 years, however, it is unlikely that NPB technology will be able to put more than ten percent of the primary energy into the particle beam itself. Such low efficiency means that a space-based NPB would probably require a nuclear power source, development of which would delay the possible deployment of a system.

In addition to the usual target acquisition and tracking problems, a defense based on neutral particle beams must address several other critical tasks. The magnet necessary to point the beam before its neutralization is likely to be heavy—and expensive—to put into space. The tasks of developing an ion source capable of operation over some minutes and of achieving the necessary pointing accuracy will be difficult. Even more difficult is tracking the beam, since it gives off almost no signal in space. Finally, the system will need to find ways to detect the effect on the target, through nuclear emanations from it, because at the full range of a successful NPB attack, the target would not be physically destroyed. Even where NPBs cannot be used to kill targets, however, they might ultimately prove useful in discriminating among them, because the nuclear emanations from an object hit by an NPB would depend on the object's weight.

For chemical lasers several technological problems still need to be solved. One is getting high enough power while maintaining a low enough beam divergence. Another is the very large weight of chemical reactants required for providing the energy. A third is the feasibility of the large optical systems required. There are, however, some promising technologies under development for chemical and other lasers. Among them are: various phase-compensation techniques to improve the quality and stability of the beam; phase-locking separate lasers together to increase the overall brightness; using adaptive optics (rapid adjustment of segments of a mirror), both to compensate for atmospheric dispersion for ground-based lasers and to ease the problems of creating large aperture mirrors for space-based ones; and phased arrays of lasers to increase intensity and to steer them more rapidly through a small angle, so as to move quickly from target to target. But some of these technologies have yet to reach full demonstration of the physical principles involved, and all are still far from being developed.

IV

Less technologically developed, and therefore more suitable for consideration of full-scale deployment beginning 20–25 years from now, is the use of ground-based *excimer* and *free-electron lasers* (FEL)[4] to be used with mirrors in space as components of a system for boost-phase intercept. Both are now many orders of magnitude away from achieving the intensity necessary for the required lethality, the free-electron laser further away than the excimer laser, at present. But the free-electron laser's device weight is lighter and its efficiency greater (and thus, its fuel weight lighter) than that of the excimer laser. The FEL might perhaps therefore be deployable in space. But the weights of these lasers and of their energy supplies more probably would require either to be ground based. The laser wavelength for both would allow the beams to penetrate the atmosphere, if the atmospheric distortion problem is solved. Thus both seem more suitable for ground deployment along with mirrors in space. Other problems for the ground-based lasers are the large optics required, both on the ground and for the synchronous-altitude steering mirrors, and obtaining the same high power in each of a long series of repetitive pulses.

These two systems might also be suitable for "active" discrimination—also called "interactive" or "perturbing"—in the mid-course phase of a strategic defense. That is, they could impart energy or momentum to very large numbers of objects in mid-course being tracked by some of the more established technologies already discussed. The resulting changes in the objects being tracked, or in their trajectory, could offer some limited opportunities for discrimination of reentry vehicles from decoys and debris.

Significant technological disagreement exists about the potential of ground-based lasers (free-electron or excimer) versus space-based chemical lasers. Some believe that the smaller amount and lesser complexity of hardware required to be put in space will bring the time for availability of these ground-based lasers as close as or closer than the time actually required for those entirely space-based.

Chemical lasers are more proven technologically than excimer or free-electron lasers, but many experts have dismissed their potential use because of the difficulties in designing an effective system. Chemical lasers (space-based because their wavelengths will not penetrate the atmosphere) could be of some use against ballistic missiles now deployed. They could well be severely inadequate, however, against the offensive systems (with, for example, fast-burn missiles and other countermeasures) that could be in place during the first decade of the next century, when a significant defensive laser deployment could be made. Surely such countermeasures would be put in place if defense lasers were deployed. And in light of the large weight of chemical fuel that would have to be deployed in space, the chemical laser system at present seems to fall into the category of technically feasible but ineffective as a system. New optical developments such as phased arrays and phase conjugation are now being investigated, however. These might be able to improve the brightness and stability of chemical lasers—and increase their lethal range—to the point where they would have some systems effectiveness even against a responsive threat.

X-ray lasers powered by nuclear explosions are still further off than the other types of lasers, although they seem to offer some interesting distant possibilities. X-ray lasers would have wider beam angles and higher power per unit solid angle than optical ones. This would make them suitable for destroying clouds of objects or for actively discriminating heavy objects among them, and thus effective against such counter-measures as balloons and decoys. Proof of the most basic principle has been established, in that bomb-driven X-ray lasing has been demonstrated to be possible. But there is doubt as to what intensity has been achieved; it is in any event far less than necessary for use in active discrimination, let alone target kill. Demonstration of the physics of a possible weapon is at least five (more likely ten) years off. Weaponization would involve another five or more years, and only thereafter could its incorporation into a full-scale engineering development of a defensive system begin.

Rail guns, which accelerate objects to very high speed electromagnetically, may also have promise. But they are almost as far off as X-ray lasers. Multi-kilogram payloads would need to be accelerated to speeds above 15 kilometers per second, and a system (and power source) would need to be designed that could be used for multiple shots. New guidance and propulsion systems would also have to be engineered to survive such accelerations and to do the necessary terminal homing.

While many uncertainties exist as to future laser technologies for strategic defense, all laser systems would be vulnerable to other lasers. In general, the rules of the competition are that ground-based lasers will defeat space-based ones, larger ones will defeat smaller ones, and bomb-driven X-ray lasers looking up through the fringes of the at-mosphere will defeat the same sort of X-ray lasers looking down into the fringes of the atmosphere. Vulnerabilities will also differ as between ground-based and space-based lasers. The former would have the weap-ons—or at least their energy source—on the ground, and presumably would include mirrors stored or unfolded in or popped up into space for the purpose of steering the laser beams.

As to time scale, when one is talking about time scales for deployment 25 or more years from now, corresponding to technologies whose full demonstration is more than ten years away, one really cannot know what the time scale will be to reach substantial deployment. The accompanying chart summarizes the time scales for these various systems. For the space-based systems, the pop-up systems and those with mirrors in space, lengthy technology development periods will be required. Depending on how that development is carried out, it may be possible to defer collision with the provisions of the ABM treaty until early in the process of full-scale engineering development. The calendar times differ for each technology, as shown in Figure 1.

V

A successful strategic defense would require not only kill mechanics but also a *battle management system* involving sophisticated *command, control and communications* (C^3). Estimates for the total number of lines of code of software required range from 10 million to 100 million. A measure of the effort involved can be derived by using the standard figure of $50 a line. Thus, the software costs could range from $500 million to $5 billion. The raw cost of such a system is therefore less important than the feasibility and methods of finding and correcting errors in it.

One problem would be with errors in the codes themselves. While this would not be trivial, it could be dealt with in part through automated software production and through artificial intelligence. The latter, though still mostly in the conceptual stage, nevertheless has real capabilities in terms of expert systems, and can be expected to produce real advances within the next ten years. The most fundamental problems for battle management and C^3 are: the establishment of appropriate rules of engagement; the probability of conceptual as well as mechanical error in the creation of the software, and the possibility of redundancy to compensate for it; the need to change portions of the software as new elements are introduced into the system without having the changes compromise the working of the rest of the software; and, most of all, the ability to check out the system, so as to make sure there are no conceptual errors in the software in such matters as handing over tracks of the offensive missiles, transferring automated decisions from one node of the system to another, avoiding loops in the logical sequence, and so forth.

How could such capabilities be tested? Can on-orbit testing be used? Such problems are just beginning to be addressed, and it will take a long time before conclusions can be drawn even as to what the state of this particular technology is compared with what is needed.

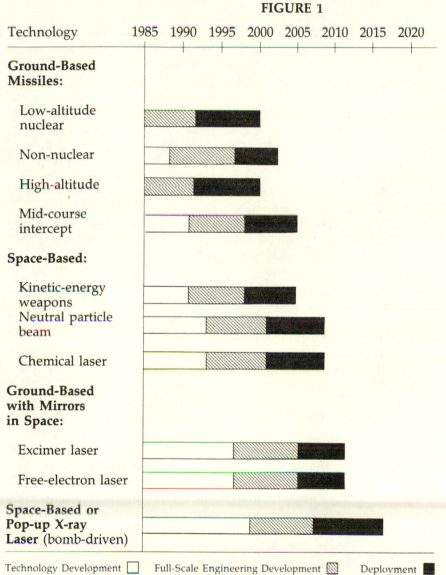

FIGURE 1

VI

In terms of future defensive technologies, what potential defense systems are technically feasible?

It is technologically feasible to create a terminal defense overlay of hard ICBM silos, deployed so that the missiles are moved among multiple silos and so that their position at any one time is unknown to the attacker. Such a defense overlay can, by preferential defense—that is, defending only the occupied silos—provide a cost-exchange ratio favorable to the defense because the attacker must attack all silos. The same is probably true of defense of moderately hardened mobile missile systems by a terminal defense of corresponding mobility and hardness. In the case of hard-silo defense, a single layer of defense by endoatmospheric ground-based interceptors would suffice. For mobile hardened missiles, a two-tier ground-based system might be needed.

Modified ground-based defenses using similar technologies could protect some other military targets, for example command and control centers. The exchange ratio at the margin will vary widely, however, among classes of such targets according to their nature (hardness, area and mobility), their number and their cost. Such defenses could also be deployed for a thin protection of some urban-industrial areas, though they must be recognized as protecting such targets, if at all, only against attacks that are both limited in size and not responsive (i.e., not modified to take account of the defenses). Terminal defenses for these categories would use two-tier ground-based interceptors, and until the early 21st century would need to carry nuclear warheads in at least the exoatmospheric long-range tier. The defenses would be accompanied by space-based early warning and tracking sensors, and by airborne optical sensors to aid in the discrimination task during the terminal phase.

Advanced versions of infrared sensors deployed near or above geosynchronous orbit (an altitude of 20,000 miles) will be needed for attack warning and assessment in any defensive system, even if no boost-phase intercept is attempted. Infrared or other sensors in lower orbits (at altitudes of hundreds of miles) would also be useful to all layers of a ballistic missile defense system for tracking and discrimination. But the sensors must be able to survive. This suggests that they be provided with some self-defense, which in turn could be the first step toward boost-phase intercept.

As to weapons, kinetic-energy rockets based in space are technologically feasible. But an ICBM using a fast-burn booster clearly defeats them, and space-based defenses are vulnerable to defense suppression. Estimates of the exchange ratio for a *boost-phase intercept* defense layer based on kinetic-energy kill range from as low as two to one adverse to the defense at the margin (assuming unresponsive offensive threats and including sunk costs for the offense) to more realistic estimates, assuming responsive offenses, of five or ten to one. Defense suppression would probably further shift the ratio in favor of the offense.

Space-based chemical lasers seem feasible in technological terms but more questionable in practical systems terms. Though likely to be faster in response than kinetic-energy weapons, they still will not be a match for fast-burn boosters of offensive missiles. They will, moreover, be vulnerable to defense suppression systems based on other space-based lasers, and also vulnerable to ground-based lasers and direct-ascent antisatellite weapons. Ground-based lasers, whether free-electron or excimer lasers, are interesting future technologies and may be more effective than chemical lasers, but it is too soon to know.

It should be noted that even though fast-burn missiles could thwart a boost-phase intercept, this still leaves the possibility of a *post-boost tier* or layer in an SDI system. The deployment by the offense of warheads and decoys cannot occur until later in the trajectory than the boost phase, at a higher altitude in order to avoid atmospheric drag. But the technology for post-boost intercept capabilities is likely to be difficult to achieve, because it will require electronic examination of images (pictures), using ordinary or infrared light, to distinguish among various components: the burned-out upper stage of the missile, the post-boost vehicle, and the various objects released from it. These requirements, the countermeasures, and the potential technological capabilities for a post-boost layer of defense are just beginning to be considered.

Which technologies would be useful in the next tier, in *mid-course intercept*, is still less understood. Presumably the defense would want to use the same kill methods (kinetic-energy and directed-energy weapons) for intercepts as in the other tiers. This has the advantage of allowing some of the absentee satellites[5] to come into play because of the longer time period involved in mid-course flight of a missile. Discrimination among possibly colossal numbers of objects would, however, be a daunting problem. There are ideas about how to address it, but no confidence in any of them; that is why there is a drive toward consideration of "active" discrimination, which would impart energy to the objects in the threat cloud in order to be able to distinguish among them by observing the effect on their behavior. Thus, mid-course intercept is unlikely to play any role in a deployed system until well after the turn of the century.

Through all of these considerations is entwined a serious problem for space-based ABMs: however effective space-based systems may be against ballistic missiles, they would appear to be more effective in suppressing defenses. And direct-ascent antisatellite systems or ground-based lasers may be still more effective than space-based systems in this latter role.

In sum, given the state of present and foreseeable technology, a boost-phase or post-boost phase intercept tier is not a realistic prospect in the face of likely offensive countermeasures and the vulnerability of those tiers to defense suppression. It will also exhibit unfavorable relative marginal costs as a contributor to defense of population at any reasonably high level of protection. These judgments apply to any system beginning deployment at least for the next 20 years, and probably considerably beyond then.

There are interesting new technologies, however, that leave open the possibility that our estimates of the offense-defense balance might change after that time, especially if some of these technologies prove to have some mid-course discrimination and intercept capability, as well as some boost-phase effectiveness. Such a shift is very unlikely, but strategic thinking should include the possibility that it might take place in terms of deployed systems some decades into the next century.

VII

What would a defense system look like if the priorities of the Reagan Administration's SDI program (boost-phase intercept and population defense) were to be combined with the technologies that will be available and a reasonable development program leading to deployment around the year 2000?

It would be likely to have space-based components. It would perhaps include, for example: a dozen satellites at one-half to two times geo-synchronous altitude to carry out boost surveillance and tracking; some tens of satellites at perhaps one thousand kilometers altitude to carry out surveillance, tracking and fire control for the attack of boosters, post-boost vehicles, and objects in the mid-course part of the trajectory, using infrared detection (short wavelength for boost, long wavelength for mid-course) and laser designation, and possibly some semiactive radar or laser radar tracking; some thousands of satellites, at altitudes of a few hundred kilometers, whose main purpose would be to carry kinetic-kill vehicles, of which there would be a total in the tens of thousands for use as actual defensive weapons.

In parallel, terminal defenses would also be deployed. These would include terminal radars and an airborne set of optical and infrared detectors. There would be some thousands each of exoatmospheric and endoatmospheric interceptors, deployed around missile (ICBM) silos, other military targets and major urban-industrial areas. Some of the endoatmospheric interceptors might even reach out into the later parts of mid-course flight. To moderate the costs of putting into orbit the space-borne component of the system, a new and advanced shuttle would be developed and put in use beginning about 1997.

A supplementary deployment or second phase could be expected to commence eight to ten years later, thus beginning somewhere between 2005 and 2010, and taking another five to seven years to complete deployment. During that phase there would be added satellites carrying chemical lasers for killing offensive targets, and lasers or neutral particle beams for discriminating in mid-course as well. Alternatively, ground-based lasers with mirrors in orbit would be deployed, perhaps as early or perhaps three to five years later still. This second phase carries us into the realm of hypothetical technologies and cloudy crystal balls; X-ray lasers and electromagnetic rail guns lie still deeper in those realms.

Whatever the system architectures, there must be consideration of the possibility—and the effect—of catastrophic failure of one layer of a multitiered defense on the subsequent layers. In both the quantity of hardware and the nature of the software (that is, the built-in operational procedures), the systems must therefore be designed to provide a way to avoid catastrophic failure of a later layer (and thus overall failure) because of a poorer-than-expected performance of earlier layers. The simple multiplication of attrition factors in a series of layers, the number of which is sometimes rather arbitrarily assumed, carries an inherent assumption of its own. The assumption is that the operation of each layer's sensors, tracking, kill mechanisms and effectiveness is completely independent of the nature, physical components and effectiveness of all the previous tiers. The architecture of the entire system has to be such as to assure that this would in fact be the case to the maximum possible extent; also, to the extent it is not, to assure that the system degrades "gracefully." This will not be an easy or inexpensive task.

VIII

What would constitute an appropriate research and development program?

Though existing technology and system concepts for terminal defense can provide an effective defense of hard ICBM silos deployed in a multiple protective shelter mode, more advanced technologies—optical trackers, more accurate interceptors and lower interceptor yields—would increase the system's cost-effectiveness. For improving the contribution of terminal defense to protection of urban-industrial areas and, possibly, of military targets other than missile silos, the technology associated with non-nuclear kill and with terminal discrimination should be pursued. These would include greater tracking accuracy, homing warheads and the airborne orbiting adjunct. Deployment of a prototype developmental version of a terminal defense complex at a test range (Kwajalein) would be extremely valuable, and consistent with the ABM treaty.

Early warning and attack assessment systems should be further developed, including those based on detection of the infrared signal from missiles in a boost phase. To this end, improvements in the present Satellite Early Warning System should be carried out. Infrared, optical and radar tracking of objects in space from distances of up to about a thousand miles will also be useful for any defensive system. The corresponding R&D should therefore be vigorously pursued.

Because kinetic-energy weapons and conventional chemical lasers will be defeated by, or suffer a severe cost-exchange disadvantage from, offensive countermeasures and defense suppression, the R&D program should concentrate on the more advanced kill mechanisms and active discrimination methods that are further off in time. Such an approach, however, is legitimately subject to the criticism that "the best is the enemy of the good." Moreover, the effectiveness of future technologies is easily overestimated simply because less is known about them.

If one judges that the good is not good enough, then it is appropriate to work on something better (and therefore usually further away in time). This conclusion depends, however, on a judgment that successful development of such an advanced technology has a good chance to improve the defense's position in the balance between defensive measures and countermeasures. This last criterion may turn out not to be met even by the more advanced technologies for active discrimination and kill. For example, it continues to appear that everything that works well as a defense also works somewhat better as a defense suppressor. But the balance between offense and defense seems even less likely to shift in favor of the defense as a result of the nearer-term technologies than as a result of the more advanced ones. Thus, it is appropriate to increase the R&D emphasis on such programs as:

- optical technology, including, *inter alia*, the following elements; adaptive optics, i.e., adjusting the wave-front shape to compensate for distortions in the laser source and in the atmosphere; locking the phase of separate lasers together so their amplitudes add, greatly increasing the brightness; using one laser to drive another; phased-array lasers (for improving intensity, steering capability and atmospheric compensation);
- combining lasers and particle beams as a way of focusing the beam better;

- excimer and (especially) free-electron lasers, and the kill mechanisms based on those technologies; application of advanced optical technologies to chemical lasers;
- ground basing of lasers, and pop-up mirrors (which should be less vulnerable) or mirrors that unfold and that can be more easily deployed to make them less vulnerable as targets;
- verification technology for computer programs, fault tolerance, expert systems and automatic programming—in order to improve confidence in software;
- active and perturbing discrimination and other mid-course signature work (since the mid-course part of the flight gives the defense a longer time to act, *if* discriminants can be found for use by the defense); and
- survivability of space-based defensive components, especially sensors.

Bomb-driven X-ray lasers could be very effective because they could achieve very high brightness and medium beam width. But they are at such an early stage that the program, while deserving support, should be confined to demonstration of those two features. Rail guns may be useful but only if they meet very ambitious goals for speed, mass and multi-shot capability. Even then, conventional rockets accelerated to equally high speeds (and with correspondingly heavy propellant weight) may be competitive with rail guns; but neither is likely to be cost-effective.

Demonstrating the technology to achieve the above goals for X-ray lasers and rail guns should precede any consideration of a systems effort for them.

IX

In the light of the considerations set forth, what should be the emphasis of the SDI program? What should be the balance among systems design, component development, experimental demonstrations, and technology? What should be deemphasized or eliminated? These questions become more acute in the light of the substantial reductions in the funding of the research and development program from the proposals formulated in the Fletcher Committee Report of 1983.[6] Though congressionally approved funding is likely to exceed $3 billion per year, the scope of the program is so ambitious that schedules set only a year ago for systems decisions appear to be slipping, and some difficult choices about priorities will have to be made.

It would seem appropriate to emphasize technology that still needs to be proven and developed, rather than "spectacular" demonstrations—though at some point demonstrations would be needed to test the technology. Some technologies are sufficiently demonstrated, and the corresponding systems concepts sufficiently clear, so that engineering development could begin on them relatively soon. But doing so would make sense only after a decision as to the detailed nature and function of the defensive system.

1. Work is indicated to define the design of a ground-based terminal defense system, which could stand by itself or be a layer of a multilayer strategic defense system. This would involve updating the Spartan and Sprint missiles, and beginning work on the design of a non-nuclear interceptor. This system should have the capability of being deployed as a defense of the U.S. ICBM force, as well as of serving as a component of a population defense if that should ever prove feasible.

Initiation of full-scale engineering development for such terminal defenses should be deferred for several years. This would allow two prior determinations. One is the technical and military feasibility (and political acceptability) of less vulnerable modes of ICBM deployment. The second is whether mutual reductions in the size of strategic offensive forces can be negotiated, to reduce the need for active defense of ICBMs. An appropriate schedule would be to get the technology ready for a possible 1989 initiation of full-scale engineering development, and a start of deployment in the 1994 time frame if such a decision is taken.

2. Space-based kinetic-energy weapons appear unpromising in the light of the almost certain offensive countermeasures, and therefore should be deemphasized, even though such a system is the only space-based one that could be reasonably well specified today. By the same logic, it would make sense to delay a decision on detailed specification of and initiation of full-scale engineering development on any boost-phase intercept system until 1994 or 1995. By that time enough ought to be known about the technology of the various directed-energy weapons to allow a more informed choice among them.

3. A full-scale technology program (phasing into development as particular technologies reach that stage) on boost-phase surveillance, mid-course surveillance and tracking is fully warranted. Boost-phase surveillance capabilities will augment early warning of attack; mid-course surveillance and tracking will augment attack assessment capabilities. These functions are justified even in the absence of a decision to proceed with active defense of population. Like the terminal defense development activities, they are consistent with restrictive interpretations of the ABM treaty. But they would also constitute the eyes of a strategic

defense of population or of military forces against ballistic missile attack, should such a defense be decided upon.

4. A full program on adaptive optics, phase compensation and phase conjugation devices, phased-array lasers and related optical technology should be emphasized strongly, since obtaining the brightness and beam accuracies required for effectiveness even in the absence of offensive countermeasures depends strongly on these technologies.

5. The electromagnetic rail gun, bomb-driven X-ray laser, and (probably) neutral particle beam programs all belong in the preliminary technology stage. If they work they would be useful in specific functional areas of a strategic defense system, but they are in too early a stage to justify putting them in the component development category.

6. The directed-energy weapons segment of the program should be tilted toward the excimer and (especially) free-electron lasers, with emphasis on ground basing the energy sources and consideration of space-based mirrors as the pointing mechanism. Work on space-based chemical lasers should emphasize ways of making them brighter—such as phased arrays—within the limitations imposed by space basing; it is probably too early to abandon chemical lasers completely.

This orientation of the program would, as a separate matter, delay conflict with the ABM treaty while permitting rapid development and even preliminary testing of technology. It corresponds to an acceptance of the judgment that the program dates are ambitious even for the more developed (and less promising) technologies, and concentrates on the less developed but more promising ones.

That approach would defer until after 1995 the decision on full-scale engineering development for the directed-energy boost-phase intercept segment of the program that could involve space-based components generating or transmitting very high energy densities. Such a schedule, however, might prompt concerns that it was so far in the future as to undermine congressional and public support for the program. But that factor works both ways. Though there is real public support for strategic defense, both the expert and congressional communities are doubtful about the vision of protecting populations from a nuclear attack by means other than deterrence through the threat of retaliation. They are also concerned about the potential negative effects of SDI on arms control. Moreover, even those defense tasks and system components that look most promising are subject to serious policy objections regarding their deployment or testing. Thus a sign of willingness to pursue a more modest track, with long-term goals, and more care about arms control, would probably favorably influence a decisive segment of congressional votes on program funding.

To sum up, the near-term prospects for ballistic missile defense capabilities are reasonably well known. Technically, they appear cost-effective for defense of some kinds of strategic retaliatory forces. For defense of populations against a responsive threat, they look poor through the year 2010 and beyond. The prognosis for the longer term for this latter objective in the contest between defense and offense is less certain. It still looks questionable, at best, for the defense, because of some fundamental problems of geometry and geography, and the physics of offensive countermeasures and defense suppression in their contest with defense.

NOTES

1. The boost phase is the period during which the ballistic missile rockets operate to bring it to (or near) its peak velocity. In the post-boost phase the warheads (and decoys) are released from the last stage of the missile. It is followed by the mid-course phase outside of the atmosphere, the lengthiest part of the trajectory. The terminal phase is the period from shortly before reentry into the atmosphere until detonation.

2. Development or testing of AOA beyond the technology platform stage, as a component of an ABM system, even of a fixed ground-based ABM system, would appear to violate the ABM treaty because the AOA is itself a mobile component.

3. For example, the chemical combination of hydrogen and fluorine. If the population of the resulting excited molecules outnumbers that of the lowest-energy ("ground") state, stimulation of emission of light of the frequency corresponding to the energy difference occurs, resulting in an intense coherent beam.

4. Excimer lasers use "excited" (higher-energy) states of molecules including a rare gas (e.g., argon) and a halogen (e.g., iodine). These excited states are quasi-stable, while the unexcited ("ground") states are not populated, because the rare gases are not chemically active in their lowest-energy states. Free-electron lasers use the effect of oscillating electromagnetic fields on electron beams to cause the electrons to emit phase-coherent (laser) radiation.

5. Satellites in nonsynchronous orbit trace out a path over the earth whose pattern and timing depends on their altitude and velocity. Absentee satellites are those whose position in their orbits, at the time when the attacking missiles are launched, puts them over parts of the earth that are distant from the offensive launch sites.

6. The work of this committee, headed by Dr. James C. Fletcher, was published in the unclassified report, "Strategic Defense Initiative: Defensive Technology Study," U.S. Department of Defense, March 1984.

6

THE MACROECONOMICS OF STRATEGIC DEFENSES

Barry M. Blechman and Victor A. Utgoff

A decision by the United States to develop and deploy a system to defend its territory against ballistic missiles would represent not only a major departure in U.S. defense strategy, but also a significant commitment of the nation's resources. Yet, in the extensive and sometimes heated debate that has followed the President's speech of March 1983, when he announced his intention to explore the possibility that new technologies might make effective missile defenses feasible, relatively little attention has been paid to either the cost of a strategic defense system or to the economic implications of such a decision.

This study is intended to initiate a process of continually improving assessments of the potential costs of strategic defenses. The estimates it provides admittedly are rough, and they are based on technical approaches to defending against missiles and aircraft that may well differ in many ways from those ultimately adopted. This means, of course, that the actual costs of the strategic defense system selected and constructed by the nation may differ significantly from the estimates made in this paper. Our estimates represent reasonable, first, detailed assessments of a set of plausible alternatives. As the investigation of alternative designs for strategic defenses proceeds, more refined estimates of costs can and should be made.

Reprinted from *International Security*, vol. 11, no. 3 (Winter 1986–87), 33–70, Barry M. Blechman and Victor A. Utgoff, "The Macroeconomics of Strategic Defenses," by permission of The MIT Press, Cambridge, Massachusetts. © 1986 by the President and Fellows of Harvard College and of the Massachusetts Institute of Technology. This article is based on the study *Fiscal and Economic Implications of Strategic Defenses* (Boulder, Colo.: Westview Press with The Johns Hopkins Foreign Policy Institute, SAIS, 1986).

In estimating strategic defense costs, it is necessary to describe a set of notional systems in relatively specific terms, determining the rough characteristics and size of the elements—sensors, weapons, and command subsystems—that would constitute each alternative. Such an analysis necessarily requires that many assumptions be made regarding the kinds of technologies to be employed in solving problems, how well the chosen approaches might work, the counteractions that the Soviet Union might take in designing and deploying the offensive forces that would face U.S. defenses, and so forth. In general, we regard the assumptions we have made to be optimistic for the United States, and this judgment is concurred in by nearly all of the many individuals who have reviewed the study. To the extent that this judgment is correct, the cost estimates should be considered optimistic as well. On the other hand, there is always the possibility of a genuine technical breakthrough that could lead to significantly less costly strategic defense systems than those described here.

The article is divided into two parts. In the first, we summarize the costs of four notional strategic defense systems intended to achieve alternative national objectives. In the second, we set these estimates in perspective, describing the potential trade-offs between expenditures of this magnitude and alternative uses, private and public, of the nation's resources.

COSTS OF NOTIONAL STRATEGIC DEFENSE SYSTEMS

We have constructed four notional strategic defense systems in this study, and estimated the costs of developing, building, and operating each one for ten years. The four systems illustrate means of achieving alternative defense objectives.

Notional Strategic Defense System "Alpha": Defense of Nuclear Retaliatory Forces

The first system would have a limited objective: to make U.S. strategic nuclear retaliatory forces militarily unattractive to attack. In operational terms, the goal would be to raise the cost of attacking the bases at which U.S. strategic nuclear forces are located to the point at which more nuclear weapons would be required to destroy each base than could be expected to be found at the base at the time the attack were executed. If this objective could be accomplished, potential adversaries would have less incentive to initiate an attack, as they would face the prospect of using up more of their own nuclear weapons in carrying out the attack than they could reasonably expect to destroy.

For the purposes of this analysis, every known location of U.S. strategic forces is considered to constitute a "base," including each individual missile silo. To assess the level of defense required at each type of base, we must first estimate the number of strategic weapons likely to be located at each of the bases at the time an attack could arrive.

These data are contained in Table 1. For each type of facility, the number of weapons expected to be present at the time of an attack is the product of the total number of missile launchers or bombers located at the base and the number of weapons deployed on each launcher or bomber, multiplied by the percentage of those types of launchers or bombers that would be maintained at too low an alert rate to escape from the base in the period between receipt of warning of an attack and its arrival (or that would be expected to ride out the attack).

The Alpha system would only employ components that the U.S. could build today or in the near future to defend the bases of its strategic forces against attacks by either ballistic missiles or air-breathing vehicles. If a decision were taken in 1987 to build the Alpha system, it could be fully deployed by about 2005.

For ballistic missile defense, the Alpha notional strategic defense system would employ combinations of ground-based missile interceptors and radars with airborne surveillance, target acquisition, and battle management systems. The missiles would include longer-range (high endo-atmospheric or HEDI) interceptors, organized into an upper layer of defense that would seek to destroy incoming reentry vehicles (RVs) carrying nuclear warheads above an altitude of 100,000 feet, plus faster, shorter-range (low endo-atmospheric or LEDI) interceptors that would constitute a lower layer of defense to destroy those few RVs that managed to penetrate the upper defense layer. Intercepts in the lower defense layer would be controlled by individual ground-based radars at each location being defended. The actions of the high endo-atmospheric interceptors would be controlled by airborne laser radar systems, assisted by the ground-based radars. The airborne laser radar systems would similarly assist intercept attempts by the LEDI interceptors.

We have assumed that a missile defense system incorporating only one or two layers of defense would not be built unless the interceptors it utilized had relatively high individual probabilities of kill against attacking reentry vehicles. Thus, in designing the Alpha system, we assumed that each interceptor would have a 90 percent chance of destroying its designated target. Such performance is conceivable, although optimistic; few things as complex as guided missiles perform so well.

TABLE 1
Average Number of Weapons Located at U.S. Strategic Bases
at the Time an Enemy Attack Could Arrive
(by type of strategic force)

Type of Strategic Force	Total Number of Launchers in Force[a]	Average Weapons per Launcher	Number of Bases[c]	Average Number of Weapons Left at Base
Trident Strategic Submarine	480	8	2	576
B-1 and ATB Bombers	240	12[b]	30	58
MX	50	10	50	10
Minuteman III	550	3	550	3
Midgetman	500	1	3	17

NOTES: Forty percent of the bomber force are presumed to be sufficiently alert to escape from their bases before an attack arrives; 70 percent of the Trident submarines are presumed to be at sea and the remainder are presumed vulnerable to attack; 90 percent of the Midgetman force are presumed to have dispersed and thus to be effectively untargetable. All of the land-based missile force is assumed to ride out any attack.

[a]Numbers of strategic launchers are the writers' projections of the force structure in the year 2005, when the Alpha system would be fully operational. It seems likely that the Poseidon submarine force would be retired by then, for example, as would the Minuteman II force, the latter in favor of Midgetman.

[b]The average number of weapons per bomber is based on an assumption that the B-1 typically carries 12 weapons, its internal capacity, even though additional weapons could be stored externally. Although the ATB is reported to have a smaller payload, its effective operational load could not be too much smaller if the new bomber is to be practical.

[c]A strategic forces "base" is defined as any location of such forces that would provide an individual aim point for an attack. Thus, although all 50 MX might be located at a single air force "base," in the normal usage of the word, they constitute 50 bases in our usage because each silo must be targeted individually.

TABLE 2
Firing Doctrines Employed by the Alpha Defense

Number of Warheads at Defended Base	Doctrine for Defense of the Base
1–3	One HEDI per defended warhead
4–35	One HEDI per defended warhead, plus one LEDI for each leaker expected through the upper defense
36–178	One HEDI per defended warhead, plus one 2-missile LEDI salvo for each of one-half of the leakers expected through the upper defense, plus one LEDI for each of the remaining leakers
179–576	One HEDI per defended warhead, plus one 3-missile LEDI salvo for each of one-third the number of leakers expected through the upper defense, plus one 2-missile LEDI salvo for a second third of the expected leakers, plus one LEDI for the remaining third of the leakers

The creation of an effective terminal defense can be made more difficult by surrounding each reentry vehicle with lightweight decoys in order to force the defense to waste interceptors. The most straightforward means to identify lightweight decoys is to wait until they begin to reenter the atmosphere, at which point the false targets will begin to be stripped away from the heavier reentry vehicles. Heavy decoys could be used to mask reentry vehicles effectively further into the atmosphere, but their greater weight means that they would use up larger amounts of the throwweight of the offensive missiles that otherwise could be used for real weapons. We assume that the defense uses this "atmospheric filtering" to achieve perfect discrimination between lightweight decoys and real reentry vehicles, and that the Soviet Union chooses not to pay the throwweight penalty required to deploy heavy decoys.

The sizing of a missile defense strong enough to extract a specified "attack price" also will depend upon the doctrine chosen for allocating defending interceptors to attacking warheads, and upon the attacker's anticipated strategy as well. In constructing the Alpha defense, we have utilized the firing doctrines listed in Table 2.

The defenses of each type of strategic base must provide sufficient interceptors to allow destruction of a number of attackers equal to the

TABLE 3
Ballistic Missile Defense Configurations Required to Make Attacks on U.S. Strategic Forces Bases Unprofitable or Minimally Profitable

Type of Strategic Force	Number of HEDI per Base[a]	Number of LEDI per Base[b]	Number of Radars per Base
Trident Strategic Submarines	576	115	1
B–1 and ATB Bombers	60	10	1
MX	10	2	0.1[c]
Minuteman III	3	0	0
Midgetman	17	3	1

[a]In several cases the numbers of HEDI have been rounded upward by 1 or 2 per base.
[b]The numbers of LEDI have been rounded up by slightly more than 1 or 2 to allow for statistical variations in the expected leakage through the upper layer.
[c]MX missiles are assumed to be located in silos that are close enough together to allow the lower layer of defense for 10 silos to be managed by a single ground-based radar.

number of U.S. warheads remaining at the base, assuming employment of the stated firing doctrine. The resultant numbers of high endo-atmospheric interceptors, low endo-atmospheric interceptors, and ground-based radars required to defend each type of base are provided in Table 3.

To estimate the number of aircraft carrying laser radars and battle management systems that would be required in the Alpha system to control intercepts by the upper layer, we have assumed that the aircraft would operate at an altitude of 35,000 feet and that all intercept attempts by the upper layer would be completed well above this altitude. The aircraft would be required to cover the entire area of the United States plus a 200 nautical mile (n.mi.) wide band of the territory of Canada adjacent to the U.S.; the potential targets of a Soviet attack would be distributed over this entire area.

The laser radar/battle management aircraft are designed to be capable of escaping from their bases upon first warning of an attack sufficiently quickly that they need not be maintained on airborne alert. Taking training and maintenance requirements into account, 40 percent of the laser radar/battle management aircraft are kept on strip alert, ready to depart their bases at first warning of a possible attack. During the course of the battle, backup aircraft would be kept airborne in each sector of the upper defense layer to guard against the collapse of missile defenses in any one sector.

The Alpha missile defense system would be complemented by an airborne system to defend against bombers and cruise missiles. High-flying aircraft carrying long-range surveillance systems would continuously patrol a barrier well to the north, and off the coasts, of the U.S. These aircraft would provide the advance warning needed to organize an outer barrier of surveillance aircraft equipped with relatively long-range air-to-air missiles. Bombers that were able to penetrate this outer barrier would be met subsequently by shorter-range interceptor aircraft directed by AWACs-type aircraft.

In sizing the air defense system, we assume that the Soviet Union deploys a force of 200 "Bear F" and "Blackjack" strategic bombers carrying an average of 10 cruise missiles each. This would represent roughly the same number of long-range bombers that the USSR has maintained in its force posture for many years, but their equipage with modern cruise missiles would constitute a major improvement in Soviet bomber capabilities. Two-thirds of the bombers are assumed to take part in the initial attack. Soviet bombers and cruise missiles are assumed to travel at high subsonic speeds and to have sufficient range to make impractical any attempt to intercept the aircraft carrying them before the missiles had been launched. We further assume that a surge effort might allow the Soviet Union to deploy 350 cruise missiles on submarines off the U.S. coasts.

The early warning aircraft used by the United States for air defense in the Alpha system would be maintained continuously in the air, sufficiently close to Soviet territory to allow two hours warning of an attack. A modified version of the TR-1 reconnaissance aircraft equipped with a long-range, conformal array radar would be suitable for the task. They would maintain a continuous barrier approximately 1,000 n.mi. to the north of the U.S. border with Canada and stretching well offshore down the U.S. coasts, a total length of roughly 7,500 n.mi.

The aircraft to be employed for the armed surveillance role would be similar to existing KC-10 cargo and tanker aircraft, but would be equipped with a powerful air surveillance radar and the equipment needed to allow a team of eight controllers to run simultaneously four intercepts each. Each aircraft would be equipped with 100 interceptor missiles with characteristics roughly comparable to existing Phoenix

(54C) missiles, but with 50 percent greater range. The attacking aircraft are assumed to attempt to penetrate the air defense barrier at low altitudes, which would create a cluttered background for the surveillance radar and constrain the range at which the attacking aircraft could be tracked and intercepted to a maximum distance of 150 n.mi. Given the cluttered radar background, the interceptor missiles would be unlikely to have single shot probabilities of kill in excess of 70 percent. Armed surveillance aircraft would be kept on strip alert, except when sufficient numbers of Soviet submarines moved close enough to U.S. coasts as to jeopardize their timely escape from bases under attack.

The effectiveness of the battle management, armed surveillance, and early warning aircraft could be improved by giving them an aerial refueling capability and providing them with tanker aircraft. All the aircraft required both for the ballistic missile and the air defense components of the Alpha defense would have to be dispersed across a set of air bases that were sufficiently well protected against ballistic missile attacks as to make the price of destroying the defense system through attacks on these bases every bit as expensive as a direct attack on U.S. strategic forces. Moreover, concrete shelters would have to be built to protect U.S. strategic bombers, as well as all types of aircraft used in the air defense system, from the effects of nuclear explosions. Otherwise, Soviet missiles could be fused so that those which penetrated the upper defense layer could detonate and destroy their targets, before they might have been successfully intercepted by the lower layer of missile defense.

Table 4 summarizes the numbers of the various elements of the ballistic missile and air defense components that would be required to make it unprofitable for an enemy to attack the bases of U.S. strategic forces. (The derivations of the size of each element are too lengthy to describe in this article, but are detailed in the full study previously referenced.) Readers should note that ballistic missile defenses are provided for each of the bases used for the aircraft that constitute the air defense component, a factor that greatly increases the size of necessary ballistic missile defense elements but that, if not provided, would offer strategies to an attacker that could nullify the basic purpose of the defense system.

The development, procurement, construction, and ten-year operating costs of each element of the Alpha system are provided in Table 5. Generally speaking, individual element costs were based on the costs of existing weapon systems of comparable designs, sometimes modified as a result of informal discussions with manufacturers. All costs in this table and the remainder of the article are given in constant 1987 prices. A key assumption in all our cost calculations is that, for those elements

TABLE 4
Alpha System Components

COMPONENTS DEPLOYED AT STRATEGIC FORCES BASES

Type of Strategic Force	Number of Bases	Total Number of HEDI	Total Number of LEDI	Total Number of Radars
Trident Strategic Submarines	2	1,152	230	2
Bombers	30	1,800	300	30
MX	50	500	100	5
Minuteman III	550	1,650	0	0
Midgetman	3	51	9	3
Air Bases for Defensive Aircraft	42	5,124	840	42
Total	677	10,277	1,479	82

UNDIFFERENTIATED COMPONENTS

Element	Number
Laser Radar/Battle Management Aircraft	40
Early Warning Air Defense Aircraft	75
Armed Surveillance Aircraft	125
Aerial Refueling Tankers	35
Air-to-Air Missiles	8,750
Air Base (additional)	32
Aircraft Shelters	435

NOTES: Excepting 10 of the 42 air bases for defensive aircraft, these figures include only those components of the strategic defense system Alpha that are not already included in the U.S. defense program. Components of the system that already exist or are planned include early warning satellites, over-the-horizon radars, 300 interceptor aircraft, 10 airborne warning and control systems, 10 bases for air defense aircraft, and existing bases for strategic submarines, land-based missiles, and strategic bombers.

TABLE 5
Costs of Strategic Defense System Alpha
(billions of 1987 dollars)

Component	R&D	Procurement	Construction	Ten-Year Operations	Total Cost
HEDI	2.0	21.0	3.1	12.0	38.1
LEDI	3.0	5.9	0.5	3.2	12.6
Ground Radars	0.5	1.6	—	2.9	5.0
Battle Management Aircraft	4.0	10.0	—	6.0	20.0
Armed Surveillance Aircraft	3.0	18.8	—	11.0	32.8
Air-to-Air Missiles	1.0	10.0	—	5.0	16.0
Early Warning Aircraft	0.5	3.8	—	1.9	6.2
Tankers	—	4.7	—	2.5	7.2
Air Bases	—	—	1.6	13.0	14.6
Aircraft Shelters	—	—	0.9	—	0.9
Other Costs	—	2.0	—	2.0	4.0
Total	14.0	77.8	6.1	59.5	157.4
Rounded Total	**10**	**80**	**10**	**60**	**160**

NOTES: The degree of precision expressed by these figures is not meant to suggest a comparable degree of certainty about the estimates. It is necessary in cumulating the costs of the system to keep track of the individual elements at this level. The final "rounded" line is the more appropriate way to think of these estimates.

that would be procured in large numbers (HEDI and LEDI interceptors, air-to-air missiles, etc.), the marginal cost of a single unit would be reduced by 10 percent for each doubling of the total number of units to be produced. Thus, for example, our sources suggest that the first HEDI missile might cost $6 million; the second HEDI is then assumed to cost $5.4 million, the fourth $4.9 million, etc. Such a "learning curve" would not be unreasonable, although it would be better than actual experience with most defense systems. It likely would require freezing the design of the element in question throughout the stated production run. Even relatively small variations in this assumption, in either direction, result in large changes in the overall costs of our four notional systems.

All told, the component of the Alpha system intended to defend against bombers and cruise missiles, along with those portions of the ballistic missile defense component used to guard the bases used by air defense aircraft, constitute nearly two-thirds of the total cost of the complete system. A decision to defend U.S. strategic forces only from ballistic missiles would reduce the ten-year cost of the Alpha system to perhaps $40 to $50 billion, depending upon the assumptions made about "learning curves" and other economies of scale. If the United States chose to defend its land-based ballistic missiles alone from attacks by only ballistic missiles, the total ten-year cost would be roughly $30 billion.

Notional Strategic Defense System "Beta":
Defense of Nuclear Retaliatory Forces Plus a Partial
Population Defense Against Small Attacks

The second strategic defense system would build upon the first, adding the elements necessary to defend the most densely populated urban areas of the United States and Canada against relatively small ballistic missile attacks. Like the Alpha system, the Beta system would utilize only weapons, sensors, and command and control systems that could be built today or in the near future. It could be fully deployed around 2005.

The Beta system would provide protection against accidental launches of small numbers of nuclear-armed missiles. It also could reduce significantly the total damage that could be inflicted on the U.S. and Canada by countries with small nuclear forces. And the Beta system also could make limited "demonstration" attacks by the Soviet Union or another major nuclear power somewhat more difficult. The light area defense component of the Beta system would not provide protection against any major attack; even a relatively small nuclear power could overcome the system by concentrating its missiles against a small number of the most important urban targets or by attacking larger numbers of undefended targets. The Beta system, however, could be used as the "last ditch" terminal layer of a more extensive ballistic missile defense system that included components that would destroy attacking missiles in space, such as the Gamma and Delta systems described below.

We have assumed that the operational goal of the light area defense would be to prevent damage from nominal one megaton yield attackers, greater than light damage to residential housing. This implies that the attackers must be prevented from getting closer than approximately 65,000 feet. With the high endo-atmospheric interceptors meeting their targets at an altitude of roughly 100,000 feet, "leakers" would have to come down only 35,000 feet further before they could defeat the defender's goal. This equates to between three and five seconds of travel time for the attacker, which is far too short a period to permit a second intercept attempt. Thus, only HEDI interceptors would be employed.

Determination of the number of interceptors necessary for a light area defense is fairly arbitrary. Should interceptors be so spread across the U.S. as to allow at least one interceptor to reach the first reentry vehicle aimed at any point in the country? Such a strategy would value the protection of all areas equally, regardless of the number of people that might be located in any particular region.

It would seem more reasonable to allow a distribution of interceptors across areas that would be proportional to the values located in that area. At the same time, there are certain threshold costs associated with setting up defenses in any particular area. Thus, for example, interceptors probably should not be located in any area whose value was so low as to merit only one or two of them.

In view of these considerations, we arbitrarily assume that HEDI interceptors intended for area defense are deployed in bases of 10 missiles each, and that one base is assigned for every 500,000 people located in the 40 largest metropolitan areas in the United States. These metropolitan areas contain approximately 110 million people. The Canadian portion of the Beta system was sized in a slightly different fashion: one base of 10 interceptors was provided for every 500,000 people within those Canadian metropolitan areas with total populations over 500,000.

Given these assumptions, 220 missile bases containing 2,200 high endo-atmospheric interceptors would be required for the light area defense component of the Beta system. This requirement is about one-fifth the number of HEDI missiles needed for the Alpha system—sufficiently small that the number of laser radar/battle management aircraft used to control outer layer intercepts would probably not have to be increased. The 40 such aircraft already purchased for that system also could manage

TABLE 6
Costs of Strategic Defense System Beta
(billions of 1987 dollars)

Element	R&D	Procurement	Construction	Ten-Year Operations	Total Cost
HEDI	—	3.0	2.0	2.5	7.5
Battle Management Modifications	0.5	—	—	—	0.5
Subtotal	0.5	3.0	2.0	2.5	8.0
Alpha System	14.0	77.8	6.1	59.5	157.4
Total	14.5	80.8	8.1	62.0	165.4
Rounded Total	**10**	**80**	**10**	**60**	**170**

the light area defense task with only modest modifications of the battle management system.

The incremental ten-year costs of the light area defense component of the Beta defense system, which are summarized in Table 6, would thus come to approximately $8 billion. This is clearly a modest expense, but the cost is so low only because the Beta system makes use of many elements that already had been acquired for the Alpha system; a "stand-alone" light area defense system would be far more expensive.

Notional Strategic Defense System "Gamma":
A Comprehensive Defense
Using Space-Based Missile Interceptors

Consisting of only a single layer of less-than-perfect defenses, any light area defense system would inevitably be "leaky," and relatively easily overwhelmed by attacking forces of even modest size. More effective area defenses require the deployment of additional layers, each of which can compound the others' individual capabilities.

We have assumed that it will prove impractical to intercept reentry vehicles with space-based defensive systems during the period from when they are deployed by the post-boost vehicle to when they begin to reenter the atmosphere—the "mid-course phase" of their trajectory.

If this assumption proves valid, the most attractive means of adding layers to a strategic defense would be to place defensive weapons systems in space where they could attack enemy ballistic missiles in the earliest phases of their trajectories—the boost and post-boost phases. In the Gamma system, we accomplish this by making use of technologies which, for the most part, are close at hand—in particular, space-based interceptor missiles. This system could probably be fully deployed around the year 2012. In the Delta system, we make use of more advanced technologies—space-based directed energy weapons; the Delta system could probably not be fully deployed until around 2020.

The required size of both the Gamma and Delta systems would vary depending on whether the purpose were to defend only against Soviet ICBMs and SLBMs, or also to defend against Soviet intermediate-range land-based ballistic missiles. In making these calculations, we have assumed a Soviet intercontinental ballistic missile force consisting of 1,400 land-based missiles equipped with an average of eight warheads each, a submarine-launched ballistic missile force of 1,000 missiles equipped with an average of four warheads each, and a force of intermediate-range, land-based ballistic missiles of 600 missiles with an average of three warheads each. This force is similar in size and structure to the existing Soviet missile force. We have, however, assumed three important changes in the characteristics of Soviet missiles deployed in the early part of the next century; each of these changes would be well within Soviet capabilities. First, the amount of time that Soviet missiles spend in the boost phase is assumed to have been reduced to near 90 seconds, as compared to the 150 to 300 seconds estimated for current and emerging Soviet missiles. Such a reduction would be relatively easy to accomplish with available technologies. Second, the Soviet Union is also assumed to shorten the post-boost phase of flight for its missiles equipped with multiple RVs, the phase during which a missile maneuvers to set all of its reentry vehicles on their separate trajectories, and dispenses associated decoys, from several minutes to 60 seconds. Third, we also assume that the Soviets would compress the area in which their land-based missiles are deployed by two-thirds. Such a concentration of the Soviet ICBM and IRBM force would greatly increase the required density of U.S. defensive weapons deployed in space and thus the potential cost of any defense system incorporating a space-based, boost-phase layer.

The space-based component of the Gamma system would consist of four elements, as summarized in Table 7.

Interceptor rockets would be fired in two waves at attacking missiles. Upon detection of an attack, the battle management system would assign interceptors to individual targets and direct them to an intercept point

TABLE 7
Incremental Elements of Strategic Defense System Gamma

Element	Number Required to Defend Against:	
	ICBMs and SLBMs	Long- and Intermediate-Range Missiles
Interceptors*	66,900	95,600
Battle Satellites*	1,335	1,915
Decoy Battle Satellites*	6,675	9,575
Battle Management Satellites	16	16
Upgraded Shuttle Flights (deployment)	580	825
Upgraded Shuttle Flights (maintenance) per Year	50	70

*A 10 percent margin is included for space systems awaiting maintenance.

in space from which they would home on the target and destroy it by direct contact. Interceptors are assumed to be capable of achieving a single shot probability of kill against any Soviet missile within range of 0.9. Additional interceptors, 10 percent as many as constituted the first wave, would be timed to arrive in the vicinity of the offensive missiles about ten seconds later. The interceptors in the second wave would be redirected by the battle management system to those attacking Soviet missiles that had been observed to survive the first wave of attacks. Assuming that the battle management system were capable of making a nearly perfect overall assignment of interceptors to target missiles, a space-based component of the type described would have a theoretical leakage rate of one percent—assuming of course that there were enough interceptors to cover all the missiles that the Soviet Union could launch.

We assume that an interceptor missile carrying a five kilogram (kg.) homing warhead and having an initial weight of 150 kg. can be built to achieve a burn-out velocity of 10 km./sec.; many experts would consider it optimistic to assume that as complex a warhead as the one needed here could be built at so light a weight. (The calculation of the requisite number of interceptor missiles is detailed in the full study, as previously referenced.)

The interceptor missiles would not be placed in space singly, of course, but clustered on *battle satellites* in low earth orbits, which would maintain them in ready-to-fire condition, report on their condition, receive initial firing instructions from the battle management satellites, and launch interceptors when necessary. The economies of scale of these support operations suggest that these battle satellites should collect together as many missiles as possible. The larger the number of interceptors based in a single satellite, however, the greater the loss if a battle satellite should fail or if it were attacked successfully by the Soviet Union. Moreover, if too many interceptors are clustered together on single satellites, large areas might be beyond the maximum range of any interceptor at particular points in time. To guard against these possibilities, we have assumed that no more than 50 interceptors would be based on each battle satellite.

The Gamma system also would include *decoy battle satellites*, which would not contain interceptors or participate in the battle, but which would reproduce the radar and all other signatures of the real battle satellites. Five decoys are assumed to be deployed for each real battle satellite and are assumed to be effectively indistinguishable from them. They thus would complicate proportionately any Soviet effort to destroy the defense. The battle satellites would be hardened to withstand attacks by current ground-based lasers. This hardening, the use of decoys, and other measures are presumed to be adequate to protect the satellites from being attacked effectively.

The *battle management satellites* would carry sensors and computers capable of detecting and tracking Soviet missiles, and projecting their trajectories with sufficient accuracy to allow the interceptors to be guided efficiently toward their targets. The sensors would include a radar with effective anti-jamming features, allowing instantaneous detection of missile launches and thus minimizing the defense reaction time. These satellites, maintained in 5,000 km. altitude orbits, would be netted together through high capacity, anti-jam communications systems, so that operations requiring the involvement of more than one battle management platform could be coordinated effectively.

The battle management satellites also would be hardened to protect them against attacks by ground-based lasers. Given their higher orbits, decoy battle management satellites, however, would not be deployed.

The final integral component of the Gamma defense system would be the *space launch capabilities* necessary to place the system in orbit and maintain it there. The total weight that would have to be placed in orbit initially to create a system to defend against the Soviet ICBM and SLBM force would be about 15.3 million kg. A system to defend against the entire Soviet long- and intermediate-range missile force would have an initial launch weight of about 21.9 million kg. We further assume that 10 percent of the initial launch weight would have to be orbited each year to allow repairs and a "rolling renewal" of the system.

The initial lift requirement for this system would not be great enough to justify the high development and associated infrastructure costs of the large unmanned booster one might otherwise choose for this task, so long as only the marginal costs of necessary shuttle flights would be incurred. Because a manned orbiter would be required for the sustaining lift tasks and could be used for the initial deployment, it would pay to upgrade the current shuttle, and we assume that one capable of orbiting twice as much payload as the current shuttle would be available at no incremental R&D cost to the Gamma system. An initial complement of 18 or 26 upgraded shuttles would be required, with the fleet tapering down to the 6 or 9 shuttles required to maintain the smaller and larger versions of the defense system, respectively.

The costs of the Gamma system are summarized in Table 8. The ten-year acquisition and operating cost for the space-based component would be about $460 billion if the system were intended to defend against ICBMs and SLBMs, and $600 billion for a system to defend against both long- and intermediate-range ballistic missiles. Roughly 60 percent of this cost would be attributable to the interceptor rockets. Adding in the costs of the Beta system, which would be reconfigured to provide less protection for strategic forces and a more uniform and heavier area defense capability to protect the population of North America from those Soviet warheads that leaked through the space-based component, we obtain the total costs described in the table.

Notional Strategic Defense System "Delta":
A Comprehensive Defense Using Space-Based Laser Weapons

The advantage of directed energy weapons is that the range at which they can be effective is not limited in the same way that it is for missile interceptors, as travel time for the energy needed to destroy the target is nearly instantaneous. Assuming that other relevant characteristics of the laser system were sufficiently capable, this means that a smaller number of battle satellites would be required and the overall cost of the system could be less than that of comparable systems depending on kinetic energy weapons.

Numerous estimates have been made in the open literature for the values that conceivably might be achieved for a laser defense system

TABLE 8
Costs of Strategic Defense System Gamma
(billions of 1987 dollars)

(Defense against ICBMs and SLBMs only/Long-
and intermediate-range ballistic missiles)

Element	R&D	Procurement	Construction	Ten-Year Operations	Total Cost
Interceptors	3	180/246	—	90/123	273/372
Battle Satellites	2	42/50	—	21/25	65/77
Decoys	1	11/13	—	5/6	17/20
Battle Management Satellites	2	20	—	10	32
Upgraded Shuttle Flights (deployment)	—	33/47	—	—	33/47
Upgraded Shuttle Flights (maintenance)	—	—	—	28/40	28/40
Other	—	5	—	5	10
Subtotal	8	291/381	—	159/209	458/598
Beta (reconfigured)	15	81	11	62	169
Total	23	372/462	11	221/271	627/767
Rounded Total	**20**	**370/460**	**10**	**220/270**	**630/770**

TABLE 9
Assumed Characteristics of a Laser Defense System and Its Target Missiles

Laser System:

Infrared laser light of 2.7 micron wavelength

Continuous power output of 25 megawatts

Sufficient fuel aboard to attack all assigned targets

Flawless focusing mirror of 10 meters diameter

.1 seconds required to slew, settle, and refocus on a new target

Negligible spot jitter

Target Missiles:

Hardness requiring delivery of 15 kJ/sq.cm. total energy

Booster effective attack exposure time of 80 seconds

and the potential vulnerabilities of future Soviet missiles. We assume the parameter values shown in Table 9; for the most part, they seem optimistic.

The main determinants of the costs of a space-based laser system are the number of lasers required, the total mass of satellites that must be launched into space, and the cost of the individual laser satellites. The costs of all other elements of the system would be more or less the same as those previously calculated for the Gamma system.

We estimate that approximately 235 of the laser satellites described above would be necessary to defend against the projected force of Soviet ICBMs and SLBMs, and that about 335 such satellites would be required to defend against the entire force of Soviet long- and intermediate-range missiles. (The calculation of these figures is specified in the full study previously referenced.)

These satellites would be placed in orbits inclined at 60 degrees to the equator. This is optimal for defending against land-based missiles in the deployment area we have described. Even so, in these orbits, each satellite would spend about 15 percent of its time with a line-of-sight range to the North Pole that would be within its maximum effective

TABLE 10
Costs of Strategic Defense System Delta
(billions of 1987 dollars)

(Defense against ICBMs and SLBMs only/Long-
and intermediate-range ballistic missiles)

Component	R&D	Procurement	Construction	Ten-Year Operations	Total Cost
Laser Satellites	15	210/280	—	105/140	330/435
Battle Management Satellites	2	20	—	10	32
Launch Costs	—	9/13	—	4/6	13/19
Other	—	5	—	5	10
Subtotal	17	244/318	—	124/161	385/496
Beta (reconfigured)	15	81	11	62	169
Total	32	325/399	11	186/223	554/665
Rounded Total	**30**	**330/400**	**10**	**190/220**	**550/670**

range. This implies that the laser satellite constellations also should be capable of dealing with SLBMs launched from the area of the North Pole.

We estimate further that the total weight of each laser satellite would be 40 tons, including an allowance to protect the satellite from enemy weapons. The total weight of the laser constellation (including the battle management satellites) required to defend against the projected Soviet ICBM and SLBM force alone would be 8.8 million kg. The weight of the constellation needed to defend against the entire projected force of Soviet long- and intermediate-range missiles would be 12.5 million kg.

On the basis of these assumptions, the costs of the several elements of the Delta system are shown in Table 10. Comparisons of these figures with the costs estimated for the Gamma system in Table 8 indicate that a space-based laser system of the kind we have described would be roughly 80 to 85 percent as expensive as a space-based missile system of a similar overall effectiveness.

We should not conclude, however, that a directed energy system would not ultimately prove to be even less costly. The technology of directed energy systems is far less mature than that for interceptor missile systems, and our sketch of how well a laser system might work, what its components might have to weigh, how many might be needed, and how much each one might cost are accordingly much less certain than for a missile interceptor system. The message that may be drawn from these estimates is that in designing a research strategy for strategic defenses, it may be preferable to aim for a directed energy system with considerably better performance parameters than we have assumed.

Critical Assumptions and Sensitivities

The more important assumptions made in estimating the costs of the four notional defense systems are listed in Table 11.

The optimistic assumptions primarily concern factors over which the U.S. may have the greater leverage. For example, while missile probabilities of kill depend in part upon how the Soviet Union designs its targets, the U.S. has an opportunity to prevail in this competition with very clever missile designs based on superior technology.

One exception is our assumption that the Soviet Union's anti-satellite effort could be countered effectively for costs on the order of those that have been described for the satellites used in the systems. There is little basis for this assumption. The potential vulnerability of defense satellites to attacks appears to be perhaps the largest unsolved problem for strategic defenses, and we have not heard of any promising solutions to it.

Another optimistic assumption that has particularly concerned some readers is our assumption that the various anti-ballistic missile interceptors employed in the several defense systems would be capable of 90 percent single shot probabilities of kill. A lower figure would clearly increase costs substantially, if the overall performance of the defense systems were to be held constant. If, for example, the HEDI and LEDI ground-based interceptors, and the space-based interceptor rocket, had single shot probabilities of kill of only 80 percent, the cost of a Gamma system of comparable overall performance would rise by about 30 percent. This would bring the cost of the thicker system intended to defend against IRBMs, as well as ICBMs and SLBMs, to more than $1 trillion.

TABLE 11
Critical Assumptions

Alpha and Beta Systems

Optimistic Assumptions

Missile characteristics: cost, reliability, probability of kill
U.S. missile sensors would be effective despite Soviet efforts at concealment
Anti-submarine sensors would give reliable warning of Soviet submarines deployed close to U.S. shores
Battle management of missile and air defenses would be efficient
Soviet Union would not increase the air threat substantially
Production costs would continue to decline with experience

Pessimistic Assumptions

Soviet bombers would launch cruise missiles from outside the effective range of U.S. air defenses
Soviet decoys would make attacks outside the atmosphere infeasible

Gamma and Delta Systems

Optimistic Assumptions

Soviet anti-satellite systems could be rendered ineffective at reasonable cost
Interceptor missile characteristics: cost, reliability, probability of kill, and weight
Laser characteristics: cost, power, retarget time, reliability, and weight
Only short decision delays would be involved before initiating attacks on missiles in the boost phase
Soviet submarines would not mass to shoot
Production costs would continue to decline with experience

Pessimistic Assumptions

Soviet boost times could be reduced by approximately 50 percent
Soviet land-based missile deployment area would be reduced by approximately two-thirds
Soviet missiles could be hardened to 15kJ/sq.cm. against laser attack
Decoys would make space-based defenses ineffective in midcourse

The pessimistic assumptions primarily concern factors over which the Soviet Union seems likely to have the greater leverage. For example, the Soviet Union alone will decide whether to move its missiles into a significantly smaller deployment area; the temptation to do so would be substantial. The costs of space-based defense systems such as those we have described would rise dramatically if the Soviets were to reduce sharply their deployment areas. Even if the Soviets were to show no interest in doing so, and were to agree formally not to, the United States would nonetheless have to be prepared to cope with such a move.

Our assumption that the use of lightweight decoys would make an effective defense impossible during the mid-course phase of the attacking missiles' flight has been criticized by some readers. In fact, the current SDI program is devoting a great deal of effort to solving this problem. The task of building an effective ballistic missile defense could be eased enormously if an effective mid-course discrimination technique could be found. Instead of having on the order of 100 seconds in the boost phase, plus perhaps 30 seconds in the terminal phase of a ballistic missile's flight, to destroy the attacking warheads, as much as 30 minutes could be available. This could greatly reduce the number of weapons and satellites necessary to achieve a given level of effectiveness.

STRATEGIC DEFENSE COSTS IN PERSPECTIVE

The estimated costs of the four notional strategic defense systems, including all investments and ten years of operations, thus would range between $160 billion and $770 billion at fiscal 1987 prices. These aggregate figures tell us relatively little about the prospective economic impact of a decision to deploy strategic defenses, however, as they do not address the key question of how costs might be spread over time. Illustrative cost schedules, based on historical patterns of expenditures for major weapon programs and assessments of when various technologies would be available, are contained in Figures 1–3.

The Alpha and Beta systems (Figure 1) are assumed to be designed and developed between 1988 and 1995; construction of necessary air bases and other installations could begin in 1994, and procurement of necessary missiles, radars, and aircraft initiated in 1995. Deployment of either system could probably begin in 2000; they could be fully operational by 2005. Budgetary demands for either system would build slowly over the fiscal 1988 through 1997 period. During their peak ten years of funding requirements, fiscal 1997 through 2006, the two systems would require annual appropriations on the order of $10 billion and $11 billion, respectively.

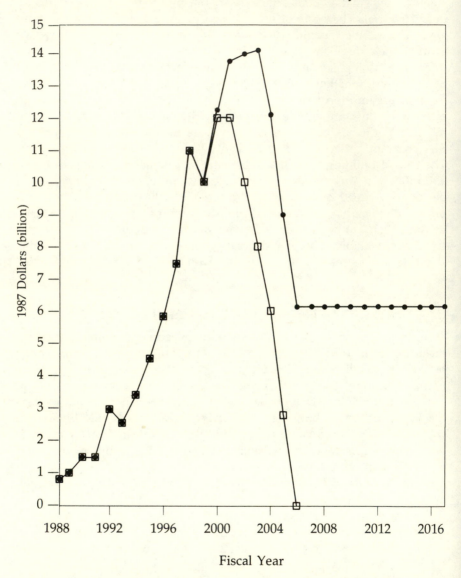

FIGURE 1: Annual Cost of Beta System

FIGURE 2: Annual Cost of Gamma System

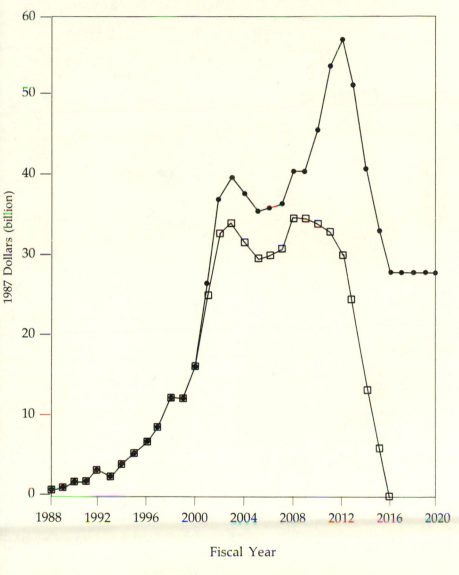

Fiscal Year

□ Investment   • Total Cost

Note: The figure includes the cost of thickening the system to defend against Soviet IRBMs.

FIGURE 3: Annual Cost of Delta System

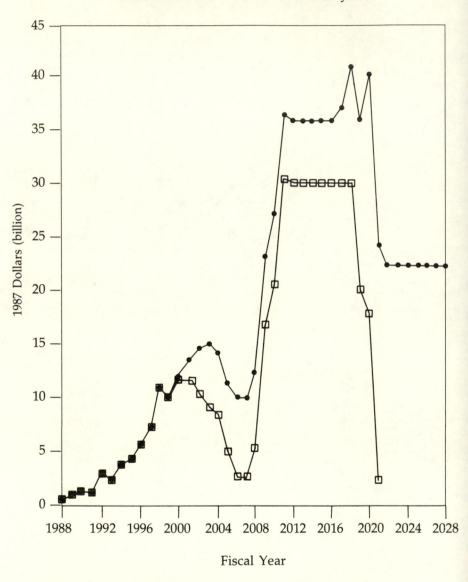

☐ Investment   ● Total Cost

NOTE: The figure includes the cost of thickening the system to defend against Soviet IRBMs.

For the Gamma system (Figure 2), we have assumed that the components of the Beta system would be deployed on the schedule described previously, and that the incremental space-based components would be developed between 1995 and 2002 and procured between 2000 and 2015. Deployment of the space-based components would begin in 2008. An initial operational capability might be achieved in 2010, and the full system could be operational in the year 2012. The budgetary requirements for Gamma would mount rapidly after the year 2000, fluctuating between $35 billion and more than $50 billion annually during the period 2002 through 2014. During its peak ten years of funding, the Gamma system would require annual appropriations averaging $44 billion.

Because it requires the solution of more difficult technological problems, the Delta system could probably not be deployed until the second decade of the new century. We have assumed in scheduling the costs of Delta that the Beta system would be deployed as described previously and that exploratory research on the space-based components would continue through the 1990s; the costs of exploratory research are not included in our estimates as such efforts are included already in the U.S. defense program. Full-scale development of the Delta system would begin in 2002 and be completed for the most part by 2010. The necessary launch capabilities and laser and battle management satellites would be acquired between 2008 and 2020. Deployment of the satellites might begin in 2016 and be completed in 2020, when the system would be fully operational. At its peak ten years of funding, 2011 through 2020, Delta would require annual appropriations on the order of $37 billion.

The first thing that should be said about these figures is that the nation could afford to deploy strategic defenses if it chose to do so. The most expensive system, Gamma, during its most demanding ten years of spending, would require annual expenditures averaging less than $50 billion. In rough terms, it would entail a commitment to allocate between one-half and one percent of the nation's resources for the purpose of strategic defense each year, and to sustain that commitment for at least fifteen years. This is not such a large financial burden as to make a deployment decision inconceivable.

The more important question, though, concerns the opportunity costs of a decision to deploy strategic defenses. Dollars spent for strategic defenses would not be available for other defense or federal civilian programs, or for private uses. Such a substantial commitment of national resources could constrain the achievement of other national goals.

Of course, the pot of resources available to the nation is not fixed for all time, and thus choices will not be zero-sum. Over time, economic growth will increase the nation's wealth; through the political process, the citizenry can decide to increase or decrease the share of resources made available to the federal government or to alter the distribution of federal programs between defense and non-defense needs.

A decision to deploy a comprehensive strategic defense system, because it would entail such a major commitment of the nation's resources, could have such effects itself, either stimulating or depressing economic growth, possibly restructuring the nation's spending priorities, and influencing the country's scientific and industrial sectors. All would depend, of course, on what economic and industrial policies were pursued during the period that the strategic defense system was being developed and deployed. Would other defense expenditures be reduced or would strategic defense costs simply be added incrementally to the defense budget? If the latter, would there be coincident cuts in federal civilian programs? If not, would federal revenues be increased to pay for the new program or would it be financed through deficit spending? If the latter, would monetary policy be adjusted to avoid any inflationary consequences and to curtail any impact on interest rates and the value of the dollar in international markets? Would coincident steps be taken to compensate for the effects of developing the strategic defense system on the scientific and industrial communities?

In the remainder of this article, we explore the potential opportunity costs of a decision to deploy strategic defenses by examining such potential expenditures in four contexts: i) the portion of the defense budget allocated to strategic forces; ii) the full defense budget; iii) the federal budget overall; and iv) the nation's economy as a whole.

Strategic Defenses in the Context
of Historical Spending Levels for Strategic Forces

As shown in Table 12, the level of funding for strategic forces has varied widely over the years, depending primarily on the stage of U.S. efforts to modernize or expand its nuclear capabilities. Strategic forces have been most important in budgetary terms in the 1950s, when the nation first deployed nuclear-armed long-range missiles, modernized its force of strategic bombers, and constructed a substantial air defense system. Annual appropriations for strategic forces averaged $47 billion when expressed in 1987 prices during this period, accounting for roughly one-fifth of all defense spending. Appropriations for strategic forces declined substantially over the next twenty years, a trend that bottomed out in fiscal 1979, when appropriations for strategic forces amounted to only $13.5 billion, less than 7 percent of the defense budget. During the 1980s, annual appropriations for strategic forces have returned to near $30 billion.

TABLE 12
Levels of Appropriations for Strategic Forces
(1946–1986)

Stage of Strategic Modernization (fiscal years)	Average Share of Total Defense Budget (percent)	Yearly Average ($ billions–1987)
1946–50	10.9	15.2
1951–60	21.5	47.4
1961–68	15.3	35.1
1969–80	8.6	18.1
1981–86	8.7	23.8
1946–86	13.3	29.0

Source: Derived from Kevin N. Lewis, *The Potential Large-Scale Budget Impacts of a Comprehensive Strategic Defense Effort: Some Parametric Analyses* (Santa Monica, Calif.: The Rand Corporation, P–7253, October 1985).

Spending for strategic defenses, which is incorporated in these figures, declined sharply over this historic period. Appropriations for strategic defenses were a relatively large share of the strategic budget in the 1950s and early 1960s, when the U.S. deployed substantial defenses against Soviet bombers; but later in the period, and particularly in the early 1970s, they fell precipitously. Around this time, existing plans to modernize the U.S. strategic air defense system were scrapped and existing forces cut back substantially.

Given this history, would it be possible to fund strategic defenses within the strategic forces budget as it traditionally has been circumscribed? The answer is "yes" for the limited systems, but "no" for either comprehensive defense system.

Current modernization programs for offensive forces will require something near 5 percent real annual growth in strategic spending well into the 1990s. Even so, the roughly $10 billion per year required by the Alpha or Beta systems could be accommodated within the strategic forces portion of the budget, if that budgetary element were increased to its 1950s level—in excess of $40 billion per year. Any new increase in the cost of offensive weapons modernization programs, of course, would greatly complicate the funding situation. And a comprehensive strategic defense system like Gamma or Delta would be too expensive to be accommodated within the strategic forces portion of the budget under any realistic circumstances.

In its cost implications, constructing one of the limited strategic defense systems would be equivalent to adding a fourth major component to the current three legs of the U.S. strategic posture. Total investment required for the Trident program, for example, including 20 submarines and two generations of missiles, will probably come to around $80 billion (in 1987 prices) over a 25 to 30-year period. The investment necessary to develop and construct the U.S. bomber force that will operate in the first decade of the next century, including 100 B-1 bombers, 144 Advanced Technology Bombers, and the cruise missiles and other armaments with which they will be equipped, will probably come close to $100 billion at 1987 prices over a 20-year period of time. Total investment for the Alpha system would be around $100 billion, spread over an 18-year period. If constraints on defense spending necessitated trade-offs with offensive forces in order to deploy strategic defenses, this is the magnitude of what might have to be given up.

Spending $40 to $50 billion per year on strategic forces to accommodate the Alpha or Beta systems, moreover, would mean sustaining at least a 60 percent real increase in this portion of the budget in the 1990s, on top of the 67 percent increase that has already taken place in the 1980s. If total defense spending remained constant in real terms over the deployment period, it would suggest an increase in the strategic forces' share of the overall defense budget from its low of 7 percent in 1979 to perhaps 14 to 16 percent in the mid-1990s. What might have to be given up to accommodate such growth in spending for strategic forces without raising the overall level of defense appropriations is examined in the next section.

Strategic Defenses in the Context of the Overall Defense Budget

Like spending for strategic forces, the defense budget has exhibited considerable volatility over the postwar period. Even factoring out the incremental costs of the Korean and Vietnamese wars, however, the overall trend in defense spending has been upward, with real growth in defense appropriations averaging slightly less than 2 percent each year between fiscal 1946 and 1986.

Defense spending has not risen nearly as fast as overall federal spending nor kept pace with the nation's overall economic growth. As a share of total federal outlays, defense spending has declined from an average in excess of 50 percent during the period between 1945 and

1965, to a figure around 25 percent during the past 20 years. This reflects, of course, the great expansion of domestic entitlement programs and growth in the federal government's interest payments, rather than any absolute cut in defense appropriations. The attempted restructuring of the nation's spending priorities during the Reagan Administration has altered this trend, but not in a major way. Defense spending as a share of federal revenues increased from 22.5 percent in fiscal 1980 to 26.4 percent in fiscal 1986.

As a share of the nation's overall resources, defense declined fairly steadily from the 1950s, when it accounted for about 9 percent of the nation's resources, through the 1970s, reaching 4.8 percent of GNP in fiscal 1978 and 1979; the Vietnam period provided a temporary deviation from this trend, of course. The trend was reversed in the 1980s, and defense spending as a share of GNP rose swiftly to around 6 percent, where it now seems to have stabilized.

What is the likely future trend? In submitting the fiscal 1987 budget, the President proposed to increase the defense budget by about 5 percent in real terms in the coming year, and projected 3 percent real annual growth through fiscal 1991. The Congress appears unwilling to permit defense appropriations to grow in real terms, however, and barring some major international crisis, this situation seems likely to prevail at least through fiscal 1991, by which time a balanced budget is supposed to be achieved. Even with the prospect of constant budgets in the near term, however, the nation's historical proclivity to sustain real increases in defense spending, and the virtual certainty of at least modest economic growth in the future, should result in rising defense budgets over the longer term. Three such possibilities are shown in Figure 4.

The low projection assumes that defense spending will increase on average over the next 25 years—in real terms, at about the same rate at which it grew over the past 40 years: 1.75 percent per year. At such a pace, defense outlays could be roughly $413 billion in the year 2010, $145 billion or 54 percent larger than they were in fiscal 1986. Even with such growth, defense would probably account for smaller shares of both federal expenditures and the nation's total resources than it does today.

The mid-range projection shows one logical outcome of the current congressional process. It assumes that for the period between fiscal 1986 and 1991, the nation's economy and federal revenues increase as projected by the Congressional Budget Office in its February 1986 report, but that, as required by the Gramm-Rudman-Hollings legislation, federal spending is gradually reduced in order to eliminate the federal deficit. We assume further that budgetary reductions are taken proportionately in all programs. Beyond 1991, we assume that the nation's economy

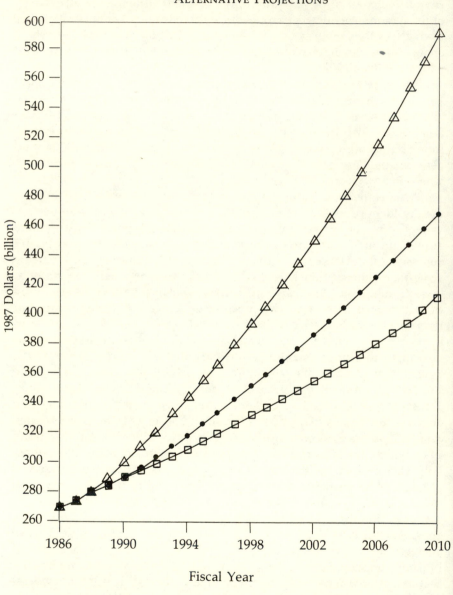

FIGURE 4: Defense Spending Trends
ALTERNATIVE PROJECTIONS

□ 1.75%   • 2.5%   △ 3.5%

grows annually at an average rate of 2.5 percent, that federal revenues are frozen at their projected 1991 level (19 percent of GNP), that federal spending does not exceed revenues, and that defense spending remains proportionate to other federal programs, meaning that it would increase only with growth in GNP. In this scenario, defense outlays would amount to $468 billion in 2010, an increase of $200 billion (75 percent) as compared to fiscal 1986; defense's share of total resources would be roughly 5.7 percent as compared to the current 6.2 percent.

The high projection shows the trend in defense spending if the President's program were fully implemented between now and fiscal 1991, and then defense's share of the nation's overall resources were held constant at 6 percent. It assumes further a 3.5 percent real growth rate in GNP. This means that domestic programs would have to take disproportionate cuts to reduce the deficit and that defense would rise to about 33 percent of total federal outlays, its level in the 1960s. At the end of the period, the defense budget would total $594 billion at 1987 prices, more than doubling fiscal 1986 spending.

The wedges under the three curves represent the incremental funds that could be made available for new defense initiatives. The growth projected for all three trends would be sufficient to absorb the incremental costs of deploying any of the four notional strategic defense systems, even Gamma, the most expensive. In principle, normal growth that can be anticipated in the defense budget should be sufficient to fund the development and procurement of even a comprehensive strategic defense system.

This first-order analysis neglects the possibility of competing demands on the defense budget, however. Strategic defenses are certain not to be the only claimant for anticipated growth in defense appropriations. Defense spending had tended to increase in real terms in the past because the nation has perceived rising needs for U.S. military power, and because the real cost of acquiring and maintaining any given quantity of military capability has tended to rise throughout the postwar period. Any real growth in defense spending allocated for strategic defenses would not be available to fulfill these other requirements. A complete answer to the question of the adequacy of predictable growth in defense spending for the cost of strategic defenses, therefore, depends on the prospects for additional or reduced demands on the aggregate defense budget.

One implicit factor inevitably will drive defense costs higher. As technology advances, the capabilities of individual weapon systems improve measurably; so too, however, do the salaries and training costs of the individuals who operate them, the cost of maintaining the systems, and the investment necessary to replace them. Estimates of the annual real budget growth necessary simply to maintain the current force posture—without increases in force levels or additional missions—typically range between 2 and 4 percent. In the absence of such added expenditures, either the size of the forces or their readiness for combat would have to decline. As we have noted, annual real growth in U.S. defense budgets has averaged less than 2 percent in the past and, indeed, U.S. combatant force levels have tended to decline over much of the postwar period.

One factor that might mitigate the demand for incremental defense expenditures simply to maintain current forces is the reforms now being instituted to streamline the weapons acquisition process. But the potential here is limited; reformers would be delighted if these measures managed to reduce acquisition costs by 20 percent, meaning savings on the order of $25 billion at today's levels of expenditures.

World conditions also will determine whether demands for U.S. military capabilities, and thus defense spending, will rise or fall. Conflicts and threats to Western interests in the Third World have been rising, for example, and show little evidence of subsiding in the future. They must be considered likely to constitute a continuing demand for rising defense budgets. If allies were to increase their spending on defense, on the other hand, it might be possible for the U.S. to decrease its spending.

The U.S. decision to deploy strategic defenses itself would affect aggregate demand on U.S. military capabilities and overall defense budgets. On the negative side, a need to improve certain capabilities for the defense of NATO would follow logically from a decision to deploy comprehensive defenses. The possible costs of such initiatives are estimated in our full study; they come to around $160 billion. On the other hand, deployment of strategic defenses conceivably could lead to a breakthrough in relations with the Soviet Union and far-reaching arms control agreements—perhaps specifying a transition to a defense-dominated strategic regime involving much smaller offensive forces, as well as reductions in forces in Europe. These changes of course would lead to reduced defense budgets.

What the net result of these contradictory possibilities might be is impossible to predict. It does seem safe to forecast that demands for real growth in defense spending, even without a decision to deploy strategic defenses, are likely to exceed the 1.75 percent average annual growth rate assumed in our low projection. This suggests that if the defense budget were to grow at only its historical rate, expenditures for strategic defenses could be made only at the cost of not fulfilling other defense needs. This brings us back to the issue with which we ended the previous section: the potential trade-offs between deploying strategic defenses and other defense programs. For $160 billion dollars, the cost of the Alpha system, for example, the nation could build eight aircraft carrier battle groups and operate them for ten years. Alternatively, the ten-year systems cost of the Alpha system is the equivalent of the ten-year systems cost of 27 wings of F-15s or 14 armored divisions.

To look at the worst case, deploying the Gamma comprehensive defense system would require a national commitment, in rough terms, to sustain annual expenditures between $35 billion and more than $50 billion for a period of fifteen years, and then nearly $30 billion per year indefinitely to operate the system. To put these figures in some perspective, consider that over the past five years, the U.S. has appropriated, in fiscal 1987 dollars, on average, $30 billion for all defense research and development accounts. Total procurement for all three military services has been running about $94 billion per year. If $40 billion per year were allocated for strategic defenses, roughly the amount necessary during the peak ten years of funding for the Delta system, this one mission would cost about the same amount as the Navy's or Air Force's total investment budget in fiscal 1986, and about twice as much as the Army invested that year. To the extent that the nation were willing to increase defense spending beyond its historical trend, these difficult trade-offs would be eased. Such a decision, however, would require reductions in other federal programs, or in private consumption, as described in the next sections.

Strategic Defenses in the Context of Total Federal Expenditures

Most federal civilian programs do not begin to approach the prospective cost of deploying strategic defenses. The Tennessee Tom-Big-Bee Waterway, for example, one of the largest recent projects of its kind, cost less than $3 billion, at 1987 prices, over a 14-year period. Somewhat more comparable have been the nation's largest space efforts. The "Apollo" program, for example, cost about $66 billion when expressed in fiscal 1987 prices, over a twelve-year period. This would exceed, but not be dissimilar to, the cost of the missile defense component of the Alpha system. Closer to the full cost of the Alpha system would be the expense of rebuilding the nation's interstate highway system. From its start in 1956 through 1985, the current federal road network cost about $140 billion in fiscal 1987 prices.

The civilian programs that begin to approximate the potential cost of comprehensive strategic defenses are those that involve substantial expenditures on a continuing basis. Agricultural subsidies from 1945 through the current fiscal year, for example, will have accounted for

TABLE 13
Average Annual Expenditures During Peak Funding for
Notional Strategic Defense Systems and Federal Outlays
in 1986 for Selected Civilian Programs

Program	Amount ($ billions–1987)
Water Resources	4
Community Development	5
Higher Education	9
Alpha System	**10**
Beta System	**11**
Ground Transportation	19
Farm Income Stabilization	25
Medicaid	26
Health Care Services	30
Delta System	**37**
Gamma System	**44**
Medicare	71
Social Security	208

Source: OMB, *Historical Tables, Budget of the United States Government*, FY 1987.

about $330 billion in federal outlays at fiscal 1987 prices. From its
inception in 1967 through 1986, the nation has paid 10 percent more
for the entire Medicare program than we estimated would be required
for the "Gamma" system, $770 billion. The relative magnitude of potential
annual expenditures for strategic defenses as compared to federal civilian
programs can perhaps be seen most clearly in Table 13, which lists
both the average annual peak ten-year funding levels for the notional
strategic defense systems and the actual expenditures for a sampling of
federal programs.

It should be clear from these relative magnitudes that increasing the defense budget to accommodate the cost of strategic defenses, without also raising the level of overall federal spending, would necessitate extremely difficult choices between defense and civilian programs. Indeed, the experience of the first five years of the Reagan Administration suggests that this strategy for financing strategic defenses simply would be impracticable.

A concerted effort on the part of the Administration to restructure national priorities has resulted in a reduction in the portion of federal spending accounted for by non-defense programs from 77.5 percent in fiscal 1980, the last complete Carter budget, to 73.6 percent in fiscal 1986. Repeating such a shift in federal spending priorities to accommodate a new increase in defense budgets would appear to be an unlikely prospect. The potential base for such reductions is no longer large. The largest portion of non-defense spending (60 percent) is used for entitlements, like social security, and other mandatory spending programs. There is virtually no support for cuts in any of these programs. Factoring out entitlements and net interest payments leaves around $180 billion (in fiscal 1987 prices) for annual, discretionary, non-defense spending. Funding the Delta system in its peak years solely by reducing these expenditures would require cutting one-fifth of discretionary non-defense programs—a most unlikely prospect.

Federal revenues will increase, of course, along with economic growth, permitting increases in federal spending without the accumulation of new deficits. If the nation's economy grew at an average long-term annual rate of 2 percent, for example, a figure on the conservative side of most economic projections, and federal revenues remained at their current 19 percent of national resources, annual federal outlays could be 50 percent larger in 2006 without incurring additional deficits. Assuming that defense retained its current share of federal spending, the defense budget could be $110 billion greater in 2006.

There will be many other claimants on future increases in federal revenues, however. Some experts have argued, for example, that for many years the nation has not invested sufficient amounts to maintain its economic infrastructure adequately. Others have argued that the federal government should be investing more heavily in the nation's educational system and in civilian research and development, in order to maintain the United States in a competitive position in modern industrial technologies and basic sciences.

The gradual increase in the average age of the U.S. population will both pose new demands for non-defense spending and constrain the potential growth in federal revenues. An aging population means that the fiscal requirements of many entitlement programs will increase more rapidly. An aging population, moreover, means that the ratio of the active work force to the community of retired individuals is likely to diminish, a trend that can reduce the prospective size of federal revenues and, thus, diminish the increase in federal spending that might otherwise be made possible by economic growth.

These factors seem likely to limit annual real growth in the defense budget, on average, to no more than its historical rate near 2 percent, even if the overall federal budget grows more rapidly, meaning that increases in defense spending would not be sufficient to fund the development and deployment of a comprehensive strategic defense system without compensating reductions in other military forces.

One obvious alternative would be to increase federal revenues beyond the levels that can be anticipated as a result of economic growth—in other words, to increase the government's share of the nation's resources in order to accommodate the fiscal requirements of strategic defenses along with the other defense and non-defense demands on the federal budget. A second alternative would be to finance strategic defenses by permitting federal deficits to increase, a decision to postpone the problem rather than face it at the same time as the defense system were being constructed. Both possibilities are examined below.

Strategic Defenses in the Context of the Nation's Economy

If tax revenues were not increased to pay for strategic defenses, the federal policies established to help contain any adverse economic effects would be of first-order importance. Other factors, some of which are relatively uncontrollable in the short term, such as trends in the cost of basic commodities, the international competitive position of American industries, and the relative strength of national currencies, also would play determining roles. Consider two examples.

From fiscal 1965 to 1969, defense spending increased from $51 to $83 billion, a nearly one-third increase in real terms, as the nation escalated its involvement in Vietnam; this rise increased defense's share of GNP by one full percentage point (6.8 to 7.8 percent). This defense increase, moreover, took place at the same time as other parts of the federal budget were growing rapidly; total federal outlays increased from 17.6 to 19.8 percent of GNP over these five years. Additionally, President Johnson chose to permit these spending increases without raising taxes. Together, these actions had major economic effects: the overall expansion in government spending, defense and non-defense, stimulated a surge in output that cut the unemployment rate substantially, but also resulted in major inflationary pressures.

Between 1979 and 1983, on the other hand, defense spending rose from $116 to $210 billion, also a real increase of about one-third over a five-year period, as the nation acted to correct what it perceived to be a decline in U.S. military capabilities relative to those of the USSR. Although federal non-defense spending was constrained during this period, tax revenues were cut sharply. Despite the fact that in this case defense spending as a percentage of GNP increased by one and one-half percentage points (4.7 to 6.2 percent), a larger relative increase than the Vietnam case, opposite economic trends obtained: GNP growth slowed, unemployment remained high, and inflation subsided.

Thus, in two situations that are analogous to the magnitude of the increase in defense spending that might be associated with the deployment of comprehensive strategic defenses, the near-term macroeconomic consequences of defense budgetary decisions were dominated by other dimensions of federal policy. Although overall federal spending was more stimulative in the early 1980s than in the late 1960s, primarily because of the coincident cut in federal taxes, monetary policy was more restrained in the 1980s than in the 1960s. This seems to have overwhelmed any potential effects of the defense run-up on inflation. The strength of the dollar relative to other currencies in the early 1980s also was important in determining the economic situation, as it depressed U.S. exports and encouraged imports, thus contributing to the poor employment record. In short, the immediate macroeconomic effects of changes in defense spending—even of the magnitude envisioned to deploy strategic defenses—are likely to be overwhelmed by other considerations.

If comprehensive strategic defenses were financed on a "pay-as-you-go" basis, many near-term adverse macroeconomic effects, such as greater inflation, might be avoided altogether. Such a "pay-as-you-go" policy would require, however, in the case of the Gamma system, an increase of about 5.6 percent in the current annual level of federal revenues. This amount might be raised by increasing revenues from individual income taxes by about 11 percent. In 1986, such a raise would mean, on average, an increase of about $570 in the yearly federal tax bill of a family earning between $30,000 and $50,000 per year. A family earning between $20,000 and $30,000 would pay, on average, an additional $260 in federal income taxes each year. Alternatively, under current tax codes, revenues from corporate income taxes could be increased by 50 percent, or the income from excise taxes more than doubled, or some combination of new taxes installed.

Because federal revenues will increase as a result of economic growth regardless of such possible surcharges to pay for strategic defenses, the relative incremental tax burden would be smaller at the time a strategic defense system actually would be acquired. If we assume a 2 percent average annual real increase in federal revenues, for example, financing the Gamma system in the first decade of the next century would require an increase of 3 to 4 percent in federal revenues each year, as compared to the 5.6 percent for the federal tax base in 1986.

In short, if the nation decided to deploy a comprehensive strategic defense system and to increase the magnitude of the federal budget to pay for it, it would appear that any potentially adverse economic consequences could probably be minimized, assuming that uncontrollable economic circumstances were not severely negative, by establishing additional taxes, and by setting fiscal and monetary policies to take account of these new circumstances.

Greater difficulty might be encountered in seeking to contain the effects of such a gigantic federal program on specific industrial sectors. The consequences of the major research projects and huge procurement programs we have described for the electronic and aerospace industries, for example, could be quite severe if compensating measures were not taken in a timely manner. Shortages of trained engineers, computer programmers, and other occupations could result, for example, or shortages could develop in supplies of certain types of materials and electronic components. Depending on the overall economic situation, these problems could lead to sharp increases in the price of certain types of civilian goods, and to a slower rate of development of civilian technologies, at least in the near term, which could have an adverse impact on the nation's economic growth. These effects could be ameliorated over time, and perhaps ultimately reversed, if the technologies developed for strategic defense spun off advances in civilian technologies and industrial techniques. Assessing these prospective effects requires detailed studies of individual industries.

CONCLUSION

In all likelihood, if the nation does decide to build a comprehensive strategic defense system, it would be financed through a mixture of the various means we have discussed. Spending for other defense needs would be somewhat lower than in other circumstances, as would federal spending for non-defense programs. Individual, corporate, and federal excise taxes might be somewhat higher than they could have been in other circumstances. The rate of inflation might be slightly greater and the rate of economic growth perhaps a little lower.

Because the costs of the system would be distributed among these various means, they would not likely be so visible. But whatever the precise means adopted to pay for a strategic defense system, the dollars spent on it would be real. They would represent forgone opportunities for the nation, either as taxpayers, individually, or as a society, collectively.

As a shorthand, the income tax surcharge mentioned above ($570 per year for the average family earning $30,000 to $50,000 annually, at the current level of federal revenues and under current tax laws) is probably the most direct way of understanding the opportunity cost of deploying a comprehensive strategic defense system. Whether such a tax would actually be imposed or strategic defenses financed through some other means, that figure represents the opportunity cost of the system.

In aggregate economic terms, it is feasible for the United States to develop and build comprehensive strategic defenses—assuming that the technical problems identified in the previous sections were solved and that costs were held to levels not significantly greater than those estimated in this paper. Still, the opportunity costs of the project would be substantial. The issue for all citizens is whether the potential benefits of strategic defenses would be great enough to warrant these forgone opportunities for other private or collective enterprises.

7

IS SDI POLITICALLY DURABLE?

Dave McCurdy

Politics is harder than physics.
　　　　　—Einstein

Einstein's dictum is especially meaningful to members of Congress who are confronting the difficult choices related to potential development and deployment of a strategic defensive system. Ronald Reagan no doubt wishes that his dream to eliminate the threat posed by strategic nuclear weapons could be limited by the laws of physics only. But defense policy is made by the laws of man, and it is as much a creature of politics as of science. The two are interrelated and in competition as policymakers try to determine whether President Reagan's Strategic Defense Initiative (SDI) will be fully funded, eliminated, or supported at some intermediate level.

Members of Congress, especially those on the armed services and appropriations committees, are challenged to examine thoroughly the merits of the science in the context of overall strategic doctrine, the Soviet threat, strategic advances, defense budgets and priorities, and the U.S. economy. Yet it is difficult to assign relative importance to the various factors in the SDI debate because each is unique. Analysis is further complicated by the alternative goals envisaged for the program and the potential levels of success attributed to it.

As with most policy initiatives, the fight over SDI involves not only proponents and opponents but active moderates and undecided individuals as well. Proponents—Ronald Reagan and his ideological soul mates as well as parents of the idea, such as Dr. Edward Teller and General Daniel Graham, and their political followers—have made the leap of faith necessary to believe that SDI will work. They are committed to pursuing the dream. Opponents, mostly liberals, coalesce around arms control and antinuclear positions and generally oppose Department of Defense (DOD) policy. They, too, have made a leap of faith to believe that SDI *cannot,* or at least should not, work. Moderates (or pragmatists, for lack of a better term) are generally less ideological and tend to evaluate the program in terms of technological arguments, economic realities, and implications for U.S. foreign policy. Finally, about 95 percent of the American public appear undecided.

During the past few years much of the SDI debate has centered on practical questions of technology and cost. Today more questions are being asked about SDI's impact on U.S. foreign policy and the relative priority assigned to the program vis-à-vis other costly and competing weapons systems. In the absence of a policy suggesting how SDI will relate to arms control and U.S. offensive systems, Congress has been asked to support everything—offensive and defensive. Clearly this is no longer possible.

Making the right choices on SDI, however, is extremely difficult when the answers to technological questions are years away. But judgments cannot be made solely on the basis of technology. The public— and a few members of Congress—seem unaware that SDI is not merely a proposal to build some new military hardware but a basic revision of strategic doctrine. For forty years the United States has maintained stability in the nuclear world by a policy of deterrence, which derives from mutual vulnerability to nuclear attack. SDI is intended to keep the peace through mutual defense from nuclear attack. Policymakers must now answer the question: Would SDI make nuclear war more, or less, likely? The arguments advanced thus far are rooted in basic strategic theory; all were thoroughly explored during the antiballistic missile (ABM) debate of the 1960s.[1]

Since the United States first began to deploy an ABM the Soviets have stressed the dangers of a contest in missile defenses (contrary to premier Kosygin's earlier statement, made at the 1967 Glassboro summit with president Johnson, that purely defensive weapons were unobjectionable). Now a U.S. effort to mount a new system of strategic defense has again become the driving force behind arms control and raises an issue critical to moderate members of Congress, who may cast the determining votes on the fate of SDI. Is SDI a poker chip, or is it the pot? Is SDI upon us for the sake of arms control, or is arms control upon us for the sake of SDI? Now we have to violate a treaty to get into SDI, runs a liberal critique, but if SDI was enshrined in an arms agreement, we would have to violate a treaty to get out of it. Hence the program would become politically unimpeachable.[2] "The President says that under no circumstances will he willingly abandon his vision," says Representative Edward J. Markey. "At the same time, he tells Congress that it cannot reduce funding for Star Wars because that would reduce his leverage over the Soviet Union. Star Wars has now become the ultimate oxymoron: a non-negotiable bargaining chip."[3]

To liberals, Reykjavík showed that only the surrender of SDI will make the Soviets amenable to deep reductions and that a commitment to SDI will probably spur the Soviets to build up their own nuclear arsenal.[4] But to the president's supporters in the New Right, Ronald Reagan became the first president in history to walk away from a bad arms-control deal.[5] Ironically, the theoretical case for Reagan's population shield rests, finally, on effecting in advance of deployment a basic change in the U.S.-Soviet political relationship: that the two nations will begin to resolve their political differences and develop the trust in one another that would be required to permit a phasing-in of strategic defenses and limits on offensive weapons, without seeking all means possible to defeat the other's defenses. Many of the true believers in SDI explicitly reject that such a change is possible, and for good reason.[6]

The so-called moderates agree with James Schlesinger that "for Western security, the nuclear deterrent continues to represent the ultimate reality." Although this group has voted to fund SDI research, in the eyes of the true believers we pragmatists—rather than the liberals who favor arms control—are the real enemy because we have yet to make the leap of faith that is required to see SDI as the ultimate solution. "Yes, there has been some bipartisan support," Representative Jack Kemp acknowledges, but "far from being enthusiasts for SDI, these more moderate Democrats . . . would fund *needed* conventional force improvements, but *at the expense* of strategic programs, including SDI."[7]

In fact, a consensus has emerged in Congress that recognizes the strategic importance of improving conventional forces as an alternative to nuclear first use. General Bernard Rogers, supreme commander of NATO forces, reinforced this awareness when he explained the "trip wire" strategy in effect in Europe: After three days of fighting at current force levels he would have two choices—theater nuclear war or surrender.

The European problem, however, cannot be resolved solely by upgrading conventional forces and providing new weapons. Questions of extended deterrence remain. To many Europeans, who already fear that the United States is not fully committed to their defense, SDI inherently possesses the potential to decouple the defense of Western Europe from that of the United States. From their perspective, SDI is decidedly destabilizing.[8] Following the Reykjavík summit, even President Reagan's former national-security adviser, Robert McFarlane, charged that "the Administration has overturned forty years of alliance strategy by offering to abandon offensive missiles."

The 1987 defense authorization and appropriations acts demonstrate congressional interest in ameliorating this problem by establishing a new Conventional Defense Initiatives (CDI) program to develop SDI technologies with conventional defense applications. The Senate Committee on Appropriations cited as a "prime example" the antitactical ballistic missile (ATBM) defense, which it described as "an issue of much importance to the United States and our European allies."[9] An ATBM capability presumably would be for NATO what SDI is for the continental United States, and SDI opponents seem to view it as a bribe to dampen opposition within the alliance to the Reagan plan. They note that "conceptually, the development of such a capability is not needed for SDI. Politically, however, it is likely to be unavoidable unless we wish to do without allies in the future."[10]

To survive politically, SDI must overcome challenges to its technological feasibility and affordability and build a base of popular support. Already, technical and fiscal constraints are forcing changes in emphasis and direction. They have compelled program managers to narrow the focus, downgrade some technologies that once seemed promising, and delay deadlines. The $1 billion national test bed that is a foundation of SDI will be delayed as much as one year because of serious differences between program managers and computer experts over how best to define major design tasks. "It's not budget cuts, it's not political pressures, it's just a tough nut to crack," said one SDI program official. The program is at such an early stage that no one has a clear idea of how well it is proceeding, and there are no yardsticks to measure progress.[11]

These problems have led Congress to provide statutory guidance. Notably, in FY 1987 the program is to be refocused on "developing survivable and cost-effective defensive options for enhancing the survivability of U.S. retaliatory forces and command, control, and communications systems." This new orientation is meant to shift the program from what Senator Sam Nunn called the "grandiose and unrealistic idea" embodied in President Reagan's dream of a population space shield.[12] While technological breakthroughs on specific elements of strategic defensive weapons systems probably can be anticipated, it remains uncertain whether the requisite variety of weapons and sensors can be combined in a *system* that is reliable, under human control, survivable, and cost-effective.[13]

Few members of Congress feel comfortable with the physics of SDI, but all are familiar with serious fiscal problems. For many members the priority for national survival may become a different "SDI"—a Strategic Deficit Initiative. The realization is growing that tens of billions of dollars will not be found in the defense budget to deal with the deficit, and there is a demonstrated lack of support for cutting important domestic programs. Thus, it is likely that increases in SDI funding (if any) will come at the expense of current DOD programs. As expressed by forty-nine senators in May 1986 in a joint letter to the leadership of the Committee on Armed Services:

> Our concern is that the Strategic Defense Initiative has received excessive and inappropriate emphasis in DOD's budget. It is difficult to conceive of a sound rationale for increasing the combined DOD/DOE SDI budget by 77 percent while the entire DOD budget will likely be frozen at zero real growth and other vital military research programs are facing budget cuts. Not only are the goals of the research effort unclear, but the need for accelerated funding for a long-range program such as SDI has not been demonstrated.
>
> We support a vigorous ballistic missile defense research program which conducts research into innovative technologies. Such a program is necessary to hedge against Soviet breakout from the ABM Treaty, to protect the U.S. from technological surprises, and to maintain an array of strategic options including strategic defense.
>
> We are concerned, however, that the SDI program is being rushed to a premature development decision in the early 1990's in order to meet an unrealistic schedule. . . .
>
> By any measure budget growth in the SDI has outpaced the progress of technology and, more importantly, has begun to impinge on other military research and development. The FY 1986 SDI budget is twice as large as the combined Advanced Technology budgets of the three military services and is nearly as large as the Technology Base budget of the entire Department of Defense.
>
> For these and other reasons, we question whether the combined DOD/DOE SDI program should be funded for FY 1987 at a level higher than that which would allow for approximately three percent real growth. Such an increase, after all, is equal to the increase the President is seeking for all military programs.

In fact, Congress nearly approved *zero* real growth in SDI for FY 1987 before settling on 13 percent under intense pressure from the Reagan administration not to undermine the president's negotiating position at the Reykjavík summit—the same kind of lobbying effort was undertaken the previous year before the Geneva summit. In FY 1985–87, SDI (DOD/DOE) has been funded at $1.621 billion, $3.109 billion, and $3.530 billion. These amounts were, respectively, 19 percent, 22.5 percent, and 35 percent below administration requests, but they provided year-to-year increases of 92 percent and 13.5 percent. Given the known inability of research programs to absorb efficiently increases of more than 30 to 35 percent per year, it was assumed that the requested huge increases over previous year appropriations (147 percent from FY 1985 to 1986; 74 percent from FY 1986 to 1987) related more to President

Reagan's desire to make a political statement than to any urgent defense requirement.

In his appearances before Congress, Lt. General James A. Abrahamson, director of the Pentagon's Strategic Defense Initiative Organization, has been in the difficult position of insisting on the importance of full funding while trying to convince members that "on the other hand, we have made substantial progress" with what has been appropriated.[14] Thus far, conferees have split the difference between the higher figures passed by the Republican-controlled Senate and the lower amounts approved by the Democratic-controlled House of Representatives. Majorities in both houses have generally supported their committees' recommendations.

In August 1986, however, the Senate twice came within one vote of making additional cuts in authorization levels. While the debate focused on the program's merits, the actual political maneuvering more closely resembled a bidding war, with SDI critics vying to produce a magic figure below the committee-approved amount that could command a majority. In the following week the House voted by 239 to 176 to hold the FY 1987 authorization for SDI to zero real growth. Although the vote was mostly along party lines—33 Republicans voted for the cut and 34 Democrats opposed it—the substantial majority included several strong "pro-defense" conservatives, and many members cited budget constraints as the reason they voted for the lowest authorization proposed.

Future funding increases seem unlikely. The administration's request for a $500 million FY 1987 supplemental to recoup previous SDI cuts was never taken seriously, and it will be miraculous if Congress approves an increase of just 1 percent real growth in the 1988 defense budget. Even before the FY 1988 budget was formally submitted, Representative William L. Dickinson, the senior Republican on the armed services committee and a strong Reagan supporter, released a letter he sent to Secretary Caspar Weinberger denouncing the Pentagon's plans:

> I consider it unwise to sacrifice conventional Army capability in favor of requests for large, unobtainable increases in the SDI program. . . . There is no way that such funding can or should be approved, particularly when it is requested at the expense of needed conventional capabilities. . . . If my facts are correct, I want you to know that neither I nor many of your traditionally strongest supporters will be able to stand behind the proposals for the fiscal year 1988 defense budget.[15]

The potential long-term costs of the SDI program are also likely to inhibit greater budgetary commitments. For instance, at a meeting of the House defense appropriations subcommittee, Representative Bill Hefner raised the worrisome factor of transportation costs: "I don't understand all the technology . . . but I do vaguely understand the problems of the transportation and putting it into place. My concern is that . . . we get to the point where it goes into space, then we look back and say we have a bill of $100 billion just for transportation."[16] The fundamental cost question is whether the United States will be spending billions to develop and deploy a system that the Soviets will be able to counter through measures costing only millions. Generally, as the director of the Soviet Space Research Institute said with respect to SDI, "Cost efficiency favors countermeasures by a big margin," especially since their actual development could wait until the directions of the U.S. program become clearer.[17]

But selling the public on SDI, as the president intuitively understands, depends precisely on not playing by the ordinary rules. "Isn't it worth every investment necessary to free the world from the threat of nuclear war?" he asked in his original SDI speech. "We know it is."[18] The question exemplifies Ronald Reagan's political genius at work. Most members of Congress would find it far easier to explain a vote *for* SDI by asking this question than to defend a vote *against* SDI by citing offense-defense cost-exchange ratios.

Administration officials have even attempted to suit notions of cost-effectiveness to the demands of SDI. They blundered early by stipulating that any deployable strategic defense must be "cost-effective at the margin." Now, Secretary Weinberger and General Abrahamson say that cost-effectiveness should be replaced with a criterion of "affordability," which is "more than an economic concept" but includes a variety of measurable and nonquantifiable issues.[19] What this means is that the president was right in the first place: If we have to have it, it's affordable.

Of course, we are a long way from knowing just what "it" is. Liberal arms controllers want to slow or stop the program, although most liberals concede the need for some type of research. Senator Joseph Biden, who has labeled SDI a "fantasy and a false alternative to arms control," argues that SDI must be clearly restricted to "a genuine research program intended to hedge against and deter any Soviet 'breakout' from the ABM treaty, and to examine the possibilities of stabilizing point defenses." In the words of another liberal, Representative George Brown, concerned members of Congress have generally delayed the decision-making process to place a decision on the program's scope and pace in the hands of the next administration.[20] Attempts to create a majority opposition thus far have been hindered by an estimated $150 billion Soviet investment in strategic defense during the past decade (about fifteen times the amount spent by the United States for similar work) and by obvious Soviet "creep-out" from the ABM treaty and the strong possibility of clear violations.

Moderates feel that neither arms control nor strategic defense, by itself, can be expected to "save the world." Instead, they believe that the way out of the nuclear dilemma lies between the extremes, in trying to negotiate a new generation of arms-control agreements that combine reductions in offensive weapons and gradually loosen restraints on missile defense.[21] In fact, the so-called grand compromise of Reykjavík, if it ever came about, would scarcely represent a whole new approach to strategic arms but would "reaffirm not only SALT II, but SALT I by linking limits on strategic defense with restrictions on strategic offense."[22] Because moderates also fear a Soviet breakout from the ABM treaty, they advocate investments in strategic modernization and improved conventional force capabilities. Consequently, while they are the group most concerned about reducing the deficit, they are in danger of becoming the biggest spenders.

Ironically, the loudest complaints about the current SDI program come from the president's hard-core supporters on the New Right, who want to secure a national commitment to strategic defense before Ronald Reagan leaves office. Although many experts say that in ten years we could not deploy anything that would provide an effective defense, members of the House, including Jack Kemp, Jim Courter, and Henry Hyde, and senators including Malcolm Wallop and Pete Wilson, insist, "We need it now." SDI supporters are deeply concerned that a research program that has no definite consequences for the defense of America and its allies within the next ten years will not be politically sustainable. According to their critique, SDI as presently constituted "is, in effect, a decision to postpone until the 1990s any serious consideration of what, if anything, the United States shall do to prevent Soviet missiles, once launched, from landing in the United States."[23] This tracks with criticism from the Left that the Reagan administration "seems to hold strategic doctrine in contempt, and is taking steps to weaken its influence even before there is any certainty of an adequate successor."[24]

According to General Abrahamson, a decision to deploy SDI must be preceded by a determination of what is an acceptable level of confidence in the system. One cannot, as with other weapons, ask simply if it works. "Any effort to redirect the SDI towards a development and deployment program," he continues, "could have a substantial and negative impact on our ability to develop the . . . concepts necessary to support an informed decision in the early 1990s on whether to develop and deploy defenses against ballistic missiles."[25]

At a minimum, early deployment of some type of advanced strategic defense would require concurrency of development and deployment, which has almost always proved to be a mistake with major systems. (A case in point is the B-1B bomber.) More important, the political effort required to achieve early deployment might provide SDI opponents with the rallying point they need to galvanize public opinion against the program. Although the Right has tried to "force" other controversial issues in the past to make moderate and undecided members choose sides, such an effort would be pointless without support from their own congressional leadership and the administration.

In the three weeks following the Reykjavík summit, President Reagan himself was unable to make SDI an issue in the 1986 congressional campaigns. Representative Kemp noted unhappily that while Democrats were unwilling to present a firm opposition to SDI, Republicans did not unite to champion the program. Thus, the most important quality of public opinion on SDI may be that it is not very strong. While there is some public interest in the military budget, few members of Congress feel pressed to take a stand on strategic defense.[26] As SDI's supporters recognize, the public is not heavily interested in twenty-year research projects, and the more drawn out the research phase, the more political inertia SDI will have to overcome.

Within the defense establishment, programmatic uncertainty has weakened private industry's willingness to support SDI, while increasingly intense intramural budgetary competition has eroded the no-less-essential support of the military services. A retired air force general observed that "the military will follow when they are ordered to support SDI, but that will change once [Secretary Weinberger] is gone."[27] Opinions received through unofficial channels from sources like these are extremely influential in congressional policymaking, particularly on defense-related issues.

Regardless of the opposition, however, it is unlikely that President Reagan will scale back his vision of "a world free from the threat of nuclear war." He has already made his decision. Speaking to a group of SDI supporters in August 1986, he said, "When the time has come and the research is complete, yes, we're going to deploy."[28] But at this point in his presidency Reagan is no longer a controlling factor in the process, and Congress has shown no willingness to make major changes in the scope of the program before his successor takes office.

The budgetary, political, and arms-control environments strongly suggest an even more concerted legislative effort to redefine SDI along lines compatible with fiscal realities and arms-control possibilities. While the conferees on the 1987 defense authorization act supported a "robust SDI research program" to aid our negotiators in Geneva, they stated their belief that "leverage for arms control negotiations comes only from real defense programs which are aimed at realistic objectives, adequately funded and broadly supported by a bipartisan consensus."[29] As this statement suggests, moderate and undecided members of Congress are anxious to avoid sending the wrong signals to the Soviet Union by sharply reducing support for SDI. The report of the Senate appropriations committee on the FY 1987 defense spending bill noted testimony from former secretary of defense Harold Brown that it found "particularly instructive" in this regard: "The Soviets are clearly watching what Congress will do. . . . They would certainly like to see the strategic defense program, about which they worry for some good reasons and some bad reasons, decrease without having to pay anything for it. If the Congress were to level it or decrease it, that would certainly reduce the price they might be willing to pay."[30]

Thus, Congress is likely to continue to support SDI as a high-priority research project from which certain prospective elements may prove practical by the turn of the century. Funding probably will not exceed FY 1987 levels and may be reduced by small amounts if required by budget realities. Although program managers will retain considerable discretion in the allocation of funds among the program's scientific components, Congress will seek new ways to exploit SDI research for near-term payoffs in areas related to conventional defense.

Unlike their mentor, Ronald Reagan's ideological heirs in Congress are oriented toward technology rather than utopia; they tend to seek "hardware" solutions to what others see as fundamentally political problems. Their effort to achieve early deployment of a less-than-perfect strategic defense is stalled and suggests that President Reagan's dream of an ultimate system cannot continue to be politically viable. More modest goals, such as a selective defense of U.S. land-based forces, do in fact seem technically plausible in the near term and could conceivably appeal to moderates, although they must be compared with alternatives such as the small mobile missile.[31]

As we think about SDI we might ponder the sorry state of our once-proud civilian space program. Too much emphasis, it seems, was placed on short-term accomplishments, such as developing shuttles and flying specific satellite missions. Little thought was given to long-term goals and to a sustained commitment to the programs and technologies required to achieve them.[32] The debate over SDI will serve a useful purpose if it concentrates our attention on the importance of defining long-term national-security goals and finding the most effective ways to achieve them.

NOTES

1. Robert E. Hunter, "SDI: Return to Basics," *The Washington Quarterly*, 9 (Winter 1986), 159, 164.

2. Leon Wieseltier, "The Ungrand Compromise," *The New Republic*, November 17, 1986, 31.

3. Edward J. Markey, "The Packaging and Sale of 'Star Wars,'" *Christian Science Monitor*, November 20, 1986.

4. Paul B. Stares, "Limitations of Space," *The New Republic*, November 3, 1986, 41.

5. Jack Kemp, "The Politics of SDI," *National Review*, December 31, 1986, 28.

6. Hunter, "SDI: Return to Basics," 164.

7. Kemp, "The Politics of SDI," 28.

8. David E. Windmiller, "SDI: A Strategy for Peace and Stability or the End to Deterrence?" *Parameters*, Journal of the U.S. Army War College, XVI, no. 2, 22.

9. Report of the Senate Committee on Appropriations, *Department of Defense Appropriations Bill, 1987*, 99th Cong., 2d sess., S. Rept. 99–446, 335.

10. Senator Albert Gore, *Congressional Record*, June 9, 1986, 99th Cong., 2d sess., S7091.

11. *The New York Times*, October 19, 1986, 1; *Defense News*, December 15, 1986, 1.

12. Conference report, *National Defense Authorization Act for Fiscal Year 1987*, 99th Cong., 2d sess., H. Rept. 99–1001, 450.

13. Cosmo DiMaggio, Arthur F. Manfredi, Jr., and Steven A. Hildreth, "The Strategic Defense Initiative: Program Description and Major Issues," Congressional Research Service, Library of Congress, Report No. 86–8 SPR, January 7, 1986, 23.

14. Testimony of Lt. Gen. James A. Abrahamson, *Department of Defense Appropriations for 1987*, hearings before the House Defense Appropriations Subcommittee, May 1, 1986, part 5, 99th Cong., 2d sess., 629.

15. Representative William L. Dickinson's letter was attached to the news release, House Armed Services Committee, "Ranking Republican Decries Weinberger Budget Plan," December 31, 1986.

16. *Department of Defense Appropriations for 1987*, 603.

17. *The New York Times*, December 18, 1986, A15.

18. Public Papers of the Presidents of the United States, Administration of Ronald Reagan, 1983 (March 23), 443.

19. *Report to the Congress on the Strategic Defense Initiative*, Department of Defense (June 1986), IV–2.

20. Remarks by Senator Joseph R. Biden, Jr., to the National Press Club, September 10, 1986, printed in the *Congressional Record*, September 17, 1986, 99th Cong., 2d sess., S12729; Representative George E. Brown, Jr., quoted in *National Journal*, October 25, 1986, 2545.

21. John Walcott, "Approach to Arms Control Combines Missile Reductions, Work on Defense," *The Wall Street Journal*, October 20, 1986.

22. Michael Mandelbaum and Strobe Talbott, "Reykjavík and Beyond," *Foreign Affairs* (Winter 1986/87), 235.

23. Angelo M. Codevilla, "How SDI Is Being Undone From Within," *Commentary*, May 1986, 27.

24. Senator Albert Gore, *Congressional Record*, May 20, 1986, 99th Cong., 2d sess., S6165.

25. *Department of Defense Appropriations for 1987*, 616–17, 634.

26. Kemp, "The Politics of SDI," 28; *Congressional Quarterly*, January 25, 1986, 146.

27. David C. Morrison, "Shooting Down Star Wars," *National Journal*, October 25, 1986, 2544.

28. Public Papers of the Presidents of the United States, Administration of Ronald Reagan, 1986 (August 6), 1053.

29. *National Defense Authorization Act for Fiscal Year 1987*, 450.

30. *Department of Defense Appropriations Bill, 1987*, 333.

31. Joseph S. Nye and James A. Schear, "SDI: A Lever We Should Use," *The Washington Post*, December 15, 1986, A15.

32. John Noble Wilford, "Threat to Nation's Lead in Space Is Seen in Lack of Guiding Policy," *The New York Times*, December 30, 1986, A1.

Part Three

IS SDI DESIRABLE?

8

SOVIET POLICY TOWARD BMD AND SDI

Bruce Parrott

THE CENTRAL ISSUES

Paradoxically, although the Strategic Defense Initiative (SDI) is meant to cope with the strategic threat from the Soviet Union, the recent American debate over SDI has devoted little systematic attention to the Soviet dimension of the problem. Despite the existence of a substantial body of pertinent Western scholarship, the public discussion of SDI has given only sporadic attention to Soviet views and policies toward ballistic missile defense (BMD).[1] A number of U.S. officials, omitting the Soviet perspective entirely or assuming that Soviet policy is already permanently fixed, have implicitly discounted the need to consider possible Soviet responses to U.S. strategic undertakings. More wisely, other observers have examined Soviet policy options, but by focusing on the specific military programs the USSR has already begun or might begin in response to the U.S. SDI program, they have neglected the vital question of how BMD fits into broader Soviet conceptions of international politics and military strategy. The commentators who have actually pursued this question, however, have frequently been so eager to use Soviet statements as ammunition in the American debate over SDI that they have made little effort to distinguish Soviet propaganda from real Soviet beliefs.

The failure to devote sustained attention to the Soviet approach to ballistic missile defense is a critical deficiency of the Western public debate over U.S. policy and may lead Western policymakers to make serious misjudgments. For instance, U.S. officials, relying on Soviet

This chapter is expanded in *The Soviet Union and Ballistic Missile Defense* (Boulder, Colo.: Westview Press with The Johns Hopkins Foreign Policy Institute, SAIS, 1987). The author wishes to express his appreciation to Anne Herr for her assistance in preparing this article.

doctrinal statements drawn from the the 1960s rather than from later years, have suggested that the USSR is already committed to deploying its own large-scale BMD system, whatever the United States may do.[2] Such ahistorical analyses of Soviet military doctrine invite anachronistic evaluations of current Soviet intentions and may obscure the interaction between U.S. and Soviet strategic decisions. In addition, a narrow focus on Soviet military options neglects the nonmilitary factors that may exert a decisive influence on Soviet policy toward strategic defense. Just as important, a "grab bag" approach to Soviet sources runs the risk of mistaking minority Soviet views for established policy. Only careful sifting can distinguish the strands of Soviet policy discourse and differentiate statements of policy from propaganda.

Distinguishing real from feigned Soviet beliefs is no easy matter, and Western observers of Soviet military affairs differ over how to balance Soviet public statements against such observable Soviet behavior as weapons tests and deployments. This chapter assumes that both Soviet words and deeds are indispensable data for understanding Soviet conduct. Soviet weapons programs must be carefully analyzed to discern Soviet military capabilities and the possible range of Soviet strategic intentions. But Soviet statements must also be studied to understand the frequent cases in which these "hard" data do not resolve questions about underlying Soviet aims. The further ahead we try to see, the less conclusive becomes the evidence derived from existing Soviet military programs. In the long run, Western analysts must ask not simply, "What can the Soviets now do militarily?" but "What are the Soviets determined to be able to do in the future?"

Observers pondering this question can learn much from Soviet speeches and writings. Although the USSR often disseminates misleading propaganda, the party Politburo must explain its policies not only to foreign and domestic publics but also to other members of the elite, who must understand those policies if they are to implement them.[3] Even speeches and articles that are widely distributed at home and abroad frequently contain guidelines to policy, although they are commonly stated in veiled terms. In addition, the regime issues many specialized books and periodicals, including foreign-policy and military journals, which are intended primarily for members of the domestic elite and which shed more light on operational Soviet policy than do mass-circulation publications. By comparing these sources with the contents of military writings prepared solely for the confidential use of Soviet officers (such as the General Staff journal *Military Thought*), Western analysts can further refine their understanding of Soviet strategic thinking—thinking that, on the whole, has been mirrored in the specialized published literature.[4] Finally, the views expressed in Soviet publications sometimes contradict one another and occasionally spark open polemics, which can give outside observers further insight into the real issues occupying the attention of Soviet decisionmakers.

The remainder of this chapter is divided into five sections. First the chapter surveys Soviet views of the superpowers' shifting geopolitical relationship and BMD's impact on the relationship. Next it summarizes the evolution of Soviet policies toward Soviet BMD and the introduction of weapons into space. Turning from the international to the domestic context, the chapter then sketches the resource allocation debate that will affect future Soviet decisions on strategic defense and space systems. After outlining possible Soviet responses to SDI, it draws some lessons for U.S. policy.

SOVIET VIEWS OF THE GEOPOLITICAL CONTEXT

To understand Soviet policies toward ballistic missile defense and the military uses of space, we must examine the overall context in which the Soviets evaluate trends in military relations between the superpowers. In contrast to the humanitarian justifications of the Strategic Defense Initiative advanced by American proponents, Soviet observers regard SDI as a disturbing extension of a superpower competition that has recently taken several turns inimical to Soviet security.

For the Soviets, the dominant international fact of the 1980s has been the geopolitical resurgence of the United States and the decline of superpower détente. Although the greater assertiveness of the United States strikes many Western observers as an inevitable consequence of Soviet actions during the 1970s, it has perplexed Soviet policymakers, who believed during the 1970s that they had discovered a workable formula for managing relations with the United States through a mix of military power, arms negotiations, and diplomacy.

Introduced under Brezhnev's aegis about 1970, this two-track approach generated intermittent conflict within the Soviet leadership for the next four or five years. The tensions centered on the wisdom of the détente policy, including the pursuit of arms control, and on the Soviet decision in the mid-1970s to slow the growth of the military budget.[5] But during the second half of the decade a policy consensus took hold, and there were few signs of serious dissatisfaction within the military and foreign-policy establishments. Based on a combination of cooperation and competition with the West, Brezhnev's dual-track approach helped consolidate the USSR's standing as a military superpower and produced major geopolitical gains in Europe and the Third World. It also satisfied the basic institutional and budgetary interests of most components of the elite.

By the end of the decade, however, Soviet decisionmakers discovered that the dual-track formula for East-West détente was in danger of failure. During the late 1970s U.S. political circles, unaware of the slowdown in the growth of Soviet defense spending and alarmed by such Soviet Third World ventures as Angola and Afghanistan, became increasingly critical of the USSR. In the second half of the Carter presidency the U.S. defense budget, after declining for several years in real terms, began to increase. Moreover, in 1980 Ronald Reagan was elected president on a party platform that explicitly called for the United States to regain military superiority over the USSR. While demonstrating little interest in arms-control negotiations, the Reagan administration enunciated an ambitious new military strategy and sharply accelerated the U.S. military buildup begun under president Carter. Although the Reagan administration has cautiously avoided direct military confrontations with the USSR, its military policies and rhetoric have prompted Soviet officials to ask whether the Soviet policies of the 1970s were mistaken and whether the possibility of Soviet-American détente has been irretrievably lost.

Since about 1980 Soviet ruling circles have engaged in a running debate over this question. Virtually all Soviet officials and specialists have accepted the notion that the United States is striving to reestablish military superiority over the USSR and that the danger of war has increased. However, Soviet officials and foreign-policy experts have disagreed about the depth of U.S. hostility and about whether the Reagan administration and its successors can sustain the push for superiority over the long haul.[6]

Guided by these contrasting diagnoses of the current situation, Soviet decisionmakers have favored divergent policy prescriptions. Broadly speaking, during the 1980s all party general secretaries have expressed the belief that superpower détente can be revived and have favored an approach calculated to deflect the United States onto a less assertive path through political rather than military means.[7] A minority within the leadership, however, has dissented from this position. Backed by high-level party leaders, elements of the military high command have suggested that Soviet-American détente cannot be reestablished on acceptable terms, leaving no alternative except prolonged political hostility and an all-out arms race with the United States. Voiced with particular vehemence by Marshal Nikolai Ogarkov, such hard-line sentiments have gathered enough support within the elite that the Soviet proponents of détente have felt compelled to reply publicly, issuing condemnations of "well-intentioned skeptics" that clearly have been directed at domestic critics.[8]

The recurrence and timing of such polemics demonstrate that on certain crucial matters a hard-line minority has lobbied vigorously for a more confrontational policy toward the United States. To date, more measured views have usually prevailed, but during the past five years the critique of established policy from Soviet conservatives has put such leaders as Brezhnev and Chernenko on the political defensive, and similar pressures are now being exerted on Gorbachev.[9] As shown below, the question of how to respond to SDI has been one of the sources of internal political friction.

Despite their disagreements about how to cope with U.S. assertiveness, virtually all Soviet observers agree that the United States has embarked on a major drive to overturn the international position that the USSR attained through immense effort, and they view the Strategic Defense Initiative as part of that campaign. On the political level, SDI symbolizes a threat to the USSR's standing as a superpower—a position which depends heavily on military instrumentalities and the possession of weapons comparable to those of the United States. At the same time, SDI constitutes a challenge to the technological dynamism of the Soviet system, because it raises serious questions about whether the Soviet economy will prove able to generate the types of technology now being incorporated into Western military plans.

In the final analysis, of course, the urgency of responding to these political and economic challenges stems from the potential military implications of SDI. More than any other U.S. military program, SDI exemplifies an emerging U.S. effort to outflank the USSR by shifting the arms competition to new realms of technology.[10] The strategic uncertainties introduced by SDI seem especially large to Soviet observers because they are convinced that SDI will be used not to supplant but to augment other U.S. weapons programs.[11]

For this reason, virtually all Soviet commentators dismiss U.S. assurances that a deployed SDI system would be strictly defensive. Iury Andropov contended that SDI and the U.S. offensive buildup were complementary policies designed to give the United States a capacity to launch with impunity a disarming nuclear strike against the USSR.[12] Soviet strategists find little consolation in the notion that the United States probably cannot devise a "leak proof" BMD system, because they believe that possession of a less-than-perfect BMD system could still influence the conduct of U.S. decisionmakers pondering whether to use nuclear weapons against the USSR or to try to fight a limited nuclear war in Europe.

Consistent with their skepticism that SDI is intended to serve a defensive purpose, the Soviets claim that a U.S. BMD system will ultimately be designed to strike not only Soviet missiles in flight but

Soviet terrestrial targets. While cautioning against the offensive potential of exotic weapons technologies whose feasibility will not be ascertainable for many years, Soviet experts have also warned that orbiting battle stations might be fitted with special nuclear missiles able to deliver rapid attacks on enemy targets below. In other words, space-based systems might become direct, rather than indirect, instruments of a U.S. first strike against the USSR—one that could be delivered almost instantaneously, without the ten to thirty minutes' warning currently afforded by the trajectories of submarine-launched ballistic missiles (SLBMs) and intercontinental ballistic missiles (ICBMs).[13]

For all these reasons, Soviet policymakers contend that a competition in building and deploying large BMD systems will mark a watershed in Soviet-American relations. Gorbachev, for instance, has warned that the introduction of weapons into space would mark "a qualitatively new jump in the arms race which would inevitably lead to the disappearance of the very concept of strategic stability" and could cause a "universal catastrophy" through human miscalculation or technical malfunction.[14]

Although Soviet officials often try to erect political obstacles to American weapons programs through such public condemnations, it is improbable that Gorbachev's exceptionally stark statements about the implications of SDI are simply public posturing designed to serve Soviet negotiating tactics. This explanation fails to explain the absence of such categorical expressions of alarm before the deployment of other American weapons, such as the Pershing II, which the Soviets have similarly opposed. It also fails to consider the negative political impact of such statements on the Soviet bargaining position at superpower arms talks. Expressions of apprehension may elicit supportive responses from relatively sympathetic Western groups opposed to SDI. But they may also encourage the Reagan administration's more assertive members to press forward with SDI and the more moderate members to demand radical Soviet military concessions in exchange for limiting the program.[15] Taken together with the other evidence of Soviet soul-searching and apprehension cited above, the special force of Soviet pronouncements on SDI suggests that Soviet policymakers do indeed view the program as the potential harbinger of a new era of unstable strategic relations with the United States and that they regard this prospect with genuine alarm.

SOVIET POLICY TOWARD SOVIET BMD
AND THE MILITARY USES OF SPACE

The USSR's policies toward the use of BMD and space-based weapons for its own defense have been shaped by long-standing strategic goals.

Historically, the Soviet leadership has been cautious about risking wars that might endanger the Soviet system. At the same time, it has striven to build a military establishment capable of deterring attack and defeating any state that launches a war against the USSR. A further goal, grounded in memories of the Nazi invasion, has been to minimize war damage to Soviet society by building strong strategic defenses. Finally, in the past two decades the regime has sought to avoid engaging potential enemies in arms races militarily disadvantageous to the USSR.

At the practical level, however, such strategic goals are often incompatible with one another, and policymakers must decide which to give primacy. They must, for instance, weigh a desire for forces capable of protecting their homeland and defeating the enemy against a desire to avoid forms of arms competition that may ultimately put them at a military disadvantage. Soviet analysts and officials concerned with BMD have sometimes disagreed about such matters, and the prevailing Soviet attitude toward BMD has changed over time.

As late as the mid-1960s Soviet proponents of BMD were inclined to treat mutual nuclear vulnerability as a destabilizing factor. An effective antiballistic missile (ABM) system would "substantially increase the stability of mutual deterrence," they maintained, while a policy of deterrence through mutual vulnerability would leave the Soviet Union dependent "on the goodwill of the other side."[16] In a 1967 news conference prime minister Aleksei Kosygin reportedly suggested that, in contrast to offensive arms, ABM weaponry does not give rise to international tensions but "prevents attack" and is intended "not to kill people, but to save human lives." As printed by *Pravda*, Kosygin's remarks also clearly implied that ABM systems would not contribute to the arms race by fueling an action-reaction cycle between defensive and offensive weaponry.[17] The party newspaper's inaccurate rendering of Kosygin's tape-recorded remarks suggests that by 1967 the Soviet debate over entering Soviet-American talks on strategic arms had become intertwined with an internal debate over BMD.[18] But publication of the emended text also shows that the prevailing view continued to be that BMD was beneficial rather than harmful.

Pravda's account reflected the assumptions guiding the postwar construction of the Soviet air defense network. During the 1950s the USSR developed and deployed an extensive system of interceptor aircraft and surface-to-air missiles (SAMs) to counter enemy bombers; in the mid-1950s the government also began to develop its first BMD components. In the early 1960s it started to build a ring of defensive missiles intended, perhaps, to protect the city of Leningrad against enemy ballistic missiles, and within a few more years it began building a different system, unsophisticated and extremely costly, to provide antimissile defense for the Moscow region.

During the first half of the 1960s the Soviet predisposition to favor ballistic missile defenses was reinforced by the strong sense of technological optimism fostered under Khrushchev. Despite occasional dissenting voices, Soviet commentators appeared confident that effective ABM systems could be devised and that the Soviet Union was better able to develop such a system than was the United States.[19] In a period when Soviet socialism seemed technologically more dynamic than American capitalism, the question of diplomatic control over the progress of military weaponry was not pressing. In any event, at the time there were few encouraging precedents for negotiated limitations on the deployment of new weapons.

By the final third of the 1960s Soviet judgments about BMD's impact on superpower relations during crises began to change markedly. As the USSR came closer to strategic parity, Soviet decisionmakers became more confident of the ability of Soviet offensive weapons to deter a U.S. nuclear strike and began to downgrade the value of BMD, accepting that it might undermine crisis stability.[20] While the theory of mutual assured destruction remained ideologically unpalatable, Soviet officials did publicly acknowledge the existence of mutual strategic vulnerability, and privately some spokesmen went so far as to state that ABM systems, if deployed, might be destabilizing because they would undermine the certainty of devastating retaliation against a first strike.[21] As the 1970s progressed these views began to be expressed publicly.[22]

Soviet views on the connection between BMD systems and the arms race also shifted. In 1972 two of the Soviet SALT negotiators approvingly cited the view that without large BMD systems there would be no stimulus for either side to develop more powerful offensive systems.[23] Most Soviet officials did not endorse such a categorical view of the action-reaction cycle, which excluded the possibility that one cause of the arms race could be the contest for advantage between the offensive weapons of each side. But numerous officials, such as Politburo member N. V. Podgornyi, deputy foreign minister Kuznetsov, and minister of defense Grechko, did suggest that a limit on ABM systems would slow the pace of the superpower weapons competition, although Grechko was also obviously reluctant to cut back Soviet R and D in this realm.[24]

The post-1967 appraisal of the role of ABM weaponry in the arms race was linked to new Soviet doubts about the feasibility of building effective missile defenses. In the mid-1960s a debate flared up in the confidential General Staff journal *Military Thought*, in which spokesmen for the National Air Defense Forces pushed for the construction of a large ABM system.[25] Because of the difficulty of destroying enemy ballistic missiles through preemptive attack, they contended, Soviet offensive nuclear forces could not defend the USSR against U.S. missiles; only a Soviet ABM system could perform this function.[26] Other officers, including officers of the Strategic Rocket Forces (SRF), voiced doubt about the feasibility of building a Soviet ABM system and advocated countering U.S. strategic power through a further expansion of Soviet offensive forces. One military analysis of U.S. ABM programs, for example, strongly implied that an effective Soviet ABM system could not be built for some time.[27]

This internal debate was linked to the Soviet decision to halt construction of some of the BMD installations being built around Moscow. Although eight interceptor missile complexes were originally planned for the Moscow BMD system, only four were finally completed.[28] This failure to follow through with full deployment plans indicates that domestic critics had a tangible effect on Soviet BMD policy. By the end of the 1960s most Soviet military spokesmen, even senior air defense commanders, began to describe the mission of the National Air Defense Forces as defense against enemy aircraft only.[29]

The shift in BMD policy was influenced by an economic reappraisal that questioned Soviet capacities for technological innovation and carried worrisome implications for the USSR's ability to compete with the United States in developing missile defenses. During the late 1960s some Soviet economists reached the unorthodox conclusion that the USSR was less technologically dynamic than the West, and as this view filtered into the outlook of foreign-policy specialists and some Politburo members, it influenced Soviet decisions about weapons policy and the desirability of beginning arms limitation talks. In these internal deliberations the proponents of arms talks were usually pessimistic about the Soviet technological future, whereas the opponents of negotiation remained optimistic about the USSR's prospects of surpassing the West technologically.[30] The pessimistic view of Soviet technological capabilities was a large factor in the decisions to begin strategic arms negotiations and subsequently to sign the Anti-Ballistic Missile Treaty limiting Soviet BMD activities. Another contributing factor was the Soviet leadership's increasing acknowledgment of the existence of Western officials and influential social groups interested in slowing the arms race.[31]

These far-reaching changes in Soviet attitudes toward BMD sparked considerable internal disagreement, particularly after Brezhnev took steps to slow the growth of the overall military budget in the mid-1970s. One key document in the dispute over BMD was a book written by the military writer V. M. Bondarenko and published in mid-1976 by the Ministry of Defense. In contrast to Brezhnev's growing stress on the security benefits of East-West détente, Bondarenko emphasized the persisting influence of "reactionary" Western circles and warned that the threat of overwhelming retaliation might not deter a Western nuclear attack on the USSR. Bondarenko also asserted that defenses against ballistic missiles would sooner or later become feasible and lobbied for stepped-up R and D in this area.[32] Plainly he did not share the prevailing Soviet assumption that the West had a rational self-interest in survival and that the continuing vulnerability of the superpowers contributed to the military stability of their relationship.

The proposal to work toward an extensive Soviet BMD system engendered resistance as well as support within the military establishment. Air defense reviewers of Bondarenko's book were unqualifiedly enthusiastic, but officers from other military branches expressed reservations that were strengthened by the proposal's infringement on their own institutional missions, especially that of the Strategic Rocket Forces. In a book published at the same time as Bondarenko's, a group of air defense theorists headed by G. V. Zimin argued for an expanded BMD system and implicitly denigrated the role of the SRF. Asserting that Soviet counterforce strikes would be insufficient to protect the USSR from devastation or to ensure military success, the writers contended that a defense capable of destroying incoming ballistic missiles and enemy satellites was necessary.[33]

Probably under political pressure, this open doctrinal challenge was quickly muted. Marshal P. F. Batitskii, the commander of the National Air Defense Forces, who had contributed a foreword implicitly endorsing the Zimin book's arguments for BMD, soon published a pamphlet that studiously ignored any mention of Western ballistic missiles or the need to counter them.[34] Apparently, however, this about-face came too late. By 1978 Batitskii had been demoted from his post and the budget of the National Air Defense Forces had begun to shrink, along with the budget of the Strategic Rocket Forces.[35]

The doctrinal challenge over BMD thus failed to affect basic Soviet policy toward strategic defense, although it may have exerted a narrower influence on policy toward R and D on antisatellite (ASAT) and BMD weapons. In 1976, when the challenge occurred, work on a primitive ASAT system, suspended at the end of 1971, was resumed. Nevertheless, ASAT weapons evidently still ranked as a low Soviet priority, and the renewed suspension of ASAT tests in 1978 in conjunction with bilateral ASAT talks showed that the Soviet government was not committed to a rapid upgrading of the largely ineffectual system it had already created or to the rapid development of a more effective alternative. In early 1980, when the United States declined to continue the talks in response to the Soviet invasion of Afghanistan, the USSR again resumed ASAT tests, but in June 1982 it once more suspended the tests and soon declared an ASAT test moratorium that remained in effect at the start of 1987.[36]

In the late 1970s and early 1980s the Soviets undertook a significant modernization of the Moscow ABM system and pursued an active program of BMD research and development. Although the USSR refrained from raising the number of ABM interceptors in the Moscow ABM system to the ceiling permitted by the ABM treaty, it did develop new transportable phased-array radars and improved types of interceptor missiles. In the late 1970s it also began to upgrade the Moscow ABM system by replacing Galosh launchers with the new interceptors and upgrading the system's radar capacities. In addition, during the early 1980s the regime began developing an antitactical ballistic missile (ATBM) designed for use against missiles with shorter ranges than SLBMs and ICBMs.[37] Meanwhile the Kremlin has maintained an extensive R and D effort that reportedly involves more than 10,000 specialists and is intended to reveal the feasibility of applying high-energy lasers and particle beams to ballistic missile defense.[38]

The upgrading of the Moscow system has improved only marginally the Soviets' ability to defend their capital from U.S. missiles and would have little utility against a massive U.S. strategic attack.[39] While in theory Soviet ATBMs may ultimately have some limited effectiveness against U.S. SLBMs, this would also depend on developing a sophisticated radar and control system, and ATBMs would still be ineffective against ICBM reentry vehicles, which are less vulnerable than SLBM reentry vehicles. The prospects for obtaining advantageous results from Soviet research into exotic BMD technologies also remain uncertain. Soviet work on ground-based lasers and space-based particle beam weapons faces serious technical obstacles. Administration claims that the Soviet Union leads the United States in research on space-based BMD are misleading. The USSR, though abreast of the United States in directed-energy research, trails in many complementary technologies that would be essential to transform directed-energy weapons into effective BMD systems.[40]

In the early 1980s the balance of Soviet elite opinion toward BMD was little changed. Soviet commentators suggested that the risk of nuclear devastation was an effective deterrent against Western nuclear attack, and they claimed that the introduction of BMD systems would undermine the stability of the superpower relationship.[41] They also reiterated that the absence of BMD systems helps to curb the arms race.

Perhaps the most vital question for Soviet decisionmakers was the technological feasibility of building an effective BMD system. In a book published before the unveiling of SDI, two Soviet specialists argued that effective strategic defenses were unlikely to be devised in the foreseeable future.[42] This view encountered reservations among some important military figures, such as Marshal Ogarkov. In 1978 Ogarkov, hinting that he favored more vigorous BMD research, dismissed the idea that the spiral between offensive and defensive weapons could be halted. The historical alternation in the development of offensive and defensive armaments, he asserted, demonstrated that an effective defense against ballistic missiles would eventually appear.[43] Ogarkov's statement was not a call for the immediate development and deployment of an extensive Soviet BMD system, because it implied that offensive weapons still enjoyed a decisive advantage over defensive systems. But it clearly suggested that in the long run this advantage might not be preserved.

Although unsettling, the announcement of SDI does not appear to have persuaded most military men that the USSR should immediately commit itself to develop a large BMD system of its own. Ogarkov, in theory the senior military policymaker most likely to push for such a system, warned stridently in 1984 against the West's stepped-up development of sophisticated weapons based on "new physical principles" and asserted that Soviet counterprograms must immediately be launched. However, he does not appear to have favored a commitment to build an extensive Soviet BMD system. Although in 1984 he emphasized the threat from exotic technologies, he highlighted the threat from sophisticated Western conventional weapons systems and did not refer to SDI.[44] In a pamphlet published the following year, he omitted his earlier observation that the offense-defense dialectic applies to nuclear missiles, thereby implicitly downgrading the case for giving high priority to Soviet BMD programs. Although oblique evidence suggests that the Air Defense Forces may have wished to proceed with a major expansion of the Soviet BMD system,[45] this opinion was probably not shared by most senior officers and certainly not by the party leadership as a whole.

Some Western observers have pointed to the construction of a large phased-array radar (LPAR) in central Siberia at Abalakovo, near Krasnoyarsk, as evidence of a Soviet intention to build an extensive BMD system. While the siting and orientation of the radar manifestly violate the ABM treaty, construction of the installation does not prove that the USSR has decided to deploy an extensive BMD. A detailed CIA appraisal suggests that the radar has the wrong technical characteristics to serve as an ABM engagement radar. It will operate on the wrong frequencies, is pointed too near to the horizon, and covers too narrow an approach corridor to play such a role effectively.[46] A more plausible explanation is that the Soviet government built the radar to fill a gap in its early-warning radar coverage, which it had already decided to upgrade by building peripheral LPARs at Pechora and other sites permitted under the terms of the ABM treaty. Although the optimal site for such a network would have been on the east coast of the Soviet Union, this probably would have required two rather than one of these extremely expensive radars and would have posed forbidding construction problems. Moreover, because the Abalakovo site provides as much warning of an attack from the east as the other LPARs would furnish of an attack from other directions, it constitutes an integral part of a perimeter of early-warning radars centered on Moscow even though it is not located on the Soviet border. This interpretation is buttressed by the belief of most Western experts that the other Soviet LPARs begun after the start of the construction at Abalakovo conform to the requirements of the ABM treaty.[47]

Taken as a whole, the evidence indicates that, despite minority views within the elite, the Soviet leadership wishes to avoid a commitment to build a large BMD system. Even if we accept the dubious proposition that Ogarkov privately championed such a step, his demotion in 1984 was hardly a vote of confidence in the idea. More to the point, the leadership is now far more pessimistic about Soviet technological capacities vis-à-vis the West than it was twenty years ago. Gorbachev has presented a much franker and more worrisome picture of Soviet economic troubles than Brezhnev ever did, and his pronouncements show a deep respect for U.S. capacities for technological innovation. Finally, an acute shortage of resources is already generating serious domestic strains, and the elite has compelling economic reasons to try to avoid an all-out competition in BMD and space weaponry.

THE RESOURCE ALLOCATION DEBATE
AND SOVIET BMD DECISIONS

The party chiefs have resisted a commitment to develop and deploy an extensive BMD because they fear the economic as well as the military consequences of competition in this realm. In recent years the central fact of the Soviet domestic scene has been the further deterioration of the country's economic performance. While the economy is not in danger of collapse, it is growing slowly, and the rate of expansion may decline still more in the coming years. Moreover, the USSR's weaknesses in promoting advanced technologies are increasingly evident. Because of the shortage of resources Soviet economic strategists find themselves under mounting pressures that are already formidable even in the absence of an all-out race in BMD.

To understand these pressures, we must glance back at the budgetary decisions of the mid-1970s. Around 1974, after a decade of rapid Soviet military expansion, the Brezhnev leadership adjusted its spending priorities. The causes of this adjustment included a more positive appraisal of the Soviet security situation and possibly the need to deal with internal economic problems that were beginning to worsen. By comparison with the preceding ten years, the regime's new resource allocation formula entailed slower growth of both military spending and economic investment and a continuation of the relatively high growth rate of popular consumption.[48]

Since about 1980, however, the declining performance of the domestic economy and the sharp deterioration of superpower relations have undermined this formula for resource allocation. To a far greater extent than during the past two decades, Soviet economic planners now face fundamental conflicts among divergent needs to invest in future economic growth, to improve consumer welfare, and to spend more on military programs.

In the 1980s these hard budgetary choices have sparked serious debates within the Soviet political elite. Well before President Reagan announced SDI, signs of controversy over the level of Soviet military spending appeared. Backed by a Politburo faction that probably included G. V. Romanov and V. V. Shcherbitskii, Marshal Ogarkov and other professional officers urged that military spending be sharply increased.[49] By contrast, Brezhnev and such top-level allies as Konstantin Chernenko resisted a drastic increase in military spending. Instead, prompted partly by fears of a Soviet domestic upheaval like that in Poland, they advocated high priority for the consumer sectors.[50] Meanwhile, yet another group within the elite argued for a sharp rise of economic investment, especially in heavy industry.[51]

The resistance of the dominant Politburo coalition to demands for a jump in military spending sparked new objections from senior officers. Shortly after becoming general secretary, Chernenko explicitly rejected a proposal for a special public campaign to support a larger military effort and instead focused attention on the needs of agriculture and consumer welfare. Ogarkov responded with a hard-hitting warning that Western military programs were proceeding at a breakneck pace and that failure to respond promptly would be "a serious error" which would undermine Soviet security.[52] Nonetheless, Chernenko spurned such advice and told a meeting of military servicemen that the Soviet regime was doing "everything" required to ensure peaceful relations with the West.[53] In the 1980s open clashes of this kind have provoked sharp tensions in Soviet civil-military relations, and they clearly contributed to the decision in the fall of 1984 to demote Ogarkov.

The controversy over priorities has encompassed not only the standard forms of economic resources but also the orientation of the national R and D effort. In 1980–81 Brezhnev, calling for negotiated restraints on the creation of "qualitatively new" types of weapons, demanded that Soviet military R and D programs make a greater contribution to civilian needs and instituted an administrative review that apparently tried to implement this injunction.[54] By contrast, Ogarkov and some other military men argued for the acceleration of military R and D, particularly work on novel weapons.[55] Near the end of 1982 Brezhnev met with the military high command and grudgingly acknowledged a need to step up military R and D programs, although not military production; but members of the officer corps have continued to press for a further enlargement of the military share of R and D.[56]

The object lesson of Ogarkov's demotion has made the champions of military spending more cautious but has not eliminated tensions over the size of the defense budget. Gorbachev's ambitious targets for the rapid growth of investments have intensified short-term demands on resources and have strengthened the temptation to divert inputs earmarked for military spending.[57] The new general secretary has shown little inclination to underwrite a drastic expansion of the defense effort. Rather, he has asserted that the USSR's future depends on accelerating the economy's growth and expanding its high-technology sectors.[58] In response, some officers have begun pressing for a stronger commitment to military needs, forcing Gorbachev to reassure "many of our people" that the USSR is not falling behind the United States militarily.[59] One recent manifestation of this pressure was the publication of an article by Ogarkov reiterating the importance of increasing high-technology weaponry.[60]

Such tensions shed important light on the connections between Gorbachev's economic strategy and the task of countering SDI. A number of Western analysts have suggested that Gorbachev's emphasis on strengthening the economy's advanced sectors has won widespread military support because it offers a ready-made prescription for matching the United States in a long-term competition in BMD and other sophisticated weapons systems. Struck by the apparent fit between the challenge of SDI and the campaign to modernize high-technology sectors of the economy, a few Western scholars have suggested that Gorbachev secretly welcomes SDI as a means of forcing through the drastic domestic economic reform he desires.[61]

However, the creation of a space-based BMD and the promotion of general economic modernization are incompatible goals, and the Soviet response to SDI is not a simple by-product of Gorbachev's domestic political agenda. Although economic modernization is indispensable for faster Soviet progress in developing space-based defenses, a crash campaign to match U.S. advances in this field will complicate and quite possibly defeat the modernization effort. The party is plainly striving to invigorate several branches of scientific research that would be necessary to compete with the United States in space-based BMD. But even if the programs of basic research necessary for an expanded BMD program and for general economic modernization prove more or less compatible, the requirements of the two goals will diverge as the development and engineering of BMD components consume a mounting share of the R and D resources essential for revitalizing the economy as a whole.[62]

Moreover, in the longer run SDI poses a direct threat to economic modernization. Even if the regime develops satisfactory prototypes of the necessary BMD components, it will face an enormous drain on conventional economic resources when the time comes to manufacture and deploy the system. Most knowledgeable Western economists believe that the USSR lacks the investment resources to fulfill Gorbachev's targets for economic growth, and some foresee an impending conflict between the need for extensive civilian investment and the need to begin renovating the defense industries at the end of the 1980s.[63] It is virtually certain that this shortage of resources cannot be overcome in time to shoulder an exponential increase in BMD production and deployment costs in the 1990s. Since Gorbachev has a realistic prospect of remaining general secretary well into the next century, he has every incentive to avoid the tremendous pressures that a commitment to an extensive BMD would put on the political system and on him personally.

Scarcely less important than the costs of BMD to civilian programs are the costs to other military programs. In a period of constrained growth of military budgets, a substantial share of the R and D and economic resources allocated to BMD will have to be taken from the programs of the other military services. Soviet observers are aware of the revolution in computer and microelectronic technology spreading through all parts of the Western armed forces, and there are already signs of disagreement over the priority to be assigned to the missions of the various Soviet armed services.[64] Under these conditions the Air Defense Forces may champion the development and deployment of a large BMD system, but other services will probably resist the idea, and interservice rivalries are likely to have a sizable impact on Soviet decisions. Some military observers have already expressed oblique differences over whether SDI or trends in intermediate-range nuclear forces (INF) and conventional forces constitute the most threatening Western military programs. As the debate becomes more intense, civilian opponents of a large Soviet BMD system will enjoy a substantial advantage if they have part of the military establishment on their side.

There are thus strong internal forces working against a Soviet decision to enter into an all-out race with the United States in BMD technology.

This, in turn, will influence the ways in which the Soviets respond to the further evolution of the U.S. SDI program.

SOVIET RESPONSES TO THE
STRATEGIC DEFENSE INITIATIVE

Since the United States will probably deploy an enlarged BMD system no sooner than the mid-1990s and the USSR is already experiencing serious resource strains, Moscow's preferred response is to counter SDI through energetic diplomacy meant to produce strengthened arms limitations. On the one hand, the Soviets are trying to use direct contacts and more flexible arms-control proposals to convince U.S. policymakers that SDI should be restricted. On the other, they are striving through public diplomacy to generate pressure on administration officials who resist this idea. Only if political approaches fail will the party leadership turn to major new military deployments as the chief method of countering the U.S. strategic defense program. At the same time, however, this accent on negotiation and political maneuver is encountering internal Soviet resistance that will probably limit the additional military concessions Gorbachev can make in arms talks. In combination with U.S. field tests and deadlines posed by the Soviet military procurement cycle, conservative uneasiness will gradually increase pressures within the elite for a shift from a predominantly political to a predominantly military response to SDI.

The USSR's initial reaction to the announcement of SDI was swift. In March 1983, immediately after President Reagan unveiled the program, general secretary Andropov launched the anti-SDI campaign with a hard-hitting speech. In August the Soviet delegation to the United Nations tabled the draft of a multilateral treaty prohibiting the use of force in outer space and from space against the earth. Not simply a political improvisation, the draft embodied several features of a similar treaty that the USSR had submitted to the UN two years earlier, but it widened the proposed coverage to prohibit air-launched and ground-based ASAT systems as well. Shortly afterward, Andropov announced a moratorium on Soviet ASAT tests and promised that it would be observed as long as the United States refrained from further tests of its own ASAT system.[65]

The issue of how to respond to SDI soon became entangled with the other military questions facing Moscow and provoked internal discord. The announcement of SDI came in the midst of the Soviet political struggle to block the deployment of U.S. INF missiles in Europe, and when the deployments began, the USSR broke off Soviet-American negotiations over INF and strategic arms limitations. During 1984, however, it became apparent that such leaders as Chernenko were eager to return to the bargaining table, partly in order to take up the issue of SDI, whereas others, such as Romanov, felt that the USSR should continue to demand a Western commitment to roll back the INF deployments before negotiations were renewed.[66] Nearly a year passed between Chernenko's first attempt to resume negotiations and the Soviet offer that led to a new cycle of arms-control talks, which got under way without any INF rollbacks. The decision to pursue a new round of negotiations clearly provoked serious disagreement within the Soviet leadership, and it was resolved at the same time as Marshal Ogarkov was demoted to a lower military post.[67]

In January 1985 the United States and the USSR announced that the new cycle of negotiations would be conducted at Geneva in three parallel sets of talks, dealing respectively with strategic offensive, intermediate offensive, and space weapons. The agreement to hold new talks papered over fundamental Soviet-American differences on the relationship between offensive and defensive arms limitations, and parts of the Reagan administration continued to oppose the linkage sought by the Soviets between new restrictions on offensive weapons and on SDI. In the first half of 1985, as the depth of the persisting gap between the Soviet and U.S. positions became evident, there were further hints of internal controversy on the Soviet side, as Ogarkov and other military leaders warned that Soviet security should not be jeopardized.[68]

These events shed some light on the evolution of Soviet policy since the Geneva talks got under way in March 1985. In his first months as general secretary, Gorbachev adopted a rather hard public line, twice suggesting that the negotiations might be broken off if the United States failed to agree to linkage between limits on SDI and on offensive nuclear arms.[69] After forcing Romanov, his leading conservative rival, out of the Politburo, Gorbachev began to show more flexibility. In July he confirmed that he had agreed to a summit meeting with President Reagan in the fall and announced that a five-month moratorium on Soviet nuclear tests would begin in August. These steps coincided with signs that Gorbachev was seeking to limit the growth of Soviet military spending.[70]

At the same time, Gorbachev attempted to take advantage of differences within the NATO alliance to impede SDI. On balance, this attempt proved unsuccessful, as the Reagan administration persuaded most of the major West European governments to support, or at least not to oppose, the first phase of the program. But even if the Soviet attempt to turn Europe against SDI yields better results in the future, this effort can play no more than a subordinate role in the campaign against SDI, because West European attitudes are not decisive for the continuation of the program. During the controversy over the prospective

U.S. INF deployments, the Soviet propaganda campaign in Western Europe had a real chance of eliciting a European decision that would have blocked the deployments. In contrast, even if West European governments firmly oppose SDI, the United States can proceed to develop and deploy the system.

For this reason, the Soviet Union has recently concentrated on encouraging domestic U.S. opposition to SDI and convincing U.S. policymakers to conclude a new arms agreement restricting BMD. Although a few Western analysts have suggested that the frustrations of dealing with the Reagan administration may prompt Gorbachev to shift to a "Eurocentric" foreign policy that downgrades the priority of Soviet-American relations, U.S. military power and the overriding importance of SDI dictate that Soviet diplomacy must continue to center on the United States. Time pressure sharpens the need to deal directly with the United States. In order to be prepared to deploy adequate countermeasures to U.S. BMD seven to ten years in the future, Soviet policymakers must soon begin making difficult strategic and economic decisions. To avoid the adoption of expensive military programs, Gorbachev must elicit a change of U.S. policy within, perhaps, two or three years.

To augment the political campaign against SDI, in October 1985 Soviet negotiators put forward a new arms-control proposal that entailed major substantative concessions, as well as provisions manifestly unacceptable to the United States. The offer called for 50 percent reductions in strategic weapons and vehicles, including subceilings that would necessitate sizable cuts in the Soviet ICBM force and considerably reduce the Soviet advantage in ICBM throw weight. This concession, however, was predicated on the prohibition of all SDI research (as well as development and field testing) and on the inclusion of U.S. INF and other forward-based forces in the category of "strategic" weapons.[71]

At the November summit with President Reagan, Gorbachev tried again to extract a U.S. agreement to negotiate restrictions on SDI, but the United States refused to acquiesce, and the final communiqué issued by the two sides presented a statement of general principles rather than any concrete agreements. Nonetheless, in his report on the summit, Gorbachev described the meeting as a political milestone. The Soviet leader underscored the importance of the statement of principles adopted at the summit, particularly the leaders' mutual disavowal of the pursuit of military superiority, and he went out of his way to rebut the notion that the meeting had been useless or premature.[72] Obviously he viewed the summit as part of an urgent political struggle to defeat SDI, and he appeared to be trying to persuade persons who doubted that it had been as successful and significant as he claimed.

Important officials were manifestly skeptical. Politburo member Shcherbitskii, for instance, remarked pointedly that the Reagan administration still intended to pursue military superiority and that possibilities for reaching a common understanding with the United States on fundamental questions of arms control "do not exist."[73] Although Gorbachev had previously indicated that it might be possible to decouple SDI from an agreement on intermediate-range nuclear forces, Shcherbitskii appeared to be registering opposition to any move in this direction. His skepticism was echoed in the statements of some military commentators, who highlighted the U.S. failure to follow the Soviet lead by adopting moratoriums on ASAT and nuclear weapons tests.[74] These internal differences help explain why at the end of 1985 Western observers found the Soviet position on the INF-SDI linkage ambiguous.[75]

In January 1986 Gorbachev redoubled the campaign against SDI and injected additional, novel elements into the Soviet arms-control posture. Bidding to wrest the vision of a nuclear-free world from the proponents of SDI, he unveiled a sweeping proposal for the elimination of nuclear arms by the year 2000 and announced a renewal of the Soviet moratorium on nuclear test explosions. Softening the previous Soviet stance, the proposal called for the British and French nuclear arsenals to be frozen rather than cut. Although ambiguity about the SDI-INF linkage remained, the package also echoed Gorbachev's past hints that the two issues might be decoupled—a hint he explicitly confirmed soon afterward.[76]

In addition, in May Soviet negotiators acknowledged that they would accept SDI research as part of a new set of limits on BMD but would seek to reinforce the ABM treaty limitations on the field testing and deployment of an SDI system. They also sought a new agreement under which both sides would be bound not to withdraw from the treaty for a minimum of fifteen to twenty years.[77] By delaying SDI field tests for at least ten years, this would substantially slow the program, perhaps ultimately halting it, and would provide a cushion against a possible U.S. "breakout" in BMD before Soviet military countermeasures could be implemented.

As an aid to countering SDI through far-reaching arms-control proposals and test moratoriums, Gorbachev has sought to make Soviet diplomacy more flexible. A joint Soviet-American nuclear test moratorium would benefit the USSR by hampering the development of U.S. offensive nuclear forces and some of the more promising SDI technologies, but the first year of persistent Soviet effort failed to maneuver the Reagan administration into accepting the moratorium. Apparently the hope of achieving this goal was one of Gorbachev's motives for engineering a drastic shake-up of the Soviet diplomatic corps in mid-1986. The shake-up, which strengthened Party Secretary Dobrynin's control of foreign policy, was reportedly intended to make Soviet diplomacy more agile and dispel the image of intransigence from which it had long suffered in the West.[78]

Soviet military men, however, have had doubts about the utility of diplomatic gestures and apparently resisted the nuclear test moratorium on the grounds that its continuation would harm Soviet weapons programs. Evidence for this proposition comes both from Soviet statements and from improbable delays in renewals of the moratorium, which was extended several times during 1986. Early in 1986 Marshal Akhromeev, hinting that he was dissatisfied, remarked that unilateral steps such as the test moratorium were "not endless."[79] Three days after Gorbachev announced the May renewal, one proponent of the extension commented that "we prolonged our moratorium, but I am not at all convinced that our military comrades are particularly happy about this." About the same time Dobrynin, in a discussion of the moratorium implying that the extension had met internal resistance, referred to the need for "a certain daring" and to "fierce collisions, sharp discussions, and painful disagreements" that had arisen in implementing the new Soviet approach to international affairs.[80] Moreover, an additional extension in late August was announced about two weeks after the previous phase had lapsed and well after the anniversary of the U.S. bombing of Hiroshima, thereby sacrificing the sort of propaganda opportunity that had prompted the Soviets to announce the original moratorium on the eve of the Hiroshima anniversary in 1985. The most plausible explanation is that some members of the elite tried unsuccessfully to block the August renewal on the grounds that the political benefits were not worth the military costs. Whether the Soviet Union fulfills its December 1986 promise to resume nuclear testing immediately after the first U.S. test in 1987 will be an additional index of elite sentiment on such trade-offs.

Evidently, members of the military and political leadership have also opposed other aspects of Gorbachev's approach to arms control. About the same time that Soviet negotiators in Geneva offered further concessions on offensive nuclear arms in exchange for limits on SDI, an article by Dobrynin, rebutting opponents of disarmament, hinted at the existence of internal opposition to reductions in offensive nuclear weapons.[81] In view of an earlier assertion by Akhromeev that the preservation of peace hinged on increasing the USSR's military might, an unprecedented call by Dobrynin for the creation of civilian centers of military-political expertise inside the Soviet Union suggests that the party secretary was taking issue with Soviet officers who had expressed doubts about Soviet proposals for drastic reductions in offensive nuclear arms.[82]

Conflicting Soviet views of how to manage the military competition with the United States may help account for Soviet conduct at the Reykjavík meeting between Gorbachev and Reagan in the fall of 1986. At the meeting the Soviet delegates presented a comprehensive arms-control proposal and made major concessions, offering an unprecedented "zero-zero" trade that would eliminate all the SS-20 missiles targeted on Europe. However, they demanded that the United States agree to postpone testing of SDI components for a least ten years and took the position that limitations on SDI were a precondition for agreement not only on strategic but on intermediate-range nuclear forces. They thereby reversed their offer of almost a year's standing to decouple INF from SDI.

The recoupling of INF and SDI may conceivably have been a policy option, worked out long before the Reykjavík meeting, to arouse Western hopes for an INF agreement and then place the onus for any failure on the Reagan administration's refusal to limit SDI. Alternatively, it may have been a last-minute policy shift occasioned by internal Soviet dissatisfaction with Gorbachev's sweeping arms-control offers. After the meeting one Soviet commentator indicated that Marshal Akhromeev, the chief Soviet military representative at Reykjavík, had resisted Gorbachev's proposals to eliminate nuclear missiles, and Gorbachev's own remarks implied that there was top-level disagreement over the Soviet negotiating position.[83]

Whatever the precise explanation of the shifts in the Soviet position at Reykjavík, Gorbachev will almost certainly continue to hold out the possibility of another superpower summit and will try to use this prospect as a political lever to induce changes in the American position on SDI. He is unlikely to slow the pace of arms-control negotiations in the hope that the next administration will be easier to deal with. He and his supporters fear the political momentum that SDI may acquire, particularly now that SDI proponents within the U.S. Congress and Department of Defense are attempting to "lock in" the program by adopting a commitment to phased deployment starting in the early 1990s. Moreover, the beginning of the new U.S. administration will coincide with the preparation of the Thirteenth Soviet Five-Year Plan, and it might prove difficult to reach an arms-control accord with a new administration in time for it to affect major Soviet decisions about the level of military research and production for the period 1991–95. Finally, during the late 1980s the United States is scheduled to begin field tests that, from the Soviet standpoint, will clearly contravene the ABM treaty and will increase the pressure for major new Soviet weapons programs.[84]

Gorbachev thus has two to three years in which to find an effective political response to SDI; after that time, under a mounting sense of urgency, Soviet policymakers are likely to focus increasingly on military responses.

In theory, Soviet decisionmakers might adopt any of several political approaches to SDI. One alternative is to demand limits on SDI as a precondition for continued arms-control negotiations, thereby increasing the political pressure on the Reagan administration to restrict the program unilaterally. However, such an approach failed to defeat the U.S. INF deployments and is at odds with Gorbachev's preference for diplomatic flexibility and maneuver. By creating a more confrontational atmosphere, it could increase public support for defense spending in the United States; it would also strengthen the Soviet military's case for an immediate surge in Soviet defense outlays.

A second alternative is to accept the need for negotiations but to persist in refusing to limit offensive nuclear arms without a U.S. agreement to restrict SDI. This would help allay the concerns of Soviet conservatives and would demonstrate the seriousness of Soviet concern about SDI. But this position, too, would make the USSR look less flexible in the eyes of the American public, and it might not achieve the apparent Soviet goal of eliciting West European pressure to sacrifice SDI in exchange for INF reductions.[85]

A third alternative is to reverse field and follow through with the decoupling of INF from SDI. Reaching an agreement on INF would demonstrate that the Soviet Union is serious about arms control, but it could weaken the Western opposition to SDI by fostering an impression that the USSR might ultimately accept limits on strategic offensive weapons as well without obtaining restrictions on SDI.

A fourth alternative, to accept limits on offensive strategic arms without new restrictions on SDI, is unlikely to occur. Unless Soviet negotiators can ensure that BMD systems will continue to be restricted, the fear of SDI will lead them to resist such cuts more strongly than in the past because ballistic missile forces would be a necessary means for countering a future large U.S. BMD system. Moreover, an agreement to limit strategic offenses without limits on SDI would be nearly impossible to justify to members of the Soviet national-security establishment and would probably intensify demands for the USSR to accelerate the development and deployment of its own BMD system.

Finally, the Soviets might consider negotiating a controlled introduction of BMD systems on both sides. One option would be to negotiate the deployment of ground-based point defenses in both countries but to prohibit the deployment of space-based systems. This approach could prove advantageous to the Soviet Union, if accepted by the United

States, because it would foreclose U.S. deployment of space-based BMD systems, which the Soviets clearly regard as more destabilizing than ground-based systems.[86] It offers a further advantage because the USSR is considerably stronger relative to the United States in ground-based than in space-based BMD technologies. Nevertheless, such an approach would be extremely expensive and suffers from a key political deficiency. By implicitly admitting the value of BMD, it would undermine the Soviet political campaign against SDI. Yet the U.S. champions of SDI would be extremely unlikely to settle for terminal-phase defenses alone, which would require them to abandon the dream of defending the U.S. population and might well shift the net advantage from parallel BMD deployments in favor of the USSR.

Even more remote is the possibility of a negotiated transition to space-based BMD systems, which presupposes either that the Soviets and Americans deploy their defensive systems in step with one another or that they prevent the lack of simultaneous deployment from unleashing an unregulated competition in strategic weapons. Historically, however, the superpowers have not deployed new types of weapons, such as ICBMs or MIRVs, at precisely the same time, and these asynchronous deployments have been a major spur to the arms race. Because space-based weapons will take an exceptionally long period to develop and will be extraordinarily complex, timing will be an even more serious problem in this case. No less significant, the complexity and untestability of the deployed systems will make it extremely difficult to agree on what components will give each side a comparable BMD capability at any given stage of the transition.

Since the United States leads in most of the technologies that will be required for space-based weapons, it might in theory cope with these difficulties by slowing the SDI program to match Soviet progress or by sharing U.S. SDI technology with the USSR. However, the USSR will never gamble its security on the goodwill of the Reagan administration, which has waged a vigorous struggle to restrict Soviet acquisition of other technologies having far less military significance, or on the goodwill of the unknown future administrations whose backing would be required to carry out such a policy. Rather, the Soviet leaders will prepare militarily to overcome an enlarged U.S. BMD system.

If the U.S. commitment to SDI still seems firm in the late 1980s, the first Soviet military response is likely to be to develop and prepare to deploy effective and relatively inexpensive defense-suppression weaponry that could attack a space-based BMD system directly, either from space or from the earth. The timing of such a program would be important because it could undermine the claim that the USSR opposes the militarization of space and is not working toward space-based defenses of its own. If the Soviets have not already done so, they will certainly accelerate the laboratory research and development programs required for more effective space-launched ASAT weapons and may also step up development work on ground-based lasers for this purpose. At present, large-scale testing of such weapons is unlikely to begin before the end of the 1980s; but if officials favoring military responses gain greater influence, it could start sooner.

If SDI moves further along the road from research to deployment, Soviet policymakers will have to decide whether to expand their offensive nuclear arsenal or to create an extensive BMD system of their own, and they are already jockeying over which response would be preferable. Gorbachev appears to favor offensive over defensive programs. Apprehensive that the costs of matching the U.S. military buildup could injure the economy and harm Soviet national security in the process, he has stressed that the USSR would find a relatively inexpensive and "asymmetrical" response to SDI.[87] Some officials, however, seem more prepared to try to match SDI with a large Soviet BMD system. Shcherbitskii has implied that the Soviet response would include an extensive Soviet BMD, and Marshal Akhromeev has promised that the USSR will deploy missile defenses as well as offensive countermeasures, even at the expense of economic revitalization.[88]

Despite pressures to respond to SDI with a large Soviet BMD, the USSR's first major military response will probably be to build an upgraded offensive strategic force powerful enough to overwhelm the planned U.S. system. General B. M. Shabanov, the principal overseer of weapons development and procurement at the Ministry of Defense, has indicated a preference for this course of action, and officers of the Strategic Rocket Forces and most other services will probably also support it.[89] The upgrading of offensive weaponry could take several forms, including the development of new penetration aids and decoys for offensive missiles, the deployment of decoy boosters without warheads, an increase in the number of fully armed missiles, and the development of fast-burn boosters able to degrade the capacity of a U.S. space-based BMD system. Depending on how the SDI program evolves, the Soviet offensive response may also involve accelerated production of cruise missiles and intercontinental bombers, since a BMD system alone would not protect against such threats.[90]

Budgetary pressures notwithstanding, such offensive improvements would be quite feasible. The Soviet program to modernize strategic offensive forces could be substantially accelerated, especially if the USSR elects not to observe the SALT II treaty limits, and by the mid-1990s the number of warheads could reach at least 21,000.[91] Thus, in considerably less time than the United States would require to deploy an

extensive BMD, Soviet strategic planners will have the option of increasing
the projected number of nuclear warheads targeted on the United States
by at least 60 percent. Here, too, the timing of steps to expand Soviet
strategic offensive forces could have a substantial impact on the Soviet
political campaign against SDI. If the U.S. government continues to
equivocate about its factual adherence to the SALT II ceilings, a public
Soviet decision to abandon the agreement and to expand offensive forces
could easily cripple the campaign by raising the specter in the United
States of a new "window of vulnerability." As far as possible, the Soviets
will probably try to have it both ways by beginning with countermeasures
that do not entail a breach of the SALT II ceilings and only later
intensifying the expansion of their offensive strategic arsenal.

Soviet and Western opponents of SDI sometimes claim that because
of the availability of such offensive countermeasures the USSR will
allow the United States to squander resources on developing the system
without seeking to create a comparable Soviet defense. This claim may
be rational from a technical standpoint, and it appeals to the opponents
of BMD in both East and West. It is, however, probably incorrect. If
the SDI program moves into the stages of field testing and design, the
USSR is nearly sure to accelerate BMD research and development with
the aim of ultimately deploying a similar system of its own. Despite
the likelihood that space-based BMD will prove only marginally effective,
Soviet force planners cannot afford to write off a weapon that might
conceivably radically alter the strategic balance and make their country
extraordinarily vulnerable to a U.S. attack. Historically, Western military
R and D has frequently surmounted formidable technical obstacles and
produced novel weapons that the USSR lacked. There is, moreover, a
genuine possibility that space-based weapons, even if they prove unable
to destroy large numbers of enemy missiles in flight, may ultimately
offer a new means of direct offensive attack against terrestrial targets.
The Soviets manifestly fear this possibility, and it will probably spur
them, reluctantly and with some delay, to seek to meet the continued
progress of SDI with a full-fledged effort to develop and deploy extensive
space weapons of their own. Each step along this path would inflict
progressively higher economic costs and political pressures on the Soviet
system, but there can be little doubt that in the absence of U.S. restraint
the Soviet leadership will launch and attempt to carry out such a
program.

U.S. POLICY AND THE FUTURE
OF THE SUPERPOWER ARMS COMPETITION

Broadly speaking, the Strategic Defense Initiative has four possible
justifications. SDI's proponents sometimes assert that the USSR is already

committed to building an extensive BMD system and that SDI is merely a U.S. effort to stay abreast of Soviet military progress. Alternatively, it is sometimes said that the United States can achieve greater security, for the USSR as well as for itself, by steering a reluctant Soviet regime into a world dominated by strategic defenses rather than by offensive nuclear weapons. Another alternative, rarely voiced in public but sometimes espoused in private, is that the United States can outstrip the USSR technologically and will therefore gain a decisive strategic advantage from an unregulated race in BMD and space-based weaponry. A contrasting justification is that SDI might be used as a bargaining chip to gain U.S. strategic benefits through tightened restrictions on Soviet offensive and defensive weapons.

Although wartime experiences and Soviet military doctrine predispose the USSR to favor strong strategic defenses, a careful examination of the evidence does not support the claim that the USSR is already committed to developing and deploying a large BMD system. Since the late 1960s most Soviet policymakers have recognized that the construction of such a system would entail major drawbacks including tremendous costs, the availability of inexpensive countermeasures, the likelihood that the United States would muster its superior technological capacities to win the resulting weapons competition even if the USSR initially took the lead, and the prospect that the mutual possession of space-based weapons might increase rather than decrease the chances of war between the superpowers.

Viewed in the light of Soviet discussions of BMD, Soviet weapons programs appear less ominous than abstract speculation might suggest. Over the past two decades the USSR has slowly developed a primitive ASAT capability, and it is conducting research on particle-beam and laser technology with potential applications to space weaponry. It is also continuing to deploy upgraded "gray area" surface-to-air antiaircraft missiles and is developing antitactical ballistic missiles. However, Soviet gray-area weapons do not appear to constitute calculated violations of the ABM treaty, and they will not produce a major improvement in the USSR's marginal capacity to defend against strategic missile attacks. Construction of the Abalakovo radar, the USSR's one clear violation of the treaty, was an aberration from the general pattern of Soviet treaty compliance. When completed, the radar will not substantially enhance the Soviet BMD capacity, and the Soviet LPARs begun since Abalakovo appear to satisfy treaty requirements.

On balance, the evidence examined in this chapter strongly suggests that the principal motivation for Soviet work on BMD and space weapons is to guard against the contingency of an unexpected technological breakthrough followed by a sudden U.S. deployment of an extensive BMD system. Most Soviet officials are more apprehensive than enthusiastic about the possible strategic consequences of new BMD weapons. If anything, the USSR today feels more trepidation about an unrestrained competition in BMD than it did twenty years ago, and there is no likelihood of a reversal of the superpowers' economic and technological fortunes sufficient to change this attitude during the next ten or fifteen years. Fearful of losing a race in space-based weapons, the USSR has taken such initiatives as the four-year moratorium on Soviet ASAT testing and the unilateral moratorium on nuclear test explosions. These measures, which entail genuine sacrifices in the development of Soviet military capacities, constitute an attempt to elicit a reciprocal U.S. decision against building an extensive BMD system. The United States thus has a real opportunity to prevent the deployment of any large BMD system, Soviet as well as American, for a long time.

Although the United States has such an option, SDI can still be justified if it will facilitate a cooperative superpower transition to a more secure world of space-based defenses. This alternative rationale rests on the critical assumption that the United States can persuade the USSR to follow a U.S. scenario involving fundamental changes in the military doctrines and weapons systems of both countries. This optimistic assumption, however, is extremely unlikely to be confirmed. Soviet military doctrine, for all its stress on strategic defense, has customarily put greater emphasis on maintaining powerful strategic offensive forces, and U.S. attempts to convince the Soviets to shift to a defense-dominated world are likely to founder on this offensive orientation.[92] The task will be all the harder because the United States is proposing a transition to a new category of weapons in which it possesses a large technological advantage and which the Soviets believe will eventually be utilized to bolster U.S. offensive forces rather than for strictly defensive purposes. Because the future capabilities of space-based weapons remain in the realm of speculation, negotiating an agreement on the functions and deployment of such armaments is likely to prove extraordinarily difficult and probably impossible.

Under these conditions an attempt to compel the USSR to accept a joint transition to space-based BMD is more likely to destroy nuclear arms control than to strengthen it. The evolution of the Soviet negotiating posture during the past two years suggests that the Soviets are now prepared to agree to major cuts in offensive arms. The record, however, also suggests that they will make such concessions only in exchange for strengthened curbs on BMD and space-based weapons. Without such curbs Soviet policymakers are extremely unlikely to agree to any limitations, not to mention reductions, of offensive strategic arms. Instead they will probably launch an accelerated drive to develop ASAT and other defense-suppression weapons and will drastically upgrade their strategic offensive forces while moving toward deployment of a large BMD system of their own.

This brings us to the third major rationale for SDI—the proposition that an unregulated race in space will enable the United States, through its superior technological prowess, to improve its security position vis-à-vis the Soviet Union. There can be no doubt that today the United States enjoys a substantial lead over the USSR in most fields of technology with potential military applications. Nor can there be any doubt that the United States, if it bends all its efforts to the task, will be able to deploy space-based defenses at any given level of effectiveness well before the USSR will. In the United States, however, the main impediment to the development of weapons is not technological but political. SDI has an extraordinarily long time horizon, and even if it proves feasible technically, future administrations may lack the determination or political power to carry it through. The Soviet Union, by contrast, is technologically weaker but politically dogged. The United States conceivably could pursue SDI long enough to provoke an enduring Soviet response but not long enough to bring the American program to fruition, and the outcome might well be a U.S. security situation more perilous than the one that exists today.

Even if the United States maintains SDI's momentum and rapidly deploys the resulting weapons, the ultimate consequences of space-based BMD will in all probability outweigh any shorter-term gains. As we try to imagine the future, we must beware of the soothing assumption that the strategic competition between the superpowers will cease once the United States deploys a space-based defense. The competition is virtually certain to continue at an accelerated pace, and this prospect demands that American policymakers ponder what may happen in the stages that follow U.S. BMD deployments. Although daunting, the prospect of a rapid expansion of the Soviet ballistic missile arsenal is but one of the possibilities requiring attention. Assuming that the United States enjoyed a monopoly on space weapons for the first decade or longer, how should this temporary advantage be weighed against the subsequent Soviet acquisition of similar weapons and the destabilizing effects this situation would produce? In particular, if BMD developments pave the way for powerful space-based weapons able to deliver direct strikes against the earth nearly instantaneously, would we wish the Soviet Union to acquire such weapons, and how would the mutual possession of such capabilities affect the likelihood of general war? Owing partly to the defensive rationale advanced for SDI, the recent American debate has scarcely broached, let alone answered, these vital strategic questions.

If such questions do not receive attention now, the development of BMD technology—Soviet as well as American—may decide them by default. Because of the different technical requirements of attacking enemy missiles in flight and attacking terrestrial targets, the deficiencies of Soviet technology may constitute a smaller barrier to the creation of offensive space weapons than to the creation of space-based BMD.[93] Despite the Soviet economic system's many technological flaws, Western analysts would be mistaken to assume that the USSR will prove unable, over the long run, to obtain and deploy weapons comparable to those devised in the United States. This judgment is not supported by the history of conventional weapons, of the atomic and hydrogen bombs, of ballistic missiles, or of MIRVs. Although correct in a narrow sense, Americans who celebrate only U.S. technological dynamism and superiority over the USSR reflect an outlook that future historians may judge to be as politically shortsighted as Nikita Khrushchev's triumphant proclamations of Soviet technological superiority in the 1950s. Over the long term, it is quite likely that the attempt to capitalize on U.S. technological superiority by deploying space-based weapons will lead to a strategic situation that will sharply reduce rather than increase U.S. military security.

If it is true that the United States has compelling reasons to prevent the introduction of weapons into space, then the main value of SDI is as a hedge against unpredictable Soviet behavior and as a bargaining chip in superpower arms negotiations. It follows that the United States should be prepared to scale down SDI and pursue further BMD research on a contingency basis only. For reasons of prudence, U.S. BMD research should not be entirely abandoned. As shown above, since the signing of the ABM treaty some influential Soviet officers have maintained that BMD will eventually become technologically feasible, and a few air defense officials have actively pushed for a decision to build such a system. Although this view has not been accepted by the top party leadership, it coincides with the long-standing Soviet enthusiasm for the general idea of strategic defense, and if the feasibility of BMD improved radically during the next decade or two, it might gain a more receptive hearing in Soviet ruling circles. The United States can best ensure that this does not occur by maintaining a limited program of laboratory research to maintain its lead in most of the technologies that might be employed in future BMD systems.

At the same time, the United States should quickly make use of the Soviet fear of SDI to strengthen existing limits on offensive as well as defensive armaments. In launching SDI the Reagan administration has created a bargaining chip of extraordinary value—if the administration will trade it. The offer to restrict SDI should be used to obtain major offensive nuclear cuts that reduce the size of the Soviet arsenal and that are structured to increase crisis stability. In addition to such reductions, the United States should pursue tighter restrictions on Soviet gray-area weapons. These restrictions should spell out clearer definitions of permissible and impermissible radar installations and impose tighter limits on Soviet SAM and ATBM programs. The Soviets may resist SAM limits because they face an increasing air-breathing threat from U.S. cruise missiles and from the Stealth bomber now under development. They may also resist limits on ATBMs, which they have developed largely as a defense against Pershing II missiles and which they are now preparing to deploy. Nevertheless, the threat posed by SDI is so large that the Soviets will probably make concessions on the SAM issue as well as on ATBMs, particularly if the superpowers reach an INF agreement providing for drastic reductions in the Pershing IIs. In exchange for Soviet offensive and defensive concessions the United States should reaffirm the principles of the ABM treaty and accept tighter definitions of critical treaty concepts, such as ABM testing and ABM components, as well as a longer period of notification of withdrawal from the treaty. This would reassure Soviet leaders and strategic planners that the United States does not intend to transform its own research findings into an extensive BMD system unless the USSR first embarks upon such a course. By making such an offer, the United States could avoid a paradoxical policy that threatens to stimulate the USSR to enlarge the very danger that U.S. policy is intended to reduce.

NOTES

1. Sayre Stevens, "The Soviet BMD Program," and Raymond L. Garthoff, "BMD and East-West Relations," in Ashton B. Carter and David N. Schwartz, eds., *Ballistic Missile Defense* (Washington, D.C.: The Brookings Institution, 1984), 182–220, 275–329; Mary C. FitzGerald, "The Other Side of SDI: What Does Moscow Say?" in Graham Vernon, ed., *Soviet Perceptions of War and Peace* (forthcoming); Mary C. FitzGerald, "The Soviet Military on SDI," *Soviet Armed Forces Review Annual* 10 (forthcoming); David Holloway, "The Strategic Defense Initiative and the Soviet Union," *Daedalus* 114, no. 3 (Summer 1985), 257–79; Stephen M. Meyer, "Soviet Strategic Programmes and the US SDI," *Survival,* (November/December 1985), 274–92; and Rebecca V. Strode, "Space-Based Lasers for Ballistic Missile Defense: Soviet Policy Options," in Keith B. Payne, ed., *Laser Weapons in Space: Policy and Doctrine* (Boulder, Colo.: Westview Press, 1983), 106–61. Useful earlier writings on Soviet strategic defense and military activities in space include Michael J. Deane, *The Role of Strategic Defense in Soviet Strategy* (Washington, D.C.: Advanced International Studies Institute, 1980); Lawrence Freedman, "The Soviet Union and 'Anti-Space Defence,'" *Survival,* no. 1 (January 1977); Stephen M. Meyer, "Anti-satellite Weapons and Arms

Control: Incentives and Disincentives from the Soviet and American Perspectives," *International Journal* (Summer 1981), 460–84; and Stephen M. Meyer, "Space and Soviet Military Planning," in William J. Durch, ed., *National Interests and the Military Use of Space* (Cambridge, Mass.: Ballinger Publishing Co., 1984).

2. *Soviet Strategic Defense Programs* (Washington, D.C.: U.S. Department of State, 1985), 5–7, and "Text of Reagan's Broadcast Address on Talks with Gorbachev in Iceland," *The New York Times*, October 14, 1986, A10; James M. McConnell, *Analyzing the Soviet Press—Spot Report No. 1: The Irrelevance Today of Sokolovskiy's Book 'Military Strategy'* (Washington, D.C.: Center for Naval Analyses, May 1985).

3. James M. McConnell, "Shifts in Soviet Views on the Proper Focus of Military Development," *World Politics* 37, no. 3 (April 1985), 319.

4. Raymond L. Garthoff, "Mutual Deterrence and Strategic Arms Limitation in Soviet Policy," *International Security* (Summer 1978), 117, 146.

5. Bruce Parrott, *Politics and Technology in the Soviet Union* (Cambridge, Mass.: MIT Press, 1983), 192–202, 242–43, 251–55; Grey Hodnett, "Ukrainian Politics and the Purge of Shelest," paper prepared for the annual meeting of the Midwest Slavic Conference, Ann Arbor, Michigan, May 5–7, 1977; Bruce Parrott, *The Soviet Union and Ballistic Missile Defense* (Boulder, Colo.: Westview Press with The Johns Hopkins Foreign Policy Institute, SAIS, 1987), 10.

6. See "Formirovanie voenno-politicheskoi strategii administratsii Reigana," *SShA: ekonomika, politika, ideologiia*, no. 5, 1982, 119–26, and no. 6, 1982, 119, 127, and Bruce Parrott, *The Politics of Soviet Defense Spending* (Bloomington, Ind.: Indiana University Press, forthcoming).

7. Bruce Parrott, "Soviet Policy toward the United States: A Fork in the Road?" *SAIS Review* 5, no. 1 (Winter-Spring 1985), 110–11 and passim.

8. E. Rybkin, "V. I. Lenin, KPSS ob imperializme kak postoiannom istochnike voennoi opasnosti," *Voenno-istoricheskii zhurnal*, no. 4, 1983, 3, 7–9.

9. Nikolai Ogarkov, "Na strazhe mirnogo truda," *Kommunist*, no. 10, 1981, 81–82, and "Zashchita sotsializma: opyt istorii i sovremennost'," *Krasnaia zvezda*, May 9, 1984, 2–3; A. A. Gromyko, "V. I. Lenin i vneshniaia politika Sovetskogo gosudarstva," *Kommunist*, no. 6, 1983, 11–33; Iu. Molchanov, "Razriadka: istoki i vozmozhnosti," *Kommunist*, no. 13, 1984, 109–10, 112.

10. A. Dobrynin, "Za bez"iadernyi mir, navstrechu XXI veku," *Kommunist*, no. 9, 1986, 24–25.

11. A. Dvoretskii, "Kosmos v planakh Pentagona," *Vestnik protivovozdushnoi oborony*, no. 7, 1983, 82.

12. Iu. V. Andropov, *Izbrannye rechi i stat'i*, 2d ed. (Moscow: Politizdat, 1983), 250–53; General-lieutenant I. Rudnev, "Usilenie agressivnosti voennoi doktriny SShA," *Zarubezhnoe voennoe obozrenie*, no. 6, 1985, 7–12.

13. Andropov, *Izbrannye rechi i stat'i*, 250–53; Yevgeni Velikhov, Roald Sagdeyev, and Andrei Kokoshin, *Weaponry in Space: The Dilemma of Security* (Moscow: Mir, 1986), 76.

14. FitzGerald, "The Soviet Military on SDI"; A. A. Arbatov, *Voenno-strategicheskii paritet i politika SShA* (Moscow: Politicheskaia Literatura, 1984), 235–36, as quoted in FitzGerald, "The Other Side of SDI"; "Doklad General'nogo sekretaria TsK KPSS deputata M. S. Gorbacheva," *Kommunist*, no. 17, 1985, 41.

15. Parrott, *The Soviet Union and Ballistic Missile Defense*, 19–21.

16. N. Talensky, "Anti-Missile Systems and Disarmament," *International Affairs*, no. 10 (October 1964), 18, as quoted in Garthoff, "BMD and East-West Relations," 293.

17. "Vazhnye problemy: Vystuplenie A. N. Kosygina pered angliiskimi i inostrannymi zhurnalistami," *Pravda*, February 11, 1967, 1, 3.

18. See Garthoff, "BMD and East-West Relations," 295–96. On the broader Soviet debate over the wisdom of entering SALT negotiations, see Parrott, *Politics and Technology in the Soviet Union*, 192–202.

19. Thomas Wolfe, *Soviet Strategy at the Crossroads* (Cambridge, Mass.: Harvard University Press, 1964), 190–93; Deane, *The Role of Strategic Defense in Soviet Strategy*, 25–28, 33–34.

20. Holloway, "The Strategic Defense Initiative and the Soviet Union," 259; V. D. Sokolovskiy, *Soviet Military Strategy*, 3d ed., edited by Harriet Fast Scott (New York: Crane, Russak & Company), 169–70, 258–59.

21. Garthoff, "Mutual Deterrence and Strategic Arms Limitation in Soviet Policy"; Robert L. Arnett, "Soviet Attitudes Towards Nuclear War: Do They Really Think They Can Win?" *Journal of Strategic Studies* 2, no. 2 (September 1979), 172–91.

22. Garthoff, "BMD and East-West Relations," 302.

23. O. Grinev and V. Pavlov, "Vazhnyi shag k obuzdaniiu gonki vooruzhenii," *Pravda*, June 22, 1972; Garthoff, "BMD and East-West Relations," 307.

24. "Vazhnyi vklad v ukreplenie mira i bezopasnosti," *Pravda*, September 30, 1972, 1–2; *Izvestiia*, August 24, 1972.

25. Colonel General of Aviation G. Zimin, "PVO Strany Troops in the Great Patriotic War," *Voennaia mysl'*, no. 5, 1965, CIA Foreign Press Digest 949, November 5, 1966, 116.

26. I. Zav'yalov, "An Answer to Opponents," *Voennaia mysl'*, no. 10, 1965, CIA Foreign Documents Division, no. 955, March 25, 1966, 53–54; Major General I. Anureyev, "Determining the Correlation of Forces in Terms of Nuclear Weapons," *Voennaia mysl'*, no. 6, 1967, CIA Foreign Press Digest 0112/68, July 11, 1968, 37–39.

27. V. Aleksandrov, "The Search for a Solution to the Problems of Antimissile Defense in the US," *Voennaia mysl'*, no. 9, 1965, CIA Foreign Press Digest 952, March 2, 1966, 19–20; Holloway, "The Strategic Defense Initiative and the Soviet Union," 259.

28. Stevens, "The Soviet BMD Program," 200–1.

29. Deane, *The Role of Strategic Defense in Soviet Strategy*, 52–55; Garthoff, "BMD and East-West Relations," 298–99, 313; P. F. Batitskii et al., *Voiska protivovozdushnoi oborony strany: istoricheskii ocherk* (Moscow: Voenizdat, 1968), 362, 370.

30. Parrott, *Politics and Technology in the Soviet Union*, 181–202; Colonel B. Trushin and Colonel M. Gladkov, "The Economic Foundation of the Military-Technical Policy of a Country," *Voennaia mysl'*, no. 12, 1968, CIA Foreign Press Digest 0102/69, November 3, 1969, 36–38.

31. Parrott, *Politics and Technology in the Soviet Union*, 194–98, 201–2, 232–36.

32. V. M. Bondarenko, *Sovremennaia nauka i razvitie voennogo dela* (Moscow: Voenizdat, 1976), 32, 41, 46–49, 62, 64, 130–32, 184.

33. Marshal of Aviation G. V. Zimin et al., *Razvitie protivovozdushnoi oborony* (Moscow: Voenizdat, 1976), 61–67, 87, 91–92, 100–102, 183–86, 191–92.

34. P. F. Batitskii, *Voiska protivovozdushnoi oborony strany* (Moscow: Znanie, 1977), 35, 42, 48, 50.

35. According to CIA estimates, spending for both the Strategic Rocket Forces and the National Air Defense Forces dropped in absolute terms after 1977. U.S. Congress, Joint Economic Committee, *Allocation of Resources in the Soviet Union and China—1984* (Washington, D.C.: GPO, 1985), 53–54.

36. Donald L. Hafner, "Averting a Brobdingnagian Skeet Shoot: Arms Control Measures for Anti-Satellite Weapons," *International Security* 5, no. 3 (Winter 1980–1981), 41–42; Robert Bowman, *Star Wars: A Defense Expert's Case Against the Strategic Defense Initiative* (Los Angeles, Calif.: Jeremy P. Tarcher, Inc., 1986), 16.

37. Stevens, "The Soviet BMD Program," 213–16.

38. *Soviet Strategic Defense Programs* (Washington, D.C.: U.S. Department of State, 1985), 12–16.

39. Holloway, "The Strategic Defense Initiative and the Soviet Union," 262.

40. Office of Technology Assessment, *Ballistic Missile Defense Technologies* (Washington, D.C.: GPO, 1985), 217–18; Walter Pincus, "U.S., Soviet at Odds on 'Star Wars,'" *The Washington Post*, September 30, 1985, A1, A4; B. Jeffrey Smith, "U.S. Tops Soviets in Key Weapons Technology," *Science*, May 7, 1986, 1063–64.

41. G. Trofimenko, "Voennaia strategiia SShA—orudie agressivnoi politiki," *SShA: ekonomika, politika, ideologiia*, no. 1, 1985, 12. See also L. Semeiko, "U opasnoi cherty," *Krasnaia zvezda*, January 23, 1986, 3.

42. V. I. Zamkovoi and M. N. Filatov, *Filosofiia agressii* (Alma-Ata: Kazakhstan, 1981), 197, 213–14, 230, 270, 276, 287, 303.

43. N. Ogarkov, "Voennaia nauka i zashchita sotsialisticheskogo otechestva," *Kommunist*, no. 7, 1978, 117.

44. "Zashchita sotsializma: opyt istorii i sovremennost'," 2–3.

45. Parrott, *The Soviet Union and Ballistic Missile Defense*, 41.

46. Michael R. Gordon, "CIA Is Skeptical that New Soviet Radar Is Part of an ABM Defense System," *National Journal*, March 9, 1985, 523–26.

47. Michael R. Gordon, "Soviet Building 2 Big Radars," *The New York Times*, August 16, 1986.

48. See Richard F. Kaufman, "Causes of the Slowdown in Soviet Defense," along with the commentaries on this article, in *Soviet Economy* 1, no. 1 (January–March 1985), 9–32, and U.S. Congress, Joint Economic Committee, *Allocation of Resources in the Soviet Union and China—1985* (Washington, D.C.: GPO, 1986), 101.

49. Ogarkov, "Na strazhe mirnogo truda," 81–82, 89–91.

50. Leonid Brezhnev, *Leninskim kursom*, VIII (Moscow: Politizdat, 1981), 469–73; *XXVI s"ezd KPSS: stenograficheskii otchet* (Moscow: Politizdat, 1981), I, 63; Konstantin Chernenko, "Leninskaia strategiia rukovodstva," *Kommunist*, no. 13, 1981, 11, 14.

51. G. Sorokin, "Intensifikatsiia i razvitie dvukh podrazdelenii obshchest-vennogo proizvodstva," *Planovoe khoziaistvo*, no. 5, 1982, 25–28.

52. *Krasnaia zvezda*, May 9, 1984, 2–3.

53. "Rech' tovarishcha K. U. Chernenko na vstreche s rabochimi moskovskogo metallurgicheskogo zavoda 'Serp i molot' 29 aprelia 1984 goda," 15–17, and "Po-leninski zhit', rabotat', borot'sia," *Kommunist*, no. 9, 1984, 4.

54. *XXVI s"ezd KPSS*, 43–44, 62; Parrott, *Politics and Technology in the Soviet Union*, 406n.

55. V. Ermanchenkov, "Deiatel'nost' KPSS po ukrepleniiu oboronosposob-nosti strany na sovremennom etape," *Kommunist Vooruzhennykh Sil*, no. 15, 1980, 68; Ogarkov, *Vsegda v gotovnosti k zashchite otechestva*, 30.

56. *Pravda*, October 28, 1982, 1; V. Bondarenko, "Edinaia nauchno-tekhni-cheskaia politika KPSS," *Kommunist Vooruzhennykh Sil*, no. 19, 1984, 14.

57. Jan Vanous and Bryan Roberts, "Time to Choose Between Tanks and Tractors: Why Gorbachev Must Come to the Negotiating Table or Face a Collapse of His Ambitious Modernization Program," *PlanEcon Report: Developments in the Economies of the Soviet Union and Eastern Europe* II, nos. 25–26, 1–16.

58. "Doklad General'nogo sekretaria TsK KPSS M. S. Gorbacheva," *Pravda*, April 24, 1985, 1.

59. "Programma Kommunisticheskoi partii Sovetskogo Soiuza (novaia re-daktsiia)," *Kommunist*, no. 16, 1985, 35; *XXVII s"ezd KPSS: stenograficheskii otchet* (Moscow: Politizdat, 1986), I, 595–96; "Rech' tovarishcha Gorbacheva M. S. na vstreche s trudiashchimisia goroda Tol'iatti," *Pravda*, April 9, 1986, 2.

60. Gary Lee, "Soviet Marshal Issues Call for High-Technology Arms," *The Washington Post*, October 28, 1986, A21.

61. Jerry Hough, "Soviet Interpretation and Response," in *Arms Control and the Strategic Defense Initiative: Three Perspectives*, Occasional Paper 36 (Muscatine, Iowa: The Stanley Foundation, October 1985), 7–12.

62. *Allocation of Resources in the Soviet Union and China—1985*, 53, 115; Robert Campbell, "Resource Stringency and the Civilian-Military Resource Allocation," unpublished paper, 15–16.

63. *Allocation of Resources in the Soviet Union and China—1985*, 9, 55–57, 118.

64. V. V. Lipaev and A. I. Potapov, "Programmnoe obespechenie dlia EVM voennogo naznacheniia," *SShA: ekonomika, politika, ideologiia*, no. 4, 1985, 113–18; Colonel S. Bartenev, "Vroven' s progressom ekonomiki, nauki, tekhniki," *Kommunist Vooruzhennykh Sil*, no. 5, 1983, 21; McConnell, *Analyzing the Soviet Press*, 2–3, 5–6, 10–11; William Odom, "Soviet Force Posture: Dilemmas and Decisions," *Problems of Communism* 34, no. 4 (July-August 1985), 8–11.

65. "Priem Iu. V. Andropovym amerikanskikh senatorov," *SShA: ekonomika, politika, ideologiia*, no. 10, 1983, 6. For the texts of the draft treaties, see Foreign Broadcast Information Service, *Daily Report: Soviet Union*, August 12, 1981, AA16–18, and U.S. Congress, Office of Technology Assessment, *Anti-Satellite Weapons, Countermeasures, and Arms Control* (Washington, D.C.: GPO, 1985), 145–46.

66. Parrott, *The Soviet Union and Ballistic Missile Defense*, 55–56.

67. Ibid.

68. S. Akhromeev, "Dogovor po PRO—pregrada na puti gonki strategi-cheskikh vooruzhenii," *Pravda*, June 14, 1985, 4; N. V. Ogarkov, *Istoriia uchit bditel'nosti* (Moscow: Voenizdat, 1985), 27–28, 32–33, 36.

69. "Doklad General'nogo sekretaria TsK KPSS M. S. Gorbacheva," 2; Dusko Doder, "Gorbachev Says Talks Could Collapse," *The Washington Post*, June 25, 1985, A32.

70. Dale R. Herspring, "The Soviet Military in the Aftermath of the 27th Party Congress," *Orbis* 30, no. 2 (Summer 1986), 311; Campbell, "Resource Stringency and the Civilian-Military Resource Allocation," 25–26.

71. Arnold L. Horelick and Edward L. Warner III, "U.S.-Soviet Nuclear Arms Control: The Next Phase," in Arnold L. Horelick, ed., *U.S.-Soviet Relations: The Next Phase* (Ithaca, N.Y.: Cornell University Press, 1986), 232–33, 245–46.

72. "Doklad General'nogo sekretaria TsK KPSS deputata M. S. Gorbacheva," 35–43.

73. "Rech' deputata V. V. Shcherbitskogo," *Izvestiia*, November 28, 1985, 3.

74. V. Pustov, "Zheneva: do i posle," *Krasnaia zvezda*, November 24, 1985, 3.

75. "U.S. Not Sure if Soviet Links Missile Accord to 'Star Wars,'" *The New York Times*, February 6, 1986, A10.

76. Parrott, *The Soviet Union and Ballistic Missile Defense*, 114n; *The New York Times*, February 8, 1986.

77. *The New York Times*, May 31, 1986; June 14, 1986; and June 17, 1986.

78. Alexander Rahr, "Winds of Change Hit Foreign Ministry," *Radio Liberty Research Bulletin*, RL 274/86, no. 30 (July 23, 1986), 1–10; Serge Schmemann, "Gorbachev Convenes Aides and Gives a Critique of Foreign Policy," *The New York Times*, May 24, 1986, 4.

79. Quoted in Herspring, "The Soviet Military in the Aftermath of the 27th Party Congress."

80. Television interview with Aleksandr Bovin, quoted in Bohdan Nahaylo, "The Soviet Military and the Kremlin's Moratorium on Nuclear Tests," *Radio Liberty Research Bulletin*, RL 381/86, no. 42 (October 15, 1986), 3; Dobrynin, "Za bez"iadernyi mir, navstrechu XXI veku," 25.

81. Dobrynin, "Za bez"iadernyi mir, navstrechu XXI veku," 19.

82. "Rech' deputata S. F. Akhromeeva," *Izvestiia*, November 28, 1985, 4; Dobrynin, "Za bez"iadernyi mir, navstrechu XXI veku," 26.

83. Interview with Valentin Falin, chief of the Novosti Press Agency, published in the Vienna *Kurier*, October 30, 1986, and reprinted in *FBIS Daily Report: Soviet Union*, October 31, 1986, R4–5; "Press-konferentsiia M. S. Gorbacheva," *Pravda*, October 14, 1986, 2. I am grateful to Dawn Mann for calling the Falin interview to my attention.

84. Thomas K. Longstreth, John E. Pike, and John B. Rhinelander, *The Impact of U.S. and Soviet Ballistic Missile Defense Programs on the ABM Treaty*, 3d ed. (Washington, D.C.: National Campaign to Save the ABM Treaty, 1985), 15, 18.

85. Karen DeYoung, "Soviet Union Loses Ground in Vienna," *The Washington Post*, November 7, 1986, A33.

86. TASS, October 17, 1986, in *FBIS Daily Report: Soviet Union*, October 21, 1986, AA14.

87. Philip Taubman, "Gorbachev Says Soviet Test Halt Is Again Extended," *The New York Times*, August 19, 1986, A1, A13; "Press-konferentsiia M. S. Gorbacheva," 2.

88. Don Oberdorfer, "Military Response Planned to 'Star Wars', Soviet Says," *The Washington Post*, March 8, 1985, A1; *Pravda*, June 14, 1985, 4. See also Philip Taubman, "Soviet Says Its Nuclear Ban Is Militarily Beneficial to U.S.," *The New York Times*, August 26, 1986, A4.

89. B. M. Shabanov in *Krasnaia zvezda*, November 14, 1985, 3.

90. John M. Collins, *U.S.-Soviet Military Balance 1980–1985* (Washington, D.C.: Pergamon-Brassey's, 1985), 55; Robert M. Gates and Lawrence K. Gershwin, "Soviet Strategic Force Developments: Testimony before a Joint Session of the Subcommittee on Strategic and Theater Nuclear Forces of the Senate Armed Services Committee and the Defense Subcommittee of the Senate Committee on Appropriations, June 26, 1985," (photocopy) 3–4.

91. According to the CIA, the deployment of 21,000 warheads "would require a substantially greater commitment of resources" but "is not a maximum [Soviet] effort." (Gates and Gershwin, "Soviet Strategic Force Developments," 4)

92. Meyer, "Soviet Strategic Programmes and the US SDI," 285.

93. One of the central problems of effective space-based BMD is to create an unprecedented information-processing capacity to identify and track large numbers of rapidly moving enemy missiles and destroy them very quickly. By contrast, terrestrial targets would be easier to target and could be subjected to a more sustained attack.

9

HEAVENLY GAINS
OR EARTHLY LOSSES?
TOWARD A BALANCE SHEET
FOR STRATEGIC DEFENSE

Richard K. Betts

Ah, but a man's reach should exceed his grasp,
Or what's a heaven for?
—Robert Browning,
Andrea del Sarto, 1855

O God, give us serenity to accept what cannot be changed, courage to change
what should be changed, and wisdom to distinguish the one from the other.
—Reinhold Niebuhr,
Prayer, 1934

The contrasting sentiments above should normally strike hardheaded strategists as pious or romantic bromides.[1] They bracket the problem of the debate over strategic defense, however, in some pithily apt ways. Like most of nuclear strategy, disputes about the Strategic Defense Initiative (SDI) are usually highly charged and often ethereal. At their best, arguments are based far more on theoretical principles and extrapolation than on empirical data; at their worst, they degenerate into retreats to dogma. The boundaries between idealism, fatalism, and realism in this debate are seldom clear. There is danger in the extremes of thinking on the question (the most ardent advocates of SDI are as naively insensitive to the constraints of political reality as are the most reckless unilateral disarmers), but there is often difficulty in distinguishing conclusions of analysis from premises of faith. Fanatical idealism can be as dangerous as helpless fatalism, but the crucial questions about strategic defense are all speculative, susceptible to discussion in terms of logic but not to very meaningful tests in advance of fateful decisions.

The most powerful argument for moving toward strategic defense is that however successful and stable mutual nuclear deterrence may have been so far, it cannot last forever and may not outlast the antagonism that keeps the superpowers in conflict. In a world of vulnerability to apocalyptic destruction, "a single serious malfunction cannot be tolerated," and strategic defense might "buy time for the alleviation and resolution of political differences."[2] Conversely, moves toward defense might as easily prolong the conflict, aggravate risks, and shake the stability of deterrence. (Deterrence and defense, of course, need not be stark alternatives but in some combinations could complement each other.)

Is the balance of terror something we cannot change and should accept with serenity, or is there a way out of deterrence, a change we should have the courage to make? SDI enthusiasts assume that the belief "that the only practical way to protect against destruction is to threaten retaliation in kind reflects not a permanent fact of technology but a choice of doctrine."[3] But where do we get the wisdom to know the difference between reasonable hope and naive faith in technical innovation or between prudent appreciation of the constraints of reality and premature resignation to them? The problem in trying to predict military possibilities is compounded by the interdependence of technological, economic, political, and diplomatic uncertainties.

That interdependence makes all simple statements about the future of strategic defense suspect. Much of the SDI debate consists of categorical assertions, which rarely consider trade-offs among more than two values. Yet most answers should be contingent on several variables, and they are matters of degree rather than "either/or" propositions. Many of the most important considerations are subjective matters of political perception and diplomatic maneuver. Since many of these are discussed in other chapters of this book, I will concentrate on a rationalistic view of the trade-offs. The number of interacting uncertainties are endless, but the crucial interdependencies can be grouped under three questions about prospective defense systems.

(1) *Effectiveness.* How well will any given system "work" at given tasks, and how sensitive will effectiveness be to potential adaptations in an adversary's offensive capability?
(2) *Symmetry.* Will the United States or the Soviet Union have a significant advantage in defense, or will both have comparable capabilities?

(3) *Opportunity Cost.* Since any dollar spent on SDI is a dollar not
spent on something else (or subtracted from taxes or national
debt), what other objectives will be compromised in order to
procure and sustain the defense?

The following sections will examine the principal elements that
should be considered in assessing each of these questions, although no
assessment is conclusive in isolation from any other. Unless otherwise
stated, analysis assumes that Soviet deployment of a defense system
beyond that allowed by the Anti-Ballistic Missile (ABM) Treaty is not
inevitable and that the USSR is not close to breaking out of the treaty.
This contradicts arguments by some alarmists who use the specter to
discredit arguments against SDI, but no firm evidence has been made
public to support either charge.[4]

My analysis is skeptical of both the pro-SDI zealots' arguments and
the anti-SDI curmudgeons'. Both tend to focus too intently on the issue
within the limits of the nuclear calculus alone. The curmudgeons overstate
the dangers of strategic defense to crisis stability in the narrow sense—
incentives to strike first for fear of being struck first. It is hard to argue
simultaneously, as some curmudgeons do, that SDI "will never work,"
but that it would be dangerous because the Russians would be scared
enough by it to mount a preventive attack. The zealots get too much
mileage out of the other sort of argument—that if SDI upsets the Russians
terribly, it cannot be bad for us. It is quite possible that an offense-
defense competition would more or less preserve an equilibrium of
vulnerability similar to what exists now, thus burdening both sides
economically while benefiting neither side militarily.

The balance of judgment, however, tilts toward a jaundiced view
of strategic defense investments because they imply a weakening of
security as a whole when opportunity costs for conventional defense
and deterrence are considered. When the U.S. Air Force long ago
succeeded, by an act of semantic imperialism, in co-opting the term
"strategic" and identifying it with specific sorts of nuclear capability[5]
(as if conventional forces had nothing to do with strategy), terminology
came to have a refractory effect on thinking. But except for the long-
shot eventuality of near-perfect defense of the United States combined
with sustained Soviet vulnerability to U.S. nuclear attack, nuclear forces
of all sorts are likely to remain far less strategic (in the proper Clau-
sewitzian sense) than is conventional military power. Thus the third
section below is the most important.

Since the conclusion of this chapter will be critical of the promise
of SDI, therefore, the reasons emphasized will be more hawkish than
dovish. This choice provides the stronger critical argument. Some dovish

concerns, however, still have merit. The fifth section will return to a discussion of the nuclear balance to explore how defenses might lose as much for security by complicating possibilities for negotiated solutions as they gain by providing unilateral improvements.

EFFECTIVENESS

How well a defense system "works" can be seen as a combination of performance in several dimensions:

1. *Breadth.* What classes of targets could a defense system cover—point or area targets or, more generally, military or civilian? (When not otherwise specified, "military" targets will refer to hardened intercontinental ballistic missiles [ICBMs] or command and control facilities or small areas such as airfields, and effectiveness against air-breathing vehicles will be assumed at least as great as against ballistic missiles. The latter point is not generally assumed by SDI proponents *or* opponents, and the implications of a return to offenses based on air-breathers can be interpreted either favorably or unfavorably.[6] It strains belief, however, that the technical problem of air defense would ultimately prove less malleable than that of destroying ballistic missiles.)

A defense covering civilian targets would change the strategic equation far more significantly than would point defense. If the West alone had such a defense, Soviet basic deterrence would be weakened, which would thus reinvigorate Western extended deterrence; if the Soviet Union also possessed such a system, the problems of the North Atlantic Treaty Organization (NATO) would become even greater than they have been so far. Alternatively, defense of offensive military capabilities would not overturn the recent configuration of deterrence but only reinforce it, and in some cases it would do so by creating a balance of retaliatory capacity that might also be achieved as easily by passive measures for protection (such as mobility and concealment) or by negotiated constraints on offensive capabilities.

2. *Leakage.* Against how large an attack could the defense protect a given target; that is, what are the percentage chances of intercepting all offensive warheads aimed at the target? A defense that is likely to knock down nine out of ten warheads aimed at each military target should be considered more effective than one that can exact the same attrition against warheads aimed at urban-industrial concentrations, since the greater value of cities makes it more economical for the enemy to "waste" ten or more warheads against those targets.

3. *Competitive efficiency.* How sensitive is effectiveness to changes in the offensive threat against a defense system; how great an effort would the enemy have to make to overcome the defense; and how

durable is cost-effectiveness over time? Paul Nitze, one of the administration's spokesmen, has endorsed cost-effectiveness at the margin as a necessary condition for a strategic defense.[7] If the increments of defense necessary to keep pace with the opponent's offense adjustments cost less than the additional offense, it should be attractive. It might still be attractive if the relative cost of defense is greater,[8] as long as the margin of difference is not wide. However, a defense that can be neutralized by enemy initiatives costing substantially less than the defense, and which can be completed soon after completion of the defense, should be unattractive. We certainly should not assume the primitive "action-reaction" model of arms competition. In the past, some nations' major initiatives have not provoked significant reaction, or countering action lagged so far behind that the initiating side enjoyed a long period of significant advantage.[9] Yet when contemplating commitment to huge expenditures, it would be no more wise to rest on the premise that there will *not* be a timely and effective reaction.

It is easier to envisage effective defense of military targets than effective defense of population. Military targets could capitalize on supporting passive protection (hardening, concealment, mobility) and could tolerate more leakage, and the physics of at least part of the defense system (such as ground-based interceptors) would be more conducive to covering points than large areas. In any case competitive efficiency is the most crucial dimension of effectiveness, since devising a defense against the current threat is only the necessary condition, not a sufficient one. The central question about maintaining a satisfactory "cost-exchange ratio" involves prospective countermeasures, and these are what critics cite as invalidating any comparisons between SDI and other daunting scientific challenges.[10]

The "anything is possible" argument for faith in SDI can also be turned on its head. If dismissing highly effective strategic defense as outlandish is as foolish as saying in 1902 that man would never fly, it would be equally foolish to assume that the Soviet Union could not devise a cheap means to circumvent whatever the United States produces. Some SDI proponents tend to cite critics as technologically defeatist for refusing to take seriously possibilities for defense that seem ridiculous while also dismissing arguments about countermeasures as unrealistic. This inconsistency is implied in a tongue-in-cheek suggestion that for boost-phase intercept (BPI), "The easiest approach would be to place a rapid-firing cannon right next to each Soviet silo and fire on the missile as it rises from it. But this system would be assuredly subject to rather effective countermeasures and therefore is not considered a viable system."[11]

Critical scientists' discussions of SDI countermeasures have been devastating. The 1984 study of the Office of Technology Assessment concluded, "For every defense concept proposed or imagined . . . a countermeasure has already been identified." The study also argued that most countermeasures are more feasible in terms of current technology than are the defense concepts themselves, that "the costs of the countermeasures can be estimated and shown to be relatively low, whereas the costs of the defense are unknown but seem likely to be high," and that technologies proposed for defense systems will also be effective for attacking the defense.[12]

A basic reason for greater sensitivity of a defense system is that it must cope with all potential counters, while an attacker can focus counterefforts against a defense already identified.[13] In addition, designs of defensive systems may also be "locked in" years in advance of deployment, giving an opponent more time to work on counters and further reducing the system's effective life span. Such design commitments would be very hard to keep completely secret in the United States, given the high level of political controversy over the issue, but might well be kept secret in the USSR. Thus the Soviet Union might be able to deploy countermeasures soon after an American defensive deployment, while the United States would not be as well positioned to respond promptly to a similar Soviet deployment. To hawks who fear that Moscow is laying the groundwork for a defensive breakout anyway, this consideration supports the case for expeditious U.S. movement to strategic defense; for doves who believe that the Soviets are sincere when they profess to want to save the ABM treaty, it argues against provoking them to give up on the treaty.

Defense supporters argue that the complexity of a deployed defense would prevent an enemy from negating it with simple counters because defensive redundancy would create difficulties for restoring confidence in the timing and consequences of an attack on the system. Complex defense "architectures give the aggressor problems similar to those he encounters from the triad of U.S. strategic forces which prevent him from being able to eliminate any one kind of force without warning the others."[14] Countermeasures "that could be effective against the first layer of defense may not be effective against the second or third layers."[15]

To the extent that the defense is meant to complicate the planning of an attack, these points have some merit. Otherwise, they are weakened by the fact that one particular layer of the prospective defense—the first, for boost-phase intercept—provides the crucial leverage for the whole system. Especially with defense suppression, most reasonable observers still believe the exchange ratio favors the offense.[16] As Peter Zimmerman notes, simple compounding of leakage rates from different layers of the defense obscures their interdependence, which may lead failure of one layer to swamp the others:

> Paradoxically, the high leverage of a layered defense is also the system's Achilles' Heel, easily exploitable by the offense. . . . [S]cenarios . . . are predicated on . . . an anti-Murphy's Law: "If anything can go wrong, it won't". . . . The layers of a defense will be so tightly linked that if the threat is increased by only 20 or 30 per cent, the defense will collapse in a classic display of the hazards of leveraging. Any incorporation of successful countermeasures against boost-phase interception will put the offense right back in nearly the same dominant position.[17]

The simplest Soviet way of coping with a deployed defense would be direct attack on the U.S. system (for example, with antisatellite [ASAT] weapons or space mines). The standard passive BPI countermeasures envisaged (jinking, fast-burning, coating or shielding, rotation, and proliferation of unarmed decoy boosters) would be expensive adjustments to the Soviet missile force but not nearly as expensive as the defense system itself.[18] Soviet spokesmen have discussed a large number of active and passive options for defeating SDI.[19] Unless one assumes an array of redundant BPI concepts grander than those yet discussed in public, and an uncharacteristically lethargic Soviet military establishment, the probability of a highly effective defense of population centers seems very low—something most SDI proponents concede. The issues then become how valuable a limited defense of cities or a more substantial defense of ICBMs might be and which side would benefit from an increase in uncertainty about the results of attack.

A defense of population that would marginally reduce likely casualties—for instance, by 10 to 20 percent—would be a useful hedge against the possibility of all-out war but would not plausibly affect the strength of deterrence. Decisionmakers' risk propensities are not likely to vary much if prospective fatalities fall from well over a hundred million to barely over a hundred million. If anticipated losses were cut from present levels by 50 percent or more, however, it might begin to affect some leaders' risk calculations—at least those of the high rollers.[20] In either case the opportunity cost of the defense system would be the prime consideration. The first alternative is a weak hedge against a low-probability event, and the second alternative is more substantial insurance against failure of deterrence. Is either one worth decreasing conventional military capacity, which might in turn slightly raise the odds that deterrence might fail?

The more developed arguments for SDI focus on the advantages of complicating a Soviet counterforce attack. There is little danger of a rational decision in Moscow to strike first against cities, since that "would be akin to a wanton terrorist act. It is precisely against such irrational acts that an exclusive reliance on deterrence would offer no protection at all."[21] Substantial leakage would be more tolerable in defending military as opposed to civilian targets because an attacker would want a high degree of confidence in the ability to minimize retaliation by the victim. Defenses of uncertain effectiveness would weaken that confidence more than no defenses at all—and an attacker's natural bias would be to overestimate the defense's effectiveness. The victim's option for preferential defense would also require further redundancy in the attacking force to preserve damage expectancy. Moreover, defenses for military targets would protect co-located civilians too, and if isolated military targets are less heavily defended than those in built-up areas, the enemy would be induced to focus on the isolated ones to increase the efficiency of the attack. This contrasts with SDI critics' arguments that defending military installations would increase the enemy's incentive to concentrate warheads on urban areas. "When we understand that the problem of protecting civilians is primarily the problem of dealing with collateral damage, it becomes clear that we do not need leakproof defenses to achieve useful results."[22]

The counterargument is that a cautious Soviet leadership that would be deterred by uncertainty will not decide to launch an attack anyway because great uncertainties already exist. Given the prospective survivability of at least several thousand U.S. warheads, one would have to presume a risk-prone or overconfident enemy that, rather than indulging in worst-case planning, overestimated its own offensive capacity and underestimated the effectiveness of the victim's defense.[23]

SDI critics often argue that highly effective defense is impossible because the full, deployed system would have numerous "bugs" (especially in unimaginably complex software), yet while it could never be tested as a fully integrated whole, the system would have to work perfectly the first time it was used. This is unpersuasive if increased uncertainty increases disincentives to contemplate attack. Proponents who note this are convincing, however, only if they presume a low opportunity cost for a limited defense system, since the disincentives will be only incrementally greater than at present. And if the Soviet Union has comparable defenses, it is not at all clear that the United States would gain any increase in deliverable retaliatory capability over the present situation of partial vulnerability to preemption.

SYMMETRY

In the best of outcomes, the United States alone would possess a highly effective defense. Except to those who worry more about American than Soviet malfeasance, there is no automatic advantage in reducing Soviet vulnerability. The dovish argument that asymmetrical vulnerability would tempt frightened Russians to launch a first strike is bizarrely inconsistent with the logic of mutual assured destruction (MAD), since the Soviets would face the same prospect of suicide from striking first before, during, and after a transition to a defended America as they face at present; indeed the weight of U.S. retaliation would be even more awesome after unilateral deployment of defenses, since they would preserve some of the forces that a Soviet strike today might be able to destroy.[24]

There is one important exception to nonchalant notions of a safe unilateral U.S. movement to defense: the incentive the Soviets might have to attack the system in space as it was deployed. Such an action, not involving damage to territory on earth, might not seem as likely to draw nuclear retaliation. Moreover, there is a legal rationale available to Moscow for such attack—the notion that outer space is an extension of airspace and that intrusions over one's national territory may be interdicted forcibly.

The USSR indeed held this position explicitly in the early 1960s[25] and has never formally abandoned it. Moscow implicitly shifted when it agreed in Article XII of the ABM treaty not to interfere with "national technical means of verification" (NTM) that are "consistent with generally recognized principles of international law." A U.S. defense system, however, would not be NTM, and its deployment would make the treaty that embodied the Soviet acceptance of any overflight in space a dead letter. The incentive for such high-risk preventive action would be particularly heightened to the extent that Kremlin leaders believe (as there is no special reason they should not) in the revolutionary offensive capability that Soviet spokesmen have sometimes imputed to "space strike" weapons—the capacity to hit targets in the opponent's homeland instantaneously, cutting warning time to zero. If one can seriously believe in the feasibility of space-based lasers that could destroy thousands of missiles in flight, it takes little imagination to envisage an ancillary capacity to destroy missiles on the ground (*pre*-boost-phase intercept) or to incinerate the Kremlin.

The next possibility in strategic defense deployment—a one-sided, modestly effective U.S. defense sensitive to changes in the offensive threat—might seem at least better than nothing if all else is equal, but as with all the important questions in the debate, that "if" is the crucial qualification. It is not clear how much such a defense would be worth. In one sense it might offer a return to the good old days of asymmetrical vulnerability in the 1950s. Despite many strategists' nostalgia for this era, however, American leaders had far less confidence in the possibility of preventing unacceptable damage—even with a U.S. first strike—than later folklore implies.[26]

If the cost-exchange ratio clearly favored offense, and the Soviets restored their penetration capacity with missile improvements far cheaper than the defense, Moscow would gain the advantage. SDI proponents sometimes cite the extraordinary Soviet investment in air defenses as evidence of their value, even given a bad cost-exchange ratio. For example, Fred Iklé reports that the USSR has spent more on active defenses than on nuclear offensive capabilities since signing the ABM treaty, and according to Keith Payne, "Soviet expenditures on defense against U.S. strategic bombers are much greater than the cost of the U.S. bombers."[27] So who has been smarter? Has the air force been stupid in estimating for so long that U.S. bombers would suffer little attrition by defenses? Would the United States have been better off if all the rubles pumped into the PVO had instead been spent on ICBMs or tanks or MiGs? Even Secretary of Defense Weinberger implicitly cited the cost-ineffectiveness of Soviet air defenses when he justified U.S. spending for "stealth" technologies because of the "enormous investment in new defensive systems" they would induce the Soviets to make.[28]

Perhaps the most cynically captious brief for SDI is one by a commentator who suggested that with typical faddishness the United States will give up on the effort after a few years but by then will have panicked the Russians into a crash program of their own, which will absorb huge amounts of the Soviet defense budget and provide no better protection against ballistic missiles than the PVO does against air-breathers. Just as likely, however, is the more worrisome possibility that the United States would give up after provoking the Russians into a defense program of their own that is *not* totally ineffective.

Consider in more detail the possibilities of higher symmetry, for example, deployment by both sides of defenses for ICBMs. The standard criticism of this option is that it would be a wash, providing no net improvement because greater survivability at the victim's end would be canceled by the reduced ability of the surviving retaliatory forces to penetrate the attacker's defense. In fact, for counterforce exchanges site defense would benefit the Soviets disproportionately because a much larger portion of their offensive force comprises ICBMs. This contradicts the view of the window of vulnerability that became conventional wisdom at the end of the 1970s, but without defenses preferential targeting of Minuteman III and MX missiles on Soviet heavy ICBMs would put a larger proportion of Soviet warheads and megatonnage under threat than the Soviets could threaten on the American side by their ability to destroy almost all U.S. ICBMs (which carry less than a quarter of U.S. warheads and megatonnage). In an ICBM duel in which defenses on both sides shifted the ratio of penetrating warheads to launchers, U.S. missiles would be exhausted before the Soviets'.

If mutual ICBM defenses neutralized the counterforce capability of those missiles and compelled both sides to target ICBMs on unprotected assets, there might be a gain in terms of MAD norms of stability, but reinforcement of MAD is seldom the justification offered for the promise of SDI. If securing MAD were the objective, it would be easier to achieve by proscribing defenses altogether. Counterforce equivalence might be endangered by ICBM vulnerability, but MAD is not, given the thousands of warheads on more survivable submarine-launched ballistic missiles (SLBMs) and bombers. If ICBMs were still wanted for striking soft targets, their survival might just as well be arranged by mobile deployment schemes—something the Soviets have moved on more expeditiously than has the United States.

One reason cited for defense of ICBMs is to prevent becoming dependent on submarine-launched ballistic missiles because such dependence "would significantly reduce Soviet defense requirements."[29] As a hedge against a Soviet breakthrough in antisubmarine warfare, this point has some merit, but otherwise it has the problem completely backward. The United States has more than 5,000 SLBM warheads (more than 3,000 on day-to-day alert), which now are less vulnerable to a Soviet first strike than any other system and face no significant barriers to penetration. Even limited site defenses would offer some spillover protection against SLBMs. To the extent that a Soviet defense system became more effective or expanded, the deterrent capacity not only of U.S. ICBMs being defended but also of the most important (sea-based) leg of the U.S. triad would be degraded.[30] Moreover, without Soviet defenses the deployment of D-5 SLBMs in the next decade would give the United States an invulnerable capability against Soviet hard targets and a major advantage in relative counterforce; confronting Soviet defenses, D-5s would be an expensive modernization with scant purpose, since they would offer little more in targeting options than does the current combination of secure soft-target capability in SLBMs, slow hard-target capability in bombers and cruise missiles, and vulnerable fast counterforce capability in silo-based missiles.

Is the prognosis better for symmetrical defenses that cover an appreciable portion of population? All else equal, again, significantly reduced vulnerability of American civilians would certainly be worth the price of reduced vulnerability of Soviet citizens. The crucial question lurking in the ceteris paribus clause is whether the price also would include a higher probability of conventional war. If defense replaced deterrence, the potential consequences of war would become less apocalyptic, so the constraints against daring to risk it would be loosened (see the next section).

In any case, the Soviets would derive one asymmetrical benefit from symmetrical defenses—protection against French, British, and Chinese forces. A prudent security planner in Moscow faces four independent decision centers that might have an interest in inflicting unacceptable damage on his society; Washington faces only one. This makes the Soviet risk calculus more complicated in any potential decision to challenge the credibility of Western deterrence. While the odds may be high that any one of those capitals would be cowed, the cumulative probability that *all* three (or four, if the dispute also involved the Chinese) would be deterred is far lower.[31] Given the small size of the nonsuperpower forces, a leaky Soviet defense would offer substantial protection against 75 percent of the potential decisions to launch nuclear weapons against the USSR, while a comparably leaky American defense would offer minimal protection against any threat the United States faced. Finally, even if the superpowers returned to symmetrical defenses limited to military targets, the Soviet Union would gain more than the United States. The French and British plan to equip their forces with multiple independently targeted reentry vehicles (MIRVs), which will yield a large growth in those countries' warheads. This will give those countries some targeting flexibility and limited attack options against military targets as long as the ABM treaty ensures penetration to target; with effective Soviet defenses those options would be vitiated.[32]

OPPORTUNITY COST

Cost-effectiveness of strategic defense proposals is usually considered in terms of the cost-exchange ratio between offense and defense in the nuclear calculus, or the percentage of targets that a system can protect for a given price. SDI has faced an uphill battle in convincing skeptics of its potential even within this limited frame of reference, although scary figures of up to a trillion dollars—roughly half of what the United States spent on offensive nuclear forces in the four decades after Nagasaki—are not so daunting if they would really make nuclear weapons "impotent and obsolete."[33] Even skeptics have provided an estimate, based on thoughtful analysis, that suggests the most expensive comprehensive defense of population might be purchased for an average of less than 1 percent of U.S. gross national product (GNP) per year—without doubt an affordable amount.[34] As they note, however, this does not prove in itself that the investment would be wise. As with any military system, *the questions "do we want it" or "can we afford it" are meaningless in themselves; the meaningful question is, "compared to what?"*

The full range of potential opportunity costs is impossible to grapple with here, ranging across general economic and political trade-offs in taxation, aggregate government expenditures, domestic social programs, and budgets for other military capabilities, as well as political aspects of relations with allies and adversaries. Perhaps the clearest and most useful way to focus the issue is to speculate on the consequences of strategic defense for other objectives of military policy alone. What would the United States lose strategically, what dangers to security would grow, as a result of investment in a strategic defense system? If the answer is "very little," it becomes harder to oppose the promise of SDI. If the answer predicts something more substantial, however, anti-military opponents of SDI spending would be reinforced by pro-military constituencies. The crucial potential trade-offs are among expenditures for offensive nuclear forces, strategic defense, and conventional forces. Except where otherwise stipulated, the following discussion assumes highly symmetrical deployment of U.S. and Soviet population defenses.

Historically, offensive nuclear forces have been comparatively cheap, in many recent years consuming less than 15 percent of the U.S. defense budget. The exception was in the early years of the nuclear buildup in the 1950s. The greater share of the defense budget allocated to developing offensive nuclear forces, under Eisenhower's New Look, however, was still rationalized by comparative cheapness; nuclear forces were cast explicitly as a substitute for ruinously expensive conventional military power. In the 1950s the United States also "spent about two-thirds as much on air defenses as on nuclear offensive forces, some $200 billion in ten years (in today's dollars). In 1960, the United States actually allocated more to its defenses against Soviet nuclear attack than to its nuclear offensive forces."[35]

Well, what did the United States get for these efforts? American nuclear superiority was useful, but air defenses did little to preserve it; growth in Soviet offensive forces steadily outpaced improvements in U.S. defenses, and American leaders never had confidence that air defenses could knock down a high percentage of attacking bombers.[36] What the United States got instead was rising vulnerability, regular confirmations of the high advantage of penetration technique against defensive technologies, Strategic Air Command war plans and air force procurement efforts focused on a preemptive first-strike option, reductions in conventional ground forces, Soviet squeezes on West Berlin, and a NATO establishment thoroughly convinced of the futility of nonnuclear resistance to Soviet aggression. If the $200 billion spent on air defenses in the 1950s had been pumped instead into the Seventh Army in Germany—in contrast with the reductions in conventional forces that Eisenhower continued even in early 1959 at the height of the Berlin

Deadline crisis—would the West have been worse off? Would Khrushchev have been as emboldened as readily as he was to try again on Berlin in 1961? Of course we cannot know, and in any case the Soviets were chastened by 1962. The chastening, however, came from offensive deterrence and coercion—the amplified threats of U.S. nuclear attack if the Soviets moved against Berlin and of conventional attack on Cuba in response to Soviet missiles there—*not* by U.S. air defenses.

If the 1950s provide any useful analogy, it does not obviously indicate a high payoff for investment in active defenses. An offense-defense race in the future also would proceed from a baseline Soviet offensive capability (both in existing launchers and payload and in hot production lines) far higher than that of the 1950s. If preventing nuclear devastation of the United States is all that is at issue, nevertheless, investment in any effective defense makes more sense than spending the money on better deterrent forces. Given the high baseline of offensive capabilities on both sides, the elasticity of *basic*, mutual deterrence of attacks against homelands is not very great. There was some logic—a bit military, mostly political—in the sound and fury of the recent past about the delicacy of the relative balance of forces, or the window of vulnerability. But it obscured the fact that the absolute increase in weapons gave the United States more survivable warheads in the 1980s, the anxious age of nuclear parity, than it had in the early 1960s, the vaunted era of U.S. superiority.[37] (The more significant change in the interim was the decline of U.S. *first*-strike capability.) At these high levels, increments of retaliatory capacity to buttress deterrence offer less change in the strategic equation than decrements of prospective casualties in the event that deterrence fails. The trade-off between offensive and defensive nuclear investments under current circumstances, therefore, is not crucial in terms of deterring an unprovoked Soviet strike on the continental United States.

Basic deterrence, however, is not all that is at issue. What always has been the more difficult American commitment is extended deterrence—the reliance on threats of nuclear escalation to prevent Soviet conventional military action against Western Europe. A highly effective U.S. strategic defense, unmatched by the USSR, would tremendously reinforce the badly frayed credibility of extended deterrence, since it would diminish the suicidal quality of the commitment. (Some Europeans worry that invulnerability would encourage a "fortress America" mentality and U.S. isolationism. This concern is peculiar, since American leaders would be crazy if they were *more* willing to defend Europe when the commitment risked annihilation of the United States than when it did not.)

Deployment of highly effective defenses on both sides, however, would have the reverse effect, by giving immunity to Soviet territory. As Payne correctly notes, this situation would exchange the current high capability and low credibility of the U.S. extended deterrent for the opposite combination.[38] This would not be an even trade, however. Payne argues that on balance the switch would enhance extended deterrence; for some unexplained reason he assumes that the diminution of capability would be less than the increase of credibility.[39] It is more likely that the switch would be a net loss for extended deterrence. With high capability and low credibility for the U.S. deterrent, Soviet leaders contemplating invasion of Western Europe would have to bank everything on the accuracy of their own subjective judgment—they would have to bet the survival of their entire society on their estimate of American rationality, self-control, and will (as well as the probability that authorities in London and Paris would remain equally unwilling to honor their doctrines). With an effective defense, however, the danger the Soviet Union would face from possible miscalculation would be far less. For a rational gambler, propensity to bet against a low-probability disaster should vary inversely with the magnitude of the disaster. In which situation would a Russian leader be more willing to play Russian roulette—when the gun is pointed at his head or at his foot?

A counterargument contends that the USSR is unlikely to attack Western Europe unless it has "very high confidence in its defenses."[40] Yet this argument actually undermines the notion that strategic defenses would enhance extended deterrence: Obviously the best way to prevent high confidence in defenses (and thereby reduce the probability of a Soviet attack on Europe) is to proscribe the defenses. Moreover, the best way to minimize the danger of a Soviet nuclear strike on the United States is to prevent a war between the superpowers elsewhere, as in Europe. No lesser conflict provides any rational motive for Moscow to strike U.S. home territory.

A third alternative to consider is a unilateral U.S. defense of only modest effectiveness. This would ease but not solve the dilemma inherent in the first-use policy. After all, critics of massive retaliation felt driven to flexible response and greater reliance on conventional forces nearly three decades ago, when the Soviets would have been lucky to deliver more than a hundred warheads in retaliation after a U.S. first strike. The critical question is whether a marginal increase in the credibility of extended nuclear deterrence would be purchased by a decrease in conventional deterrence as the strategic defense spends dollars otherwise available for tanks, artillery, tactical aircraft, and military manpower. The trade-off probably would be worthwhile only if the increments of effectiveness of the strategic defense were appreciably greater than the decrements to effectiveness of NATO's conventional defense, because the probability of successful conventional defense is far more sensitive to marginal changes in force balances than is the probability of successful nuclear deterrence.

The final combination of strategic defensive forces would consist of partially effective systems on both sides. Some worry that this would prevent NATO from exercising limited nuclear options (LNOs), since many more offensive weapons per expected detonation would have to be launched.[41] It is unclear, however, that more launches per se should be significantly more dangerous unless there is a huge difference in the amount of uncertainty about how many of the larger number of warheads would explode on target. (Others argue that inhibitions on LNOs are good because they will prevent the Soviets from using them against the West and thus decrease the overall probability of nuclear exchange,[42] but NATO doctrine historically has relied more on nuclear first use than has Soviet doctrine.) In general this fourth combination should represent a wash for extended deterrence *provided that* the opportunity cost for the Soviets' conventional force is comparable with that for NATO's.

To assume the latter condition, however, contradicts official U.S. estimates of relative military spending and capability. Although Moscow outspent Washington for many years, the Atlantic Alliance as a whole has outspent the Warsaw Pact as a whole. Yet official net assessments always cite Pact forces as superior. Either the standard assessments of expenditure or capability are somehow spurious,[43] or—despite how much it contradicts other stereotypes—the East is more efficient in converting economic inputs into military outputs.

A different argument, often heard from Reaganite strategists, holds that Moscow is already stretched to its limits, has no more capacity to invest in military competition, and could not match additional effort by the United States. There are two problems with this view. First, it is indeed evident that the Soviets do not *wish* to accelerate the arms competition; Gorbachev's political and economic initiatives point toward reducing the military burden. There is no evidence, however, that the Russians lack the *capacity* to keep pace or even spurt ahead if they feel the need. U.S. intelligence estimates in 1986 confirmed this, and some even predicted that the Soviets' military spending may grow faster than their economy in the 1990s.[44] Second, the argument blithely ignores *U.S.* economic constraints, most obviously a national debt that, after 200 years, more than doubled in the one administration that gave us SDI. There is no evidence that the American electorate has the will to force the pace by raising (or even maintaining) recent levels of military spending.

To argue that SDI will spur improvements in Western conventional forces[45] is as ahistorically naive about the internal dynamics of democratic polities as are advocates of unilateral disarmament about the external dynamics of international relations. The U.S. defense budget grew roughly 50 percent in the first half-dozen years of the Reagan presidency, exceeding past peacetime records for sustained expansion, but also, in the process, exhausting the consensus for further increases. If Americans and Europeans lack the will to improve conventional defenses any more now, when the West is still completely vulnerable to nuclear destruction, what conceivable reason is there to believe that the same people will have any greater desire to do so when they are less vulnerable? If a conventional defense that offers high confidence of adequacy is too expensive to buy now, how can it not slip even further out of reach if billions of dollars are being sunk into a strategic defense?

Barring a crisis that provoked allocation of more than 7 to 8 percent of GNP for defense spending, it is overwhelmingly probable that the bulk of funds for strategic defense deployments would turn out to be extracted from other elements of the current defense budget. It is unlikely that even very limited strategic defense systems could be funded within percentages of the defense budget allocated to offensive nuclear forces during most of the post-Nagasaki era.[46] Even if the United States elected to dispense completely with *both* basic and extended deterrence, therefore, funding would have to be diverted from conventional forces.

Conventional deterrence and extended nuclear deterrence compensate somewhat for each other's deficiencies, so in the past when one has been considered dangerously weak, initiatives have been taken to bolster the other. The New Look nuclear buildup did this in the 1950s when defense budgets went down; the flexible response conventional buildup did this with reverse emphasis in the 1960s when budgets went up. Unless the prospective American strategic defense is unilateral and highly effective (the least probable of the four possibilities previously discussed), it would do little for aggregate deterrence. In the past, financial constraints prompted increased reliance on extended deterrence; with investment in strategic defense, financial constraints would *increase the need* for extended deterrence at the same time that Soviet strategic defense would *reduce the capability* for it.

Even if defense budgets expanded to allow procurement of a limited defense system while maintaining baseline conventional forces, *neither* conventional *nor* extended deterrence would be notably increased. In the more likely case that strategic defenses were obtained from defense budget diversions, both forms of deterrence would be weakened at the same time. If this was the price of effective protection of most of the American population, it would be a worthwhile one to pay. A Fortress

America concept was shortsighted and pernicious around the time of
World War II, when America could promote its interests by joining allies
against a common enemy without suffering any awesome devastation
at home; it is harder to argue against when World War III would wash
away that impunity. For anything less, however, the dangers that are
reduced probably would be exceeded by those that are increased—and
highly effective population defense is the least probable outcome of
commitment to strategic defense.

PRIORITIES AND ALTERNATIVES:
SUMMARY COMPARISON

Thinking in terms of opportunity cost highlights the difference
between "nice-to-have" programs and "need-to-have" ones, and it comes
into better focus when potential capabilities are ranked by priority. Such
exercises in integrated analysis are rarely encouraged by the structure
and process of U.S. defense policymaking, which is most often disag-
gregated along lines of military service or congressional subcommittee.
Analysts may attempt broader comparisons, but more often within
general categories (such as nuclear or conventional forces) than between
them.

Tackling the whole range of interests and choices in military policy
risks superficial assessment, but it is the only real, logical sense in which
the relative attractions of SDI potentials can be weighed. The more
detailed the range of choices, the less agreement there will be about
their relative priority; incommensurabilities between priorities and costs,
and different ways in which some goals can subsume others, further
complicate the feasibility of ordering functions in a hierarchy of desirability. With these methodological inhibitions noted, however, I offer
the following rough and incomplete list of my own preferences. It serves
to illustrate the analytical point about trade-offs and choices, even if
the reader has a different order of preferences. If we temporarily hold
in abeyance the crucial questions of feasibility and cost, the ideal order
of priority for attainment of U.S. military capabilities might be:

1. Highly effective and unilateral strategic defense of U.S. population (the national "astrodome," without comparable Soviet
   defense).
2. Highly effective strategic defense of population, with matching
   Soviet capability.
3. Finite nuclear deterrent capability to inflict severe damage (likely
   to prove "unacceptable") in a second strike—for example, capacity to kill 10 percent of enemy population.

4. Better-than-hopeless NATO conventional defense.
5. Conventional power projection forces for a small war (sometimes known in jargon as a "half war") outside Europe.
6. Serious civil defense program.
7. Stronger nuclear deterrent—"assured destruction" capability—and at least rough parity with USSR in countervalue second-strike forces.
8. Limited ground-based defense of Washington, D.C. (and possibly other selected command, control, and communications [C^3] sites), as hedge against accidental enemy launch.
9. Moderately effective and unilateral strategic defense of U.S. population.
10. Conventional forces for an additional "half war."
11. Conventional parity with the Warsaw Pact in Europe.
12. Moderately effective and symmetrical U.S. and Soviet population defenses, but in an overall configuration that does not increase first-strike incentives (that is, avoiding defenses that would be weak against counterforce attacks but strong against ragged retaliation aimed at cities).
13. Equality with the USSR in nuclear counterforce capability.
14. Highly effective defense of U.S. ICBMs *without* matching Soviet capability (marginal U.S. superiority in offensive forces).
15. NATO conventional forces superior to those of Warsaw Pact.
16. Conventional forces for a third "half war."
17. Substantial U.S. offensive nuclear superiority.
18. Highly effective defense of U.S. ICBMs *with* matching Soviet capability.

As noted, this notional list would require many qualifications in practice—for example, some of the lower priorities listed might be more desirable to procure than higher ones if they cost far less—but let it stand for heuristic purposes. Of the capabilities listed, 3, 4, 5, and 7 clearly exist, and 13 probably does (although hawks, when they limit the force comparison to ICBMs, disagree). The other options have so far been foreclosed by financial, political, or technological constraints. The first two hypothetical priorities are strategic defense systems, but, because their feasibility is diminished by all three dimensions of constraint, they are the longest of long-shot bets. Both of the next listed defense options (6 and 8) are technically feasible and insignificant in financial cost, but they have not been pursued for domestic political reasons. (There have been periodic efforts to promote civil defense, but they have never progressed very far because initial publicity provoked backlash. In strict terms of strategic logic it has been nonsensical to

spend billions of dollars for offensive nuclear forces capable of discriminating attacks, and to promote doctrines for extended deterrence, limited
first use, and escalation control, without also maximizing the cheap
means to limit damage at the margins.)[47]

The next sort of strategic defense on the list is item 9—moderately
effective U.S. population defense. If its absolute cost was not horrendous,
it also should not impinge on the ability to fund other capabilities
assumed to be higher priorities, such as the basic conventional force
objectives (4 and 5) or the offensive nuclear deterrent (7). It also would
represent an improvement over the current situation of vulnerability,
but only in the sense of a hedge against the worst case—the finite
probability that war could occur despite all attempts to avoid it. If
anticipated U.S. fatalities were cut by, for instance, 25 percent, the
absolute number saved in the event of war would be significant. When
it came to crisis decisions on risks and options, however, it would be
hardly enough to override the significance of the huge remaining losses.

The real reason to doubt the value of item 9, however, is that it
would be surprising if Moscow were unable or disinclined to match it.
In that case it would turn into option 12, whose opportunity cost, in
contrast with number 9, probably would be excessive. A unilateral partial
defense might be worth more than improved conventional capabilities
because nuclear risks are a more potent deterrent than conventional
ones and the Soviets would have to face disproportionate nuclear risks.
(Even then, the choice would be a close call, as the earlier consideration
of the opportunity cost of air defense in the 1950s suggested.) The
symmetrical partial defense, in contrast, would restore equality of nuclear
risks, while the conventional options that were forgone (items 10 and
11) would be worth more for deterrence and denial. From anything like
current baselines, conventional parity in Europe as well as forces for
two other small wars probably are unaffordable already and would
certainly be so if more funds were diverted to strategic defense.

STABILITY AND ARMS CONTROL

The prevalent argument that unequal vulnerability in itself would
be destabilizing is not the best criticism of strategic defense. When we
canonize stability as a value it is pertinent to ask, stability for whom?
Technical criteria associated with the notion of crisis stability are not
the whole story. Since the danger of war is a function of capabilities
multiplied by intentions, the difference in antagonists' intentions has
to figure in the equation. If the status quo power in a conflict has a
great military advantage, the situation is eminently stable. By the same
token, if nuclear stability becomes so absolutely assured that conventional

power can be used with acceptable risk, then the revisionist power has an advantage. A unilateral advantage for the United States, therefore, should hardly be unstable in the terms that matter to us.

In general, SDI critics have overstated the dangers of strategic defense for stability in the nuclear dimension of U.S.-Soviet interaction, while proponents have understated the danger for stability in the overall security equation that embraces conventional power as well. The preceding discussion emphasized the latter point. Yet the knowledge that deterrence cannot last forever, and that any chance of preventing nuclear destruction is worth serious attention, still provides powerful arguments for SDI. In some ways, however, critics do not overstate the dangers of SDI to nuclear stability, and these exceptions should be noted before concluding that opportunity costs outside the nuclear calculus alone are the primary reasons for skepticism about the promise of strategic defense.

The best argument against SDI, in terms of crisis stability, cites the danger that both sides would deploy defenses that would be ineffective against a large-scale attack but that could effectively blunt a "ragged retaliation" following a first strike on the opponents' forces—a so-called mop-up defense. This would create the classic reciprocal fear of surprise attack in the same way that completely vulnerable offensive forces would in a world without defenses. This situation is conceivable but does not seem the most likely consequence of effective defenses deployed by both sides on a similar scale, unless first-strike counterforce capability also increases to a degree that SDI opponents should consider destabilizing in itself.

For the feared situation to develop, an attacker would need a combination of offensive first-strike capacity and defensive capacity against countervalue retaliation that would be able to reduce detonations on his own cities to a low level (for the sake of rough argument, no more than 100 warheads). Assume also that both sides have a peacetime inventory of deployed warheads near current levels—for instance, 10,000 apiece. (My criticism becomes even stronger if the peacetime numbers of offensive warheads increase while the percentage effectiveness of first-strike and defense capabilities remain the same.)

If the mop-up defense deployed by both sides could intercept 90 percent of the warheads in a ragged retaliation by the opponent, then first-strike capability would have to be good enough to destroy at least 90 percent of the other side's starting number of warheads if the combination were to limit total penetrating retaliatory warheads to 100. This presumes dramatic improvements in antisubmarine warfare capability for the side striking first, improvements beyond what most SDI critics usually consider probable. It also presumes very poor effectiveness for active defenses of land-based forces (remember that my criticism assumes symmetrical, not unilateral, defense deployments) and little ability to limit ICBM vulnerability through other adaptations, such as mobility and concealment.[48] Otherwise, if first-strike capability is lower, an attacker's mop-up defense must be better—capable of intercepting more than 90 percent of more than 1,000 warheads.

In either case, the SDI opponents' position has problems. If first-strike counterforce capability can develop to the point of destroying 90 percent of an opponent's total retaliatory force, most observers—even many of the MAD supporters associated with the mop-up argument—would begin to worry irrespective of whether defenses were deployed too. (Remember the anxiety over ICBM vulnerability that became a consensus by the end of the 1970s, even though that vulnerability left the United States with far more than 10 percent of its warheads secure against attack.) However, to the extent that the mop-up defense could intercept more than 90 percent of warheads at some level over 1,000 of such retaliating weapons, such a defense would begin to appear more attractive in its own right.

A thornier problem is the improbability that space-based systems would not be vulnerable to each other. Antisatellite systems could blind early warning and battle management sensors, and SDI systems are likely to be more effective against satellites than against missiles. "Thus ASAT threatens ABM but ABM developments contribute to ASAT."[49] According to the criteria announced in Paul Nitze's speech on June 3, 1986, however, a defense should not be deployed unless it is survivable.[50] This avoids the question, though, of how vulnerabilities could change after deployment.

This concern reflects a more general problem—the fragility of expensive systems in the face of change over time, or the problem of maintenance as opposed to development. "A situation in which both superpowers were invulnerable to nuclear attack would be extremely sensitive to even small improvements in the ability of one country's offense to penetrate the adversary's defense," as Charles Glaser notes; the side with ten warheads capable of penetrating would reap a large advantage over an opponent with none. Under the current situation of redundant assured destruction, in contrast, there is little sensitivity to change at the margins.[51]

Even if crisis stability is less of a reason to condemn strategic defense than opponents usually suggest, ample problems exist in the realm of arms race stability. Arms control in the past, through the Strategic Arms Limitation Talks (SALT) process, proved difficult enough, and it does not appear very durable today. Yet the currency of negotiation in SALT was comparatively simple—and trade-offs were eased by the ABM treaty, which reduced the marginal return from increases in offensive capacity.

It is hard to conceive of how negotiating mechanisms could cope as well, let alone any better, with the higher order of complexity that defense systems would inject into the calculus. Domestic pressures could be even more problematic:

> [T]here would always be arguments that the United States needed additional defense to improve its protection against Soviet attacks and as a hedge against Soviet breakthroughs. The strength of these arguments would be greater than those made about the inadequacy of today's offensive forces since defensive capability would start to become redundant only once the defenses were perfect. The existence of uncertainties would be likely to result in unrelenting requests for additional defenses, yet fulfilling these requests would yield little satisfaction and add little to the public's sense of security.[52]

A reasonably practical compromise solution might be a negotiated defense-dominant balance. The public demands suggested above might be more effectively met by constraints on Soviet offenses than by a continuous unilateral countering effort. The efficacy of most potential defense systems is also likely to be low unless offensive forces and countermeasures are kept in check. This probability leads some to point out, however, that a similar result theoretically could be reached without defenses, just by negotiating more radical reductions in offensive forces. This, indeed, is what Gorbachev maintained at Reykjavík. (The best approach in such an effort would be to reduce the ratio of warheads to launchers—deMIRVing—which would passively produce the same leverage as boost-phase intercept.)

A fair argument for complementing radical offensive reductions with defenses is that the latter would ease verification requirements (which would present insurmountable problems if the agreed reductions decreased offensive forces to extremely low levels) by making small violations militarily insignificant.[53] The record of more than two decades of arms-control efforts offers no good reason to guess that such a defense-dominant order could be successfully negotiated, ratified, and maintained. But without clear commitment to neutering offensive forces, a practical basis for determining an agreed balance would almost certainly prove too complex and thus elusive—and without limits on offenses, the value of prospective defensive systems is likely to be circumscribed, hence less arguably cost-effective and dubiously attractive. Thus it seems that while SDI has complicated arms control, its best hope also lies in arms control.

CONCLUSION

The payoffs from defense systems that are likely to be most feasible
seem to be the payoffs that are the least certainly positive. The choices
at either end of the range of hypothetical possibilities—highly effective
population defense or no significant defenses at all—are easier to endorse
than those in between. The latter extreme, which was generally accepted
as holy writ until President Reagan's 1983 speech introducing SDI, now
strikes many as unduly fatalistic and as a dead end, as the United States
has proved unable to stanch the erosion of its position in the balance
of offensive forces. The former extreme strikes others as dangerous in
the manner of all zealotry. Reaching for the stars, for something beyond
our grasp, is not necessarily innocent aspiration if the consequences
entail damage to security in the dimensions that we *can* change.

The intermediate possibilities would be good for security if they did
not cost much, but bad for security if they did. (The one that assuredly
would be worth the financial cost—limited defense of Washington, D.C.,
against accidental attack—has scarcely any constituency and obvious
domestic political liabilities.) A limited population defense that could
not prevent damage far above the unacceptable level would offer a
useful marginal hedge against disaster but not much impact on basic
stability unless it were asymmetrical. To the extent that the effectiveness
rose or symmetry declined enough to make an appreciable rather than
marginal difference, the absolute cost would be high, which in turn
would make the opportunity cost severe. Similarly, a limited defense
of ICBMs would offer limited benefits if it were asymmetrical, thus
insuring a net increase in retaliatory American warheads that could land
on target. Such limited benefit (defense of ICBMs would protect only
about 20 percent of U.S. intercontinental-range warheads) is worth a
small cost, but probable Soviet attempts to match the system (they are
currently far better positioned to launch a competition in ground-based
defense deployments)[54] make the prospect of maintaining simultaneously
the asymmetrical effectiveness and low cost almost nil.

In an unconstrained competition in offensive and defensive nuclear
forces the United States could, if it has the will to sacrifice, achieve a
net advantage over the Soviet Union. Many of those disillusioned with
arms control as a means to progress, therefore, relish the unilateral
alternative for boosting security. The problem is that even without
constraint, the U.S. advantage that plausibly could be achieved would
be at best only one of degree (making the United States proportionally
less vulnerable than the Soviet Union), not one of kind (making the
United States and only the United States nearly invulnerable). The degree

of advantage in the nuclear dimension, in turn, would vary directly with the opportunity cost to conventional defense, and it is in the dimension of conventional conflict and power that the least unlikely sources of war—and hence of nuclear danger—lie. Modest improvements in nuclear vulnerability have less effect on the overall stability of deterrence than does modest deterioration of relative conventional capability. To purchase the former at the price of the latter would yield a net decline in safety.

So if SDI seems so much less promising than its advocates assert, why are the Russians not encouraging Washington to proceed with it? Perhaps they have as much naive faith in American technology as Ronald Reagan does. Or, if they do not wish to invade Western Europe, the opportunity cost to U.S. extended and conventional deterrence may not strike them as an important gain. Or maybe they just do not want to spend the rubles necessary to compete in a new dimension of military capacity. (Just because the United States could beggar them economically in an arms race—leaving aside the obvious asymmetry of domestic political barriers to belt-tightening—this does not mean that it is in American interest to do so. The purpose of security policy is not to damage the adversary's prosperity but to protect one's own.) Or perhaps the Russians believe in the capacity of offensive arms control to reach the same outcomes foreseen in Reagan's starry-eyed visions of defense.

Indeed, SDI proponents might argue, arms control has been good for the Russians, so they have more reason to like it. But however dispiriting has been the legacy of SALT, there is no reason whatever to believe that a better balance of vulnerability or a less onerous defense burden can flow more easily from active moves toward strategic defense than from negotiated reductions of offensive capabilities. This is particularly true when one considers the concessions offered by the Soviets in negotiations of recent years, surpassing anything the West might have hoped for in earlier negotiations. Since these were largely responses to SDI, the president's program clearly could be judged a stroke of genius were he to use it, finally, as leverage for an arms-control deal.

For that purpose, SDI would be properly seen as an instance of wisdom about what can be changed, and as a courageous initiative. To refuse to trade any prospective defense options for any amount of concessions on offensive capacity, on the other hand, is to reach too far. Ignoring the probable difference between what can and cannot be achieved—reaching for the stars no matter what the obstacles—is noble or innocent only as long as doing so does not weaken one's footing on the nuclear precipice.

NOTES

1. I am grateful to Charles Fairbanks, Bruce Blair, Paul Stares, and Simon Serfaty for helpful criticisms of an earlier draft of this chapter.

2. Colin S. Gray, "A Case for Strategic Defense," *Survival* 27, no. 2 (March/April 1985), 51.

3. Fred Charles Iklé, "Nuclear Strategy: Can There Be a Happy Ending?" *Foreign Affairs* 63, no. 4 (Spring 1985), 811.

4. The official brochure *Soviet Strategic Defense Programs* (Washington, D.C.: U.S. Department of Defense, October 1985) emphasizes how Soviet defensive efforts have been "far more extensive than those of the United States," but the bulk of those cited are in air defense, civil defense, and the Moscow ABM system permitted by the treaty. The Abalakova/Krasnoyarsk radar, which will violate the treaty when activated, is generally believed in the West to be designed for early warning, although it can be seen as a foot in the door toward a defensive battle management system. (The Soviets also challenge the compliance of U.S. radar innovations near Thule, Greenland, and Fylingdales Moor, United Kingdom, with ABM treaty provisions.) See Thomas K. Longstreth, John E. Pike, and John B. Rhinelander, *The Impact of U.S. and Soviet Ballistic Missile Defense Programs on the ABM Treaty*, 3d ed. (Washington, D.C.: National Campaign to Save the ABM Treaty, March 1985), 37–41. See also Raymond L. Garthoff, "U.S.-Soviet Radar Dispute Tests Treaty Good Faith," *The New York Times*, February 14, 1987, 26. There are fragmentary indications of Soviet activities that *could* be compatible with initial preparations to break out of the ABM treaty but none reported in public that are not explicable in other terms. Complacency about the danger of breakout would be foolish, but so would the assumption that it is probable—or that American activities in that direction would not induce the Soviets to begin efforts from which they would otherwise refrain.

5. Consider the percentage of cases in which the adjectives "nuclear" or "intercontinental" could be substituted for "strategic" without changing the meaning.

6. Pro-SDI views emphasize that air-breathing systems, being slow, are more stabilizing than ballistic missiles (although this was certainly not the uniform view a quarter-century ago). Critics note that geography gives the Soviets an advantage because of the proximity of critical U.S. targets to seacoasts, making them vulnerable to quick attack by sea-launched cruise missiles.

7. Paul H. Nitze, "SDI, Arms Control, and Stability: Toward a New Synthesis," June 3, 1986 (Washington, D.C.: U.S. Department of State, Bureau of Public Affairs Current Policy No. 845), 2.

8. Michael F. Altfeld notes this in "Strategic Defense and the 'Cost-Exchange Ratio,'" *Strategic Review* 14, no. 4 (Fall 1986), 23, but does not indicate how far the cost-exchange ratio could move in favor of the offense before investments in defense lost their value. He notes that a defense with a high probability of kill (pk) would be desirable even if less efficient than the offense, but he does not deal with the dynamic problem of declines in pk resulting from cheaper offensive adaptations.

9. Charles H. Fairbanks, Jr., "Arms Races: The Metaphor & the Facts," *National Interest* no. 1 (Fall 1985), 86–89.

10. For example, "all optimistic parallels to the Wright brothers, the Manhattan Project, or the U.S. manned lunar landing break down. Those were races against nature, not against a scientifically advanced adversary bent on overcoming an American program." Joshua M. Epstein, *The 1987 Defense Budget* (Washington, D.C.: The Brookings Institution, 1986), 12. Or, "the moon didn't fight back. The Russians will." Scott D. Sagan, "Arms and Ideas," *New Republic*, September 8, 1986, 38.

11. Kosta Tsipis, "Technical Impediments to a Workable Defense System," in Dorinda G. Dallmeyer, ed., *The Strategic Defense Initiative: New Perspectives on Deterrence* (Boulder, Colo.: Westview Press, 1986), 35.

12. Ashton B. Carter, *Directed Energy Missile Defense in Space*, Background Paper (Washington, D.C.: Office of Technology Assessment, April 1984), 69–70. See also Sidney D. Drell, Philip J. Farley, and David Holloway, "Preserving the ABM Treaty: A Critique of the Reagan Strategic Defense Initiative," *International Security* 9, no. 2 (Fall 1984), 89, and 62, which notes a Soviet Academy of Sciences report concluding that means for destroying space-based defensive systems would be far cheaper to develop.

13. Charles L. Glaser, "Why Even Good Defenses May Be Bad," *International Security* 9, no. 2 (Fall 1984), 111–13.

14. Tom Blau, "SDI and Space Basing," *NATO's Sixteen Nations* 31, no. 2 (April 1986), 41.

15. Keith B. Payne, *Strategic Defense: "Star Wars" in Perspective* (Lanham, Md.: Hamilton Press, 1986), 77.

16. See the chapter by Harold Brown, 15–19; James R. Schlesinger, "Rhetoric and Realities in the Star Wars Debate," *International Security* 10, no. 1 (Summer 1985), 7–8.

17. Peter D. Zimmerman, "Pork Bellies and SDI," *Foreign Policy* no. 63 (Summer 1986), 77–82.

18. Consider the last, for example. The Soviets have excess capacity for producing boosters. If they began stockpiling soon, "several thousand units might be accumulated by the time a US SDI became operational. The marginal cost of these boosters would be comparatively low . . . because warheads and associated front-end components (e.g. guidance systems) would not be procured. . . . [They would be the] boost-phase equivalent of penetration aids." (Stephen M. Meyer, "Soviet Views on SDI," *Survival* 27, no. 6 [November/December 1985], 286) The problem would be even worse, considering that the Soviets probably already have a number of spares, if (as would comport with their typical aversion to throwing away hardware) the Soviets stockpiled boosters for older missile launchers that were retired, such as SS-9s and SS-11s.

19. Philip Taubman, "Moscow Planning Anti-'Star Wars,'" *The New York Times*, December 18, 1986, A15.

20. Remember the legendary exchange: Herman Kahn: "If we deploy a full-scale anti-ballistic missile system, we can save 50 million lives." Bernard Brodie: "Herman, in order to save 50 million lives, you've got to have a war." (Quoted

in Robert E. Hunter, "SDI: Return to Basics," *Washington Quarterly* 9, no. 1 [Winter 1986], 155 [emphasis deleted])

21. Iklé, "Nuclear Strategy," 825.

22. Fred S. Hoffman, "The SDI in U.S. Nuclear Strategy: Senate Testimony," *International Security* 10, no. 1 (Summer 1985), 19–21.

23. Charles L. Glaser, "Do We Want the Missile Defenses We Can Build?" *International Security* 10, no. 1 (Summer 1985), 36–37.

24. For related arguments, see Colin S. Gray's testimony in hearings before the U.S. Senate Committee on Armed Services, *Department of Defense Authorization for Appropriations for Fiscal Year 1985*, part 6, 98th Cong., 2d sess., 1984, 3081.

25. See Paul B. Stares, *The Militarization of Space* (Ithaca, N.Y.: Cornell University Press, 1985), 71.

26. See the record of estimates compiled in Richard K. Betts, *Nuclear Blackmail and Nuclear Balance* (Washington, D.C.: The Brookings Institution, 1987), chap. 4.

27. Iklé, "Nuclear Strategy," 814; Payne, *Strategic Defense*, 47.

28. Quoted in George C. Wilson, "'Stealth' Weapons Emphasized," *The Washington Post*, January 11, 1987, A5.

29. Payne, *Strategic Defense*, 50–51.

30. See Drell, Farley, and Holloway, "Preserving the ABM Treaty," 84.

31. See Richard K. Betts, "Compound Deterrence vs. No-First-Use: What's Wrong Is What's Right," *Orbis* 28, no. 4 (Winter 1985), 707–11.

32. John Prados, Joel S. Wit, and Michael J. Zagurek, Jr., "The Strategic Nuclear Forces of Britain and France," *Scientific American* 255, no. 2 (August 1986), 38.

33. See Colin S. Gray, "Strategic Forces," in Joseph Kruzel, ed., *American Defense Annual 1986–1987* (Lexington, Mass.: Lexington Books, 1986), 82–83. Gray notes that total cost would be cushioned by incremental procurement over two or more decades. By the same token, however, total costs for maintaining a system over such time, and modernizing it in the face of progressive countermeasures, probably would prove higher than construction estimates for the initial architecture.

34. Barry M. Blechman and Victor A. Utgoff, *Fiscal and Economic Implications of Strategic Defenses*, SAIS Papers in International Affairs No. 12 (Boulder, Colo.: Westview Press with The Johns Hopkins Foreign Policy Institute, SAIS, 1986), 114. On crucial uncertainties and sensitivities of their estimates, see 101–6.

35. Iklé, "Nuclear Strategy," 813.

36. See Betts, *Nuclear Blackmail and Nuclear Balance*, chap. 4.

37. See Warner R. Schilling, "U.S. Strategic Nuclear Concepts in the 1970s: The Search for Sufficiently Equivalent Countervailing Parity," *International Security* 6, no. 2 (Fall 1981), 50.

38. Payne, *Strategic Defense*, 113–14.

39. Ibid., 115.

40. Ibid., 112.

41. See David S. Yost, "Ballistic Missile Defense and the Atlantic Alliance," *International Security* 7, no. 2 (Fall 1982), 153, 156.

42. John C. Toomay, "The Case for Ballistic Missile Defense," *Daedalus* 114, no. 3 (Summer 1985), 228, 232.

43. For elaboration on the anomaly, see Epstein, *1987 Defense Budget*, 29–31, and Barry R. Posen, "Measuring the European Conventional Balance: Coping with Complexity in Threat Assessment," *International Security* 9, no. 3 (Winter 1984), 51–54.

44. See descriptions of reports by the Central Intelligence Agency and Defense Intelligence Agency in Stephen Engelberg, "U.S. Reports Deny Soviet Is Pressed," *The New York Times*, September 16, 1986, A7.

45. For example, Payne, *Strategic Defense*, 114–16.

46. Blechman and Utgoff, *Fiscal and Economic Implications of Strategic Defenses*, 120–22.

47. See Harold Brown, "The Strategic Defense Initiative," *Survival* 27, no. 2 (March/April 1985), 59. Brown also notes that site defenses could not protect C^3 centers because their small numbers would allow the offense to saturate them (page 60). This would be true of a dedicated attack, but the limited defense of National Command Authority suggested above would be a modest-cost way to reduce the chance that accidental attack would unleash all-out war; if the top of the chain of command were destroyed, it would be harder to limit retaliation or negotiate.

48. Naturally this simple an illustrative argument has qualifications. For example, the side striking first could assume that the victim would not be able to reprogram the targets for his surviving missiles and bombers, and would not know which 10 percent of his warheads would survive, so would have to cross-target large numbers on each city in order to have a high probability of 100 non-overlapping detonations in his retaliatory strike. If the second-striker's ability to proliferate the peacetime number of his offensive warheads for this purpose could not keep well ahead of the other side's first-strike capability, my criticism would not hold as well. Nevertheless, the side striking first would still have to confront uncertainty—and given the stakes, still awesome risk—concerning the probability that many of the retaliating warheads would land in the same place.

49. Drell, Farley, and Holloway, "Preserving the ABM Treaty," 79. See also Albert Carnesale, "The Strategic Defense Initiative," in George E. Hudson and Joseph Kruzel, eds., *American Defense Annual 1985–1986* (Lexington, Mass.: D.C. Heath, 1985), 203.

50. Nitze, "SDI, Arms Control, and Stability," 2.

51. Glaser, "Why Even Good Defenses May Be Bad," 98–99, 112.

52. Ibid., 120–21.

53. Hoffman, "The SDI in U.S. Nuclear Strategy," 23; Payne, *Strategic Defense*, 145.

54. Sayre Stevens, "The Soviet BMD Program," in Ashton B. Carter and David N. Schwartz, eds., *Ballistic Missile Defense* (Washington, D.C.: The Brookings Institution, 1984).

10

THE IMPLICATIONS OF SDI FOR U.S.-EUROPEAN RELATIONS

Robert E. Osgood

TOWARD CRISIS OR ASSIMILATION?

The Strategic Defense Initiative (SDI) impinges on the whole range of issues that have bedeviled the security and cohesion of the Atlantic alliance since NATO—the alliance's integrated military organization—was created amidst the panic following the outbreak of the Korean War. These are the issues of military strategy (particularly the conventional-nuclear relationship and U.S. extended nuclear deterrence), arms control, East-West relations, defense expenditures, technology sharing, and the independent British and French nuclear forces.

These issues are deep-rooted. They will be with us for a long time. At this point the controversies surrounding them are latent. In so far as they are connected to SDI they are largely confined to sharing the technology. But they may grow more intense if they become focused on the procurement and deployment of specific weapons for the United States or NATO or if they become central to arms-control policies on which differing U.S. and allied priorities and differing views within Europe are a matter of lively domestic political contention.

SDI is likely to become a divisive source of transatlantic controversies to the extent that its organizing purpose remains the creation of national population shields intended to abolish nuclear deterrence. However, SDI may cease to serve this purpose after the one great champion of this vision, President Reagan, has left office. As a leak-proof population-defense system, it may then, like the multinational nuclear force (MLF), rapidly fade away for a combination of technological, economic, and

---

This chapter is expanded in Robert W. Tucker et al., *SDI and U.S. Foreign Policy* (Boulder, Colo.: Westview Press with The Johns Hopkins Foreign Policy Institute, SAIS, 1987).

political reasons. If so, SDI, for practical purposes, will become a system
to defend land-based military targets—primarily, ICBMs and command,
control, and communications centers (C^3).

Even as a system to protect U.S. retaliatory forces SDI will impinge
on a number of the contentious issues at the root of transatlantic tension.
But, like the flexible-response doctrine and intermediate-range nuclear
forces (INF), it would probably be gradually assimilated into the East-
West arms competition and the familiar pattern of intra-alliance relations.
The ease of assimilation, however, will depend on whether the transition
to a more balanced mix of offensive and defensive weapons can be
achieved within the framework of an arms agreement (or successive
agreements) limiting strategic defense weapons and reducing strategic
nuclear warheads.

An assimilated SDI would constitute a landmark in the evolution
of NATO's military posture, but it would not transform the alliance. It
would not overcome the dilemma of extended deterrence—that is,
Europe's dependence on nuclear deterrence—which compels the allies
to embrace and reaffirm the U.S. nuclear protectorate even though, given
the specter of nuclear war in Europe, they are as fearful as they are
doubtful that it would be used in their behalf. President Reagan's vision
of SDI promises to abolish this dilemma by restructuring both direct
and extended deterrence to depend on mutual assured defense against
nuclear attacks. But SDI as a system to protect military targets can, at
best, only mitigate NATO's nuclear dilemma. Nevertheless, SDI, assimilated or not, could aggravate as well as mitigate this dilemma. Indeed,
its initial impact sent a sharp shockwave throughout NATO. The potentially disruptive effect of SDI on U.S.-European relations is now
muted only because the program is still in its formative stage, far short
of deployment, and because its full implications for arms control, whether
as an obstacle or a lever, are only beginning to unfold.

Several developments in the last fifteen or twenty years have ac-
centuated NATO's nuclear dilemma at the root of extended deterrence:
the growth of Soviet strategic and theater nuclear capabilities and the
strengthening of the Soviet capacity for a conventional blitzkrieg; the
growing capacity of antinuclear groups for political mobilization, as
revealed in the INF deployment crisis; the decline of the center and
ascendance of the Left in the German Social Democratic party (SDP)
and the leftward turn of the British Labour party in the wake of the
INF crisis; and the collapse of U.S.-Soviet détente, followed by the
Reagan administration's drive to revitalize containment, in the face of
allied efforts to salvage and enhance détente. These developments activate
the anxieties with which the European allies view the slightest sign of
a weakening of will on the part of the United States to couple its full

nuclear deterrent to their defense. They make any change in the military status quo, especially one that affects the nuclear balance, subject to organized popular opposition. To counter these effects the United States presses its allies to raise NATO's nuclear threshold by strengthening conventional capabilities, and it champions arms control as the centerpiece in the improvement of East-West relations. The administration's peace initiative in Reagan's second term has somewhat softened transatlantic differences over the conduct of East-West relations. But keeping these differences under control depends, eventually, on a mutually satisfactory outcome of arms negotiations. Yet, the obstacles to achieving a comprehensive arms agreement are formidable.

EUROPEAN RESPONSES TO SDI

The intensification of NATO's nuclear dilemma, aggravated by the developments in U.S.-allied relations just outlined, made it certain that any major change in NATO's military posture and strategy initiated by the United States would activate all the strategic anxieties, diplomatic concerns, and transatlantic tensions that the dilemma chronically generates. The substance, method, and timing of President Reagan's enunciation of SDI in March 1983 guaranteed that this program would be extremely disturbing to allied governments.

Proclaimed without previous consultation with (as opposed to notification of) the allies, defined as a program intended to abolish nuclear deterrence, and justified on the highest grounds of morality and international security, SDI burst into public attention as an extraordinarily large research program designed to transform the military foundation of Western security. The instrument of transformation was to be anti-nuclear shields for both East and West, which would render nuclear weapons "impotent and obsolete" and enable mutual deterrence to depend on the protection of national populations from nuclear strikes instead of on the vulnerability of national populations to nuclear retaliatory destruction. And this proposed strategic transformation, with its implied denigration of nuclear deterrence, was presented to Europe in the midst of the NATO-wide effort, in the face of intense domestic opposition, to deploy intermediate-range missiles on European soil in order to assure the coupling of U.S. strategic nuclear forces to the defense of Europe.

The initial shock with which allied governments reacted to President Reagan's announcement, however, was followed by more complex reactions as the SDI program was shaped by the diverse forces of technological developments, defense budgets, the arms-control dialogue, domestic politics, and prospects of industrial-technological spin-offs. Several con-

ditions have suppressed the initial shock caused by Reagan's announcement, muted official opposition to SDI in Western Europe, and prevented
SDI from becoming a focus of popular protest: (1) the abstract and
remote quality of SDI's ultimate goal, (2) the prospect that this goal
will become practically irrelevant as technological and economic difficulties mount and Reagan leaves the presidency, (3) the fact that SDI
is still only a research program, (4) the tendency of different groups
and individuals engaged in this program to emphasize a variety of
objectives short of creating population shields, (5) the fact that the
United States swears adherence to the ABM treaty while it seeks agreed
reductions of nuclear strike weapons, including the medium-range missiles in Europe, and (6) official U.S. assurances (as in the Reagan-
Thatcher accords) that SDI aims to stabilize a strategic balance, not to
achieve strategic superiority, and that the United States will not deploy
defensive weapons beyond the ABM treaty restrictions without consulting
its allies and negotiating with the Soviets. Moreover, unlike INF, SDI
remains largely the concern of governments and experts, since, for the
time being, it poses a set of esoteric technical issues and complicated,
hypothetical strategic, political, and economic issues, but nothing visible
to demonstrate against.

Nevertheless, future developments might again activate some of the
initial European concerns, so it is important to understand them. They
fall into several categories, as explained below.

Military Security

Universally, allied governments, as soon as they understood that
Reagan meant what he said, viewed SDI with dismay on the grounds
that, as announced, it would undermine the rationale of extended nuclear
deterrence, which had given them forty years of unprecedented peace
and security. The French were particularly vehement on this point, just
as they have been particularly disturbed by the U.S. emphasis on
reducing NATO's reliance on nuclear first-use by strengthening conventional options.

The corollary of this fear of nuclear nakedness was the fear that
rendering nuclear weapons impotent and obsolete would make Europe
safe for conventional war. Forced to rely entirely on conventional denial
capabilities (and on chemical weapons, in the absence of an effective
ban against them) instead of on a conventional "tripwire" or "pause"
plus nuclear escalation, the European allies feared that they would have
to spend unaffordable (or, at least, entirely unacceptable) funds on
conventional defense, which would still be incapable of withstanding
a Soviet blitzkrieg, in order to compensate for denuclearization.

Next in prominence among early adverse strategic reactions in Western Europe to President Reagan's SDI proclamation was the fear that shielding Americans from Soviet nuclear attacks would lead the United States to return to Fortress America or, at least, to decouple its strategic nuclear forces from the defense of Europe. This fear runs directly contrary to U.S. strategic logic and underestimates the strength of the U.S. self-interested commitment to the security of Western Europe, which crystallized during World War II and has been consolidated by a powerful set of entanglements since the creation of NATO in 1949. But the fear is not so implausible as it sounds. Europeans are conscious of the historical correlation of U.S. physical invulnerability with isolationism; U.S. vulnerability to Soviet retaliation gives the United States a stake in deterring aggression against Europe. The expectation of invulnerability may relieve the United States of that incentive, especially because the United States has acquired extensive global commitments that compete for the support of scarce resources.

If the American logic that correlates reduced U.S. vulnerability with the enhanced credibility of nuclear first-use is correct, however, it tends to support a more plausible European strategic anxiety: that the superpowers, protected by national shields, would spare each other from attack while waging a nuclear or conventional war in the relatively vulnerable European theater; or at least that Europe's geographical proximity to a great number and variety of Soviet strike weapons would lead the Soviets to concentrate on theater attacks rather than on the less profitable targets in the United States. Although Americans have a material interest in limiting an East-West war to Europe, Europeans are inclined to view any war in Europe as a catastrophic repetition of World War II.

If the SDI research program had been announced as an effort to catch up with the Soviet strategic defense program and guard against a Soviet breakout from the ABM treaty, or even as an effort to explore the feasibility of reducing the vulnerability of U.S. land-based retaliation forces—rationales that were prominent in the U.S. military establishment and national-security community—the adverse reaction would have been less intense and sweeping and SDI might even have attracted some early support among allied governments. Fears would then have focused on the possibility that SDI, given its huge funding and scope, would accelerate the arms race, disturb East-West relations, obstruct an arms agreement, and jeopardize the ABM treaty. But there would have been—indeed, there is now—considerable understanding and support for a U.S. program to reduce the vulnerability of U.S. land-based retaliatory forces, especially if the program was confined to terminal ballistic missile defense (BMD).

President Reagan's insistence on justifying SDI exclusively in terms of its ultimate goal keeps the initial strategic anxieties alive. Nonetheless, these anxieties have been muted by skeptical second thoughts about the technological and budgetary feasibility of population shields (at least for the next twenty or thirty years); U.S. assurances about maintaining nuclear deterrence as long as necessary; a U.S. promise to consult the allies and negotiate with the Soviets before deciding to deploy new BMDs; European hopes that at least the development and testing of space-based weapons may be banned or suspended in return for nuclear offensive reductions; favorable (if puzzling) signals from the U.S. bureaucracy and the contracting research laboratories about SDI's more proximate and less worrisome goal of protecting intercontinental ballistic missiles (ICBMs) and command, control, communications, and intelligence facilities (C^3I); and, as mentioned earlier, the possibility that when Reagan leaves the presidency the official commitment to his ultimate SDI goal will disappear.

These European second thoughts about the strategic significance of SDI are well advised on practical grounds. They argue for a calm and pragmatic approach to real policy choices instead of the initial alarm in reaction to remote and hypothetical possibilities. But a rounded evaluation should nevertheless consider the implications of these hypothetical possibilities because they will persist as part of the background of allied responses to SDI as long as the U.S. government justifies SDI in terms of the ultimate goal President Reagan proclaimed.

Feasibility of SDI

It is an open question as to whether Europeans could be convinced of the virtue of Reagan's vision of protective shields for Europe and the superpowers if they thought it was feasible and not too costly. Polls in Europe, as in the United States, indicate popular approval of the idea in the abstract. But the fact of the matter is that people in Western Europe with informed opinions about the technological feasibility and affordability of nearly perfect antinuclear shields are almost universally skeptical for all the reasons that induce skepticism among American scientists and technologists. There is equal skepticism about the possibility that the Soviets would help to alleviate the technological problems by cooperating with the United States in fostering a transition toward the ultimate goal through a series of arms agreements that would constrain offensive and antidefensive measures.

Suffice it here to say that profound skepticism about the feasibility of ever achieving nearly perfect shields against all kinds of nuclear attacks seems justified on technological and political grounds. Even if such protection was feasible for the superpowers, extending the same degree of protection to Western Europe would seem technically impossible, considering the variety of Soviet weapons with nuclear (and interchangeable conventional) warheads of all ranges and considering their speed of delivery and mobility. Only if conventional weapons eventually replaced nuclear weapons for all counterforce functions might the problem of Europe's differential vulnerability to nuclear weapons be overcome, but then only at the price of establishing an adequate conventional balance.

Under the most favorable conditions that can be reasonably imagined, nearly perfect shields could be achieved only through the constraints of an extremely comprehensive arms agreement, reached through a series of transitional agreements, that reliably abolished all kinds of nuclear weapons. But everything we know about the difficulties the United States and the Soviet Union had in SALT I and II agreeing on comprehensive limitations of their strategic forces—limitations that essentially only ratified the status quo—militates against these armed adversaries agreeing to the radical restructuring of their forces that the ultimate goal of SDI requires.

Perhaps, a better case can be made for 70 or 50 percent effective defensive systems in an offense-defense mix that would leave a minimum number of long- and medium-range nuclear weapons for escalatory and countervalue retaliatory purposes, while counterforce functions were largely performed by conventional weapons. Such partial defense against nuclear and conventional missiles would be more feasible; it should be more acceptable to the European allies, especially if they could gain comparable protection to that which the superpowers enjoyed. In the long run a preponderantly nonnuclear and antioffensive military structure may be congruent with the current trend toward the conventionalization of tactical and strategic nuclear forces. But these are hypothetical speculations that cannot be appraised in operational terms for decades.

Meanwhile, European skepticism about the feasibility of SDI as nearly perfect defensive shields is certainly warranted. However, the effect of this skepticism on U.S.-allied relations cuts different ways. On the one hand, zealous U.S. championing of such an improbable vision is unsettling to Europeans, who cannot dismiss a projected $26 billion program (from 1985 through 1989) as just another flight of American utopianism, even if Congress cuts the funding in half. Whether or not the concept of mutual assured defense is infeasible, it will leave its unpredictable imprint on military doctrine, defense budgets, and arms control; and the European allies are always upset by change. On the other hand, the incredibility of nearly perfect antinuclear shields encourages allied governments to focus on proximate and real aspects of

SDI and hope that the fantasy will fade. In other words, the unreality of the vision helps the allies to accept SDI with equanimity as long as the United States does not push it beyond the research stage.

Stability of the Military Balance

Regardless of the technological feasibility or infeasibility of SDI, government and other leaders in Western Europe generally oppose SDI for a more important reason: its supposed stimulus to the arms race and its allegedly destabilizing effect on the East-West military balance and East-West relations in general. This opposition is particularly intense among left-wing groups. Its most significant impact is in West Germany, where the longing for East-West détente runs strong and the government must make allowances for the latent antimilitary sentiment revealed during the INF crisis.

In Europe, more than in the United States, governments tend to defer to popular sentiment in their view of the "arms race" (more accurately, the competition for military strength through quantitative and qualitative improvements in weapons) as an ever-increasing, self-perpetuating, technologically determined accumulation of ever-more-deadly nuclear arsenals, which, if not halted, will lead to Armageddon. Europeans generally believe that through arms agreements and détente the arms race can be curbed and its dangers suppressed. They regard the SALT agreements of the 1970s as the most significant remission of the arms race malady, and they are naturally anxious to preserve them. This means, among other things, preserving the ABM treaty's severe restrictions on strategic defense weapons, in accordance with the theory that invulnerable nuclear forces clearly capable of inflicting unacceptable retaliatory damage on vulnerable populations are the best guarantee of peace.

According to this view, any proposal to introduce new or additional BMD weapons into the strategic equation, especially if not in the context of a negotiable comprehensive arms agreement, threatens to touch off a new round of the arms race in a mounting defensive-offensive competition that will destabilize the nuclear balance. Space-based BMDs are regarded as particularly pernicious because of the mystique (and myth) of space as a weaponless sanctuary, the extraordinary variety of exotic weapons that space promises to spawn, the uncertain and untestable wartime effects of these weapons and their components operating in conjunction with each other, and the presumed insurmountable vulnerability of such weapons to countermeasures. Furthermore, increasing the proportion of strategic defensive to strategic offensive weapons, it is feared, might mislead one side or the other to think that it possessed a rational first-strike capability because BMD could impair a ragged retaliatory strike. Clearly, the persistent Soviet criticism of SDI on these grounds, coupled with the Soviet threat to counter defensive weapons with an increase in offensive as well as defensive capabilities, reinforces these concerns.

These European concerns, at the least, exaggerate reality. The dynamics of East-West arms competition are much more complex and less ominous than the stereotyped view of the arms race. Budgetary constraints, the general quality of East-West relations, and many other factors, in addition to the invention and production of new weapons, affect the intensity of the arms competition. Despite occasional waves of fear in the United States that new weapons will upset the strategic balance—the erroneous post-*Sputnik* fear of a "missile gap" is the most notable—the history of the post-World War II arms competition shows that technological gains by either side are offset by compensating measures on the other side long before either obtains a decisive advantage. Indeed, the high rate of technological innovation, along with the quantitative surplus of nuclear striking power, makes truly destabilizing weapons innovations—that is, those that dangerously enhance the likelihood of a first strike—quite unlikely, although they may intensify the competition and make it more expensive.

Why, then, should the incremental introduction of BMD into the superpowers' arsenals over the next three or four decades, whether within the constraints of the proposed transitional arms agreements or not, be more destabilizing than the introduction of ICBMs or cruise missiles? To be sure, the element of uncertainty about the actual performance of BMD in warfare would be greater, but logic and common sense suggest that this uncertainty will be a stronger deterrent to the side contemplating a disarming first strike against protected retaliatory forces than to the side retaliating against either counterforce or countervalue targets. If space-based BMDs are substantially more vulnerable to countermeasures than, say, land-based ICBMs, which is not necessarily the case, would their vulnerability attract a first strike against them in a crisis, on the assumption that nuclear retaliation would be less likely or costly? Such a lapse of risk-taking constraint, given the uncertainties of technological performance and adversary behavior involved, seems implausible. If what is envisaged, nevertheless, is a war of attrition in space, such a war would at least seem to be more subject to limitation and early termination than nuclear exchanges on land under current conditions (in which, incidentally, space-based sensors would also be targets).

Insofar as reasoned speculation can penetrate the incalculable hypothetical realities of the effect of new and additional BMDs on the arms competition and the military balance, the fears of Europeans and others about the consequences of abandoning the present offense-heavy structure of deterrence seem, at the least, exaggerated. But the fears are nonetheless real and will probably persist, considering the popular anxieties that would be excited by major alteration of the familiar basis of deterrence, which lies in the mutual vulnerability of the superpowers and their allies to retaliatory destruction. European governments and populations regard this mutual vulnerability as both unavoidable and exceedingly dangerous to try to alter.

Only under two conditions might the European allies find it acceptable to increase substantially the proportion of strategic defensive weapons compared with strategic offensive weapons: (1) the change must take place in the context of a comprehensive agreement that promises to curb the arms race and enhance the stability of the military balance, (2) the change must not weaken the credibility of NATO's nuclear first-use strategy or substantially increase the burden of the nonnuclear defense of Western Europe.

Arms Control

As organized popular anxieties about nuclear weapons and weapons competition have increased, arms control—if only in the form of negotiations that hold some promise of an agreement—has become more necessary to allay anxieties and to gain acceptance of major nuclear weapons programs and support of defense budgets. This political truth was both revealed and enhanced by allied insistence on the "two-track" approach to the deployment of INF. It is even more compelling with respect to SDI, which envisages a radical restructuring of deterrence and an extension of the arms competition into a much larger realm of new, more powerful weapons.

Conscious of this role of arms control, the Reagan administration, despite its condemnation of the SALT agreements and its skepticism about the utility of strategic arms control in general, has proposed that the new world of mutual assured defense and survival be achieved in cooperation with the Soviet Union by means of transitional arms agreements. The agreements would begin with the deep reduction of strategic nuclear warheads (and of medium-range nuclear weapons in the European theater), especially on those ICBMs with multiple independently targeted reentry vehicles (MIRVs) capable, hypothetically, of knocking out most U.S. land-based ICBMs on a first strike. The Reagan administration postulates these agreements as steps toward the world of nearly perfect antinuclear shields. Yet all European governments and almost all security specialists devoutly hope that the United States, having helped induce the Soviets to return to the strategic arms talks in order to curb SDI, will use SDI as a bargaining chip by offering to ban development and testing, as well as deployment, of new strategic defense weapons (especially those based in space), and antisatellite weapons (ASATs) too, while reaffirming and tightening up the ABM treaty restrictions.

In addition, some Europeans—especially those in the left-wing parties of West Germany, Britain, and the Netherlands—look toward the elimination or at least an equitable reduction of intermediate-range missiles in the European theater. European governments, however, are now more worried that a superpower arms deal might "denuclearize" Europe than that it would make Europe more vulnerable to a nuclear attack, and even the antinuclear Left no longer worries so vociferously that INF will endanger the peace.

The Soviets, appreciating the European apprehensions about SDI and European reliance on arms control as an instrument of détente, concentrate on condemning SDI as the sole obstacle to nuclear reductions. By impressing anxious Europeans (and Americans) with the "generosity" of their concessions on offensive reductions, the visceral appeal of a complete ban on testing of nuclear weapons, and the alluring goal of abolishing all nuclear weapons, the Soviets hope to emphasize the obstacle that SDI poses to arms reductions and détente. Thereby, they hope to stimulate allied and congressional pressure against the program, while exploiting U.S.-allied differences, without having to pay anything in terms of constraints on their own military programs in an arms agreement.

To counter this Soviet tactic the United States must, at least, propose an attractive and plausible (that is, seemingly negotiable) arms agreement and place the onus on the Soviets for rejecting it. But such an arms agreement is unlikely so long as the United States lacks carrots or sticks to induce the Soviets to limit the heavy offensive weapons that threaten U.S. ICBMs, in which they have a quantitative advantage, while the United States holds open the option of eventually deploying new kinds of defensive weapons, in which it has a technological lead. The United States has no persuasive concession to offer—probably not even a limit on ASATs, which it rejects anyway—so long as it bars any restriction on SDI development and testing that is not consistent with its interpretation of the ABM treaty. Yet as long as the United States is also reluctant to threaten unilateral development, testing, or deployment of SDI beyond the restrictive definition of the ABM treaty, it lacks bargaining penalties to impose.

Even aside from the SDI problem, it is extremely difficult to achieve the kind of stabilizing reductions in nuclear forces that the United States seeks. This is because of the asymmetrical nuclear force structures (with the USSR heavily dependent on ICBMs and the United States relatively more dependent on sea- and air-launched ballistic and cruise missiles), the projected Soviet gains in relative nuclear striking power with or without arms restrictions, and the new technical problems of verification (for example, the problem of verifying limits on mobile missiles and missiles with interchangeable conventional and nuclear warheads). Under these conditions the prospect for arms negotiations is stalemate.

The allies will tend to blame an arms stalemate on President Reagan's refusal to use SDI as a bargaining chip unless Soviet intransigence is conspicuous. In time, if the U.S. position seems like a big obstacle to détente and arms control in Europe, the kind of popular and political protest that INF engendered (minus the on-site demonstrations) could be sparked. As against this prospect of stalemate, Europeans yearn for a "grand bargain" in which the United States will trade SDI for nuclear reductions, but it is not evident that either side is prepared to make any such bargain.

Neither the opening gambits in strategic force bargaining set forth by the two heads of state in the summer of 1986 nor the dramatic concessions that they seemed to be offering at the preparatory talks at Reykjavík in October demonstrated that a grand bargain is likely or imminent. What they did demonstrate is that both sides seek the moral high ground in order to persuade the American and West European publics of the justice of opposing positions on SDI. It remains to be seen whether the Soviet and American leaders, advertising these positions as the final solution to all nuclear anxieties, culminating in the elimination of all nuclear weapons (or at least all nuclear ballistic missiles, as in the U.S. position tabled at Reykjavík), have infused new energy into the hard bargaining for military advantage that is always at the crux of arms negotiations. But the impression they conveyed of a quick and sweeping resolution of the dozens of intractable issues entailed in reaching a mutually satisfactory and reliably verifiable military balance at a drastically reduced or zero level of nuclear forces, in addition to resolving their differences over SDI, is surely an illusion. This illusion will eventually dissolve in stalemated or failed negotiations or in protracted bargaining about much more limited changes in the asymmetrical structures of U.S. and Soviet strategic forces, such as the approximately 30 percent reductions in strategic offensive weapons that both sides accepted at Reykjavík for the first five-year phase.

Although the most likely prospect for strategic arms negotiations seems to be protracted bargaining or a stalemate, it is theoretically much easier to achieve a reduction and limitation of land-based medium-range missiles in the European theater, since the military significance of the numbers of these missiles is diminished by the existence of both shorter- and longer-range nuclear weapons relevant to the theater balance and by the fact that this balance is only part of a global balance. In practice, however, it is not clear whether the contest between the superpowers for the favor of West European sentiment will facilitate or obstruct an INF agreement.

Both superpowers' declared aim of eliminating all medium-range missiles as a step toward eliminating all nuclear (or all ballistic nuclear) weapons is surely propaganda, not bargaining. Moreover, it is propaganda that is likely to backfire in U.S.-allied relations, since, like President Reagan's vision of SDI, it confronts the allies with the specter of having to rely on a nonnuclear military balance. In contrast, an "interim" agreement, in which both sides would retain a reduced but moderate number of missiles, might very well be negotiated if the problem of limiting Soviet short-range INF (the SS-21, SS-22, and SS-23) and the SS-20s deployed in Soviet Asia could be resolved.

This kind of agreement, however, presupposes that the Soviets would calculate that it promoted their overriding objective of mobilizing European sentiment against SDI. They are more likely to seek this objective by trying to convince U.S. allies that American insistence on developing, testing, and eventually deploying SDI is the sole obstacle to achieving an irresistible INF agreement. Apparently, the latter calculation prevailed at Reykjavík, since General Secretary Gorbachev prescribed, contrary to previous Soviet statements that an INF agreement could be considered separately from SDI, that such an agreement must be part of a package including strategic weapons reductions. He also stated that Soviet acceptance of this package must be conditional upon the restriction of SDI to research in laboratories during a ten-year extension of the nonwithdrawal period from the ABM treaty, with no presumption in favor of revising the treaty's restrictions at the end of this period.

European governments could barely suppress their relief at being saved by Gorbachev's reversal from confronting the unacceptable implications of Reykjavík for the nonnuclear defense of Europe and a credible U.S. deterrent. They were further reassured when, in mid-November 1986, President Reagan concurred with Prime Minister Thatcher that the "priority" in negotiations with the Soviet Union should be placed on seeking only a 50 percent cut in all strategic nuclear forces, a sharp reduction (but not elimination) of medium-range missiles, with restraints on short-range missiles, and a ban on chemical weapons, while taking steps toward eliminating Soviet advantages in nonnuclear forces.

If, as a result of these modifications of the U.S. arms-control position, the propaganda contest at Reykjavík gives way to serious bargaining at

Geneva on the reduction of medium-range and long-range nuclear weapons, it will become obvious that the original U.S. concept of reaching the world of mutual assured defense and nuclear obsolescence by means of a "cooperative transition" is too ambitious a goal to be attainable and too radical a change in the structure of deterrence to be acceptable. This point is well understood by allied governments, although they diplomatically choose not to argue it. The goal of constructing a nuclear-free, defense-dominant structure is, on the one hand, too ambitious and incredible to attract the support of arms-control enthusiasts but, on the other hand, too linked with a vast military program to appeal to visionary nuclear abolitionists. Indeed, SDI, as President Reagan has presented it, is an odd marriage of a nuclear pacifist vision with an extraordinarily ambitious arms program, the first and most practical application of which will almost surely be the protection of military sites, not national populations. The irony is that, whereas the objective of countering nuclear strike forces with BMD might (at some stage when the technology has matured) be incorporated into a negotiable arms-control position that the allies could support, the goal of creating population shields presupposes a degree of Soviet cooperation and of multinational dependence on arms control that only the most ardent believers in disarmament believe possible.

British and French Nuclear Forces

The British and French have a special reason for deploring SDI. Although not even the French wish to represent their opposition to SDI as a special national interest, they obviously do have such an interest: to preserve the utility of their independent nuclear forces. Their fear is that U.S. strategic defense deployments will lead to similar Soviet deployments, which will degrade the value of the independent nuclear forces in which the French and British have invested large funds for the highest political stakes.

The reasoning behind this view seems strained because it assumes (1) that the Soviet threat to the independent nuclear forces is only a function of the Soviet response to U.S. deployments, (2) that the United States will disregard the ABM treaty and reject any other arms restrictions in order to deploy strategic defense weapons to which the Soviets will respond in kind, (3) that these weapons will be deployed to protect cities, (4) that MIRVs and penetration aids will not enable British and French weapons to retain countercity capabilities, and (5) that Soviet deployments will therefore provide such effective protection of cities as to negate the deterrent and political values the British and French now attribute to their independent forces. None of these assumptions is necessarily, or even probably, true. But it is understandable that the British and French should assume the worst instead of the best outcome of uncertain scenarios based on a radically new structure of deterrence. Moreover, the British, at least, have reason to fear that the domestic opponents of an independent nuclear force will exploit the worst-case scenario to reinforce their case. And even French security experts argue that SDI, if vigorously promoted, may undermine the fragile domestic consensus supporting the whole range of French nuclear policies.

To prevent the extension of East-West arms competition into anti-nuclear defense systems, the British and French rely on the ABM treaty. They will be particularly sensitive, therefore, to any signs of U.S. withdrawal from the treaty or of superpower revision of the treaty, unless it is in the context of a new comprehensive arms agreement that protects the British and French independent nuclear forces while reducing the level of superpower forces. Only in that context, moreover, would they consider a proportionate reduction of their own forces. The Soviets, however, have given only the slightest hint that they might accommodate any such solution to British and French concerns.

From the time the INF negotiations began, until the fall of 1986, the Soviets insisted that the British and French nuclear forces be counted against the numbers of Western INF missiles in any INF reduction, knowing that the British and French regard their forces as strategic weapons, not as INF. When the Soviets conceded that medium-range missiles in the European theater could be reduced to zero without requiring a ban on SDI, they made this concession contingent on freezing the numbers of British and French nuclear forces, which are scheduled to be augmented by about 1,200 warheads through MIRVs. Soviet statements in the fall of 1986, however, indicated that Moscow would no longer regard the British and French nuclear forces as medium-range missiles to be counted in INF reductions. This concession was interpreted in the West as greatly enhancing the prospect of an early INF agreement. But at the preparatory summit talks in Reykjavík in November 1986 Gorbachev's insistence on including an INF agreement in the total package of agreements that must be linked to resolution of SDI restrictions on his terms in effect made Moscow's concession on INF contingent on a ban on SDI that is unacceptable to Washington. The British and French governments were relieved that Gorbachev's intransigence blocked the prospect of superpower agreement on schemes for denuclearizing the strategic and regional balance. But the Thatcher government could hardly ignore the encouragement that the failure of arms control might offer to the Labour party, which is committed to unilateral British nuclear disarmament.

SDI's Implications for Defense Expenditures

As the limits of SDI and the remoteness and unlikelihood of the achievement of its ultimate goal become apparent, allied concerns tend to focus on more proximate issues and choices. One of these concerns is SDI's implications for defense expenditures.

Allied governments expect a program funded on the immense scale of SDI to gather political and bureaucratic momentum and powerful sponsors. Whatever its tangible military results, they believe SDI, as a multifaceted weapons program, is here to stay. Some members of the European defense community worry that the resulting expenditures and the human and material resources they consume will be a diversion of funds from higher-priority needs, such as strengthening conventional defense capabilities on NATO's central front. The supreme allied commander in Europe, General Bernard Rogers, has loudly lent his voice to this view. This apprehension is part of a larger concern that springs from the fact that allied governments are being urged—and most of them now agree with the proposed goal, in principle—to raise NATO's nuclear threshold with strengthened conventional capabilities, including costly deep-attack missiles and C^3I technology, at a time in which budget austerity and high rates of unemployment virtually preclude increased defense expenditures.

SDI as a Technological Enterprise

The other side of the concerns the NATO allies have expressed about the adverse impact of SDI on defense expenditures is their desire to share the benefits of high-technology enterprise that the immense investments in SDI research are presumed to offer. As of now the economic desire far outweighs the economic apprehension in its influence on European positions on SDI. Reconciled to the fact that the SDI program is here to stay, most European government and industry leaders are disposed to get aboard the train of technological bounties before it leaves the station. Although the European share of contracts may be disappointing, European industries can at least look forward to gaining access to technological know-how.

This disposition toward participation is reinforced by the concern that Western Europe, afflicted with structural deficiencies that impede its competitiveness in modern high-technological enterprise, is in danger of forfeiting to the United States and Japan the economic benefits of the new technological boom, while suffering a brain drain of its best scientists to U.S. corporations. Already painfully impressed by U.S. dominance of the high-technology military marketplace and resentful of the U.S. failure to establish a true two-way street in military procurement and trade, European governments and entrepreneurs are all the more determined to get a fair share of SDI technology, with its promise of civilian spin-offs.

The U.S. government, conscious of these European feelings and sensing an opportunity to elicit European support of at least one aspect of SDI, has encouraged European governments and industries to join the United States in this vast research program. General James Abrahamson, head of the SDI organization in the Pentagon, has forecast significant civilian spin-offs and formed the Office of Education and Civil Applications to foster them. This facet of SDI began with Defense Secretary Caspar Weinberger's personal initiative of March 1985, inviting the allies to join SDI research. It was followed by a memorandum of understanding with Britain in December outlining the research areas and the principles and structure for managing technological participation. This cleared the way for a similar agreement in March 1986 with West Germany, notwithstanding the opposition of the Social Democratic party and Foreign Minister Hans-Dietrich Genscher on political grounds and the opposition of Finance Minister Gerhard Stoltenberg on financial grounds. This agreement, in turn, assures an agreement with Italy.

However, France has taken the lead in opposing such official participation in SDI. In the name of independent European cooperation it has tried to organize a European surrogate based on a Franco-German foundation. Efforts supported by Great Britain and West Germany to organize the collective participation of British, West German, French, and Italian companies in SDI failed at the economic summit in Bonn in May 1985. This failure left European countries free to participate in an independent counterpart to SDI. Predictably, France seized this opportunity.

The French government, whose officials were initially the most outspoken critics of SDI, rejected government-to-government participation. Instead, it proposed in April 1985 an ostensibly nonmilitary cooperative high-technology program, Eureka (European Research Coordination Agency). Eureka—a loosely organized, open-ended association intended to attract industrial participation and investment—is supposed to give European countries, and West Germany in particular, a multinational civilian alternative to SDI research (although, in fact, most of the projects envisaged are dual-use, that is, military and commercial). Nevertheless, France gave the green light to its government-owned electronics and weapons companies, notably Matra and Thomson, to compete for SDI contracts. Although President Mitterrand continued to oppose French participation on grounds of national independence, Prime Minister Chirac, whose conservative coalition gained him a power-sharing role in the parliamentary elections of March 1986, took the position that France could not afford to remain aloof from SDI research.

At the same time, there was a growing sentiment among French political and industrial leaders that France should follow the U.S. example and develop its own space-defense program, independently or with European cooperation. The goal was not to gain perfect protection for the nation but to enhance deterrence by countering Soviet offensive missiles, including the SS-20. To give this goal a European dimension, the Mitterrand government presented it as part of a European Defense Initiative (EDI) and explored, within the framework of emerging Franco-German defense cooperation, collaborative programs with West Germany, which expressed interest in developing a European shield against cruise missiles and short-range nuclear missiles.

This prospect has attracted considerable German interest in a general way. German Defense Minister Manfred Worner has welcomed French cooperation in developing an ATBM, although he has proposed under-taking this cooperation in the context of a revitalized Western European Union (WEU) in order to assure its compatibility with the Federal Republic's commitment to NATO. Former chancellor Helmut Schmidt, in a notable speech in the Bundestag (on June 28, 1984), called for a joint Franco-German industrial program, an expanded Franco-German conventional defense effort, and a French nuclear guarantee to cover West German territory.

Nevertheless, whether Eureka and EDI can provide the best of three worlds—a competitive European surrogate for SDI, along with an independent French program and unofficial industrial participation in the U.S. program—is problematical. In June 1985 the four largest European electronics companies—Siemens, Philips, General Electric, and Thomson—signed a statement of intent to cooperate on several different projects within the framework of Eureka. Some contracts have been signed. But the British, notwithstanding successful collaboration with the French on the Airbus and the Arianne space launcher, are drawn more toward cooperation with the United States than with France. West Germany is ambivalent. It must preserve its strong U.S. ties in all security matters. It also wants closer French cooperation; but the French have given no tangible signs of willingness to extend such cooperation to the nuclear level, and no Germans believe that French cooperation could in any way be a substitute for the U.S. connection. Under these circumstances, the German government is afraid that the exclusivist bias of Eureka, in combination with U.S. pressure to join SDI research, will jeopardize one or both of its security ties. At the same time, it must heed strong domestic opposition from the Social Democratic party against participation in either a European or a U.S. military program associated with SDI.

As things now stand, in spite of political opposition to SDI in the German Social Democratic and the British Labour parties, all the *major* European governments except France have accepted (or, in the case of Italy, probably will soon accept) official participation in SDI research. Concomitantly, allied governments have muted their overt criticism of SDI's strategic implications and emphasized the necessity of SDI research for developing hard-point defense and for gaining civilian as well as military technological spin-offs. In this way, SDI as a technological enterprise has enabled most of the allies to reconcile the program with allied solidarity—particularly, for the sake of good relations with the United States but also out of reluctance to lend credence to the Soviet campaign to muster European opposition to SDI.

Nevertheless, there is considerable and well-founded skepticism in Europe (1) that the United States will award the most lucrative contracts to European instead of U.S. companies; (2) that the European share of contracts for weapons systems and major components, as opposed to subcontracts, will be more than a token; and (3) that the U.S. government, considering its emphasis on preventing the leak of critical technologies to the East, will share the most advanced technologies with Europe. Some Europeans estimate that only about 1 percent of the total contracted funds will go to European companies.

Unless European industries, whether through Eureka or otherwise, can combine their resources in an economically efficient way to overcome the artificially fragmented European market, they are likely to remain very junior partners in the production of SDI-related technology. Europeans, however, have learned to live with their skepticism about the extent of U.S. commercial and financial cooperation while making the most of it for the sake of the overriding benefits of security cooperation. European accommodation to SDI as a technological enterprise, however, does not mean European approval of SDI as a U.S. military program to restructure deterrence. The allies have accepted SDI as a research program and, perhaps, as a technological resource that might some day protect European military sites but not as a test of loyalty to President Reagan's vision, which they profoundly oppose.

Antitactical Ballistic Missiles

As the various facets of SDI materialize, there is one kind of weapon in the vast array of antinuclear defensive weapons technologies that is likely to have special significance for European military security, although it was not originally envisaged as part of a multilayered defense system:

ATBMs. The ATBM category could encompass a variety of missiles with conventional warheads, theoretically capable of intercepting and destroying incoming ballistic and cruise missiles of "tactical" rather than "strategic" range (and, therefore, not prohibited by the ABM treaty as long as they have not been tested in an ABM mode and do not use components transferred from ABMs). Some have already been developed. Improvements through further research and development are likely to give them a useful military role in defending military targets on land in the European theater long before a useful system of layered defense to protect national populations in the United States or the Soviet Union could be developed, let alone deployed as a cost-effective and affordable system. Against the SS-20, with its exo-atmospheric trajectory, longer-range BMD would be required in order to distinguish armed warheads from decoys in midcourse as part of a layered defense (although the lower payload of the SS-20 would leave less room for decoys than would be the case with long-range missiles). But against the so-called short-range INF (SS-21, SS-22, and SS-23)—accurate dual-capable missiles with ranges of 75, 550, and 300 miles, respectively—ATBMs would be appropriate because the problem of effective terminal interceptors is simplified by the slower velocity and the largely or entirely atmospheric trajectory.

As an outgrowth of their surface-to-air missile technology, the Soviets have already developed and tested and are in the process of deploying at least one first-generation ATBM: the mobile SA-X-12. (U.S. officials do not credit the anticruise missile SA-10 with an ATBM capability, although it might be upgraded for this purpose.) At the current rate of development, Soviet ATBMs, working together with improved ABMs, will give the Soviets a significant terminal-defense capability in Europe before the year 2000. The United States, in contrast, has no deployable ATBM. The likeliest candidate is the surface-to-surface Patriot, but the Patriot would have to be redesigned with new sensors and a C^3I network in order to acquire a useful ATBM capability; and even then, according to some sources, it would be very expensive and of marginal utility with a conventional warhead, which is politically indispensable.

The potential military significance of ATBMs arises from the Soviet emphasis since the late 1960s on an initial, conventional blitzkrieg capability, combined with the proliferation of mobile nuclear and non-nuclear strike missiles. These Soviet military developments are intended to nullify NATO's nuclear first-use option while overwhelming its minimal conventional defense capability. Soviet ATBMs can contribute to Soviet theater capabilities by countering INF and by protecting the Soviets' enormous and increasing lead in nuclear warheads deliverable on theater targets. This lead results from large and continuing SS-20 deployments (at the end of 1985, 441 launchers with three warheads each), the initial deployments of the SS-21s, SS-22s, and SS-23s, added to the older longer-range SS-11s and SS-9s, and the greatly expanded force of Soviet theater nuclear aircraft. No less significant in the long run may be the role of ATBMs in protecting the Soviets' new generation of deep-interdiction missiles with conventional warheads, part of a burgeoning Soviet emerging technology program.

From the U.S. standpoint the principal military role of ATBMs would be to diminish the great and growing vulnerability of concentrations of general purpose forces and critical military targets in Western Europe, including air and missile bases, to Soviet ballistic and cruise missiles. The overriding objective of protecting these targets would be to strengthen the implementation of the conventional and the limited nuclear options postulated in the 1967 NATO doctrine of flexible and controlled response (MC 14/3), by denying the Soviets a decisive first-strike capability and enhancing the survival of INF and other retaliatory forces.

The principal political objective of ATBM deployments would be to enhance the credibility of an effective conventional response to a conventional attack, demonstrate the commitment of U.S. SDI efforts to the defense of Europe, validate the U.S. commitment to provide equal protection for the allies as a counterpart to SDI, and counter any diversion of Soviet targeting from U.S. to European targets that might result from extended ABM or other SDI deployments in the United States. The validity of these objectives is reinforced by evidence of an independent European interest in ATBMs. Some British and French defense experts and officials regard ATBMs as an attractive means of protecting their independent nuclear forces. German defense officials and politicians have expressed interest in ATBMs to counter Soviet cruise missiles and short-range nuclear missiles. French and German spokesmen, with German Defense Minister Manfred Worner taking the lead, have indicated that the European allies might develop their own ATBM, probably with U.S. assistance, as part of a transatlantic division of labor. This collective project would give the allies the technological benefits of a major weapon system directly related to their own security, as opposed to mere subcontracts in the SDI program.

European enthusiasm for ATBMs, however, may be based more on political hopes than technological and economic realities. At a time of declining expenditures on conventional forces allied governments are unlikely to launch an expensive ATBM development program, and the United States is unlikely to subsidize such a program. Furthermore, U.S. promotion of ATBMs, in response to official European requests, could, like U.S. sponsorship of INF, provoke a popular opposition to deployments that would turn a political dividend into a political crisis.

The reason is that ATBMs, because they are closely related to ABMs and other strategic defense weapons and because they would be visible targets for antinuclear demonstrators, raise potentially explosive political issues in domestic politics and East-West relations.

One issue arises because of the ambiguity of the distinction between ABMs and ATBMs. The technology of some ATBMs is not much different from that of ABMs. ATBMs—the SA-X-12 is an example—could be given an ABM range and function. Politically, this ambiguity cuts two ways. On the one hand, the similarity of ATBMs to ABMs might take some of the political onus off land-based SDI and help to link U.S. strategic defense to European tactical defense. On the other hand, the development and deployment of ATBMs will probably be regarded by antimilitary parties and groups in Europe as a dangerous circumvention of the ABM treaty and a stalking horse for SDI. (With this in mind, the Soviets deny that they have an ATBM and warn that any Western effort to develop one would be contrary to the ABM treaty.) ATBMs will also be condemned in these quarters as contributions to a warfighting strategy, which will raise the likelihood of a catastrophic war on European soil.

Such public opposition to ATBMs might also raise the contentious issue of an ATBM ban or limitation to prevent an arms race in Europe between offensive and defensive weapons, especially if an INF arms agreement is reached or seems likely. In the short run, the Soviet advantage in ATBM development may be an argument for seeking an ATBM ban, perhaps in the context of a tightening of the ABM treaty's restrictions; but in the longer run NATO's great vulnerability to Soviet nuclear weapons and the general trend toward converting theater nuclear forces into conventional forces argues for investing in ATBMs as part of a badly needed effort to strengthen air defense in Western Europe. In any case, a ban or moratorium would freeze a Soviet advantage in ATBMs at this stage of Western underdevelopment of the technology.

Whatever may be the military case for linking SDI to the defense of Western Europe, the political effect might be to arouse public opinion in Europe against absorption into an allegedly provocative U.S. SDI program. However, if SDI can be dissociated from either a strategy of population defense or war fighting and if SDI can also be integrated into an arms-control position that the allies can identify with their special interests and perspectives, its extension to Europe and its linkage to ATBMs might be a political asset. A revision of the ABM treaty might facilitate such an integration of SDI into an arms limitation by permitting expanded land-based terminal defense deployments and banning the testing and deployment of space-based systems for a period of years. In the context of an agreement on offensive warhead reductions, this revision would also provide the basis for the limitation of other nuclear weapons in Europe at reduced levels. It might also provide the basis for clarifying the distinction between ATBMs and ABMs in order to prevent a divisive conflict on this question in European domestic politics.

Of course, such speculations about the military and political significance of ATBMs are inconclusive until much more is known about the technology and its cost, as compared to alternatives for achieving the same military objectives, such as a combination of passive defense and counterforce measures. Nevertheless, it is possible that if the Soviet ATBM program continues to progress at the same pace, this development, added to the large conventional and nuclear advantage the Soviets have already attained in the European theater, could affect the fate of SDI at least as much as the vulnerability of the land-based leg of the U.S. strategic triad. In any case, the emergence of ATBM issues seems likely to be one of several factors that will turn European and U.S. SDI concerns increasingly toward terminal defense of land-based targets intended to enhance the existing basis of direct and extended deterrence, while the goal of population shields recedes into the background as a dramatic expression of the inveterate longing to escape the nuclear dilemma.

THE FUTURE

Judging from the course of SDI in transatlantic relations thus far, the widespread opposition to its ultimate goal among defense specialists and governments probably will remain subordinate to the equally widespread desire to avoid transatlantic dissension and reap the benefits of technological enterprise. Therefore, SDI does not seem likely to trigger the kind of popular opposition that INF did or to be a major source of transatlantic dissension. SDI might even be a source of transatlantic cohesion if it seems to be a lever for progress in arms control, a source of technological enrichment, and, eventually, a program from which ATBM technology relevant to the conventional defense of Europe can be derived.

However, this judgment is contingent on three questionable conditions: (1) that SDI remains a research program rather than a program of developing, testing, or deploying BMD beyond the restrictive interpretation of the ABM treaty; (2) that holding open the option of such a BMD deployment seems compatible with fruitful arms negotiations and an eventual arms agreement that will stabilize nuclear deterrence at a lower level of forces; and (3) that the prospect of expanded BMD deployments in the United States is compatible with European wishes for equal protection without provocation.

A number of developments might contravene these conditions and serve as catalysts for crisis:

1. Because SDI is a research program aimed at deployment, sooner or later the decision of whether to test and deploy SDI weapons will arise. A positive decision could raise and amplify all the strategic, operational, military, and arms-control issues that were foreshadowed in the initial alarms touched off by President Reagan's proclamation. These issues would be brought to a head if they entailed U.S. abrogation of or withdrawal from the ABM treaty rather than its agreed revision. If U.S. deployment of BMDs leads to the deployment of SDI weapons in Europe or even only over Europe (that is, the sensors and satellites serving U.S.-based BMD), SDI could become a matter of public controversy and of INF-like tensions between the United States and its allies. Unlike the INF crisis, an SDI or SDI-ATBM crisis might mobilize European governments as well as the antinuclear activists against U.S. policies.

2. The most likely reason the United States might decide to deploy SDI before the end of this century would be to protect its land-based missiles and C^3I because there appeared to be no other politically as well as technologically and economically feasible way to rescue a survivable land-based ICBM force in the face of a growing Soviet advantage in hard-target-kill ICBMs. The impact of this deployment decision on U.S.-allied relations would depend, among other things, on whether projected deployments were confined to ABMs rather than extended to space-based weapons and whether they were made cooperatively by revision of the ABM treaty instead of unilaterally in defiance of the treaty. If neither of the latter conditions obtained, U.S. BMD deployments could lead to a major transatlantic crisis.

3. In the next couple of decades the infusion of ATBM competition into the East-West military confrontation in Europe, along with the conversion of many tactical and perhaps some strategic functions from nuclear to conventional weapons, could so cloud the distinction between ATBMs and ABMs and between the roles of nuclear and conventional missiles as to make the strategic rationale of the ABM treaty—crisis stability through the severe limitation of defense against missiles and the unalterable vulnerability of nations to nuclear devastation—obsolete. Just the Soviet deployment of mobile ATBMs—integrated with ABMs upgradable to ABM ranges and assigned to protect military targets enmeshed with urban centers—could obliterate the distinctions on which the treaty's restrictions were based. The politically troublesome question of whether to revise or abandon the ABM treaty may therefore arise before long. Whether the deployment of ATBMs would facilitate or obstruct the revision of the ABM treaty will depend on a number of

factors, not the least of which is the official U.S. rationale for SDI and the way the United States relates SDI to strategic arms reductions. But, unless the treaty is revised in East-West agreement, the proliferation of ATBMs and the conversion of nuclear to conventional functions would almost surely make the ABM treaty the focal point of a divisive transatlantic strategic debate. This debate may be foreshadowed in the issues raised by the very prospect of ATBM development, testing, and deployment before the end of this century. The debate would be complicated by the achievement, or just the lively prospect of the achievement, of an INF reduction and limitation, since ATBMs would then seem all the greater threat to the military balance that an INF agreement was supposed to stabilize.

4. Although the United States may continue to adhere to the ABM treaty while seeking reductions of SS-18s and other Soviet ICBMs, the Soviets might, at some point, reach the conclusion that their effort to curb the SDI program through public diplomacy and arms control had failed and decide to deploy a full-scale, nationwide BMD system in a sudden "breakout" or perhaps a "creep-out," on the grounds that the United States had rejected all reasonable arms-control proposals and was preparing to seek strategic superiority through SDI deployments. Or the Soviets might threaten to do this in order to strengthen their leverage for special restrictions on ASATs and space-based BMD development and testing. The first course would compel the United States to respond with offensive and defensive measures. If the Soviet breakout or creep-out was confined to land-based systems, the United States would have to choose whether to respond with the full range of layered-defense weapons or with only a reciprocally limited land-based program. A Soviet threat of breakout as a bargaining lever would compel the United States to choose among making a simple counterthreat, accepting the Soviet arms-control position, or proposing some other alternative.

5. The Soviets, unable to stop the U.S. program aimed at space-based deployments, might propose an arms agreement to permit extended land-based ABM deployments but ban space-based deployments while reducing the number of offensive nuclear warheads on terms that would give the Soviets a strategic advantage (for example, by permitting mobile ICBMs with MIRVs) and leave the European allies vulnerable (for example, by banning ABMs in Europe). The United States would then have to face, in the context of arms negotiations foreshadowing superpower collusion, the potentially disruptive SDI issues that spring from the differential vulnerability of Europe. It might also face the heightened prospect of a Soviet ABM breakout if it rejected Soviet terms. Nevertheless, the United States might well turn a Soviet proposal to revise the ABM treaty to its advantage if it was prepared to incorporate a limited

extension of ABM deployments into a grand arms bargain entailing deep reductions in offensive missiles and bombers and extended restrictions on space-based systems.

6. If the Soviets maintain their present negotiating tactics, as seems likely for at least the next several years, and the U.S. government (even after the Reagan administration) both adheres to the ABM treaty and rejects any additional restrictions on space-based SDI as a bargaining lever, the Soviets may succeed in convincing European countries and their publics (and important segments of the U.S. Congress, too) that U.S. insistence on pursuing population shields to make nuclear deterrence obsolete is the principal obstacle to reductions of long-range and medium-range offensive weapons. Alternatively, the Soviets might accept such deep reductions of SS-18 missiles that the United States could not refuse a ten- or fifteen-year ban on SDI development, testing, and deployment, which, after President Reagan is out of office, might be tantamount to a permanent ban.

7. A Labour party victory in Great Britain and, less likely, an SPD return to power in West Germany would strengthen antimilitary forces throughout Western Europe and would greatly enhance the influence on governments of the Soviet campaign to represent SDI and any related Western military program as the sole obstacle to disarmament and détente.

8. If, contrary to present indications, deep reductions or the elimination of whole classes of nuclear weapons are reached in a comprehensive East-West agreement, without unacceptable (from the American standpoint) restrictions on SDI development and testing or against future SDI deployments, European opposition to any strategic or tactical defense programs that are inconsistent with a restrictive interpretation of the ABM treaty would be greatly strengthened. But, simultaneously, the United States might be plunged into a vociferous BMD debate, or the U.S. government might be engaged in a desperate campaign against European (and probably congressional) opposition to keep alive the SDI options technically permitted by the postulated arms agreement. The divisive effect upon U.S.-European relations could be greater than any effect of strategic differences in the absence of a treaty.

None of these developments is inevitable or necessarily the stuff of crisis if it should occur. All of these developments can be either prevented or managed. Some might be turned to the benefit of NATO. But any of them could seriously aggravate rather than mitigate the dilemma of Europe's nuclear dependence if SDI is not approached in the context of an integrated defense and arms-control policy that reconciles U.S. and European perspectives, as outlined in this chapter.

The wisest policies, however, will not entirely solve Europe's nuclear dilemma, which any major change in NATO's military posture or strategy—and certainly the changes inherent in SDI—is bound to accentuate. The beginning of wisdom is to accept this fact as long as NATO serves its central purposes. Instinctively, the allied governments do accept the dilemma. Sooner or later, visions of population shields notwithstanding, it will become evident that the U.S. government also accepts the dilemma as unavoidable. Only on this basis can the allies effectively cope with the practical policy issues of applying the new BMD technology toward reducing NATO's dependence on nuclear retaliation. Without the disruptive distraction of antinuclear shields, NATO may gradually assimilate the practical elements of SDI to the endless task of alleviating its nuclear dilemma rather than strain its fabric of cohesion in a futile effort to abolish the dilemma. Military assimilation presupposes the continuing political adaptation of the requirements of transatlantic collaboration to the European allies' search for a greater measure of control over their collective security, but that is a subject beyond the scope of this chapter.

ABOUT THE CONTRIBUTORS

Harold Brown is chairman of The Johns Hopkins Foreign Policy Institute, School of Advanced International Studies, in Washington, D.C. Previously, Dr. Brown was secretary of defense (1977–81); president of the California Institute of Technology (1969–77); a member of the U.S. delegation to the Strategic Arms Limitation Talks (1969–77); secretary of the air force (1965–69); director of defense research and engineering (1961–65); and director of the Lawrence Livermore Laboratory (1960–61). Dr. Brown is a consultant to, and director of, various corporations and is author of *Thinking About National Security: Defense and Foreign Policy in a Dangerous World* (1983).

Richard K. Betts is a senior Fellow at The Brookings Institution and visiting professor of government at Harvard University. He has taught at Columbia University and The Johns Hopkins University and has served on the staffs of the Senate Select Committee on Intelligence and the National Security Council. Dr. Betts is the author of *Soldiers, Statesmen, and Cold War Crises* (1977), *Surprise Attack* (1982), and other works.

Barry M. Blechman is president of Defense Forecasts, Inc., and a Fellow of The Johns Hopkins Foreign Policy Institute. He served as assistant director of the U.S. Arms Control and Disarmament Agency from 1977 to 1980; prior to that he was director of the Defense Analysis Program at The Brookings Institution. He is coauthor of *Force Without War* (1977) and author of *U.S. Security in the Twenty-first Century* (1986), among other publications.

Stephen J. Hadley is a partner in the Washington, D.C., law firm of Shea & Gardner. After receiving his law degree from Yale Law School, he served in the Department of Defense from 1972 to 1974. He was a member of the National Security Council staff from 1974 to 1977. In

1979 he was a consultant to the Senate Foreign Relations Committee on the SALT II treaty. More recently he was counsel to the President's Special Review Board on the arms sales to Iran (the Tower Commission).

George Liska, an associate of The Johns Hopkins Foreign Policy Institute, holds a joint appointment as professor of political science at The Johns Hopkins University in Baltimore, Maryland, and The Johns Hopkins School of Advanced International Studies in Washington, D.C. Before coming to the United States in 1949, he served in the General Secretariat of the Czechoslovak Ministry of Foreign Affairs. Dr. Liska is the author of *Nations in Alliance* (1962), *Imperial America* (1967), and *Russia and World Order* (1980), among other works. His latest book is a collection of essays, *Rethinking U.S.-Soviet Relations* (1987).

Dave McCurdy has been Democratic congressman from Oklahoma since 1980. In 1983 he became the only member of congress to serve simultaneously on the House Armed Services Committee, the Science, Space and Technology Committee, and the Permanent Select Committee on Intelligence. As a senior member of the Armed Services Subcommittee on Research and Development and chairman of the Subcommittee on Transportation, Aviation and Materials, Congressman McCurdy has almost exclusive jurisdiction in the House over U.S. civil and military aviation research and development programs. Within the Armed Services Committee he has been an active leader in formulating defense policy reforms.

Robert E. Osgood was the Christian A. Herter Professor of American Foreign Policy at The Johns Hopkins School of Advanced International Studies (SAIS) from 1961 until his untimely passing in December 1986. After coming to SAIS in 1961, he served as dean, as director of The Washington Center of Foreign Policy Research, and as director of the school's American foreign-policy program and codirector of security studies. A prolific writer, Dr. Osgood authored, among other books, *Ideals and Self-Interest in America's Foreign Relations* (1953), *NATO: The Entangling Alliance* (1962), and *Limited War Revisited* (1979).

Bruce Parrott is director of Soviet studies at The Johns Hopkins School of Advanced International Studies. He received his B.A. from Pomona College and his Ph.D. from Columbia University. His writings include *Information Transfer in Soviet Science and Engineering* (1981), *Politics and Technology in the Soviet Union* (1983), and *Trade, Technology, and Soviet-American Relations* (1985, editor and contributor). Dr. Parrott is currently researching a book on Soviet debates over defense spending and is preparing a study of consensus and conflict in the Soviet leadership under Gorbachev.

Robert W. Tucker is the Christian A. Herter Professor of American Foreign Policy and director of American foreign-policy studies at The Johns Hopkins School of Advanced International Studies. A graduate of the U.S. Naval Academy, he received his M.A. and Ph.D. from the University of California. Dr. Tucker taught political science at The Johns Hopkins University from 1954 to 1983 and has served as a member of the staff of the Naval War College. He also has been a consultant to the departments of state and defense. His most recent books include *The Purposes of American Power* (1981), *The Fall of the First British Empire: Origins of the War of American Independence* (1982, coauthor), and *The Nuclear Debate: Deterrence and the Lapse of Faith* (1985).

Victor A. Utgoff is a deputy director of the Strategy, Forces and Resources Division of the Institute for Defense Analyses. He received advanced degrees in engineering from Purdue University and the Massachusetts Institute of Technology and served as senior defense specialist on the staff of the National Security Council from 1977 to 1980.

Michael Vlahos is research professor and codirector of security studies at The Johns Hopkins School of Advanced International Studies and an associate of its Foreign Policy Institute. He received his A.B. from Yale College and his M.A. and Ph.D. from the Fletcher School of Law and Diplomacy. From 1977 to 1979 Dr. Vlahos served as a strategic analyst with the Central Intelligence Agency, where he focused on Soviet naval doctrine. Author of *The BLUE Sword: The Naval War College and the American Mission, 1919–1941* (1981) and *America: Images of Empire* (1982), Dr. Vlahos appears regularly as a commentator for the Cable News Network.

**Publications of
The Johns Hopkins University
Foreign Policy Institute**

FPI CASE STUDIES*

1. *The Panama Canal Negotiations,* Wm. Mark Habeeb and I. William Zartman (1986), $3.50
2. *The New GATT Trade Round,* Charles Pearson and Nils Johnson (1986), $3.50
3. *The U.S.-Soviet Conventional Arms Transfer Negotiations,* Barry M. Blechman and Janne E. Nolan (1987), $3.50
4. *The 1982 Mexican Debt Negotiations: Response to a Financial Crisis,* Roger S. Leeds and Gale Thompson (1987), $3.50
5. *Negotiations on The French Withdrawal from NATO,* Michael M. Harrison and Mark G. McDonough (1987), $3.50
6. *SALT I: The Limitations of Arms Negotiations,* Jonathan Haslam and Theresa Osborne, (1987), $3.50

FPI POLICY STUDY GROUPS*

Iran's Future: Crises, Contingencies, and Continuities, Barry Rubin, July 1987, $3.95.
Trade Policy, Three Issues, Isaiah Frank, ed. (1986) (out of print)
U.S. Soviet Relations, Simon Serfaty, ed. (1985), $5.00.

FPI POLICY BRIEFS*

Technical Means of Verifying Chemical Weapons Arms-Control Agreements, Franklin E. Walker, April 1987, $3.95
Pakistan: Internal Developments and the U.S. Interest, Thomas Perry Thornton, March 1987, $3.95
Arms Control: A Skeptical Appraisal and a Modest Proposal, Robert E. Osgood, April 1986, $3.95
Thinking About SDI, Stephen J. Hadley, March 1986, $3.95

*To order copies of these publications contact the FPI Publications Program, School of Advanced International Studies, The Johns Hopkins University, 1740 Massachusetts Avenue, N.W., Washington, D.C. 20036 (202) 663-5765/SAIS Review (202) 663-5766.

The French Fifth Republic: Steadfast and Changing, Simon Serfaty, February 1986, $3.95

Mexico in Crisis: The Parameters of Accommodation, Bruce Michael Bagley, January 1986, $3.95

The Middle East: Timing and Process, I. William Zartman, January 1986, $3.95

Summit Diplomacy in East-West Relations, Charles H. Fairbanks, Jr., October 1985, $3.95

The Gandhi Visit: Expectations and Realities of the U.S.-Indian Relationship, Thomas Perry Thornton, May 1985 (out of print)

Lebanon: Whose Failure? Barry Rubin, May 1985 (out of print)

Living with the Summits: From Rambouillet to Bonn, Simon Serfaty and Michael M. Harrison, April 1985 (out of print)

SAIS OCCASIONAL PAPERS*

America: Images of Empire, Michael Vlahos (1982), $4.75

Tilting at Windmills: Reagan in Central America, Piero Gleijeses, Caribbean Basin Studies Program (1982), (out of print)

American and European Approaches to East-West Relations, Robert E. Osgood (1982), $3.95

A Socialist France and Western Security, Michael M. Harrison and Simon Serfaty (1981), $4.75

SAIS REVIEW*

Biannual journal of international affairs, $7.00 (subscription prices vary)

SAIS PAPERS IN INTERNATIONAL AFFAIRS**

1. *A Japanese Journalist Looks at U.S.-Japan Relations,* Yukio Matsuyama (1984), $15.50
2. *Report on Cuba: Findings of the Study Group on United States–Cuban Relations,* Central American and Caribbean Program, ed. (1984), $9.50
3. *Peacekeeping on Arab-Israeli Fronts: Lessons from the Sinai and Lebanon,* Nathan A. Pelcovits (1984), $26.50
4. *The Evolution of American Strategic Doctrine: Paul H. Nitze and the Soviet Challenge,* Steven L. Rearden (1984), $21.50
5. *Nuclear Arms Control Choices,* Harold Brown and Lynn E. Davis (1984), $11.50

**To order copies contact Westview Press, Customer Service Department, 5500 Central Avenue, Boulder, CO 80301 (303) 444-3541. All prices are subject to change and do not include postage. VISA and MasterCard accepted.

6. *International Mediation in Theory and Practice,* Saadia Touval and I. William Zartman (1985), $31.00
7. *Report on Guatemala: Findings of the Study Group on United States–Guatemalan Relations,* Central American and Caribbean Program, ed. (1985), $13.50
8. *Contadora and the Central American Peace Process: Selected Documents,* Bruce Michael Bagley, Roberto Alvarez, and Katherine J. Hagedorn, eds. (1985), $32.00
9. *The Making of Foreign Policy in China: Structure and Process,* A. Doak Barnett (1985), $24.50 (hardcover)/$12.95 (softcover)
10. *The Challenge to U.S. Policy in the Third World: Global Responsibilities and Regional Devolution,* Thomas Perry Thornton (1986), $34.50
11. *Defending the Fringe: NATO, the Mediterranean, and the Persian Gulf,* Jed C. Snyder (1987), $23.50
12. *Fiscal and Economic Implications of Strategic Defenses,* Barry M. Blechman and Victor A. Utgoff (1986), $22.75
13. *Strategic Defense and the American Ethos: Can the Nuclear World Be Changed?* Michael Vlahos (1986), $15.95
14. *The Soviet Union and Ballistic Missile Defense,* Bruce Parrott (1987), $17.95
15. *SDI and U.S. Foreign Policy,* Robert W. Tucker et al. (1987), $19.50